As Bell led the way, followed by Quan with the radio, and Smith, McDonald dropped back behind the rest of the team to cover them.

After four hundred meters, the LRRPs began to have a difficult time keeping up the pace. Just ahead lay a large, dense tract of woods, and gasping and panting for air, the four men loped into the trees. By then rounds were splitting the vegetation above them as the slowly recovering VC fired blindly in their direction. A few rounds began to zero in on the running team, and bark began to fly from the trunks of the large trees around them. As the accuracy of the enemy fire improved, McDonald, still at the rear, began zigzagging from right to left to keep large trees between himself and the incoming enemy fire. He knew the tactic would slow him down, but not as much as an AK-47 round in the back.

Suddenly, up ahead of the rest of the team, Bell's rucksack exploded on his back. The force of the blow sent him flying forward, stumbling to maintain his footing. . . .

By Gary A. Linderer
Published by The Ballantine Publishing Group:

THE EYES OF THE EAGLE: *F Company LRPs in
    Vietnam, 1968*
EYES BEHIND THE LINES: *L Company Rangers in
    Vietnam, 1969*
SIX SILENT MEN: *101st LRP/Rangers:* Book Three
PHANTOM WARRIORS: Book I: *LRRPs, LRPs, and
    Rangers in Vietnam*

PHANTOM WARRIORS

BOOK I

LRRPs, LRPs, and Rangers in Vietnam

Gary A. Linderer

BALLANTINE BOOKS • NEW YORK

A Ballantine Book
Published by The Ballantine Publishing Group
Copyright © 2000 by Gary A. Linderer
Foreword copyright © 2000 by Kenn Miller

www.randomhouse.com/BB/

Library of Congress Catalog Card Number: 99-91732

ISBN 0-8041-1601-6

Manufactured in the United States of America

First Edition: February 2000

10 9 8 7 6 5 4 3 2 1

☆ ☆ ☆ ☆ ☆

Foreword

The Vietnam War had a profound effect on all who participated. For most, the war was simply the discharge of a patriotic duty. For many, it was just a temporary interruption in the normal cycle of life. Others viewed it as an evil, unwanted conscription that bordered on indentured servitude. A few used it to promote or launch successful military careers. There were even a few callous individuals who saw it as an opportunity to obtain financial reward. But for many of those who fought and suffered, it was the beginning of a lifelong nightmare of terrible magnitude that consumed everything and everyone it touched. And for all of us, whether we are willing to admit it or not, it was a time in our youth when our values were tested, our moral convictions were challenged, and our love and hatred for our fellowman were stretched to the extreme.

Most of us who participated in combat will always carry the emotional and physical baggage of that experience as a constant reminder of those terrible days so long, long ago. Like our fathers and our grandfathers before us, we, too, had to face our "war"—that shaper and breaker of mankind. And like our fathers and our grandfathers before us, we, too, are now obligated to pass on to our children some sort of legacy of our experiences. But in doing so, we must be very wise and very cautious. We must avoid justifying the righteousness of war, for war is not a righteous thing. Nor must we expound upon the glory of combat, for there is no glory in combat. Nor must we teach our children to believe that it is their sacred duty to serve a cause that is unworthy of their sacrifice and the sacrifice of their comrades because such a cause is no cause at all.

However, we must teach our children that in the terrible crucible of battle, ordinary men will sometimes rise far above the ordinary, far above the commonplace, indeed reaching the lofty heights of true heroism. And that heroism, that unselfish sacrifice, is the one thing that gives us all hope in the goodness of our fellowman. This is why those of us who have been there still honor our fallen heroes and why we still value so deeply those bonds of brotherhood forged in the flames of the combat we shared together.

Reflecting upon the previous paragraphs, I am suddenly overcome by this feeling that you, the readers, will think this is nothing more than the corny ruminations of an aging veteran. I find myself constantly fighting an impulse to tear it to pieces and start all over again, as I've already done a dozen times before. It's easy to write a story when you've lived it and have the facts at your fingertips. But to create something profound and meaningful without sounding glib and hokey, well, that's beyond my capabilities. Yet, I have to be honest with my own feelings and convictions, so I will allow these words to stand for posterity, be they good or bad.

I am a very fortunate man. For a single year in my life, I was part of the best that America had to offer. Every moral, ethical, physical, and emotional fiber in my being was put through the toughest final exam you could imagine. Did I pass the test? Probably! I'm still here. Did I ace the damn thing? Definitely not. But I was there when some of my buddies did, and I will never forget their heroic deeds.

I am truly privileged to have witnessed real heroism in the making. Honest-to-God, all-American, pure, ball-busting heroism! It is something so rare that I have always found it difficult to describe to my friends and relatives who were not there. How do you describe a hero? How do you make people understand that you knew so many? How do you convince them they're unfortunate not being in your shoes so they can know them, too? Well, you can't. I have never been able to do it verbally, nor did showing them photos of real heroes help matters because, unfortunately, heroes never look like heroes. So, I got lucky and published a couple of books that enabled me to tell my story. Now, I'm not a hero. But at least it afforded me an opportunity to describe the actions of those heroes I have known. Thanks to a very understanding publisher, who has since become convinced that LRRPs do sell, I got another opportunity to tell of the exploits of heroes from my own unit, some whom I served with and some who served later, but still men who added to the legend.

Now, in this two-part *Phantom Warriors* series, I can finally complete my mission. I want you all to know the kind of men it took to do what these young men did, to accomplish what they accomplished. Their stories deserve to be told. This book is my tribute to each one of them, heroes all. We walked the same trails, lived the same experiences, and shared the same heart. I love you guys. *Phantom Warriors* is their story.

Gary A. Linderer
Company F, 58th Infantry (LRP)
Company L, 75th Infantry (Ranger)
101st Airborne Division

☆　☆　☆　☆　☆

Introduction

When Gary Linderer sent me his manuscript for *Phantom Warriors*, I thought I knew what to expect. I was aware that he had been working on it for a long time, and I knew that it wasn't going to be just another book about the LRP/Ranger unit we served in together during the Vietnam War. *Phantom Warriors* was going to deal with every U.S. Army LRRP/ LRP/Ranger unit that fought in Vietnam, including the very first unit of this type that established the standards and operating procedures for all such units that followed—5th Special Forces Group's Project Delta. I really thought I knew what to expect, but when I began reading the manuscript I was surprised at the amount of raw combat it contained.

Most LRRP missions did not result in combat simply because most were reconnaissance missions, where the original intent was to get in, sneak and peek around in the enemy's backyard, then get out without being discovered. Many of the missions related in *Phantom Warriors* did, in fact, begin as reconnaissance missions, but too often something went wrong and combat became unavoidable. Sometimes this was due to misfortune or to the skill of the enemy. On occasion it was due to mistakes made by the men on the teams. Sometimes, too, it was due to the fact that the LRRPs chanced upon an opportunity for direct action that was simply too good to pass up. However, the most frequent reason reconnaissance missions ended in combat was that mistakes were made by those deploying the LRRP teams or those supporting them—not by the LRRPs themselves.

When it came to their place in the command structure, the LRRP/Ranger units in Vietnam were the proverbial "redhaired stepchildren" of their parent organizations. With few exceptions, LRRP units were commanded by company-grade officers, and the individual recon teams were led by enlisted men in pay grades E-4 to E-7. The missions themselves, however, were always on behalf of some "higher" command.

In theory, the LRRPs were given a great deal of discretion when it came to planning and carrying out the missions assigned to them, with the final operational authority resting on either the team leader or his immediate commanding officer. In practice, however, staff officers and field-grade commanders, who understood neither the capabilities nor the limitations of long-range reconnaissance patrols, often took it upon themselves to interfere with the mission and disaster—or at best, near disaster—was often the outcome.

When a small and lightly armed reconnaissance team of five to twelve men, operating deep in the enemy territory, suddenly finds itself under attack, its survival depends on the courage, the tenacity, the professionalism, and the fighting skills of the individual LRRPs on the team, along with those same characteristics among the reaction forces, artillery, and air assets that the team has on call.

Unfortunately, sometimes when long-range recon patrols found themselves in desperate situations and needed the support they had been assigned, they discovered, much to their dismay, that it was unavailable. All too often, senior officers up the chain of command, who knew next to nothing about the deployment and support of long-range patrols, overrode the judgment of those directly in charge of "handling" the LRRP teams and "pre-empted" the team's support assets for "more important" activities.

Phantom Warriors is full of examples of this sort of command arrogance, ignorance, irresponsibility, malfeasance, and disregard for the established operational chain of command. That's why this book is so heavy on desperate and intense combat, and perhaps, that's why the names of the majority of the LRRPs, LRPs, and Rangers that adorn the ebony granite wall in Washington, D.C., are there.

The problem continues today. The lineage of the Vietnam War LRP/Ranger units has been passed down to the present-day battalions of the 75th Ranger Regiment, the various Long Range Surveillance detachments, and—in the case of the single Special Forces long-range patrol unit in this book, Project Delta—the current Special Forces Operational Detachment Delta. The Long Range Surveillance detachments are the current "red-haired stepsons" of the U.S. Army's special-operations forces. They do not belong to the Special Operations Command but rather are under the control of the conventional units for whom they work. This leaves them extremely vulnerable to the foibles of commanders who do not understand the intrinsic value of effective long-range reconnaissance or the principles of their deployment and support.

When it comes to matters of command and control, the Ranger battalions and "Delta Force" would seem to be in a much stronger position, at least in theory and on paper, than the Long Range Surveillance detachments. Unfortunately, Rangers and Delta operators do not serve our nation in theory or on paper. No, they serve in places like Mogadishu, where the command structure employing them failed horribly.

It might be said that the entire Vietnam experience was a terrible misuse of America's military and an unqualified failure of our command structure—beginning at the highest level. It hardly needs to be said that the command structure certainly looks no better today.

As you read Gary Linderer's *Phantom Warriors*, read it as the tribute he intended it to be; a tribute to brave men who volunteered for extreme duty, who did their best, and who all too often gave their final measure of duty and devotion on behalf of a higher command authority that was all too often unknowledgeable, unappreciative, and unworthy of their efforts and their sacrifices.

I think I've read every book about Vietnam-era U.S. Army LRRPs ever published, but I've never read one with more combat and more heroism, or one that covers so many units as well as *Phantom Warriors* does.

Kenn Miller
Author of *Tiger the LRRP Dog*
and *Six Silent Men: Book Two*

☆   ☆   ☆   ☆   ☆

B-52 (Project Delta), 5th Special Forces Group (Airborne)

Many of the standard operating procedures employed by long-range reconnaissance patrols during the Vietnam War were established by the men of Project Delta. The program started in May 1964 as an outgrowth of an earlier, covert operation known as Project Leaping Lena. Project Delta grew quickly from a single twelve-man A detachment to a battalion-size command containing nearly one hundred Special Forces personnel and more than twelve hundred indigenous soldiers.

B-52 was organized into twelve recon teams, twelve CIDG "roadrunner" teams, a Chinese Nung camp security company, and a South Vietnamese Airborne Ranger battalion as a reaction force. Their primary mission was to infiltrate hostile territories inaccessible to conventional units. Project Delta teams went into these areas to locate enemy units, gather intelligence, ambush small enemy elements, coordinate air and artillery strikes, perform bomb-damage assessments, harass and confuse the enemy, and sometimes to conduct special-purpose raids. It was because of the success of Project Delta that Gen. William Westmoreland decided to authorize the formation and utilization of special reconnaissance elements for the conventional army forces deploying to Vietnam. So he sent a directive to 5th Special Forces Group to establish a permanent three-week-long school based on the concepts developed by Project Delta. He named the school "Recondo" after three well-known terms associated with soldiering—reconnaissance, commando, and doughboy. It was the beginning of a rich history of long-range patrolling carried out during the Vietnam War.

By November 1965, the guerrilla war in South Vietnam had taken on a new face. Gen. Vo Nguyen Giap's regular North Vietnamese Army divisions had surreptitiously infiltrated into the country and were openly challenging the American and South Vietnamese divisions on numerous battlefields from the DMZ in the north to the Delta in the south. Conventional unit commanders who had been used to dealing with local VC guerrillas and the more organized VC Main Force units began to meet conventional NVA forces that demonstrated a growing propensity to stand toe-to-toe and duke it out. To be able to anticipate such confrontations, major unit commanders were begging for battlefield intelligence from beyond the range of their artillery fans. It was the assembly call for covert U.S. long-range reconnaissance patrols.

B-52 (Project Delta), 5th Special Forces Group (Airborne), based at Nha Trang, fielded small recon teams, usually two Americans and two indigenous personnel, which worked wherever they were needed in South Vietnam and, sometimes, across the border into Laos. In 1965, they were commanded by the legendary Lt. Col. Charles Beckwith.

Just before Christmas, 1965, S.Sgt. Brook Bell's patrol, consisting of Sgt. Charles McDonald at point, Quan, a Chinese Nung, and 1st Lt. Guy H. Holland II, received a warning order for a patrol into a mountainous area along the coast north of Vung Tau. The team was told to prepare for a two-day patrol, but little additional information was provided by the infantry division assigned responsibility for that area.

After the team went through all the usual preparations for the mission, the men loaded aboard a waiting helicopter late that afternoon. As the Huey approached the LZ, the pilot, flying at treetop height, inadvertently passed too close to a village along a nearby coastal road, then faked an insertion

into a large clearing not far away. He immediately com-
pounded the error by flying a little farther north before inserting the team. The sun was just setting behind the rugged
mountains to the west, and deep shadows darkened the LZ.
The large, grassy clearing was well situated on level ground
that dropped on one side into a low, heavily timbered thicket
at the bottom of the slope. On the far side of the timbered
thicket, the ground rose slightly before leveling off again at a
somewhat higher elevation than the LZ. Then it ran back
away from the LZ until it crossed the road near the village.

The chopper flared to a hover over the clearing, far from
the nearest tree line, leaving the men a long sprint across the
open before they reached cover. As the Huey lifted back into
the evening sky, McDonald, the point man, headed for the
closest tree line. At the edge of the woods, outside the trees,
McDonald discovered a well-worn trail. Stepping back
into the grass, he motioned for the team to go down, in
column. There they lay dog, listening and watching. Ten minutes after the last sounds of the Huey faded in the distance,
Bell signaled for McDonald to move on, and the four men
were up running again, crossing the trail in single file.

It wasn't long before McDonald happened across a large
thicket in the forest. They were only three hundred meters
from their insertion point, but it was getting too dark to move
about in the jungle. Taking a quick look around, he dropped
down on all fours and crawled into the dense cover, his three
teammates right behind him. Inside, the brush opened up into
a small, circular clearing perfect for the team's first "remain
overnight" (RON). The surface was covered with a thick
layer of dry leaves that protected the patrol from the damp
floor of the jungle.

Once safely inside the thicket, Bell called the command-
and-control (C & C) aircraft, circling a few miles away, and
reported that they had gotten in safely. Bell then released the
aircraft to return to base. The team was on its own, without
commo or a link to the outside until 0730 the next morning,

the time of the team's next regularly scheduled contact—unless something out of the ordinary happened during the night. The four recon men silently cleared their RON of sticks and debris, anything that might make an out-of-place sound and give their location away. Then they sat back quietly in the dark, waiting, watching, and listening over their back trail. If trouble came, it would be from that direction.

At 2130 hours, McDonald was on watch when he sensed that something was wrong; the sounds of the night insects had stopped, and in the distance, he could hear the faint barking of an animal. He was not alarmed at first, because the Asian barking deer was common to the jungles of that region. However, a few minutes later the barking was closer to their position. Then McDonald realized that the barking was not that of the diminutive deer of Indochina but that of dogs—several dogs.

Ever so quietly, McDonald reached over and gently grabbed Bell's shoulder. When he was certain that his team leader was awake, he leaned to his right and whispered that company was coming. Bell sat up and listened for a minute or two, then whispered to his point man, "I don't like the sounds of that either, but I hope you're wrong."

A large number of dogs barking had to mean that something was going on back at the village. Maybe the local VC had heard the helicopter drop off the team. If they had, it would take them a little while to organize a search party. The activity of doing so would have surely upset the dogs in the village. If that was the case, McDonald and Bell knew that it would be only a matter of time before the enemy came looking for whomever had gotten off that helicopter.

It was 2200 hours, nearly twenty minutes since the two Delta men had heard the dogs. They were both tense and alert, neither willing to go back to sleep. They had decided to forgo much-needed sleep for the sake of caution.

An hour before midnight, something rustled leaves along the trail. The sound was coming from the west, from the direction of the village and the barking dogs, and it was growing louder. Suddenly, through the thick vegetation, they spotted a tiny beam of light sweeping back and forth over the ground. The enemy was definitely looking for them.

The next few minutes passed slowly, and then they clearly heard the sounds of metal clanging together and of men talking in hushed tones.

Bell carefully reached out to touch Quan and Holland, who by then were wide awake. He wanted to assure them that he was aware of the threat. Bell knew that since no one on the team had gone on patrol together before, performance doubts were building inside each one of them. Staying cool was critical to their survival. Fortunately, the enemy soldiers moved past their position and disappeared in the night.

It was midnight, and the moon was up high overhead, casting a faint illumination through the trees. Out on the trail, it was bright enough to make out forms and shapes. No one seemed to be there, but it wasn't long before the recon team again heard the unmistakable sounds of a number of people on the trail. They could even make out the shadows of men standing between them and the clearing. Without warning, the enemy soldiers began firing their weapons on semiautomatic into the jungle to scare the team into returning fire and giving away their positions.

During the remainder of the night, at least a platoon of enemy soldiers working in small groups passed by every thirty to sixty minutes. It was certain that they had no clear idea where the American patrol was hidden, and to stomp through the jungle at night in hopes of stumbling over them was a dangerous gambit they were unwilling to take. But come morning—and light—the odds of locating the patrol would improve.

Bell decided to keep his team hidden in the thicket. To move out of their cover at night during a full moon would only give away their position. And getting hit at night would result in a long and dangerous escape and evasion (E & E) or a battle against insurmountable odds. And there was no chance for help until daylight and the return of the C & C aircraft.

The moon set in the last full hour before dawn. But soon the false dawn (BMNT, "before morning nautical twilight") began faintly illuminating the jungle around the patrol's position. This was the time that the recon men had fearfully anticipated during the long, dark night. The enemy had not given up and returned to their base camp but were probably waiting in a number of locations for the team to move. If the Americans failed to expose themselves by some predetermined time, the enemy would regroup and sweep the area.

The team members would have to break out of the trap, for to stay where they were was to risk discovery, and to be discovered was to die. They had to get free and escape.

As the sky continued to brighten in the east, the four men took salt tablets and drank lukewarm water from their canteens. There would be scant opportunity to do so later. Trying to make their RON look as natural as possible, they silently took turns brushing back into place the leaves they had raked up the night before.

The team's scheduled morning situation report (sitrep) was due at 0730 hours, but they would not be making it from their RON. They were going to have to break out before the enemy collected his forces and came after them.

A light breeze arrived with the coming dawn. It was time to go. Bell signaled for McDonald to take the point and move out east, crosswind, on an eighty-degree heading. After the first one hundred meters, he was to cut due north into the wind and maintain that general direction no matter what happened.

The four Special Forces LRRPs rose as one, slipped into file, and eased out of their RON site. Four sets of slitted eyes scanned a continuous 360-degree security circle around them. Five meters apart, weapons at the ready, the men faced their inevitable destiny. McDonald dropped to the ground, then moved forward on his hands and knees; McDonald was counting on the enemy's watching for men moving upright through the jungle. They would never expect a man to crawl on his hands and knees. It would give him an edge until the team cleared the immediate vicinity. It would also keep him down on the ground under the brush where he would be able to spot trip wires and men waiting in ambush. Behind him, five meters back, came Bell, moving in a crouch, then Quan and Holland.

Moving steadily through the thick jungle, McDonald stopped every few meters to watch and listen. There were none of the normal morning sounds of the jungle. Even the wind lay dog. Bell grimaced as his heart thumped in his chest. Surely every enemy soldier within a hundred miles could hear it.

McDonald stayed true to his heading and made good progress to the east. At one hundred meters, he broke left eighty degrees and headed north. So far, so good. A short time later, Bell signaled for his point man to stop. It was 0730 and time to make their early morning sitrep to the forward-air-controller (FAC) aircraft that would be passing high overhead.

As the four men set up in a security square, they couldn't help but notice how silent the jungle was. It wasn't normal; the enemy was out there. Bell raised the FAC quickly and reported their situation. He knew that Delta operations would be monitoring the transmission and would soon be cranking up the choppers.

Bell completed his sitrep, switched antennas, then tapped his rifle stock to signal McDonald to resume his march. But before McDonald could take a step, he spotted a slight movement up ahead near the ground. He froze instantly, causing the same response in his teammates. Ahead, a dozen birds suddenly flushed from the trees and flew directly over the patrol squawking and chirping. It had not been the American recon patrol that had alarmed them.

The LRRPs remained frozen in place while McDonald dropped down below the vegetation and flattened himself on the ground. Looking just ahead through the thick ground cover, the point man eyeballed the area for the danger he knew had to be lurking there. But he saw nothing.

After a wait of five to ten minutes, Bell leaned over to McDonald and whispered in his ear, "What do you think?"

McDonald looked slowly back over his shoulder and in hushed tones said, "I think we'd better change direction . . . right now."

Bell nodded, then indicated a new direction. McDonald took a minute to adjust the night setting on his compass, then led out again on a different azimuth. This was the "danger" time. If they were hit, they would have to try to break contact and run. If they got boxed in and cornered, they would fight to the death. They knew what capture meant.

Suddenly, McDonald held up again. He smelled stale, sour sweat, clothes permeated with incense, and unwashed people who reeked of fish sauce. They were there!

Clustered around the bases of three large anthills, the VC were just ahead of the patrol. Their claymores were well hidden off to one side. When McDonald had slammed to a halt just outside their kill zone, the VC leader panicked and gave a silent signal to initiate the ambush.

By then the team was already facedown in the dirt, praying for deliverance. It came in spades. By some miracle, the claymores missed the team. The roar of the blast deafened the four men, but failed to knock them out of action. The enemy soldiers followed up their premature ambush with a heavy volume of small-arms fire. Over the popping sounds of enemy small-arms fire, Bell bellowed, "Grenades!" Once each of his men had one in hand, he shouted for them to pull the pins on his signal, then on his second command to lob them into the enemy positions.

Seconds later, the mud-packed anthills disintegrated in a series of blinding flashes. The four deadly bombs were right on target. In the deafening silence that followed the explosions, the four men were up and running for their lives; silence and caution were no longer important. Behind them, the confused and pained voices of the enemy soldiers shouted in Vietnamese.

As Bell led the way, followed by Quan with the radio, and Holland, McDonald dropped back behind the rest of the team to cover them. After four hundred meters, they began having a difficult time keeping up the pace. They had already put good distance between themselves and the ambush site, and they had not detected any signs of pursuit.

Just ahead lay a large, dense tract of woods. Bell picked up speed and made directly for it. Thirty meters behind the team, McDonald realized that he was losing ground. At times he could no longer see his teammates. Putting his head down and pumping his legs like pistons, he dug deep into his nearly depleted energy reserves and charged after the rest of his patrol.

The four men loped into the trees, gasping and panting for air. By that time, rounds were splitting the vegetation above them, as the VC fired blindly in their direction from the ambush site. A few rounds began to focus in on the running team, and bark began to fly from the trunks of large trees around them. As the accuracy of the enemy fire improved, the LRRPs realized that the grace period was over; the enemy was in hot pursuit. Still at the rear, McDonald began zigzagging to keep large trees between himself and the incoming enemy fire. He knew the tactic would slow him down, but not as much as an AK-47 round in the back.

Suddenly, up ahead of the rest of the team, Bell's rucksack exploded on his back. The force of the blow sent him flying forward, stumbling to maintain his footing. A single enemy round had hit him in the center of his back, but had been stopped by his rucksack.

Not knowing what lay ahead, the team continued to penetrate the dense forest. They could tell from the sounds of firing behind them that they had attracted a large number of followers. And every step they took, they expected to be their last.

Still out in front of everyone else, Bell cast a quick glance back over his shoulder to see if his teammates were keeping up. At that moment, he collided with a large, mature teak tree, slamming into it and then falling backward. Before his teammates could come to his aid, the Special Forces NCO was back on his feet, recovering the distance he had just lost. The head-on collision seemed to have been rougher on the tree than on Bell; the tree was still unable to move.

As more rounds zipped around the fleeing recon team, they ran, putting more distance between themselves and their pursuers. Striving to remain together, lest they lose one another in the thick jungle, they settled into a fast pace geared to the slowest member of the team. But soon it became apparent that they were slowing down, as their exhausted bodies, now out of reserves, began to shut down. Fortunately for them, by that time the enemy had fallen so far behind that his fire had dissipated to an occasional desultory shot.

Finally, Bell halted. Quickly setting up security, he tried to make radio contact with the FAC to let him know that they were in contact and on an E & E route. When the short antenna failed to get a response, Bell quickly changed to the long pole antenna.

McDonald, breathing hard as he watched the team's back trail, soon spotted movement in the trees. The VC were still trailing them. Unable to reach the FAC, Bell pulled down the long antenna and took off once again.

The patrol had been running hard for an hour, with only a five-minute break, but the men were still hanging close together, running smoothly, settling into a comfortable pace. Ten minutes later, Bell stopped the team again and tried once more to contact the FAC. This time he was successful, and the FAC pilot was quickly informed of the team's crisis. He moved over the area to provide better commo and try to locate a pickup zone (PZ).

A short time later, the FAC pilot radioed with the bad news that there were no suitable extraction sites in their immediate vicinity. However, the Bird Dog pilot did give Bell an azimuth that he promised would eventually lead the team to a PZ. A short time later, the FAC radioed back with a bit of good news; he had a flight of A-1Es orbiting nearby, and he was going to use the propeller-driven Spads to keep the enemy off their backs.

The patrol was still a long way from being out of danger. The FAC pilot instructed them to continue their evasion plan through the woods on a zigzag pattern, marking each spot where they changed direction with a smoke grenade, and making sure that the direction of each change was exactly sixty degrees from the previous path they had followed. The FAC was going to direct air strikes on the imaginary line established between each of the last two smoke grenades on the team's back-trail.

McDonald was still back at drag, covering the patrol's rear as it fled. His job was to make sure that their pursuers didn't close in or cut off the angle of pursuit during their direction changes. Suddenly, he spotted movement in the deep shadows of the forest behind them. He slowed to make sure it hadn't just been his imagination. When he spotted the lead pursuer, it looked like the same enemy soldier who had been in the lead each time the VC had closed on them. The man had to be the tracker.

McDonald knew he had to kill the man, but when he tried to train his sights on him, he was breathing so hard that he knew he would miss. Instead, he turned and signaled the rest of the team to let them know that they had company. There was nothing left to do but continue their flight.

They ran on through the trees, still heading on the general azimuth to the PZ. It was later in the morning, and the heat of the day was taking its toll on the four men. They would not be able to continue the pace for much longer. If they didn't reach the clearing soon, they would have no choice but to turn and fight—and the odds were not in their favor.

After covering another three hundred meters, they paused again, this time sucking air and trying to recover some strength.

They took a minute to swallow a little water, and by then the enemy soldiers were already visible moving through the trees. McDonald saw one . . . two . . . three, then he knew for certain that there were many more behind them.

They ran again, but the next break came sooner; they were at the end of their energy. Suddenly, enemy rounds began snapping through the trees above them. The VC had closed again while the LRRPs were trying to regain some strength for a final sprint.

They ran once more, and that time they seemed to pick up speed. There were still untapped reserves left after all, and they had found them just in time. The team began to pull away from its pursuers, and the men suddenly began to believe that they just might survive. But it wasn't over yet.

Four hundred meters away, they pulled up once again. Bell got on the radio and the FAC told him the clearing lay only a short distance ahead. The extraction aircraft and the helicopter gunships were already on station and waiting for the team to move out of the jungle.

From the rear of the formation, McDonald reported that he could no longer see anyone on their back trail. For the final time, Bell popped a smoke and tossed it to the side, then with a quick look back over his shoulder at his teammates, he set out once again.

As the team picked up speed, anxious to reach the clearing, the A-1Es roared in over their heads and began strafing the jungle behind them with 20mm guns.

Suddenly, the jungle began to lighten up just ahead of the team. The clearing was near. It became an all-out footrace to reach the opening far enough ahead of their pursuers to allow them to get out before the VC opened fire.

McDonald caught up with his teammates just as they reached the edge of the clearing. The four men dropped to the ground just inside the tree line while Bell contacted the circling helicopters. When he was finished, he looked at McDonald and said, "McDonald, get out there a hundred meters in the open and get your panel ready." At that moment, McDonald felt that Bell had just signed his death warrant.

Seconds later and nearly a hundred meters out in the field, McDonald lay on his back and began flashing his signal panel skyward. Soon the welcome sounds of approaching helicopters coming in fast broke the silence over the clearing. As McDonald held out the panel with his arms extended, the extraction ship flew directly over his position and continued on. The Special Forces NCO fought back panic and wondered why they had not spotted him. He would later learn that they had seen McDonald and had verified his position.

Suddenly, the staccato sounds of machine guns tore across the clearing; gunships had arrived and were hovering over the trees out across the open area, covering the extraction.

As the extraction Huey touched down, the rest of the team broke out of the trees and sprinted for the waiting helicopter. McDonald leaped to his feet and joined up with his teammates as they ran past him. Seconds later, they were secure aboard the aircraft and whisked to safety.

As the Huey departed the area, the four recon men looked down and saw the rapidly blinking lights of NVA muzzle flashes scattered through the woods. The enemy soldiers who had been pursuing them and had lost the race were firing into the sky in frustration. Their quarry had escaped, and they had failed.

☆ ☆ ☆ ☆ ☆

LRRP Detachment, 1st Infantry Division

Delta Troop, 1/4 Cav had been the "eyes and ears" of the 1st Infantry Division since early 1966. Barely thirty men strong, the tiny outfit did its best to fulfill the division's reconnaissance tasks, but it was woefully small and without adequate support to accomplish its mission. In mid-1967 the unit was deactivated, and nearly half its members were transferred into a new company-size unit designated Headquarters/Headquarters Company (LRRP).

Composed mainly of volunteers from other Big Red One units, the newly formed unit had a great lack of long-range-patrolling experience. Captain London, recently transferred into the company after commanding an A team in 5th Special Forces Group, became the unit's first CO. He had been in Vietnam since 1962 and was well qualified to provide his men with the necessary training to enable them to successfully conduct long-range reconnaissance missions against the enemy.

The first thing that London did was to arrange for as many of his people as possible to attend the MACV Recondo School in Nha Trang, the quickest way to prepare troops for the grim rigors of long-range reconnaissance patrolling while minimizing their losses at the hands of the enemy.

Not long after the first of his teams had returned from Nha Trang, London received a warning order for a patrol into the Iron Triangle, a heavily fortified enemy sanctuary near the

Cambodian border. For a week, division G-2 had received numerous reports that several enemy units had been conducting night attacks against U.S. units set up in their night defense perimeters and against other elements providing security at forward fire-support bases. Scout helicopters and helicopter gunships sent to locate the enemy had encountered intense small-arms fire and had reported numerous sightings of large enemy columns on the move.

G-3 operations wanted desperately to intercept the enemy units before they could reach the well-hidden sanctuaries inside the Iron Triangle. Despite the desire for speed, the mission was scheduled to go in five days later so the newly formed long-range patrol team could have the chance to become fully operational after its return from Recondo School. It was not a warm-up mission; it was to be the real thing. And there were risks in sending out a newly trained team lacking field experience. However, since most of the unit's soldiers had yet to go through the Recondo course, the entire company was as green as the team that had been selected for the mission, the first operational long-range patrol assigned to the company.

Captain London decided to give the mission to Wildcat Three, a seven-man team led by Sp5. George Knowlton, a young NCO* who had been in Vietnam nearly eight months. He had served most of that time in a signal company before transferring to D Troop, 1/4 Cav, which at the time was on deactivation stand-down. He then volunteered for division LRRPs when that unit was first formed, and he and his teammates had recently rejoined the company after completing the Recondo course at Nha Trang. It would be Knowlton's first shot at leading a LRRP patrol in the field. He would carry a CAR-15 and walk the third slot on the patrol.

His ATL was Sp4. Bob Elsner. Elsner was not new to

---

* Formally, specialist grades are *not* NCO grades, but they functioned as such in most line units. It was a dumb system then, no less so now.

combat, having served nearly nine months as a grunt before extending six months to attend Recondo School and serve with the LRRPs. The most experienced man on the team, Elsner was the obvious choice to walk point, and made it easy by volunteering for the role. He had decided to carry an M-2 carbine, a fully automatic .30-caliber weapon, on the patrol.

Walking Elsner's slack was one of the team's two Kit Carson scouts. Rather than refer to him by his Vietnamese name, the members of Wildcat Three decided to call their slack man "Tom." It was a familiarity that Tom seemed to enjoy immensely. The plucky little Kit Carson scout had been a soldier for most of his forty-two years, and he seemed almost to enjoy the rigors of patrolling and the trials of combat. With the hard-to-find CAR-15s reserved for the Americans in the company, Tom was issued an M-16.

Wildcat Three's RTO was a private first class named Charles Pool. Pool also carried a CAR-15 to lighten the load added by the PRC-25 radio. He would walk the fourth position on the patrol directly behind the team leader.

Next came PFC Michael Randall, the patrol's grenadier. Armed with an M-79 grenade launcher and a .45 automatic pistol, Randall was the team's light artillery. The 40mm grenades of his "blooper" were the one weapon on the team that could make a real difference for the good guys in a lopsided firefight.

The sixth slot on the patrol was filled by the team's other Kit Carson scout. To avoid the appearance of favoritism, the LRRPs called this foe-turned-friend "Ken." Although he didn't look anything like a Ken, he wore his new name with pride. Like Tom, Ken also carried an M-16.

The rear-security position or drag was very ably covered by PFC Steve Sorick. Sorick's weapon of choice was the heavy, but very reliable, World War II–vintage .45-caliber Thompson submachine gun. And Sorick was good with the weapon.

The patrol's premission briefing was conducted by an officer from division intelligence (G-2). The team would be going in at last light on the evening of November 13. The primary mission was to locate the VC base camps that were harboring the enemy soldiers who had been hitting the U.S. military installations around the Iron Triangle. Once the patrol had pinpointed the sites, it was to drop back and call in air strikes and artillery to destroy them. The mission was scheduled to last five days.

To the surprise of everyone on Wildcat Three, there would be no premission overflight. Instead, the team leader would select the insertion and extraction points from recent aerial photos of the recon zone. This was not a good sign that G-2 fully understood the value of properly planning for a LRRP recon patrol.

The terrain around the LZ that Knowlton selected for the insertion was flat to rolling, with grass, scrub brush, and some single canopy. Within two thousand meters of the LZ, the terrain flattened out, changing from single- to double-canopy jungle. The weather during the mission promised to be clear, warm, and dry.

The single Huey slick moved in over the team's LZ, a small field covered with knee-high grass, and hovered three feet off the ground as the five LRRPs and two Kit Carson scouts jumped from the skids and sprinted for the scant cover of the brushy hills a hundred meters away.

When they reached the thin, single-canopy vegetation, they dropped to the ground in a tight wagon-wheel defensive perimeter and remained alert as their RTO called in a sitrep and got a commo check from the company TOC. Satisfied that they had good communication, the team lay dog for another five minutes before starting their patrol.

After moving almost a full klick to the east, the team reached an area of dense, double-canopy jungle and discovered a freshly used, high-speed trail just inside the trees. The trail was two meters wide, well camouflaged, and ran east and west. The surrounding jungle was very dense, so taking a chance, Knowlton signaled for Elsner to continue east on the trail. Elsner nodded, stepped out about twenty-five meters in front of the team, then cautiously began to move ahead.

The patrol had covered nearly five hundred meters by the time the last rays of the sun disappeared over the trees. For the last 150 meters, the vegetation had changed from double canopy to single canopy. Suddenly, Elsner held up his hand and pointed to a spot just ahead where the jungle thinned out some- what into an overgrown clearing. Just ahead another high- speed trail intersected the one they were following. However, the new one ran north and south. At the point of intersection, a third trail snaked northeast.

The team was in the middle of an obvious trail network, and it was beginning to grow dark, so Elsner scouted out a suitable spot for an OP/LP (observation point/listening post). It was fifteen meters off the trail and forty meters back from the intersection.

While the team set up a circular perimeter in the thick brush, Elsner and Sorick made a 360-degree recon around the clearing. The two LRRPs located a suitable E & E (escape and evasion) route and marked the likely points of enemy ap- proach. When they returned to the perimeter, Knowlton in- structed them to put out four claymores, two pointing toward the intersection, one on their escape-and-evasion route, and the fourth facing down the trail they had come in on.

Just after the last of the claymores had been put out, small- arms fire erupted from the north, only 150 to 200 meters away. A pair of American M-60 machine guns was exchanging fire with a number of enemy AK-47s. Then the team made out the distinct *whup . . . whup . . . whup* of an incoming Huey helicopter. It didn't take a genius to figure out that they were hearing a running gun battle between an American helicopter and an enemy ground force.

Suddenly, the sounds of battle seemed to be drawing nearer. The LRRPs knew then that the Huey gunship was chasing an enemy unit right into their laps. That posed a double danger. The team ran the risk of being forced into a firefight with an enemy unit of unknown size and of being fired upon by one of their own helicopters.

Immediately, Elsner got on the radio and called the TOC to identify the helicopter. While he waited for an answer, everyone on the team went low to the ground to stay out of sight of the helicopter and to avoid stray rounds. As Elsner was talking with his commanding officer, nearly a dozen VC suddenly appeared on the trail to their north and ran directly toward the team. A Huey slick, firing both M-60s, was coming right behind them. The enemy soldiers were less than forty meters away. Some of the VC ran in short sprints, trying to make use of the overhead cover, while others stopped to return fire at the chopper. Then, just as quickly as they had come, the VC moved past the team and disappeared into the jungle on the far side of the intersection.

At that moment, Captain London managed to reach the aviation unit and ordered it to cease fire. He told them that he had a recon team in the immediate area of the contact and requested that they pull their Huey out of the team's recon zone. After the helicopter had complied, London gave Elsner an intel update that G-2 felt that the trail running north/south was most likely the one that led directly into the suspected enemy base area. Suddenly, with the helicopter gone and the VC out of sight, everything got quiet.

Around 2100 hours, the team heard movement coming from two different directions—directly across the trail they had come in on, and south of their position on the opposite side of the intersection. The movement sounded like a lot of people trying hard to move quietly through heavy brush. It was not really close, maybe forty meters or so, but it was close enough to cause the LRRPs some major concerns. There was no talking or banging going on, just the subtle sounds of slow, deliberate movement. Knowlton put the team on 100 percent alert to see what would develop.

A short time later, Elsner decided to crawl over to Knowlton to discuss the situation. After sharing their concerns, Knowlton motioned for Tom to come over, then asked his opinion of the situation. Without giving an answer, Tom crawled down to the trail and put his ear to the ground. When he came back a few minutes later, he reported that the patrol had been compromised. He said the enemy definitely knew the team was in the area. It was his guess that the VC were setting up blockades along the trail to keep them from escaping, and then would try to surround them.

No sooner had the scout given his opinion than the team began to hear machetes hacking at trees fifty meters down the east-west trail the team had come in on. Minutes later more chopping sounded from down the main trail sixty meters to the south of the intersection.

Elsner quickly got on the radio and called in a new sitrep. After listening to the ATL's report and recommendations, Captain London authorized Elsner to call in a fire mission on the suspected enemy positions.

Elsner quickly switched frequencies to the artillery net and gave the fire-direction officer (FDO) at a distant firebase the team's coordinates. Then, using his compass, he shot an azimuth toward the sounds of the chopping out across the trail to the team's southwest. He called for a single round of HE (high explosive), and told the FDO to adjust fire on his command.

The round impacted minutes later four hundred meters from the team. Elsner then ordered the FDO to drop two hundred meters and fire a single round. While they waited for the second round to impact, the team heard heavy movement across the trail and only thirty meters away. Seconds later, more movement came from the far side of the intersection, less than forty meters from their perimeter. When Elsner reported that to the TOC, Captain London recommended putting additional artillery batteries on call.

Then as the second round landed about two hundred meters from the team's perimeter, Captain London succeeded in connecting Elsner with another FDO, this time at division level. When Elsner reported his current situation and requested a battery on each trail, the voice on the other end quickly authorized four additional batteries. Two of the batteries were giant 8-inch guns, and Elsner quickly set up preplots five hundred meters away for each of the two 8-inch batteries, one on the north/south trail south of the intersection, and the other on the east/west trail east of the intersection.

He then established another preplot five hundred meters up the north trail for a 155mm howitzer battery from another firebase. When that was confirmed Elsner set up a fourth preplot for a second 105mm battery at a spot directly across the trail but a few meters back in the jungle between the first 105 battery preplot and the 8-inch battery preplot on the trail to their south.

When this was done, one by one, he ordered each battery to fire a spotter round. As each round impacted in the distance, he shot an azimuth toward the sound of the explosion. That done he requested the first 105 battery to drop one hundred and fire for effect, then told each of the other four batteries to drop two hundred and fire for effect.

As the rounds began impacting far outside the patrol's perimeter, the enemy suddenly opened fire. From directly across the trail from the team's position, all the way down to a spot back in the jungle from across the southern trail, forming a 180-degree arc, a large number of enemy soldiers were reconning by fire. It was soon apparent that they did not know the team's exact location. It was also apparent that the encroaching artillery rounds had forced their hand much earlier than they had wanted.

The enemy fire lasted no more than a minute. Elsner couldn't understand how they had been discovered; then he realized that the VC had probably spotted the team when the Huey had chased them past the patrol's OP.

Knowlton had little combat experience, even though he had been in country for nearly eight months; therefore he was more than willing to defer leadership to Elsner during this situation. Elsner discussed the appropriate actions he wanted to take, and Knowlton quickly agreed with him. Elsner then crawled around the perimeter to instruct everyone not to open up unless they actually saw the enemy and were sure the enemy had spotted them. He told them to fire short bursts only and to save their claymores for the main assault. Then he got back on the radio and ordered the first 105 battery to drop another one hundred meters and fire for effect. At the same time, he instructed the other four batteries to drop two hundred meters and fire for effect. This move effectively had all five batteries impacting within one hundred meters of the team's perimeter at almost the same time.

After the last of the salvos had impacted, the enemy once again took advantage of the lull and opened fire. They were much nearer than before, and their fire was coming closer to the team's location.

Suddenly, four or five VC charged out of the brush just across the trail from their perimeter. The enemy soldiers were on line and running, firing and shooting as they came. Sorick and Tom were directly in their path. Calmly and deliberately, the two men took out each of the enemy soldiers with short, well-aimed bursts.

Elsner quickly got back on the radio and ordered all batteries to drop another fifty meters and fire for effect. Without waiting for the rounds to hit, he told them to drop another fifty and fire again. While this was going on the team began receiving heavy small-arms fire. Elsner was certain the enemy now knew exactly where the team was hidden. It wouldn't be long before they moved in for the kill.

Between the last two volleys, Knowlton spotted a single VC running toward the team. The team leader suddenly sat up where he could see better, took aim and fired, killing the VC instantly. But before he could drop back to the ground, the next 105 salvo landed close by. Knowlton was spun around by the blast and fell across Elsner, shouting, "I'm hit!"

Elsner screamed into the radio handset, "Cease fire, cease fire. Cancel all batteries except for gun number two. Drop fifteen meters and fire for effect, then cancel the fire mission."

Elsner then shouted for his teammates to be ready to blow their claymores when the rounds landed, except for the single claymore covering their E & E route.

While waiting for the final fire mission, the young ATL attempted to give first aid to the critically wounded team leader. Elsner quickly located the wound in Knowlton's chest by feeling around with his hands. To his dismay, he realized that Knowlton had a sucking chest wound. Elsner tore open Knowlton's camouflage shirt and tried to find the exit wound. There was none. He broke open the large bandage he carried in a pouch on his web gear. Turning the plastic wrapper inside out, he covered the wound with it, then secured the wrapper with a couple of pieces of high-speed tape. Feeling around in the dark, he applied the large dressing over the wound, tied it off with the gauze wraps, and pressed down on it for a moment or two to make sure the plastic had sealed.

Knowlton was unconscious by then, but Elsner quickly found a pulse and affirmed that the LRRP team leader was still alive and breathing. Realizing that the wounded man had probably lost a lot of blood, Elsner grabbed the team medical bag from Pool and started a serum albumin IV into one of the veins in Knowlton's arm. He hoped the blood-volume expander would help to prevent Knowlton from going into shock.

Tom and Sorick were still firing at a number of VC moving through the brush on the far side of the trail and more down by the intersection. When Elsner got word that the last fire mission was on the way, he told everyone to get down on the ground as low as possible. Soon, they heard the rounds come with a terrifying rushing noise; then there was almost a pause before the last two heavy shells smashed into the ground less than thirty meters away. The resulting blast tossed everyone into the air, then slammed them back to earth as debris and dirt began raining down upon them.

Elsner quickly got back on the radio to let Captain London know that they had just taken a casualty. He advised his company commander that the wounded man had been treated but that he needed to be medevacked immediately. This done, he once again radioed the FDO and told him to have the first 8-inch battery add fifty and fire for effect, then add one hundred and fire for effect, then continue adding a hundred and firing for effect in order to catch the enemy soldiers fleeing the area.

Elsner believed that that last volley had finally done the job. No additional enemy fire had come their way after those final rounds had impacted thirty meters from team's perimeter. The artillery had apparently broken up the enemy's attack. But the price had been great.

Elsner rolled over and told Tom and Ken to do a quick recon around the intersection. The two Kit Carson scouts nodded, then quietly slipped out of the perimeter. In the meantime, Elsner called the FDO and requested artillery flares over the intersection while the two-man recon element was out in the bush.

By that time, Gen. John H. Hay, the commanding officer of the 1st Infantry Division, had arrived on the scene in his personal helicopter, escorted by a pair of Dark Horse Huey gunships. Captain London in the C & C ship, and a medevac aircraft piloted by WO2 Bob Dillon, were also in the air orbiting high over the patrol's location. It appeared that help had finally arrived.

Tom and Ken soon returned to report that they had found numerous VC dead strewn around the area. They had detected no movement, and found no sign that any live VC were still in the vicinity. All of the trails had been interdicted by artillery fire, making passage over the trails virtually impossible.

Elsner radioed a request for the medevac to land in the

center of the trail intersection, which was large enough and open enough to handle two ships at once. The medevac pilot told Elsner that he would do a quick flyby before attempting a landing. When he had done so, he agreed with Elsner's assessment of the situation. Captain London also decided to do a last-minute flyby before releasing the medevac. He, too, was soon back on the net saying that he had seen no sign of enemy troops in the vicinity of the intersection. As Mr. Dillon was lining up for the medical extraction, General Hay then decided to do his own flyby. When his aircraft had returned to its holding pattern, the general came back up on the net and said that he totally disagreed with their assumption that the LZ was secure.

Elsner then got on the "horn" with General Hay and requested further instructions. Hay calmly said, "Listen, son, I want you to pick up your wounded and navigate down the east trail. A klick away you will find an open area that will be more secure than your present location."

Elsner immediately realized that the division's senior officer was ordering him to lead the team over their own back trail back toward their original LZ. This violated every tenet they had learned at MACV Recondo School. Hoping to make the general realize his mistake, Elsner asked him why he disagreed with the C & C and the Dustoff.

General Hay hesitated, then calmly reiterated that in his assumption the area was not secure.

Elsner quickly told him that after the artillery had been called off, he had sent out a recon element to check out the area, and it had returned a short time later to report that there were no live enemy soldiers anywhere in the vicinity of the intersection.

General Hay was still unconvinced by the young LRRP's statement. Once again, he instructed Elsner to lead his team back down the trail toward the east. Reluctantly, Elsner agreed.

Elsner then turned to his teammates to share the good news

with them. Predictably, no one was very happy with their prospects of surviving the move.

Because Knowlton was six foot three and weighed nearly 220 pounds, it took all four of the remaining Americans to carry the unconscious man. That meant that Tom had to pull point while Ken brought up the rear.

For the next fifteen minutes the team tried unsuccessfully to climb through the shell-blasted vegetation. At the end of that period of time, they had covered only fifteen to twenty meters. Calling off the effort, Elsner got back on the radio and explained to General Hay that his team had just spent the past fifteen minutes going absolutely nowhere.

General Hay said he understood, then told Elsner to try going south on the main trail about twelve hundred meters. There, he promised, they would find a large rice paddy waiting for them, large enough to handle a number of helicopters.

Elsner once again agreed to try, but when he informed his teammates what they were expected to do, he got the same reaction as before.

The team moved out cautiously toward the trail intersection less than forty meters away. When they reached the clearing, they put Knowlton down on the ground so that Elsner could check his vital signs, pulse and respiration. He was relieved to find that Knowlton was still hanging on, but he also noticed that the team leader's pulse was dropping. He kept the information to himself.

After getting their second wind, the patrol once again began moving, this time down the southern trail, but they got only twenty meters or so before hitting a major roadblock made up of roots and blasted trees.

Elsner called for a halt and got General Hay back on the radio. He told him in no uncertain terms that they had just run into the same problem as before. Elsner informed the general that it would take at least until morning to reach the rice paddy at the rate they were going. He then went on to explain that it took all four LRRPs to carry the wounded team leader, while the two *Chieu Hoi*s were walking point and drag. He stated that he was worried that if something happened, he could not really trust the Kit Carson scouts, since they had once been enemy soldiers. Elsner also reassured the general that they had just spent the last thirty minutes trying to go up both trails without hearing any noise or being fired upon by the VC. Once again, he asked the officer to reconsider allowing the medevac to land in the trail intersection. Captain London and Mr. Dillon broke in on the conversation to agree with Elsner's assessment.

The three officers then changed frequencies to hold a private discussion that the general did not want Elsner privy to. When General Hay came back on the air he immediately proved that generals always got the last word, even if it was wrong. He calmly told Elsner that they had discussed the matter and that he still wanted the team to move along the south trail to the rice paddy—even if it took until morning. "Now go ahead and move out," he said.

By this time Elsner had had enough. He refused, saying, "No, sir, I'm not going to do that and jeopardize the lives of my men."

General Hay paused for a moment, then said, "Son, I'm giving you a direct order as your commander in chief. Move out."

Elsner only repeated his first statement. "No, sir, I'm sorry, but I'm not going to do that."

The general said, "Let me speak to the assistant team leader."

Elsner replied, "Sir, I am the assistant team leader. The team leader is the man who is wounded."

General Hay growled, "Give me the next man in charge."

Elsner went off the air for a moment and told his teammates the crux of the conversation he had just had with the division commanding officer. He looked around at his fellow LRRPs and said, "Who wants to talk to the general?"

Sorick shrugged his shoulders and reached for the radio

handset. After listening to the general's diatribe for a full two minutes, he suddenly said into the handset, "Fuck you, asshole," then calmly handed the receiver back to Elsner.

Reluctantly, Elsner got back on the air and muttered into the mouthpiece, "Sorry about that, sir, we're just a little bit upset down here."

General Hay, now fully outraged, barked, "Well, I'm giving you a direct order to pick up the wounded man and move to the LZ."

Elsner calmly reiterated his previous position. "No, sir, I won't risk the lives of my men. We don't have enough security, and you can land two helicopters right here."

General Hay, still trying to recover some of his dignity, stated flatly, "You have a choice. Either follow my orders and move to the LZ, or wait until morning, and we'll send in an infantry company for you."

Elsner said in a softer tone, "Well, you're not giving me any choice. If I travel twelve hundred meters down this trail toward the rice paddy, that's the direction of the enemy base camp."

General Hay didn't seem to understand his logic, and added, "Well, you're making the decision, son."

Elsner was now thoroughly disgusted. "No, you're making the decision, and Knowlton will either live or die because of it."

General Hay had now finished with the rebellious LRRP. "Well, that's your choice," he said, and signed off the net.

Captain London then broke in over the air and told Elsner to set up a perimeter and try to keep Knowlton alive. He promised that he would be up in the air all night over the team's position.

Elsner thanked him and signed off.

It was around midnight when the patrol finally set up in a tight perimeter in the middle of the jungle, thirty meters southeast of the intersection. The LRRPs set out their one remaining claymore facing the intersection; then Elsner calmly informed everyone of the situation and told them to break out their grenades and ammo. "No one is to sleep," he said, "and everyone is to remain alert and ready."

Elsner kept checking on Knowlton every ten to fifteen minutes, but somewhere around 0130 hours Knowlton died. When Elsner checked him at 0200, he had no pulse. The young ATL performed emergency CPR and tried mouth-to-mouth resuscitation, but Knowlton was already cold.

The patrol remained in position and on full alert until the next morning. To their relief, there was no movement or any sounds in the jungle around them during the remainder of the night.

At first light, two line companies from the 1st Battalion, 16th Infantry combat assaulted into separate LZs, twelve hundred meters and fifteen hundred meters away. As soon as they got organized, they moved out in the direction of the patrol's last reported location. Delta Company reached the team first. The LRRPs had heard them approaching while they were still a hundred meters out and popped smoke to mark their position.

When the infantrymen reached the team, they secured the area before sending out patrols. One of D Company's platoon sergeants walked over to Elsner and said, "You guys have had a bad night. We counted over fifty VC bodies on the way in."

Minutes later, Captain London's C & C ship and a single medevac helicopter landed in the middle of the trail intersection. The LRRPs' CO walked up to the team and told them to put Knowlton on the medevac; then he instructed the rest of them to climb aboard the C & C for the trip back to base camp.

Twenty minutes later, they landed at Lai Khe. A vehicle was there waiting to return them to the company area. When they climbed down from the back of the truck, Captain London told the rest of the team to drop their gear at their hootch and head for the showers. He looked at Elsner and told him to report to his quarters.

When Elsner arrived at the officer's hootch and entered, the commanding officer told him to have a seat. As soon as the young LRRP had complied, Captain London said, "You did a really fine job out there. I want you to know that if it had been my decision I would have sent the medevac in."

Elsner nodded, but didn't say anything, and the officer continued. "I'm afraid I have some bad news to tell you. General Hay is putting you and Sorick up for a general court-martial, and you're restricted to the company area."

Captain London looked down at his assistant team leader and continued. "Elsner, I'll support you a hundred percent through this court-martial, and I'll get the instructors from Recondo School to come down and testify on your behalf."

The tension at the debriefing later that day was palpable. Elsner and the rest of the LRRPs didn't hold back anything when they told about the decision that had been made not to medevac Knowlton.

The general court-martial convened on 18 November and finally ended on 24 December. The decision had been made to try the two LRRPs together. Sp4. Robert Elsner was charged with refusing to obey a direct order from a superior officer in the face of the enemy, and PFC Steven Sorick was charged with gross insubordination.

At the trial, General Hay was the only witness for the prosecution. Three instructors from MACV Recondo School, Captain London, the division artillery commanding officer, the remainder of the LRRPs from Team Wildcat Three, Tom, Warrant Officer 2 Dillon, and 1st Lt. Larry Taylor, one of the gunship pilots supporting the team, all testified on behalf of Elsner and Sorick. Although the trial took nearly five weeks, it was no surprise to anyone but General Hay that the court-martial board found that both LRRPs were innocent of all charges.

Shortly after the court-martial, Maj. Gen. John H. Hay was sent back to CONUS to assume command of the 10th Mountain Division at Fort Drum, New York. Maj. Gen. Keith L. Ware replaced General Hay as commanding officer of the 1st Infantry Division in Vietnam. Captain London returned to the States and was replaced by Captain Price, who had been with the 1st Brigade of the 101st Airborne Division in Vietnam prior to his transfer.

Five weeks before the mission, Elsner had applied for a six-month extension in order to attend Recondo School. He still had a thirty-day extension leave due him. He left Vietnam on 29 December and arrived in New York on the thirty-first. He knocked on his mother's door at five minutes to midnight on New Year's Eve. They embraced, and Elsner felt awfully good to be home.

He returned to Vietnam on January 30, 1968, and arrived at the newly designated Company F, 52d Infantry (LRP) on the opening day of the enemy's 1968 Tet Offensive. It was not the welcome back he had anticipated.

LRRP Detachment, 173d Airborne Brigade (Separate)

In 1967, while conducting operations in the Central Highlands around the town of Dak To, destroying a major NVA buildup, the paratroopers of the 173d Airborne Brigade (Separate) suffered some of the heaviest casualties of any American unit in the Vietnam War. As the operations finally came to a successful end and the surviving warriors of the "Herd" began to pull back to regroup, units of the 4th Infantry Division moved in to continue providing security in the area.

On 3 December 1967, a warning order came down to the LRRP detachment of the 173d Airborne Brigade. The mission was simple. A six-man recon team was to be inserted by helicopter early on the morning of 5 December onto a II Field Force forward fire-support base that was in the process of being dismantled and abandoned. After arriving at the firebase, the team was to disembark, move past the SP (self-propelled) 175mm battery, hide in one of the perimeter bunkers, and then slip into the surrounding jungle under cover of all the activity. The team was to remain behind after everyone else was pulled out and spend the next four days monitoring enemy activity around the abandoned firebase. The mission was given to Team Delta, led by S.Sgt. Patrick Tadina.

On the afternoon of the third, Tadina took his ATL, Sgt. Lazlo Rabel, along with his point man, Sp4. Wayne Harlan, on an overflight of the mission AO. As expected, the terrain

32

was steep and mountainous and covered in double- and triple-canopy jungle. The topo map defining their recon zone (RZ) was choked with contour lines that nearly ran together.

During the briefing later that day, they were told that the weather during the four-day mission would be clear and warm. Staff Sergeant Tadina selected a plan of march that would take his team out through the northwest side of the perimeter, then straight up the slope toward the main ridge overlooking the fire-support base. On the overflight, he had spotted a distinct terrain feature near the military crest of the ridge that he thought would allow them to observe the abandoned firebase. That point was to be their goal for the first day of the mission.

Tadina took the team into the firebase at 0700, wearing olive-drab fatigues over their tiger-stripe fatigues and carrying their equipment hidden in duffel bags—just in case anyone was watching from the jungle. Once on the ground, the team mixed with the rest of the troops for a while, then unobtrusively ducked into a bunker on the perimeter line, slipped out of their ODs, applied a coat of camouflage paint, and climbed into their load-bearing equipment (LBE) harnesses and rucksacks. When that was done, they tossed their discarded ODs into the duffel bags and sat back to wait.

A short time later, an artilleryman in a tracked M-39 ammo carrier begin circling the perimeter, throwing up as much dust as he could, while the remaining redlegs began destroying the bunkers and dismantling the firebase. Under cover of the dust and activity, the team kicked out the front of the bunker, sneaked through the wire, and disappeared into the dense jungle upslope from the perimeter.

It was nearly 1100 hours before the patrol was able to move out. S.Sgt. Patrick Tadina stood clutching a Czech AK variant with a side-folding stock that he was taking to the field for the very first time. It was only the second weapon of its type captured during the war. Tadina gave the signal to go, and Sp4. Harlan, his point man, followed by Sp4. Greg Olson, slipped through the wire and sprinted up the slope toward the tree line. Harlan carried an NVA AK and a .45 automatic. Olson was a virtual arsenal with an M-16 as his primary weapon, and a sawed-off M-79 with flechette rounds and a .45 auto as backup. Behind him came Tadina and the team's senior RTO, Sp5. Raoul Santiago, followed by Sp4. Fletcher Ruckman, who was armed with a CAR-15. Santiago had recently joined the platoon from military intelligence and was being groomed as a team leader. Another veteran soldier, Sergeant Lazlo Rabel, brought up the rear, carrying an M-16.

The team raced uphill, quickly climbing the thirty-degree slope above the firebase until they reached the thick jungle. Twenty meters into the cover the team stopped, got a commo check, shot a compass heading, and moved out again. After the first two hundred meters, the slope began to grow steeper, the gradient increasing the higher they went. Their visibility in the dense vegetation was limited to little more than forty meters in any one direction.

Ten minutes out, and just shy of the military crest of the spur they were climbing, Harlan shot an enemy trail watcher. They were still within 250 meters of the FSB. Harlan had slowly been negotiating the dense jungle when he had spotted the trail watcher leaning against a tree in an open area on a slight promontory observing the activity down at the firebase. Harlan shot him with a single round at thirty-five or forty meters. The enemy soldier, wearing khaki trousers and a black pajama shirt, was carrying an SKS semiautomatic carbine.

Tadina then decided to make a hard left, paralleling the main ridgeline. He wanted only to get out of the area immediately without taking the time to search the body or recover the weapon. Their job was to observe the enemy, not to compromise the team over a single enemy KIA.

After Harlan shot the VC, Tadina switched Olson to point to give Harlan a break. The team still had to climb the major spur to reach the main ridge two hundred to three hundred

meters above them. After the team had put some distance between themselves and the dead trail watcher, Tadina signaled
his point man to make a right-hand turn and once again begin
climbing the steep slope to reach the main ridge. It proved to
be a tough climb. The patrol was forced to use a pair of Swiss
seats to assist them in their ascent.

Near the steepest part of the climb, they encountered what
appeared to be an elephant trail coming over the crest and
running down the side of the ridge. It was almost unthinkable
that elephants could traverse this degree of slope. But there it
was right in front of them, the elephant tracks standing out in
the damp soil on the side of the ridge. Tadina spotted two- or
three-day-old enemy footprints among the elephant tracks
and decided that the trail was most likely a resupply trail used
by the NVA.

The team used the elephant trail for the rest of their climb,
taking it right up to the military crest of the main ridge. When
they reached it, they turned right again and went back to the
terrain feature that Tadina had intended to use as their OP/LP
during the first day of the mission. This terrain feature was
little more than a high point on the ridge where Tadina felt the
team could monitor the basin below, where the FSB had been.

Their movement was very slow because of the thick vegetation and the steep terrain. But finally, with darkness fast approaching, they moved onto the promontory and set up in a
dense cluster of bamboo and laid out their OP/LP. There had
been no time for the team to perform an area recon. So they
quickly set out five claymores, two to the north-northwest
and northwest, one to the south along their E & E route, one
to the west, and one facing southeast. The patrol then set up in
a rough circle with their feet toward the center, with the RTO
in the middle. The RTO disconnected the handset and hooked
up a headset and detached mike. Each LRRP would use this
device during his watch, then pass it to the man who relieved
him. Tadina posted his guards beginning at 1930, one man
on, two-hour shifts, and the team settled back for the night.

Ruckman was set up on the north side of the perimeter facing uphill, and not long after Tadina posted his first guard, he fell asleep, lying on his left side facing uphill. Sometime between 2330 hours and midnight, Ruckman felt something touch his leg; then Tadina's hand clamped over his mouth. As he lay there wondering what was happening, he was startled when something brushed his hand.

Ruckman slowly eased his hand back inside the perimeter and otherwise remained motionless. It was only then that he heard and saw the column of enemy troops moving down from over the top of the ridge through the bamboo where the patrol lay hidden. The enemy soldiers were passing by in single file, every fifth or sixth man carrying a lamp made of a cartridge case.

During the next hour, as the team lay breathlessly alongside the trail, an estimated 350 enemy soldiers passed by their perimeter. The enemy troops were observing strict march discipline, but could be occasionally heard talking in low whispers. They were wearing olive-drab NVA uniforms, light rucks, and carrying AK-47s with a smattering of SKS carbines and RPD light machine guns. The LRRPs saw no heavy weapons, but there was no doubt in their minds that the enemy were NVA regulars.

The LRRPs lay beside the trail watching the feet of the enemy soldiers as they passed by. They were wearing a mixture of canvas boots and Ho Chi Minh sandals.

When the column had finally moved past their position, the LRRPs breathed easier and sat up to watch the lights move down the side of the ridge and directly into the recently abandoned U.S. fire-support base.

The team was on full alert. Over the next half hour, they observed two more enemy columns approach the firebase from different directions. Those columns were roughly the same size as the first column. The patrol watched in amazement as the enemy soldiers set up shop and began celebrating the recent withdrawal of the Americans. Unfortunately for them, they had made the fatal mistake of being right in the center of the LRRP team's artillery registration point.

Part of the original plan had been for II Field Force to pull its 175s back to a point were they could still cover their original location. Under direction of the LRRP team while they were still climbing the ridge, the battery had fired registration rounds into the recently abandoned firebase earlier that day.

At about 0230, Tadina decided it was time to call for a fire mission on the fire-support base. Because of the team's proximity to the target, he called for a 105 battery. "Higher" came back shortly and stated that it wanted to use a battery of 175s. They felt that since the 175s had preregistered on the target, the initial salvo would be right on the money. Besides, the team was not dangerously close.

Tadina agreed and called for a TOT (time on target), utilizing a full battery of 105s and a full battery of 175s. Thirty rounds of artillery, twelve from the heavier 175s, impacted right on the target. Although the team could not see the results, they knew that the artillery concentration had to be devastating.

After things had quieted down, Tadina put everyone on 50 percent alert for the remainder of the night, but no one was able to sleep.

At first light, the TOC instructed the team to hold in place while a helicopter was sent out to perform an overflight of the area of the abandoned firebase. The aircraft reported seeing many bodies still scattered around the fire-support base. The TOC radioed the team and ordered the men down to the target area to confirm the body count. Tadina balked at that.

While that subject was being discussed, the aircraft suddenly reported that it had sighted movement west of the team. The TOC ordered the patrol to check it out.

The team gathered in its claymores, sterilized the OP, then moved cautiously over the crest of the ridge and partway down the back slope. Still high enough so they could quickly move back up on top, yet low enough not to be seen against the skyline by anyone down in the valley below, the patrol began following the contour of the ridge just below the military crest. Down the slope from them, the jungle was far too thick to observe what was going on in the valley where the movement had been reported.

But the team began to hear movement below them, the sound of careless troops moving around beneath the trees. The LRRPs were unable to get a visual on the enemy soldiers, but they knew they were down there somewhere.

Olson was still on point, and Ruckman had moved up to the number-three slot. The team was still moving slowly, but in a straight line along the ridge. Every half hour or so, Tadina stopped the patrol to rest and to listen. It was nerve-racking.

Sometime after 1300 hours, the team heard more movement, but from above them, just over the top of the ridge where they had been the day before. And they were still hearing movement in the valley below them. Tadina was trying to guide the patrol into a secure position where they could monitor the movement, which was increasing by the hour.

Around 1500 hours, the patrol heard the distinct sounds of a CW transmitter sending Morse code. The LRRPs knew that only large enemy units used those sets. Tadina signaled for the team to lay dog while he tried to determine the exact direction of the commo site. He couldn't get a clear heading, so after checking some likely spots on his topo map, he plotted a number of probables for artillery interdiction.

The patrol then continued to move, and after a while the ridge began to drop into the valley below. As a precaution, Tadina decided to move the patrol back up over the top of the ridge to the other side. The team slipped into a ravine halfway down the side of the ridge, coming out on a spur overlooking a small valley that opened up into another, wider valley, which ran across the end of the ridge. At that point, the team located another RON site hidden in medium vegetation with double overhead canopy. The team put out double the normal number of claymores. Their commo was still good.

Tadina then got involved in a long discussion with the TOC. The valley they were now overlooking had a road going through its center. The TOC wanted the patrol to move down into the valley to monitor and check out the road the next morning. The team leader didn't like the way the situation was developing. Tadina didn't mind making contact, but he had always liked to call his own shots.

The night proved uneventful. Although the team heard movement on a couple of occasions, they were not sure of the source. Sometime during the night, they also heard the sound of one or two trucks back in the direction of the CW set.

At 0730 the next day, the team moved down into the valley heading northwest, but still hanging back along the edge of the jungle. About 0930, the team heard another CW set operating not far away, about fifteen hundred meters and on the opposite side of the ridge from where they had heard the last one. Tadina looked at his map and determined the only spot where the transmitter could be located. He marked the spot on his map, then called in a sitrep.

After the coordinates were confirmed, Tadina moved the team away from the second commo site. They stayed well back in the tree line paralleling the road. Suddenly, they began to hear movement in the trees above them. The sounds seemed to be paralleling the team's route of travel.

At about 1700 hours, the patrol stopped again and lay dog for a short period of time. The movement above them stopped shortly thereafter. The team advanced another three hundred meters in the direction they had been traveling to put some distance between themselves and the last place they had recorded movement. When they finally located a RON site, Tadina called in a number of preplots around their position, then set up normal security, two men on two hours at a time, and put out six claymores. The team had difficulty sleeping, but the night proved uneventful.

After checking out the road down on the valley floor, the team was scheduled to be extracted the next morning around

1100 hours. They moved out again, quickly angling toward the road, but still heading in the general direction of a trail that was marked on their maps. Olson was on point, Harlan at slack. Tadina was walking third in the patrol formation, followed by the RTO, Ruckman, and Rabel.

Their route soon opened up into seven- to eight-foot-high elephant grass and sparse single canopy. The patrol had been instructed to check out the trail before their extraction. Tadina wasn't at all happy about that, but he sent Olson south on a direct-intersect azimuth.

Twenty minutes later, Olson suddenly broke out of the tall grass overlooking the trail to find himself looking directly at a three-man NVA point element breaking out of the grass on the other side of the trail. Olson was only two meters away from the three men. The LRRP point man turned and fled; the enemy soldiers did the same thing.

By that time, Tadina was beginning to believe that they had an enemy regiment in the valley with them. Still on the move, Tadina called a fire mission on the opposite side of the trail, then turned his team away and headed back toward the road on a forty-five-degree angle. He also took the opportunity to call in a second fire mission on the far side of the road. He didn't want any surprises waiting for them when they reached it. Unfortunately, the TOC had given up the patrol's priority status, and no artillery fire was available just then. Tadina knew that the enemy column they had just run into could very well be on an intersect route with the road to their front at that very moment.

At 1100 hours, the patrol reached the road and looked up, down, and across but could see no NVA ambush waiting. The only suitable cover for the team to hide in was a large expanse of waist-high grass and scrub brush on the far side of the road. The team quickly cut across the elevated roadbed and down the embankment on the other side. A few meters away, they encountered what they first thought was another trail, until Tadina realized that it was the same trail they had just checked out on the other side of the road. To their dismay it angled across the valley and crossed the road three hundred to five hundred meters to the north, then ran parallel to the road past the spot where the team now stood. They wasted little time cutting across the trail and disappearing into a shallow depression back in the grass, fifty meters from the road and forty meters from the trail.

The patrol didn't know it at the time, but their extraction had just been canceled. When they found out several minutes later, they were irate, but no reason was offered for the change in plans. Again, they called for a fire mission, only to be turned down once more.

Tadina got on the radio and began arguing with the TOC about the situation they were being placed in. Without pulling any punches, he demanded an immediate extraction. Someone finally made the decision that the only thing that could reach them in the immediate future was a platoon of three M-48 tanks from the 4th Infantry Division. They were sent on their way accompanied by a "company" of mounted infantry from the 173d Airborne Brigade riding on the tanks. Tadina knew that this meant there would be about ten to twelve grunts on each of the M-48s—kind of light for an infantry company, but the 173d had recently been pounded pretty hard at Dak To, and most of their companies were probably less than fifty men.

There had been no movement in the valley for quite some time. The enemy appeared more concerned about vacating the area than wiping out a nosy LRRP patrol. The TOC finally radioed back and ordered Tadina to send a man out close to the road ready to place an orange signal panel across it as a marker for the tanks when they arrived.

Tadina picked Ruckman for the job, much to Ruckman's bitter disappointment. But he soon overcame his natural phobia about being left alone in the open in the middle of enemy territory, and started rummaging through his gear to find his signal panel. Tadina told Rabel to go out with

Ruckman to give him a little company, and to pull security for him while he got the panel in place.

At 1200 hours, Ruckman moved up on the bank between the trail and the road and tried to hide his full-size frame behind a miniature bush. His eyes were level with the road surface, and he expected at any moment to catch a round right between them. Rabel waited until Ruckman finished his task; then he returned to join the rest of the patrol still hidden in the shallow depression.

The plan was that at 1400 hours on the button the tanks were to arrive on the scene. The first tank was to move about seventy-five to one hundred meters past the panel that Ruckman had put out in the center of the road and come to a halt. The second tank was to move twenty-five to fifty meters past the panel and also come to a stop. The third tank was to stop twenty-five meters before it reached the panel, at which point it would rotate its turret to face the rear. The second tank was then to pivot 180 degrees and return to the panel, come to a stop, and await the LRRP patrol. At that point, the first tank was to pivot 180 degrees, keeping its turret facing up the road; then all three tanks were to withdraw in reverse order.

What actually happened was that at 1430 hours, Ruckman heard the tanks coming up the road. He remained hidden behind the bush next to the elevated roadbed. Minutes later, the first tank passed over the panel and stopped thirty meters beyond it. The second tank then stopped directly on the panel, and immediately pivoted ninety degrees, where it came to a rather unscheduled stop as the roadbed began to crumble beneath its tracks. It was now facing crosswise in the road with its main gun pointed directly at the hidden LRRP team. Only the third tank had stopped where it was supposed to. Unfortunately, the second tank was much longer than the road was wide, and soon it began teetering back and forth with its front and rear wheels overhanging the edge of the embankment.

Beneath the tracks of the wobbling behemoth, Ruckman,

on his knees, still eye-level with the road, was certain he was about to be crushed to death by friendly armor. He pushed back and flipped over hard to land flat on his back in the middle of the trail, looking directly up at the tank's right track, his mind locking in place forever the tread pattern of a U.S. M-48A2 medium tank.

Suddenly, a grunt M-60 gunner riding on the tank spotted Ruckman lying beneath the treads of the tank, and brought his gun to bear. A split second before he put a burst in the hapless LRRP's chest, his ammo bearer saw Ruckman's CAR-15 and shouted, "Don't shoot, he's a GI! Look at the gun." At which point Ruckman stood up.

The mounted infantry then turned and faced across the road, pulling security as the rest of the team broke cover and came out of the brush to mount up. The LRRPs had to literally drag the petrified Fletch Ruckman onto the tank because he was still shaking violently.

The tanks then turned and pulled back down the road to a small fire-support base occupied by troops of the 4th Infantry Division. The LRRPs were picked up later by a single Huey slick and returned to the airstrip at Dak To.

No one was there to meet them, so they bummed a ride on a three-quarter-ton truck going toward E Troop, 17th Cav's area. When they reached the troop compound, no one was there. There was nothing but plowed earth and piles of concertina wire. Someone had kidnapped their company!

Baffled by their abandonment, the LRRPs went back to the airstrip to try to find out where their unit had gone. They quickly ran into Sp4. Buschez, a LRRP from their platoon, who had just pulled up in a jeep. He had been sent to pick up the patrol at the airstrip but had shown up at the wrong chopper pad. When he spotted the team hanging around the airstrip near where the FAC pilots parked their planes, he drove up and quickly informed the LRRPs that the platoon had been pulled back to Tuy Hoa. He said that he had to hurry to catch a C-130, but that there was no room aboard for the team.

The six LRRPs accepted their fate stoically, then wandered around for a couple of hours trying to find a way out of Dak To. They finally gave up and started looking for a bite to eat and a place to sleep. They soon found an abandoned steel pot lying next to a 1st Log mess hall nearby, cleaned it out, and managed to salvage some coffee from the mess sergeant that was about to be thrown out. They also scrounged some fresh fruit off the back of a supply truck, and located a bunker at the end of the airstrip, where they crawled in over a pile of scattered tubes and crashed.

Early the next morning, a very disturbed and agitated armorer for the FAC unit awakened the soundly sleeping LRRPs to inform them that their mattress was in actuality a large pile of armed white phosphorous rockets waiting to be loaded on the FAC aircraft standing by at the airstrip. The six LRRPs were out of the bunker in short order.

Finally, late in the day, the patrol caught a hop on a C-123 Provider to Tuy Hoa. This was very likely one of the most complex extractions ever experienced by a LRRP team during the Vietnam War.

Company F, 51st Infantry (Abn) (LRP), II Field Force

Company F, 51st Infantry (Abn) Long-Range Patrol was the first long-range patrol unit to serve in that capacity for II Field Force during the Vietnam War. It was a proud unit with a proud heritage.

During the morning of 10 August 1968, Long-Range Patrol Team Two-two was alerted to prepare for a mission into a new area of operations inside the TAOR of the U.S. 25th Infantry Division, near the city of Cu Chi. It was an area of endless rubber plantations, thick jungle growth, numerous villages, and lots of enemy soldiers, most of whom lived below ground during the day, and surfaced only at night to wage war against their enemies.

The LRRPs of Team Two-two included Sgt. David Deshazo—team leader/RTO; Sp4. Reed Bonvillian—at slack; Sp4. Les Ervin—rear security; Sp4. Steve Miles—point/ATL; and Sp4. Mack Henderson, the M-60 gunner. They were told that they would be inserted along the Vam Co Dong River on the morning of 11 August while the rest of the company was in transit to Cu Chi. Sgt. Bob Defer, the team's actual patrol leader, was away on R & R when the team received the warning order for the mission. With only one NCO remaining on the team, it would have seemed that such a patrol might be a little light on experience and leadership, but that was not the case with Team Two-two. Sgt. Dave Deshazo had already proved that he was one of the finest team leaders in the outfit,

45

and Bonvillian, at twenty-seven years old, was experienced in life and cool in battle. And no one on Team Two-two was a slouch.

After a first-light briefing, the five recon soldiers boarded a Huey slick and headed out to the AO. Somehow during the flight, their pilot got confused over his instructions and inserted the team at a small Special Forces camp instead. When the team leader finally got command and control on the radio and informed them of their location and of the pilot's mistake, he was told to keep his patrol at that location for the night, and they would be picked up and reinserted the next morning.

As promised, Team Two-two was picked up early the next morning and returned to the company at Cu Chi. They arrived just in time to discover that several more patrols were scheduled to be inserted sometime during that day. Two of the patrols were designated for RZs along a canal network off the Vam Co Dong River. Teams Two-two and One-five—both light five-man recon patrols—got the missions.

Team Two-two arrived at the tarmac chopper pad to find Team One-five already waiting. There was barely enough time to exchange greetings before the ten LRRPs had to board their aircraft in preparation for their insertions. The Hueys lifted off together and headed out toward the Vam Co Dong River. Team Two-two was inserted into its recon zone first. It was approximately 1630 hours, and there wasn't a lot of daylight left.

Immediately upon insertion, Team Two-two's patrol leader, Sgt. David Deshazo, realized that they had no choice but to get well away from their LZ. There was absolutely no cover or concealment anywhere near their insertion point, and the five-man patrol was now hanging out in the open like a flashing beacon for the enemy to see.

Circling high overhead, the C & C aircraft radioed the patrol and gave them an azimuth to the nearest patch of vegetation large enough to allow them to set up a suitable RON (remain overnight). Since the patrol had not made contact on the insertion, the team leader felt they were okay and released the circling gunships.

Deshazo then ordered the team to move out toward a thin tree line seventy-five meters away. This was the spot that the C & C aircraft had selected for their RON. When they reached it a short time later, Deshazo called Charlie Relay and gave the patrol's sitrep, reporting that Team Two-two was set up in an artillery crater, where it had taken out part of a nearby dike. He added that the patrol was overlooking a large canal twenty-five or thirty meters across, and that one of his team members, Sp4. Steve Miles, had spotted some type of docking site not far away. Deshazo requested "Aloft"—a spotter plane—to fly overhead to verify the exact map coordinates in case the patrol needed air or artillery support during the night.

At about that time, the patrol heard a large amount of small-arms and machine-gun fire coming from approximately five hundred meters south of their position. Radio traffic was immediately confusing because control was unable to figure out which team was in contact. The only radio traffic that was coming through was from a new man who reported that he was one of only two members of his patrol still alive, and he wasn't even sure what team he was on. That was no help to anyone listening, and for a moment his message caused a major panic at control.

When it was finally decided that it was Team One-five that had been hit, Sergeant Deshazo immediately told his patrol to pack up and prepare to move out. They were the nearest ground element to the trapped patrol, and Two-two's team leader had decided that they were going to the rescue of One-five's survivors. When Deshazo contacted Charlie Relay to inform them that Team Two-two was going to act as a reaction force to Team One-five, Charlie Relay came back and told him that control—Lieutenant Colonel Zummo, the company commander—had ordered him to remain in place. That upset Deshazo and the rest of Team Two-two, especially Sp4. Reed Bonvillian, who seemed bothered even more than the rest of his teammates.

As the patrol waited to find out what was happening to their comrades less than half a klick away, Deshazo ordered them to set their claymores and trip flares back out to cover the approaches to their position in the artillery crater. While some members of the patrol were taking care of security, Sp4. Miles swam across the canal to the docking area, where he quickly emplaced a number of one-pound blocks of C-4, rigged them with blasting caps, then ran the detonator wire back across the canal.

After Miles had returned, Bonvillian and Deshazo left the perimeter to pull a close reconnaissance of the surrounding area. The two LRRPs came back a short time later to report everything was clear, and Deshazo called in another sitrep to Charlie Relay. The team leader reported that he had never before seen so many bunkers in one area, not even when he was with the Herd up north in the Central Highlands.

Afternoon and early evening passed uneventfully. They were marked only by Les Ervin's sudden uncontrollable sobbing. It wasn't anything to do with his manhood or his courage—he had already proven both. Sometimes in war emotions get the best of even the bravest of men.

Miles and Deshazo both asked Ervin if he was okay, and tried to comfort him. Knowing that it was only his third mission, they wanted to be sure that he could do his job if the shit hit the fan. Ervin quickly got control of himself and whispered that he was just worried about the fate of One-five, and that he would be ready to "kill as many gooks as I can, for fucking sure—you can count on me." That was good enough for Deshazo.

Deshazo put the team on 100 percent alert. Each of the LRRPs had already taken the required dose of dextroamphetamines to keep them awake and on their toes during the night; it had long been their practice to pop a dex or two when there was a likely probability of running into the enemy after dark.

Waking from a dead sleep while the bullets flew was the wrong way to enter a firefight. The patrol lay back against the sides of the crater, silently listening to the sounds of the night echoing around them and taking turns monitoring the radio and calling in sitreps.

About 1900 hours, the LRRPs began hearing movement and voices on the far side of the canal. They also observed the glare of flashlights moving around in the trees. Either the enemy knew the patrol was in the area and didn't care, or their presence in the vicinity of the enemy bunkers had gone undetected. About then it began to rain, and a light fog set in.

Around 2030 hours, the first sampan passed in front of the patrol. But because of the poor visibility the team couldn't see well enough to initiate an ambush. Deshazo attempted to call in artillery fire, but couldn't get clearance because the target was too close.

At midnight, the only other remaining team in the field called in a sitrep and reported that four or five large sampans, each with four or five enemy soldiers, had just passed their position and were headed up the canal toward Team Two-two. The other patrol was only five hundred meters north of Team Two-two. Deshazo immediately signaled his teammates to prepare for action. If the sampans made it to the patrol's location, Two-two would open fire. It was their first chance for a little payback for Team One-five, and they wanted to make the most of it.

At about 0115 hours, the silence was broken by the sounds of Vietnamese voices calling out in the distance. The enemy soldiers were making no effort to be silent. A minute or so later, the sampans were right in front of Team Two-two. The LRRPs watched in silence as the sampans pulled up to the opposite shore at the site of the enemy docking facility. By that time nearly a platoon of VC had moved out of the woods and was gathered around the site. Deshazo slowly picked up the handset, keyed it, and softly reported, "Charlie— Two-two, contact!" Dropping the handset to the ground, the team leader stood up in the crater to see over the surrounding bushes and fired an HE round from his M-79 at the cluster of enemy sampans just across the narrow canal. Surprisingly, he scored a direct hit on the lead sampan.

The enemy soldiers were going crazy trying to figure out what had just happened. Then, when a second HE round blew apart a second sampan, all hell broke loose on the enemy side of the canal. The surviving VC immediately began to recon by fire, trying to feel out their adversary's location.

The LRRPs in the crater were still trying to keep from giving away their positions. From behind a thick screen of tall shrubs and grass they began throwing grenades across the canal, pulling the pins, letting the spoons fly, and counting to four before getting rid of them. Unfortunately, they had only six frags apiece, so it didn't take long to run out of grenades. Then the team blew all of its claymores but Ervin's, which had been set up facing back toward their original LZ. Deshazo had ordered him to blow it only when the team began its escape back toward the LZ and Deshazo ordered him to do so. Hopefully, that explosion would keep the enemies' heads down long enough for them to get away.

Suddenly, Miles snatched up Deshazo's M-79 and fired a round up the canal. To his horror, the grenade hit some obstruction and bounced back toward the embattled team. The resulting explosion threw shrapnel everywhere, but no one was hit.

But minutes later, when Deshazo tried to radio for help, he discovered that the radio was no longer working. Apparently, the errant 79 round had found a target after all. Seeing that his team leader was having a problem, Miles dropped down into the bottom of the crater to help him. That was a really bad time for their commo to go tits-up because the cavalry, in the form of Huey gunships, had just arrived on the scene. But the cavalry were not the only ones to show up. Some unexpected movement on the canal bank between the crater and the water had caught the attention of Specialist Ervin: an enemy soldier was crawling up the muddy bank directly behind Miles. Without hesitating, Ervin turned and put a full magazine into the approaching VC, ruining whatever plans he had had. Ervin always made sure that the last two rounds in his magazines were tracers, so that he would know when it was time to reload. Now he was shocked when two of the rounds that had knocked the VC onto his back left trails of fire behind them; without realizing it, he had emptied an entire magazine into a single enemy target. Given the number of enemy soldiers they were still facing, that was an extravagance neither he nor his teammates could afford.

Worse, Ervin's tracers and the muzzle flash from his weapon pinpointed the team's position to the enemy soldiers across the canal, ending their confusion. But before they could take advantage of their new knowledge, the entire LRRP patrol opened up on them with everything they had, including Henderson's M-60. The U.S. long-range patrol had caught at least a full platoon or more in the open, and at that moment they were stretched out up and down the canal trying to get across to flank the Americans.

By then, fortunately, Miles and Deshazo had gotten the radio back into operation. They popped a couple of trip flares and directed the circling gunships to put gun runs around the flares that marked the friendly position.

With the gunships tearing up the countryside and the LRRPs putting out ordnance at an alarming rate, the enemy soldiers were momentarily driven to cover; no one could move in the face of that kind of firepower.

Finally, low on ammo and out of flares, the LRRPs' fire had to lessen their fire. No longer were the gunships able to provide close support without danger of hitting the patrol. The LRRPs could hear the VC once again moving around outside their perimeter, this time near Bonvillian's position.

At that point, Deshazo got word that the gunships had to return to Cu Chi to rearm and refuel, and they would be gone for quite a while. He guessed that by the time the helicopters returned the VC would be swarming all over the LZ. Things were not looking good for Team Two-two. However, the crater was a good place to make a final stand, and the five LRRPs were planning on doing just that, when suddenly a voice on the radio said, "Two-Two, this is Spooky One-six. Have 45,000 rounds. Where do you want me to put it?"

Deshazo pulled a strobe light out of his rucksack and put it down in the muzzle of his M-79. Handing it to Ervin, he told him to hold it as high as he could, then grabbed the radio handset and answered, "Spooky One-six, this is Two-two. The strobe is our position. How copy, over?"

The aircraft commander responded immediately. "Two-two, Spooky One-six. The strobe is the good guys."

With a smile on his normally serious face, Deshazo shot back, "Spooky One-six, this is Two-two. Good copy."

The pilot's response was brief and instantaneous. "Get your heads down, Two-two. Roger, out."

What followed were the most frightening moments any of the young recon men had ever experienced. Thousands of rounds of tracer ammunition impacted within ten to fifteen meters of the team's position. Anything inside the ring of death survived; anything outside it died. It was as simple as that.

By then, almost two hours after the first M-79 round initiated the battle, things began to settle down along the canal. Spooky was still circling, dropping flares to illuminate the battleground, and the gunships were back on station ready to lend their support. At that moment, up in his C & C aircraft, Colonel Zummo made one of those "command" decisions that so endeared him to the LRRPs who served under him. He radioed the team leader on the ground that he wanted an immediate body count. In addition, he ordered that the LRRPs were not to leave any wounded enemy soldiers alive in the water or on the bank.

While Deshazo stood shaking his head in disbelief, Ervin and Miles moved out on the canal bank to count bodies and finish off the wounded as their commander had ordered. The three remaining LRRPs covered them from the lip of the crater. Ervin and Miles slipped out along the bank and began shooting the wounded and counting the enemy dead, but suddenly began to take fire themselves from somewhere across the canal. Deshazo immediately ordered the two men back inside the crater. When Colonel Zummo came up on the air again and asked for a body count, Deshazo told him it wasn't safe out there and that he wasn't exposing his men to danger for the sake of a body count. That wasn't a good enough reply to satisfy Colonel Zummo, who ordered the young team leader to take his team out there to count the dead and collect any weapons and documents they could find. Deshazo radioed back, "If you want a body count or any fucking thing else, you can get your fucking chickenshit ass down here and do it yourself. We are almost out of ammo, and if we don't get picked up now, we may be overrun at any time. There are bunkers, tunnels, and gooks everywhere."

There was dead silence on the other end of the radio as Deshazo pondered his fate. He had broken the eleventh commandment, "Thou shall not refuse a direct order from a superior officer in a combat situation."

Suddenly, the radio broke squelch and Colonel Zummo's voice came over the air. "Two-two, this is Control. Mark your position and move to the LZ. Guns will cover your movement. Slicks inbound hot in five mikes. How copy? Over."

Deshazo responded, "Control, this is Two-two, position marked with strobe light. Good copy. Out."

Ervin blew his claymore and the five LRRPs took off for the LZ about fifty meters away. The two gunships moved in close to cover the team as it sprinted for the pickup point. Suddenly, a single Huey slick materialized out of the darkness right in front of the team, while both door gunners opened up with their M-60s.

On the way to the descending lift ship, Ervin, still holding the M-79 with the strobe light, disappeared from sight as he tumbled into an unseen crater. Bonvillian, laughing in spite of the gravity of the situation, reached down and pulled the embarrassed LRRP from the hole.

The aircraft flared and touched down not far away. The five men sprinted the final distance across the grass-choked clearing and leaped aboard, each amazed that he had gotten out in one piece.

When the aircraft settled down on the helipad back at the company area, it seemed as if the entire company was there waiting for them. Their brother LRRPs had been monitoring the action on their radios. The members of Team Two-two were helped off the aircraft, assisted with their equipment, and accorded the kind of treatment reserved for those who had just escaped the jaws of death. When they checked in their gear, most of the team discovered that they were down to one or two magazines apiece and a couple of smoke grenades.

As the team headed for the inevitable briefing at the TOC bunker, they decided among themselves that they would claim the docking site destroyed, four sampans wrecked, and a dozen confirmed enemy KIAs, against one friendly WIA, since Deshazo had taken a piece of shrapnel in his right leg. Colonel Zummo never mentioned the altercation over the radio net.

The next day, a reaction force from D Troop, 3/17th Cav, combat-assaulted into the area and swept the scene of the battle. They found three wounded VC, whom they took prisoner, and verified a body count of forty VC KIA. Colonel Zummo had his body count.

The two survivors of Team One-five were subsequently rescued by a squad from D Troop, 3/17th Cav. The team had suffered three KIA—including the team leader—and one WIA, seriously wounded. They had walked into an enemy bunker complex, and the team leader, RTO, and point man had been killed instantly.

Cu Chi proved to be a costly assignment for the LRRPs of Company F 51st Infantry (LRP) (Abn) Long-Range Patrol. While they were there, just three months, they suffered over 65 percent casualties.

Company F, 52d Infantry (LRP), 1st Infantry Division

On 14 June 1968, Team Wildcat Three from Company F, 52d Infantry (LRP), 1st Infantry Division, was sent to an ARVN base, thirty klicks east of Saigon, where it ran an overnight patrol outside the fire-support base. Two days later, the team was given a warning order to conduct a two-day reconnaissance of the village of Ben Suc, a suspected VC sanctuary two kilometers northeast of the firebase. Without the benefit of an overflight, the team was ordered to walk off the firebase at dusk on 18 June and patrol toward the village, reaching it by 1900 hours. Once there, they were to remain hidden until dark, then move into a gully that ran across the mouth of the horseshoe-shaped village. If they reached it unobserved, they were to set up an OP. Their mission was to monitor the village and a large rice paddy to the west between the village and the river. They were to watch for a VC company that was reportedly using the village for resupply and rest and recreation. If they spotted the enemy column, the team was to avoid contact and destroy them with artillery.

Ben Suc was a village of fifteen hundred to two thousand inhabitants about thirty klicks east of Saigon. Over the years, the village had earned a reputation for being staunchly sympathetic to the enemy.

Walking point, Sgt. Robert Elsner, Wildcat Three's team leader, led his five-man patrol out of the South Vietnamese firebase nearly an hour before dark. The weather was high overcast. It wasn't supposed to rain during the mission, but Elsner knew that the cloud cover would still have some negative effect on the starlight scope.

The team moved to the west to deceive prying eyes as to its true direction of march, then swung back around to the north and covered another 300 to 350 meters until it hit a tree line running in that direction. The terrain was flat, with a lot of brush and single canopy, and offered little cover and concealment to the long-range patrol. From his map, Elsner could see that the tree line ran north almost up to the edge of Ben Suc village.

This was not Elsner's usual team. He still had his regular assistant team leader, Sgt. Billy Cohen, walking in the fourth slot, Sp4. Charles Pool at slack, and PFC Steven Sorick with his trusty Thompson submachine gun at drag. But the patrol's RTO, Sp5. David Hill, was a dog handler who had been attached to the team the previous mission. A bad experience on that previous patrol had convinced Elsner and his teammates that the German shepherd was far too noisy to accompany a long-range patrol, and the decision had been made this time to leave him behind. But not the animal's handler; Hill was more than capable of carrying the team radio, and Elsner assigned him that role. Unfortunately, he was still an unknown factor on the team, and would be until he showed his stuff in combat. Elsner put him in the middle of the patrol for two reasons—first, because that's where he always put his RTO, and second, because he would be safer there. Hill carried his favorite weapon, an M-79 grenade launcher. Elsner appreciated having the firepower along and hoped that the man could use it if the need arose.

For that mission, Elsner was carrying a piece of very special equipment; at G-2's recommendation, he had brought along a starlight scope. The night-vision device would enable the team leader to observe the village and the adjoining rice paddy at night after they set up in their OP.

The patrol followed the tree line approximately twelve

hundred meters until it almost intersected another tree line that extended from the south wing of the U-shaped village of Ben Suc. Taking advantage of the thin brush, the team moved to within a couple hundred meters of the village, quickly set up in a circular perimeter, and remained hidden until dark.

While the sun was setting, Elsner took advantage of the shadows to scope out the approaches to the village. He could see that at the end of each leg of the village, a tree line extended westward two hundred meters or so, ending at the edge of an expansive rice paddy. He also spotted a trail that snaked from the end of the southernmost tree line and continued out across the rice paddy toward the river. Elsner guessed that was most likely the trail that the enemy used to enter and depart the village.

The team leader also spotted a waist-deep gully that separated the area inside the extended village horseshoe from the huge rice paddy to the west. The gully ran from just inside the outer tip of the southern tree line to the outer tip of the parallel tree line coming out of the north side of the village. Just before it reached the trees on the opposite side, it seemed to widen and deepen a little.

As soon as Elsner felt that it was dark enough to move closer, he led the team into the southern tree line and stopped sixty meters from the nearest point of the village. Once again the team set up in a circular perimeter. Even without the starlight scope, the LRRPs could make out the shadowy forms of the village's inhabitants moving back and forth between their hootches. They could also hear Vietnamese music, and they realized that the villagers were celebrating something. High-pitched Oriental music seemed to be coming from nearly every part of the village. There were lights in all the hootches and bonfires burning in strategic locations throughout the village.

The team remained in that position for nearly fifteen minutes while Elsner used the starlight scope to further check out the area. He could definitely make out activity inside the village, but nothing outside it.

To get a better view, Elsner led the team out of the trees and down the north-south gully. A few single-canopy trees flanked both sides of the gully as it ran across the open mouth of the U and on toward the tree line on the opposite side of the village. Within thirty meters of the hootches on the near side of the village, Elsner held up the team once again.

From their new vantage point, the LRRPs heard dogs barking in the village, but the slight breeze was blowing toward them so the domestic canines didn't seem to notice the team.

The five Americans remained hidden there for another thirty minutes, until it grew pitch-black. By then it was 2000 hours, and nothing seemed to be stirring outside the village.

Team Wildcat Three was monitoring the smaller rice paddy lying between the two wings of the village and the village proper. A large mound to their rear blocked their view of the trail that ran across the large rice paddy beyond the village. That concerned Elsner, and after a while, he whispered for his teammates to remain in place while he backtracked to the tree line to see if he could get a better view of the large rice paddy behind them. He was about thirty-five meters from the team before he found a spot where he had a good view of the large rice paddy all the way out to the river nearly a klick away. His view was hampered only by the vast distance between himself and the distant river. But even with the help of the starlight scope, he could not make out anything beyond three hundred meters. From his new vantage point, he turned back to check out the village but found that he could view only half of it.

Elsner soon decided that neither location was good enough for a suitable OP. He rejoined the team and squatted down to discuss the situation with his teammates. Elsner said that he felt they should move out into the smaller rice paddy about twenty-five meters to the front of the mound. He assured them that at that location they would be able to monitor not only the entire village, but also the large rice paddy behind them and both tree lines.

Elsner drew his teammates closer, then whispered that they would remain there until 2100 hours, then move approximately 150 meters out into the large rice paddy west of the village, where they would set up another OP. At 2200 hours, they would move another 150 meters out into the rice paddy and set up again. At 2300 hours, the patrol would repeat the process one final time, making sure that they were at least fifty meters back from the trail. This would put them out in the center of the large rice paddy, roughly halfway between the village and the river, exactly where G-2 wanted them to be at midnight. G-2 felt that they could best monitor enemy troops moving in from the river from that location.

At 2100 hours, Elsner signaled his teammates to get ready to move. Silently, with Elsner at point, they formed up five meters apart and began heading west between the two tree lines. The trail was to the patrol's left, about fifty meters away.

They had gone only ten or fifteen meters when the back of Elsner's neck suddenly began to tingle. He immediately raised a clenched fist to stop the team. Dropping to one knee, he brought up the starlight scope and peered through it to the west toward the gully and out beyond it into the large rice paddy. Running along both sides of the gully was a thin layer of scattered brush and a few isolated trees, ten to twelve inches in diameter. There, in front of one of the trees, Elsner could make out an enemy soldier sitting behind a tripod-mounted .30-caliber machine gun. The gun was set up directly in their path on the near side of the gully.

As Elsner continued scanning slowly from right to left, he counted another fifteen Viet Cong strung out along the gully on either side of the machine gun. They were obviously waiting to ambush the patrol. Some of the enemy soldiers were lying on the ground relaxing, while others were squatting in the brush.

Elsner continued panning along the gully all the way out to the tree line to the team's south and spotted another .30-caliber machine gun where the trees ended at the large rice paddy. He quickly shifted the night-vision device to the north and spotted more VC in the trees there. With the village at their backs, the team was completely boxed in.

Suddenly Elsner noticed that the music coming from the village behind the team had ceased. Somehow the enemy had spotted the patrol, and had moved quietly to trap and destroy them.

Elsner turned and whispered to the men to form up in a defensive perimeter. In a hushed but controlled voice he told them that the enemy had set up an ambush at the gully and had put flankers out in the trees on both sides of them. He instructed his teammates to put the five claymores in a circle around them, lay out their ammo, grenades, and star cluster flares, then take cover behind the low paddy dikes to their front. They had two claymores facing the gully in front of them, one to each flank, and another facing the village.

While his teammates pulled security, Elsner took a few moments to evaluate their situation. He felt certain that the enemy was not aware of their exact location. He was also sure that there would be no chance of escaping the trap without help from the outside.

Suddenly, the LRRPs detected movement in the gully to their north. Elsner told the rest of the team to wait while he went over to the gully and dumped a couple of grenades on whomever was down there.

When he reached the gully, he could hear movement and whispering close by. The LRRP NCO slowly took out a white phosphorous grenade, pulled the pin, and lobbed it into the middle of the sounds. In the resulting flash, he could see that he had caught two VC in the blast. He could also hear more of them running back up the ravine. Jumping to his feet, Elsner threw a fragmentation grenade toward the far end of the gully right where it merged with the tree line. Amazingly, the VC didn't respond. Without waiting to view the results, Elsner turned and ran back toward the team's perimeter.

By then, Hill, the RTO, had the company TOC on the radio. Elsner dropped down in the center of the perimeter and took the handset from Hill. Quickly, he gave his commanding officer a brief sitrep, reporting that they were boxed in inside the U-shaped part of the village with over thirty VC between them and the river. Without waiting for a reply, Elsner asked for gunships. The CO agreed and recommended that he call in artillery fire while the gunships were being scrambled.

Fortunately, Elsner had already preplotted each of the patrol's positions all the way up to their location, so both the TOC and the artillery FDO knew exactly where to put the rounds. Now he shot an azimuth from his position to an imaginary location about five hundred meters out along the trail toward the river, then requested a spotting round. After the appropriate wait, the LRRPs had no visual and no sound from the single marker round.

Elsner then called for a drop of five hundred meters and a second marker round. Nearly thirty seconds later, far in the distance, they spotted a flash. It was so far away that the sound of the explosion never reached them.

Something was very wrong. Suddenly, he heard Dark Horse Three-two, piloted by Captain Taylor, trying to reach the patrol on the radio. Taylor was flying the lead Cobra of the flight of gunships coming out to support them. He told Elsner that his ETA was two minutes.

Elsner immediately canceled the artillery, then switched back to the gunship push (channel or frequency) and gave Taylor a sitrep. He told the pilot that he would toss out a smoke grenade to mark his position as soon as he heard the inbound choppers. Then, when the gunships were on station, he would fire star clusters at the enemy positions around them.

At that same time, Dark Horse Three-two called the supporting artillery battery and requested aerial flares over the village.

When the LRRPs first saw the flashing of their lights, the Cobras were still a full klick out over the river. Elsner told his teammates that he and Cohen would fire star clusters at the two enemy machine-gun positions when the Cobras were five hundred meters out. Sorick was to fire his star cluster into the woods on the north where the gully intersected it, while Hill fired his into the tree line on the south side of the field. Pool would follow this up by launching his flare into the village. This would give the pilots reference points to all the enemy positions.

Elsner got back on the radio and related to Captain Taylor what was going to happen in the next few seconds. Taylor answered that he understood and told them to go ahead and pop smoke and launch the star clusters; then he would open fire.

When the LRRPs complied, everyone opened up at the same time—the VC, the gunships, and the LRRPs. Each of the star clusters was on target, marking the enemy positions for the Cobras that were roaring in, rockets firing.

The team was receiving intense small-arms fire from the gully to their front and also from the tree lines to the north and south, but nothing was coming from the village.

On the first pass, the Cobras hit the two tree lines and the gully with five or six 2.75-inch rockets each. The rockets were right on the money. Captain Taylor then did a hard turn right over the gully and sprayed it with his minigun. The other Cobra, piloted by Lieutenant Trickler, hovered right over the team's position and sprayed minigun fire from the southern tip of the U all the way around the inside of the horseshoe, including the village, and stopping at the northern tip.

While Trickler was spraying the enemy positions, Captain Taylor radioed the team that he was taking hits from a .30-caliber machine gun hidden in the tree line south of their perimeter. He said that he could actually see the gun.

Both Cobras then circled out into the large rice paddy to commence a second run. This time the two gunships came in simultaneously and made extended gun runs, each moving down a tree line, culminating their attack in the village. When the two Cobras turned outside and started their runs back down the legs of the horseshoe, they tore the trees apart with a barrage of rockets, ending up by making crisscrossing passes over the gully west of the team. Despite the hellfire raining down on them, the VC were still putting out heavy fire at the gunships and at the trapped recon team.

As the Cobras flashed past and out into the rice paddy for the second time, Lieutenant Trickler reported that he was receiving machine-gun fire from somewhere out in the paddy north of the northern tree line. He could see a large bunch of enemy soldiers attempting to reinforce the VC in the horseshoe.

As the newly arrived VC unit tried to blow the gunship out of the sky with machine-gun and small-arms fire, Trickler went around again and came back firing everything he had left, knocking out the enemy machine gun with the last of his rockets and scattering the supporting VC infantry in all directions.

Taylor and Elsner were talking on the radio. Taylor was about five hundred meters out over the large rice paddy west of the team, hovering 200 or 250 meters off the ground. Lieutenant Trickler, circling to the north, broke in to inform Taylor that he had just run dry and would have to go back to base to rearm. Taylor said that he, too, was out of rockets, but he would stay with the team and cover them with his miniguns. By then the two gunships had fired 144 rockets and nearly 16,000 rounds of minigun ammo.

For the next fifteen to twenty minutes, the LRRPs remained heavily engaged in a vicious firefight as enemy small-arms fire came at them from both tree lines. There was no longer any fire coming from the gully across their front.

Taylor called in to tell the team that he would take care of the remaining machine gun in the tree line to their south, but the team would have to handle the rest by themselves, as he was almost out of ordnance.

Fortunately, the enemy fire was coming in high over the

team's position. The VC were not using tracers, and they were having a difficult time adjusting their fire. The machine gun in the southern tree line was using tracers, but it was firing only at the remaining Cobra.

After another ten or fifteen minutes, the patrol heard and saw that another firefight was breaking out north of the village. Looking at his map, Elsner saw that a couple of kilometers downstream the river made a ninety-degree turn to the east and ran north of the village. Not far away from the bend an ARVN unit had secured a bridge over the river. It was probably that fortified position that had just been attacked by the VC.

While the new battle raged off in the distance, Taylor radioed the team that he had just run out of ammo. When the enemy, too, realized the gunship was dry, things really began to get tough.

Elsner was discussing possible escape-and-evasion options with Captain Taylor when Lieutenant Trickler broke in to say that he was less than two minutes out on his way back. Taylor immediately broke off and began to make dry runs to keep the enemy occupied and off the team's back until Trickler arrived. Wherever the LRRPs saw the flashes of enemy weapons firing at Taylor, they brought their own fire down on the enemy position.

The second Cobra arrived and first made a fast sweep around the horseshoe because the team had been receiving some fire from the village for twenty minutes or so.

While that was happening, Captain Taylor ordered Lieutenant Trickler to keep the enemy engaged inside the horseshoe, then told the LRRPs to be prepared to get up and *di di* across the gully and out into the open rice paddy as soon as Trickler made his run.

Elsner told Taylor that he understood. He said his patrol was going to fire and maneuver toward the "large terrain feature." He added that while they moved, each man on the team would have alternating areas of designated responsibility to cover so that Taylor would know what was going on.

Minutes later, in column, the team moved out at a run, each man firing toward his designated security zone. They immediately began taking fire from the tree line to their south and from the village behind them. Once they had crossed the gully, unbeknownst to Elsner, Sorick dropped off to lay down cover fire for the team with his Thompson.

The patrol was nearly a hundred meters out in the large rice paddy when they suddenly felt an intense rush of warm air coming from directly overhead; Taylor was hovering above them with his lights off.

Cohen, realizing for the first time that Sorick was not with them, turned and screamed for him to come on. Sorick leaped to his feet and began running toward the team, still seventy meters away, but he failed to see that two VC had darted out of the tree line thirty-five meters to his southwest and begun chasing him. The enemy soldiers stopped to fire.

Cohen and Hill immediately opened up on the VC and took them out before they could draw a bead on Sorick. At that point, Taylor was still fifty feet up in the night sky above the team. As Sorick rejoined the patrol, the Cobra dropped to the ground ten meters from the team's perimeter. Taylor motioned frantically for the team to climb aboard. The LRRPs stared at each other as if the pilot were nuts. But they weren't in any position to refuse his offer. Cohen and Hill quickly ran around the tail boom to the opposite side of the aircraft and climbed up on the ordnance pylon, draping themselves across the stubby "wing" on each side of the rocket pod.

On the other side of the Cobra, Elsner snapped off the pole antenna on Pool's radio to keep it from hitting the main rotor blade. Sorick got on the left ordnance pylon, while Elsner and Pool stood next to the left skid firing at the enemy weapons blinking away in the two tree lines.

As the aircraft began to lift out of the paddy, the two LRRPs still on the ground quickly secured elbow locks on the skid, then threw their legs over it as the chopper continued to climb. Taylor ascended to five hundred meters while moving steadily away from the area. He finally leveled out and headed southwest, directly toward Saigon. Fifteen minutes later, the helicopter landed near a water tower just off the runway at Tan Son Nhut Air Base.

The team ran up to the cockpit and thanked the pilot for his heroic rescue, then climbed aboard a waiting truck that took them to the MACV compound, where they got hot showers and clean clothes. After enjoying a delicious meal of barbecued chicken with all the fixings, they were debriefed, and Gen. William Westmoreland himself sat in. When it was over, he shook every LRRP's hand and told them they had done an excellent job out there. The team then spent the night at MACV headquarters.

The next day, the company commanding officer, Captain Price, and First Sergeant Morton flew to Saigon to pick up their team. They also congratulated the men and told them they had done a great job. Captain Price informed the five men that Cobra gunships had been in contact around the village all night. The VC had obviously decided the village and the surrounding area were worth fighting for, and they had stayed to contest it. That morning, two infantry companies from the 2/28th went into Ben Suc and immediately made heavy contact. They pulled back and called in an air strike that napalmed the village.

Captain Taylor, whose Cobra took sixteen hits supporting the team during the extraction, received a Distinguished Flying Cross for his heroic actions that night. Sergeant Elsner was awarded a Silver Star, while the rest of the members of the patrol received Bronze Stars with V device.

☆ ☆ ☆ ☆ ☆

Company I,
75th Infantry (Ranger),
1st Infantry Division

The 1st Infantry Division, operating out of Lai Khe in III Corps, had been given the task of protecting the north-western approaches to Saigon from large NVA and VC Main Force units operating from sanctuaries located on both sides of the border dividing South Vietnam and Cambodia. Lai Khe's large size and close proximity to those enemy strong-holds made it a prime target for large numbers of NVA/VC rocket teams. When the Bob Hope Christmas show was scheduled to appear in Lai Khe on Christmas Day 1969, a bi-lateral cease-fire went into effect, and most Big Red One and 1st Cavalry units, some twelve thousand troops, were pulled out of the field to enjoy the entertainment.

Division G-3 realized that an event of that magnitude would be impossible to keep from the prying eyes and lis-tening ears of enemy spies in and around Lai Khe, so it was decided to take a few extra precautions to ensure that enemy forces weren't able to crash the party. Operations ordered Company I, 75th Infantry (Ranger) to deploy three six-man reconnaissance patrols in a reconnaissance screen south of the Saigon River to observe and intercept any NVA/VC rocket teams moving against the base camp. Although three six-man long-range patrols hardly constituted a defense in depth, it was far better than no defense at all.

On 19 December 1969, a warning order came down from division for Company I (Ranger) to infiltrate three of its

teams into recon zones south of the Saigon River between Lai
Khe and the Long Nguyen Secret Zone. The patrols were to
go in during the early morning hours of 21 December and
stay out for five days, returning on the morning of the twenty-
sixth. The orders were a shock to the Rangers of India Company, who had been standing down from missions in order to
prepare for the coming holidays. Even though the Rangers
were aware that they were in a combat zone, the declaration
of a cease-fire had lulled them into a false sense of security—
so much so that they had been busy planning parties. For
three teams, there would be no partying that Christmas.

The team selection for the operation proved to be a bit unusual. First Sergeant Jack D. Frank had decided that the only
fair way to determine who was going to spend five long days
out in the bush and miss the Bob Hope show was to draw
names. With the names of all the team leaders in one hat, and
those of all the patrol members in another, he called a company formation. Then, while the company waited breathlessly, Top Frank selected the names of the three lucky team
leaders, who in turn drew the names of their equally fortunate teammates. When the selection process was completed,
no one, except those whose names had been drawn, seemed
disappointed at the makeup of the three patrols, nor did there
seem to be any great disparity in the talent and experience among them. For once, pure chance seemed to have
worked well.

One team, Tracker Two-two, had drawn a Kit Carson scout
as a member of its patrol, and because the scouts were considered to be part of the company, he was not pulled from the
team. To have done so would have undermined the trust and
integrity of the unit's Kit Carson scouts.

Team Tracker Two-two, led by S.Sgt. Robert Grose, drew a
recon zone just across the Saigon River from Lai Khe. Grose,
an experienced team leader, would walk the slack position,
behind his point man and senior scout, Sp4. Rich Vogel, and
carry his own radio, preset on the artillery frequency. Ty, the

team's Kit Carson scout, would walk the number-three position, behind Grose, where he could be called up quickly to the front of the column if needed. The team's senior RTO, Sp4. Dan Durr, had the fourth spot on the patrol. The junior scout, Sp4. Frank Johnson, took over the five spot, humping the team's artillery, an M-79 grenade launcher with an assortment of HE (high explosive), CS (gas), shotgun, flare, and WP (white phosphorous) rounds. Grose's ATL, Sp4. Myrn Garcia, would take the drag slot at the end of the patrol, sterilizing the team's back trail and making sure they weren't surprised from behind. What the patrol lacked in team integrity, it made up for in experience, and a few of the men had even served together before on other teams.

The overflight on the afternoon of the twentieth showed the RZ to be a vast area of rolling hills covered with lots of brush and single canopy—not a lot of concealment for a six-man reconnaissance team trying to remain hidden. Because of the lack of dense cover, Grose ordered every man on the team to carry two claymores. The antipersonnel mines were great equalizers in tight situations. They would help the team buy time if it had to break cover and run.

During the team's premission briefing, the members of Tracker Two-two were told that the weather for the next five days would remain clear and hot during the day, with the possibility of light showers at night. Showers were a mixed blessing; they could make it more difficult for the enemy to find the team, but they could also ground the Rangers' aviation assets, preventing close air support or emergency extractions.

At first light on the morning of 21 December, the seventeen Rangers and the single Kit Carson scout climbed aboard three Huey slicks. Accompanied by a command-and-control (C & C) chopper and escorted by a pair of Cobra gunships, the six-ship formation flew out toward the Saigon River, where the Hueys bearing the second and third teams went into a high orbit while the C & C aircraft and the two Cobras broke off to insert the first team.

Tracker Two-two was scheduled to go in second. Their slick soon left orbit and joined up with the gunships and the C & C ship. It was nearly 0800 hours when, after faking a couple of false insertions, their aircraft came in high and flared over the edge of a recently burned-out rice paddy. As the aircraft touched down, ashes and debris were sucked up by the chopper's prop wash, blinding the team as it leaped to the ground. Through the swirling cloud of ash, the team ran thirty meters to the edge of the wood line. After hitting the scrub brush and single-canopy trees, they moved for about another ten or fifteen meters before going to ground in a hasty wagon-wheel defensive perimeter. Each man lay silently listening and observing the area to his immediate front as the team's radio operator called in a commo check and gave their first sitrep. With the RTO's duties done, the Rangers lay dog another thirty minutes to make sure that their insertion had gone unnoticed. Finally, satisfied that they had gotten in without being detected, Grose signaled his point man to move out on patrol.

For the remainder of the day, the team patrolled slowly and deliberately through the scrub brush and low trees, constantly on the lookout for any signs of the enemy. They found nothing. After covering two thousand meters, Grose decided to start looking for a place to spend the night. It wasn't long before he spotted a good location. Signaling to his point man to mark the spot, the men moved another hundred meters or so, set up a quick night perimeter, ate their evening meal, then waited for darkness to settle in. Once it was nearly too dark to see, the team picked up and moved quietly back to the spot Grose had previously selected, their real NDP. The move after dark was designed to fool enemy scouts, and it was a simple tactic that had saved many a long-range patrol—and larger units—from ambush, attack, or annihilation. The night proved uneventful.

Day two began with the team moving out at first light. They continued patrolling through the thin vegetation until 1400 hours, when the team discovered a large, high-speed trail back under the single-canopy jungle. The trail was two meters wide and, judging by the footprints, was being heavily used by the enemy. Scratched on stumps and on nearby trees, several markings were visible along the trail. There were X marks, and others comprised of three horizontal lines. The Kit Carson scout was called up to the front of the column and became very anxious when he saw the trail and the enemy signs. Although he didn't know for certain what the signs meant, he knew that the trail was a bad place to remain. Grose agreed with him. The team backed away a safe distance and set up a wagon-wheel perimeter while Durr called in a sitrep.

After the location and direction of the trail were confirmed, the TOC ordered Tracker Two-two to parallel the trail to see where it led. That was always a dangerous sport, since it was difficult to flank a trail in the jungle without making a lot more noise than someone moving down it. But flanking it was a lot safer than walking the trail itself and risking a face-to-face confrontation with a large enemy unit.

The team followed the trail until nearly dark, then once again set up a false NDP twenty meters back from the trail. The team ate its evening meal in shifts and waited for the darkness to settle in. When it was nearly pitch-black, the team quietly moved fifty meters back to a predetermined observation point ten meters or so from the trail, and set out a dozen claymores before settling down for the night.

The patrol spent a miserable night sitting up in a slow, steady downpour. Not much to their surprise, there was no enemy traffic on the trail that night.

Day three was much the same as day two. Every time they moved up to get a closer look at the trail, they spotted more enemy signs posted along it. Then, late in the afternoon while taking a break, the team heard the muffled sounds of enemy voices down the trail in the direction they were moving. They froze in place fifteen meters back from the trail and set up security while the RTO called in the sitrep. The TOC's instructions were to wait and observe.

After about an hour, the sounds of NVA voices began to grow faint as the enemy apparently moved slowly away. Since it was far too late in the day to follow the enemy without the risk of walking into an ambush, the patrol moved a little farther along the trail, then set up the usual false NDP. More carefully than normal, the team ate the second meal of the day in two-man shifts, then moved fifty meters to a new location. They found a good spot and set up an OP/LP about twenty meters back from the trail.

Grose put the team on full alert until 0100 hours. With enemy soldiers in the immediate area, he didn't want to get caught with half the team asleep. Around 2200 hours, the patrol heard movement on the trail, and enemy soldiers began passing by in fairly substantial numbers, clanging together what sounded like metal water cans. Knowing that he had to allow his men to get some sleep, Grose took a risk and put the team on 50 percent alert a little after 0100. Fortunately for him and his Rangers, sometime after 0300 hours the enemy had quieted down and remained that way for the rest of the night.

On the fourth day, the team once again paralleled the trail. But they sensed that they were being watched and tailed. Even so, they made no contact with the enemy during the day. That evening they set up an OP/LP within fifty meters of the Saigon River, twenty to twenty-five meters off the main high-speed trail. After calling in their location and their sitrep, the team was ordered to find a good hiding place where they could remain in position on Christmas Day, then move to their extraction point at first light the following day. Grose was not very happy with his instructions: there was no longer any doubt that they were in the middle of a heavily used enemy trail network. Remaining in place for too long could be a quick invitation to a funeral. And a day and a half in an

OP less than twenty meters from a busy enemy high-speed trail was far too long.

Just before dark, Grose sent out Vogel and Durr to do a quick 360-degree recon around the team's temporary perimeter. He instructed them to locate the team's actual OP/LP for that night and all the next day, then check out the river. Grose didn't want any surprises. If they got hit while they were in their OP, he wanted to know the enemy's most likely avenues of approach and the team's best E & E route.

Right at dark, the team crawled out of its false perimeter and infiltrated to a new spot a hundred meters away. Every member of the team was trying to avoid making any unnecessary sounds as they moved through the night.

Once they were set up in their NDP, Grose ordered them to set out six claymores in a 180-degree fan facing the trail, then another on their backside in the direction of the river. His scouts reported that just behind them the river was nearly one hundred meters across and running pretty swift and muddy. It was not the best natural obstacle to have behind one's defensive perimeter.

It was nearly 2200 hours when the team heard the water cans banging once again. The sounds were not as numerous or as frequent as the night before, but Grose put his team on 100 percent alert until 0100 hours.

The next morning at first light, Grose grew more concerned about spending another entire day and night in their present location. The idea of having the river at their backs and the well-used, high-speed trail across their front was sending "red alerts" coursing through his brain. He told Durr that when he called in the team's sitrep he was to request permission to move the team to a new location just a short distance away. When Durr passed on that information the TOC immediately replied that G-3 had issued orders instructing them to remain where they were.

Day five, Christmas Day, dawned quietly. The team remained in place, but there was a feeling in the air that things were not quite right. At 1000 hours that morning, the patrol began to hear movement from the direction of the trail, but the sounds were coming from the thick brush between the trail and the team's position. To make matters worse, the sounds seemed to be moving directly toward the team.

Grose knew immediately that there was at least a full squad of NVA on line coming through the trees. That meant that the team had been compromised and was in imminent danger of making contact with a larger enemy force. While the Rangers prepared to open fire on the approaching enemy soldiers, Durr called the TOC. Once again, in defiance of common sense and violating the proven tenets of long-range patrolling, they were ordered to remain under cover and avoid contact.

Durr immediately radioed back that the team had no choice but to initiate action. Once more, orders came back—again from headquarters—not to violate the cease-fire. It was apparent that some rear-echelon "commando" would sacrifice the lives of six brave men to uphold a tenuous agreement between two combatants.

Suddenly, a dozen NVA soldiers in camouflage fatigues broke through the brush directly in front of the team's position. Durr whispered into the radio that contact was imminent. When the NVA reached the line of defensive claymores and were seconds from spotting them, Grose gave the signal to blow all the claymores. The resulting explosions killed four NVA outright and wounded several more. The surviving enemy soldiers immediately charged forward in an attempt to overpower the Rangers, but the members of Tracker Two-two opened fire, killing another two or three and sending the remaining three fleeing.

Then a larger enemy force opened up on the team from hidden positions farther up the trail. A heavy volume of small-arms fire, followed by a dozen hand grenades, ripped apart the jungle around the Rangers' perimeter.

Clearly the NVA squad that had attacked the team had

been nothing more than a bird dog trying to locate and flush the Rangers out of their cover, while the real assault force had been held back until contact had been made. With the quarry located, the larger enemy unit was swinging off the trail and pushing forward through the brush, bent on overrunning the Rangers' tiny perimeter.

Fortunately for the outnumbered Americans, the enemy fire was high, but it was only a matter of time before they realized that and made the necessary adjustments—the exact amount of time the Rangers had to survive.

Durr quickly contacted the TOC and reported that the team was in heavy contact and requested an emergency extraction. This time the Ranger TOC acted without waiting for approval from "higher." The TOC reported immediately that they were scrambling the slicks and gunships, and they would be on station in twenty minutes.

Grose knew that they didn't have twenty minutes—they didn't have ten minutes. They had to move immediately in order to survive. Escape and evasion was the only option. Over the din of combat, Grose screamed at his teammates to return fire, then throw out a couple of frags each. While the enemy troops were busy ducking, they would E & E through the narrow corridor that ran between the trail and the river. If their luck held, they just might be able to slip past the attacking NVA without being seen.

Amazingly, the plan worked, but it bought them only a few minutes. As the five Rangers and their Kit Carson scout sprinted past the enemy soldiers assaulting their old position, they were quickly spotted. Within minutes, the remainder of the NVA had wheeled about and started after them.

The enemy pursuit continued close behind for a short distance before the Rangers had to pull up to catch their breath. Panting heavily, they turned to the rear, each dropped to one knee, then opened fire in the general direction of their pursuers. Their heavy volume of fire forced the NVA to stop and regroup, buying the Rangers some time. During the brief lull in the fighting, the patrol turned and took off again, this time zigzagging away on a slightly different azimuth, but still heading in the same general direction. The enemy would soon be right behind them again, but for the moment they were all alone.

The helicopters were still not on station, and the patrol was too far outside the artillery fan to expect any help from that direction. Somehow they had to find a way to stay alive until help could arrive.

Suddenly, an OV-10 Bronco showed up overhead. It had been flying nearby and had picked up the patrol's desperate radio transmissions. Now it was on station, and the pilot was offering his help. Garcia flashed a signal mirror to mark the team's location. As they ran, the spotter plane moved in to fire the only ordnance it had—white phosphorous marker rockets—into the pursuing enemy. The ruse worked! The enemy dove for cover as the phosphorous sprayed through the jungle, some of it falling on the Rangers and burning holes in their fatigues. But the WP gave the team enough time to cut east toward the high-speed trail and some desperately needed maneuvering room.

As the patrol sprinted across the trail and dashed a full hundred meters beyond it, they unexpectedly broke into a large clearing where twelve to fifteen NVA soldiers were busy setting up a trio of 122mm rockets. The NVA were just as surprised as the Americans to find themselves in hostile company, yet they managed to recover quickly enough to get off the first shots. Fortunately for the Rangers, the enemy's aim was bad, the rounds went high, and no one was hit. Instinctively, the Rangers returned fire, and without waiting to measure the results, they cut right and disappeared back into the single canopy heading southeast.

By then the Cobra gunships had arrived on station. The team quickly marked its location and directed the gunships onto the pursuing NVA. The Cobras immediately engaged the enemy troops with rockets and miniguns, putting their ordnance right on top of the NVA. While the Cobras were busy supporting the Rangers, the OV-10 pilot pulled off and circled back to direct a newly arrived flight of F-4 fighter-bombers in to hit the enemy rocket teams.

While the Cobras and the F-4s were doing their thing, Tracker Two-two decided it best not to hang around the area. Somebody might be stupid enough to ask them to do a BDA (bomb-damage assessment) on the air strike. Instead, they continued on a southeasterly heading, still moving in the direction of their extraction point.

The surviving NVA infantry were soon back in hot pursuit, dogging the team's back trail, and there appeared to be more of them than before. Grose kept encouraging his teammates while Vogel did a miraculous job at point keeping the patrol headed in the proper direction. Unknown to the rest of the team, Garcia and Johnson kept dropping back to slow down the enemy. While Garcia hid claymore mines rigged with fifteen-second time fuses along their back trail, Johnson knelt and lobbed HE rounds from his M-79 into the pursuing NVA. While the enemy soldiers were paying the price for being impetuous, the two Rangers sprinted to catch up to their teammates.

Late in the afternoon, the team was still running and dodging enemy units in close pursuit. Grose had continued directing gunships to cover their rear and blast the jungle ahead of them in order to bust up likely ambushes. By 1500 hours, he had exhausted three pairs of gunships. The Cobras had done their job well and had been successful in keeping the NVA at bay, yet they could not prevent them from continuing the pursuit. There was little doubt among anyone involved in the action that if Tracker Two-two could not be extracted by the time the night arrived, they would never live to see the dawn of the next day. Time was running out for them.

Grose had the feeling that the enemy was attempting to push them into a box. The NVA kept trying to move up on their flanks, forcing the patrol to readjust its E & E route. However, Johnson continued putting out HE and CS rounds from his M-79, successfully discouraging the enemy's flanking maneuvers. Momentarily, the tactic seemed to be working, but nearly everyone was out of grenades and running low on ammunition. If the team was to survive, they had to reach a clearing soon.

With darkness setting in, Vogel, Grose, and Ty suddenly broke out of the jungle and into a large open area. Without thinking, the two Rangers and the Kit Carson scout turned left and raced along the edge of the clearing. When Durr, Johnson, and Garcia reached the open area a few seconds later, the first three men had already disappeared. Acting more on instinct than by design, the last three men hit the clearing and cut right to avoid the open terrain. By accident, the patrol had now split into two three-man elements moving in opposite directions.

The first element finally realized that something was wrong and began circling around a large cluster of vegetation out in the middle of the clearing. They were heading back to the right to try to find out what happened to their teammates. The second element, realizing that they had also made a mistake, had already made a swing back to the left. Now in the shadowy twilight, the two elements were heading directly for each other, with itchy fingers resting on the triggers of their weapons.

Overhead, the C & C aircraft and a pair of circling slicks saw what had happened. As Captain Wright, the Ranger commanding officer, flying overhead in the C & C, continued to work the gunships, he made contact with the two Ranger elements and told them what was happening. He directed them around the cover until they had successfully linked up once again. That took nearly thirty minutes.

By that time, the pursuing NVA had also arrived at the edge of the clearing and had begun firing out into the open terrain. There was now plenty to shoot at down on the ground, and the gunships began picking targets of opportunity. Finally, Captain Wright radioed the team and told them to prepare to extract; their slick was on final approach.

As the Huey touched down, the six members of the patrol broke from cover and dashed for the waiting aircraft, diving aboard from the right side. The pilot lifted the aircraft out of the clearing and departed the PZ in great haste, taking fire all the way out. Amazingly, the ship, its crew, and the passengers suffered no hits.

When the team finally touched down at Lai Khe, the entire company was waiting at the chopper pad to greet them. Amid much handshaking, hugging, and backslapping, the members of the patrol were ordered to throw their gear into a waiting vehicle and then climb into the first sergeant's jeep parked nearby. Still wearing their cammo fatigues and face paint, the men were then transported to a nearby NCO club, where they were treated to all the cold beer and steaks they could handle. Much to their embarrassment, the members of Tracker Two-two were being treated as celebrities. Nearly everyone they encountered seemed to have heard about the mission.

Much later that night, five grossly inebriated Rangers were escorted to their bunks to sleep off the festivities. Somewhere in the neighborhood, an unconscious Kit Carson scout was likely doing the same thing. It had been a party of gigantic proportions.

The next day, still nursing throbbing hangovers, the team was officially debriefed. Some mighty big brass had arrived for the mission debriefing, and when it was over they told the Ranger patrol that they had done an outstanding, professional job. To the men of Tracker Two-two, it had been just another day at the office. They were to receive no medals for their heroics, but to a man, they all had to admit that they really would have liked to have seen that Bob Hope show.

LRRP Detachment, 1st Cavalry Division

In the fall of 1967, the three brigades of the 1st Cavalry Division were operating out of different areas, from An Khe all the way south to Phan Thiet. The division LRRPs had been split accordingly, with four teams working out of An Khe and three teams patrolling the rolling plains outside Phan Thiet. On 15 September 1967, a warning order came down from division G-2 for an unusual reconnaissance mission in an area about twenty klicks west of Phan Thiet. The mission was assigned to Sgt. Ron Holte's five-man long-range reconnaissance patrol.

The mission called for the recon team to be flown by Huey helicopter out to a Cav firebase on the morning of 18 September. Once on the ground, the five LRRPs would accompany a platoon-size infantry patrol as it walked off the firebase and into the countryside. The LRRP patrol would then move west until it reached a point two klicks out from the firebase, where it was supposed to remain behind while the grunts continued their own patrol. Only after the infantry patrol returned to the firebase would the LRRPs' mission begin. Sounded simple!

On the afternoon of the seventeenth, Holte and his ATL, Sp4. Virgil Hoffman, made an overflight to see what they had to deal with in their area of operations. From four thousand feet, the terrain was level to rolling with lots of open ground.

Some of the open areas looked like cropped pastureland; others were covered with high elephant grass, scattered brush, and an occasional tree or two. In the wooded areas, the forests were thin and scattered, primarily single canopy. It didn't look like LRRP country to him. Holte couldn't help but wonder how enemy troops could hide in such terrain; he knew they managed to do it all the time.

Holte, whose call sign was Tough Ranger Three-Charlie, had been in country just over eight months. He had previously served a couple of years in Germany with NATO forces before being assigned to Vietnam, where he had paid his dues for six months as a squad leader with Charlie Company, 1st Battalion, 7th Cav. After volunteering for the LRRPs, he had been one of the honor graduates of the 1st Cav LRRP School and had also completed the demanding three-week MACV Recondo School at Nha Trang. Holte carried his own radio on missions and always walked slack. Like the rest of the men on his team, his basic weapon was the CAR-15, which he supplemented with a Smith & Wesson .38 for close-in work.

Virgil Hoffman was the patrol's "big man." Even Ron Holte's six-foot-two frame was dwarfed by the six-foot-four, 220-pound tight end who served as his assistant team leader. The oversize LRRP ATL was also a good man in the field. He walked the number-three slot in the patrol and carried the team's other PRC-25 radio. Hoffman had only one problem: when he first joined the team he had a nasty habit of questioning everything that Holte said or did. But Holte eventually realized that the guy was a natural and wrote off his apparent rudeness as the first sign of budding leadership.

Besides Hoffman, Holte's five-man team was made up of two Montagnards and PFC Angel Morales, a Puerto Rican LRRP who was new to the team. Holte had designated Morales the team medic, and had added an M-79 grenade launcher to the soldier's basic ordnance. Morales would patrol in the number-four slot immediately behind Hoffman.

After trying unsuccessfully to work South Vietnamese soldiers into their teams, the Cav LRRPs had settled on Montagnards and had never regretted the decision. Lich, the older
and more experienced of the two, had already earned his
place at point; he had long ago proved to Holte that he was
both courageous and loyal in the field, and the team leader
trusted him as much as any man on the patrol.

Quyen, younger than Lich, was as yet unproven. He
seemed nervous and jumpy, and bore watching. Holte didn't
really know what to expect from the Yard if the team ran into
trouble. With some reluctance he let the younger Montagnard
carry the URC-80 UHF emergency radio transmitter and the
top-secret starlight scope.

The mission was scheduled to last five days. The weather
would remain hot and clear, so it would not interfere with gunship support if it was needed. Holte hoped that it would not be.

In addition to his weapons, each member of the team also
carried two white-phosphorous grenades, four fragmentation
grenades on his belt and four to six more in his ruck, one CS
grenade, one smoke grenade, and one claymore mine. Each
man also carried a minimum load of fifteen magazines, all
loaded with tracer ammo. Even Holte's pistol was loaded
with tracer rounds. In spite of the tracer round's poorer ballis-
tics, Holte believed that the visual confusion of five magazines
of tracers converging on him at one time would be enough to
give any VC or NVA pause. It took a brave man or a fool to
stand up and return fire in the face of a hundred red tracers.

Early in the morning on 18 September 1967, Holte's team
loaded aboard a Huey slick and flew out to the tiny Cav fire-
support base. The flight took nearly twenty minutes, and when
the slick set down just inside the perimeter, they found that the
infantry patrol was just getting ready to go out. Wearing OD
jungle fatigues over their tiger stripes, the men of the long-
range patrol took their places in the center of the infantry platoon and prepared to leave the perimeter. At 0900 hours, the
patrol moved out into the countryside.

The LRRP team remained in the center of the column until 1000 hours, approximately two klicks from the firebase, when the five men suddenly dropped to the ground and let the infantry continue on with their patrol, quickly closing up the gap in the column. While the grunts put distance between themselves and the recon patrol, the LRRPs pulled off their OD fatigues and stuck them in their rucksacks. While remaining prone on the ground, they pulled out their cammo sticks and painted the exposed parts of their faces, hands, and necks.

Holte had instructed the infantry platoon leader not to come back through the team's recon zone. But just in case, he kept his team hidden in the grass for nearly a full thirty minutes while the infantry circled around to the south then headed back toward the firebase.

Holte radioed for a commo check and reported his position before leaving the cover and heading due west. The patrol moved nearly a klick before Holte signaled that it was time to lay dog. It was almost noon by then, and Holte didn't like moving in the middle of the day. He knew that the Vietnamese liked to lay up during the heat of the day. To actively patrol while the enemy was resting was a good way to walk into them without realizing where they were.

While his patrol rested in what little shade the midday sun allowed, Holte got out his binoculars and glassed the open area around them. Suddenly, an air force FAC plane flew over the edge of the team's recon zone. Something was definitely wrong with that because no one was supposed to come anywhere near a LRRP team's patrol box. Someone had screwed up their signals, and now Holte's team was in danger.

Holte instructed his men to remain hidden and not to move until the FAC left the area. When it was finally gone, he contacted his TOC and reported what had just happened. He was more than a little pissed, and he wanted the situation handled immediately.

Assured that the problem would be taken care of, Holte

signaled Lich to move out. He took the team another klick, where they crossed the bed of a seasonal creek that ran across an open field. Holte called another security stop for thirty minutes to monitor a distant wood line and some brushy spots out in the middle of the open terrain. He soon spotted a faint trail running along the edge of the nearby wood line, but there was very little cover around it.

Finally, he moved the patrol into a sheltered spot and told his teammates to take a break and eat chow if they wanted to. It was almost 1700 hours. As soon as they finished eating, Holte had everyone bury their trash and sterilize the site. When they were through, they moved out once again, this time checking some of the wooded islands out in the middle of the field.

Just before dusk they crawled into a dense, brushy area, then waited until it got totally dark before moving another one hundred meters to set up their overnight OP/LP. Holte had his men put out claymores; then he divided up the guard shift, one man on at a time, one hour per shift. Their OP/LP was in a good spot, within hearing distance of the stream and about fifty meters' line of sight from the trail. With the starlight scope, nothing could pass without being seen. The first night was uneventful.

The next morning, Holte had his team eat chow right after first light. He called in a quick sitrep, and ordered Lich to move out. They took their time going two hundred to three hundred meters, then stopped for a long security halt that lasted thirty minutes.

At 1000 hours, they encountered another streambed; this time it was dry. The air force FAC was once again flying just outside the team's AO, one thousand feet up and not more than a quarter mile away. Once again, they hid until it passed from view.

At 1100 hours the team moved out again, then took another long security halt. At 1400 hours, they were up again and patrolling once more. Then, at 1500 hours, the point man stopped the team and motioned Holte up to the front of the patrol. There in the grass were the depressions left by the bodies of twelve to fifteen men who had lain there in ambush until a short time before. Lich searched the grass until he figured out what had happened, then reported to Holte. It appeared that the enemy squad had been on a collision course with the approaching LRRP patrol. Obviously, the enemy soldiers had spotted the Americans before the Americans had spotted them. When they did, they had immediately gone on line across the path of the oncoming recon team. But for some reason, they had changed their minds before the American patrol had gotten in range, and had picked up their weapons and moved out smartly to the north. Holte reckoned that when the enemy spotted the heavily armed LRRP patrol coming through the grass, alert and heading right for them, the enemy squad leader had decided that discretion was the better part of valor, and had ordered a hasty retreat into some thick brush somewhere off in the distance. Obviously, he had considered that tackling five LRRPs in the open was more than he wanted to handle.

The LRRP team leader called in to report that he had been compromised. When asked if he wanted an extraction, Holte replied that he wanted to continue the mission.

The patrol moved past the spot where the enemy soldiers had spread out across their trail and headed for the wood line two hundred meters away, where the enemy squad's back trail disappeared. Suddenly, Lich spotted three butterfly mines lying three meters to the side of the enemy squad's trail through the grass, directly in the path of the approaching LRRPs. The mines were approximately halfway between the depressions in the grass and the edge of the woods. Lich signaled Holte up to see the mines, and when the LRRP team leader was standing to one side looking right down at them, he still could not see them. His respect for his Montagnard point man immediately increased tenfold.

Holte called in the coordinates of the mines to the TOC,

then signaled for Lich to head for the wood line a hundred meters away. Fifty meters away from the trees, Holte stopped the patrol, took Lich and moved to within twenty-five meters of the woods, then squatted down to cover Lich while the Kit Carson scout moved cautiously into the wood line. As he reached it, he turned and signaled for Holte to come up to where he stood waiting. When Holte neared the woods and saw that there was no ambush, he signaled for the rest of the team to move up quickly. As soon as everyone was together again Holte realized that they were standing at the same spot where the enemy squad had come out of the woods. Their trail down through the grass was still easy to follow.

Holte spotted a creek just ahead of them, inside the trees. Expecting a reception committee at any moment, the LRRP team leader kept three men hidden in the grass at the edge of the trees while he and Lich moved deeper into the forest to check out the area around the stream. Finding no fresh sign of enemy troops, he signaled the other three LRRPs forward, and crossed the creek. It was not a permanent stream, but there were pockets of fresh water every five to ten meters.

The patrol went another thirty meters into the woods, then buttonhooked to the left, where they encountered a smoldering fire and a piece of WD-1 commo wire strung between two trees. It had either been used as a clothesline or the enemy had draped a plastic ground cloth over it to make a shelter. On the other side of the fire, a single hammock was tied between two trees. Obviously, the long-range patrol had interrupted somebody. The team leader now knew for certain that they were compromised. Besides the near miss on an enemy patrol out in the grass, they had just run off a trail watcher or two, or perhaps maybe another enemy squad resting at the edge of the woods. Fresh trails led off in several different directions. The enemy soldiers in the area knew they had visitors.

Holte set his team up in a circular defensive perimeter while he called in a sitrep to report what they had just found.

In his patrol notebook, he had recorded everything that had been discovered, and he had taken photographs of the fire, the commo wire, and the hammock with his Penn EE 35mm camera. When he was finished, he once again moved out to the edge of the forest and glassed the field out in front of them with his binoculars. His nerves had become tense. He could almost smell the enemy close by.

Trails, streams, and clearings were always danger areas, and in their location, the LRRPs were right in the midst of all of them at one time. They would have to be extra cautious or they could find themselves in a major predicament.

Lich led them south through the woods at a right angle to the open area they had just crossed. Soon, they reached another small open field set farther back in the woods. Skirting the edge of the field for a short distance, the team moved farther south. Holte didn't like the sparse cover along the edge of the clearing. There was no place for them to hide. Then he spotted a thickly wooded island about a third of the way out in the field. Since it was getting late in the day, he decided to take an extended security halt right there along the edge of the woods until it was fully dark, then move his team out into the field and into the timbered island.

When they reached the island, they discovered that it was only thirty meters across. Holte whispered for his men not to set out their claymores. There was not a lot of cover or concealment available, and he didn't want to risk anyone back in the trees spotting them moving about in the thicket.

From where the team hid in the island, they could see 360 degrees around them, and especially the trail that ran along the edge of the trees. Holte wasted no time getting under his poncho, pulling out his map, compass, and penlight, and marking artillery preplots, back at the campfire, along the trail to their front, and at a number of points along the edge of the forest around them. If they got hit during the night, having arty on call would greatly improve their chances of survival.

Holte doubled security, posting two guards on at a time, for full one-hour shifts. He would pull the odd man's shifts himself. Even though Holte expected the worst, the night once again proved uneventful.

The third day, the team moved out early, heading southwest along the edge of the woods in broken cover. After going about a hundred meters, they stopped for a while to listen and get a commo check. Holte was being especially careful because he still had the feeling they were in grave danger.

It wasn't long before they moved out again and immediately ran into another small clearing. At around 1600 hours on the back side of the clearing, they discovered a huge high-speed trail, four to six feet wide, coming out of the woods. The trail was bare, hard-packed dirt and looked wide enough to handle motor vehicles. It ran southwest out of the main woods, then curved to the west.

Holte felt exposed there in the open next to the main trail, so he had Lich take the team in a wide circle about four hundred meters out and then come nearly all the way back again to the timbered island where the team had set up the night before. When they reached the edge of the woods along the southern edge of the field, they came up on their back trail to ambush whoever might be following.

Soon it began to grow dark, and the patrol crawled into some thick brush and set up an ambush farther back in the woods, a full hundred meters off their back trail and fifteen feet from the edge of the field. Holte had everyone put out their claymores. Feeling more secure in that location, he posted only one man on guard at a time. Once again the night passed without incident.

At first light on the fourth day, everyone ate a quick breakfast, then buried his rubbish. Holte whispered for anyone who needed it to move outside the perimeter and answer nature's call, then get ready to move out. Only Morales stepped outside the perimeter.

Holte called in his morning sitrep and was on his knees replacing the pole antenna with the short-whip antenna when a VC soldier walked down along the edge of the field about ten meters out from the wood line heading north. The VC was only about ten meters from Holte but had not yet spotted him. Not far away, back in the trees, Morales was squatting with his pants around his knees, watching the VC. Unfortunately, he had placed his CAR-15 against a tree about six feet away. Morales knew that if he shouted a warning or dove for his weapon the VC would go for his gun and shoot first.

The VC had stopped and was standing directly behind Holte when he suddenly turned and looked to his left and spotted the LRRP team leader. Slowly, the VC unshouldered his SKS carbine and took aim at the middle of Holte's back. Morales could do nothing but watch the sad tragedy unfold.

But before the Viet Cong could pull the trigger, he spotted Hoffman, Lich, and Quyen out of the corner of his eye. He must have decided at that moment that one against four were not very good odds. Carefully, he lowered his weapon and started backing slowly away until he had put some distance between himself and the men with the painted faces. Satisfied that he now had a chance to escape, he suddenly took off running toward a clump of brush out in the field three hundred meters away.

Morales had been making his personal "deposit" near a little brush line that ran from the woods directly out into the field not far from where the VC had just disappeared. When he saw the VC suddenly lower his weapon and take off for the next province, Morales quickly finished his business, snatched up his weapon (and his pants), and rushed back into the perimeter, where he whispered hoarsely to Hoffman, "A VC had the drop on Holte."

Hoffman, thinking Holte was still in danger, immediately jumped to his feet and put a ferocious flying tackle on his team leader, driving him hard into the ground. Holte landed flat on his back. Shocked and gasping for breath, he looked up at Hoffman and said, "What the hell are you doing?"

Hoffman, wild-eyed and shaking with excitement, answered, "VC!"

"Oh!" Holte replied meekly.

Holte turned slowly to the right and saw that Morales was standing there white as a sheet. Holte asked him to explain what had just happened, then proceeded to chew his ass out after hearing the full story. Wasting no more time, he called the team together, reattached the pole antenna, and called in a revised sitrep, reporting that the team had just been compromised for the third time. When Holte was asked if he wanted to extract, he told the TOC that he was going after the VC.

Taking Morales, because he had seen where the VC had gone, and Quyen, Holte started out into the field. He left Hoffman and Lich behind in the perimeter to guard the rucks and both radios. Quyen quickly cut Holte off from going out into the field, then went out in the open himself, walking directly toward the brushy cover where the VC had disappeared. Holte and Morales remained in the brush line and began moving toward the same spot. Holte held up his hand to signal Quyen to delay his advance until Holte and Morales could move up closer to the spot. The three LRRPs now had the patch of brush in a cross fire. Unfortunately, the VC was no longer there when they reached it. Keeping the brush between himself and the American recon team, he had slipped out the back side.

The three men checked out a few other nearby thickets and brushy areas, then returned to their perimeter. Once again, Holte called in sitrep. And once again, the TOC asked him if he wanted to be extracted. Remembering that Colonel Stevens, the division G-2, had previously developed a bad impression of LRRPs because he felt they had been calling for extractions for trivial reasons, Holte decided it was still not time to come out yet.

It was 0730. The team moved due west toward the spot where they had discovered the major trail the evening before.

Lich led them a third of a mile into the woods, then stopped to set up a security position.

Deciding to set up a two-man ambush out on the trail, Holte dropped his rucksack and whispered his intentions to his teammates. Hoffman immediately volunteered to go along as the second man. Holte told him that he wanted him to remain with the radios, then turned to the two Yards and asked which one was the "number-one shot." When this failed to solicit the response that Holte wanted, he pointed at Lich and emulated firing a weapon, then pointed at him and said, "Number-one shot?"

Suddenly, Quyen got very upset and pounded his chest and said, "Me numba one, me numba one." Then he pointed his weapon as if he were aiming it and repeated, "Me numba one, me numba one." Holte nodded, then turned to Hoffman and told him that if he heard any shooting, to call in and request an immediate extraction. He said that if the ambush team didn't return within fifteen minutes after he heard the gunfire, he was to head toward the rendezvous point and wait there for fifteen minutes more. If they didn't show up by then, the team was to move to the PZ and get extracted.

Holte and Quyen then dropped their packs and radios and slipped out of the perimeter. They took their time edging up to within twenty-five meters of the trail at the point where it exited the woods. In what little concealment was available, they knelt down behind some trees and took up a hasty ambush position.

Five minutes later, a single enemy soldier, carrying his AK-47 at the ready, walked out of the tree line on the trail and moved about ten meters out into the open, where he stopped. As the two LRRPs simultaneously drew beads on him, he slowly scanned the open field to his front a full 180 degrees. The enemy soldier appeared highly cautious and extremely alert. Wearing a khaki uniform, pith helmet, and a heavy ruck, he was definitely an NVA.

Then, before Holte and Quyen could squeeze the trigger,

the NVA soldier started to walk slowly down the trail, as a second NVA stepped out of the woods. This second man was maintaining a proper interval about ten meters back from the point man and scanning the open field to his right. As soon as he was ten meters out in the open, a third NVA came into sight, scanning 180 degrees to his left.

Holte could see that those guys were good. Realizing that there was probably a larger element still back in the trees, he made the snap decision to open fire before they got out in the field.

Quyen was to Holte's left, kneeling upright. Holte was bent over in a low-profile kneeling position. Suddenly, he raised his weapon, thumbed it to semiauto, and drew a bead on the lead NVA fifty meters out in the open. Holte squeezed off a shot that seemed to take the NVA high in the left thigh, then shifted his fire quickly to the second man as he switched his weapon to full automatic. However, before he could fire, Quyen had already emptied a full magazine of tracer rounds into the man's body. Seeing this, Holte continued swinging on to the third man, who had now turned around and was staring back into the trees with a stunned look on his face. Holte emptied the rest of his mag into the man, dropping him where he stood. The results of the hasty ambush were two NVA down for good, and the point man badly wounded.

The two LRRPs then turned and sprinted for the perimeter. They had only seconds before the rest of the NVA back in the woods recovered their poise and responded. Only seconds before, the hunters became the hunted.

Trying to change his Y-shaped triple-magazine configuration as he ran, Holte dropped it. Quyen was ten feet ahead of him and running full tilt at the time. Holte quickly realized that if the NVA found the three magazines taped together, they would immediately know what kind of unit they were facing and come after them like bats out of hell. He had no choice; the team leader stopped and ran back twenty feet to recover the magazine. Believing Quyen was probably in the next province by then, Holte was totally surprised when he turned back around and found his Yard kneeling at his side with his weapon at his shoulder, covering his ass.

Holte shouted, "Let's get the hell out of here," which Quyen seemed to have no trouble understanding. There was still no return fire from the enemy. The two LRRPs took advantage of that and gained another five hundred meters in the direction of their teammates.

As the two men neared the perimeter, Holte yelled ahead, "Did you call in the contact?" Hoffman said he had already done so and had asked for an extraction. Hoffman was shaking and nervous because he had no idea what had just happened, and Holte didn't have time for explanations at the moment. He screamed to his teammates that they had to get out fast, then led his four comrades in a mad dash heading east. Running through the open woods in file, they had still not taken any fire.

ARA gunships soon arrived on station, coming in just over the treetops and passing directly over the team. The first gunship confirmed the team's location, while the second aircraft, coming in a little higher, unloaded its rockets on the team's flanks and especially across their rear. By then, the first aircraft had circled around and followed up with a second attack.

The patrol soon reached the swampy area on the south side of the field where they had encountered the single VC earlier that morning. They had to wait a minute or two while the C & C tried to reach them on the radio. When he finally made contact, he told the team to remain where they were. He said that anything beyond the team's immediate perimeter was now fair game and warned them to stay away from the tree line.

The C & C then directed the extraction ship in to pick up the waiting team. The Huey soon settled down in the clearing no more than thirty meters away. On the ground, each member of the patrol fired most of a magazine into the trees around them, then broke cover and ran for the aircraft, onloading from both sides.

It was a twenty-minute flight back to Phan Thiet. As the Huey reached the company compound, Holte spotted a number of rear-echelon brass standing in a line outside a bunker near the open area where the chopper was landing. As the Huey swung around with the LRRPs now riding the skids, Holte wondered what was happening down on the ground.

After the aircraft had landed and the LRRPs had disembarked, Holte walked up to the officers and saluted each one as they extended their hands to congratulate him for a job well done. The humble team leader was both embarrassed and frustrated by all the attention he seemed to be receiving.

The five LRRPs dropped their gear at their bunker and headed for the TOC for the debriefing. It lasted only an hour. The team leader and assistant team leader compared notes in front of the company operations NCO, Staff Sergeant Campbell, who took everything down on a notepad. Afterward, the entire team shared their experiences. Then they went to clean up and grab a bite to eat.

The next day, Holte was told that two platoons of grunts had been sent into the area right after the team had been pulled out. They had made contact almost immediately and killed fifteen NVA. They were still out there looking for more.

Holte later caught hell from one of the staff officers at G-2 for not making an effort to recover the weapons and rucksacks from the three NVA they had shot. But Holte only grinned; he never let that kind of crap bother him.

Company G, 75th Infantry (Ranger), 23d (American) Infantry Division

During the height of the Vietnam War, there were always tidbits of information floating around about sightings of Communist Chinese advisers assisting North Vietnamese Army troops in battle. Everyone "knew" that it was going on; everybody knew someone who knew someone who had been on a mission that had killed a Chicom adviser. The trouble was that no one ever seemed able to get a dead one out or, better yet, capture a live one and bring him out. Christ, what a coup that would be! The top brass would probably decorate the entire team and make everyone an officer. Yeah, they would!

It only made good sense! If the Chinese and Soviets were supplying the NVA and the VC with most of their weapons and communications equipment, then they had to be advising them on how to use the stuff. Hell, we did it, why wouldn't they?

Well, after a while, it became sort of a fantasy that every LRRP or Ranger had to return from a mission with a captured Chicom adviser in tow. It meant instant gratification, instant credibility, instant fame.

So when a long-range patrol from Company G, 75th Infantry (Ranger), suddenly found itself in a position to grab a real Chinese adviser, they threw away SOP and conventional wisdom and went for the snatch.

The mission had come down from the hierarchy of the 196th Light Infantry Brigade with the added directive that the AO was particularly hot. To the men of G Company, all of their AOs had been particularly hot of late. So they took the dire warning to mean that their new AO was *exceptionally* hot. Probably because of that, the mission was assigned to Team Arkansas, under the very capable leadership of S.Sgt. Jerl "England" Freeland.

Due to a spate of excessive casualties, ETSs, DEROSs, R & Rs, and TDYs, the company had been fielding four- and five-man patrols for several months. However, the new mission would enjoy the rare luxury of a full six-man complement, leading some of its members to describe themselves as a "heavy" team. And speaking of heavy, Team Arkansas was simply chock-full of heavyweights. The Golf Company commanding officer had given his blessing to Freeland to select anyone he could con into volunteering for the mission. The tough team leader took the old man's word as gospel, and recruited the finest all-star team he could assemble. Like Freeland, sergeants Ben "Babysan" Dunham, P. J. Grossman, and Oliver "Ollie" Reamy were all experienced team leaders, assuring that leadership would not be a problem on Team Arkansas. The grenadier, Sp4. Sam "Gratis" Schreiber, was arguably the finest thumper operator in the unit; he could fire an M-79 with the accuracy of a Marine sniper. And then there was Sp4. Bobby Sedlemeyer, the first-draft choice of every team leader in G Company. There was little doubt that Freeland had put together a fine ball club. Team Arkansas might be called a Golf Company "dream team."

The patrol left late in the afternoon. The Huey slick skimmed across the treetops, zeroing in on a small hillside clearing in the middle of the jungle. Before the chopper even had a chance to touch down, the crew chief shouted over the intercom, "Go! They're out!" The aircraft commander looked back as he lifted out of the clearing, but the six Rangers had already disappeared into the jungle.

The team lay dog twenty meters off the clearing in the middle of dense underbrush. As five pairs of watchful eyes scanned the jungle outside their tiny perimeter, the team RTO got a quick commo check and gave the first mission sitrep. Three minutes on the ground, and they already had fresh intelligence for the boys back at brigade S-2—they were sitting right next to one very fresh high-speed trail. To make matters even stickier, when their aircraft had been on short final, the air crew and a couple of the Rangers had spotted three Vietnamese and a dog standing on another trail less than two hundred meters from the LZ. It was a sure bet that the team's insertion was no longer a neighborhood secret.

Under normal circumstances, being observed during an insertion would have involved the team getting both stubs punched on their round-trip ticket; the team was compromised. At worst, the team would have been flown back to base, the mission scrapped. At best, the team would have been picked up and reinserted at their secondary LZ. But they were on a top-priority mission. The intelligence people at brigade wanted the team in that AO in the worst way. There was no longer any question of there being "little people" there; brigade wanted to know how many there were and what they were doing.

Freeland quickly decided to move out immediately into the jungle, then double back on their trail to see if they were being followed. He was worried about the three dinks and their puppy less than two football fields away. If the dinks' mission was to keep their eyes on the clearing, their job was over. They could report back to their superior that the enemy had landed. If they were just three local villagers out walking their dog, well, they could still earn a lot of brownie points from the local VC commander for turning in an American long-range patrol. And the dog was a bad sign. It was hard enough to slip an enemy trail watcher. It was twice as hard to slip one with a dog.

Hiding in the brush along their back trail, it didn't take them long to discover that the three Vietnamese and their canine companion were indeed following the team. The patrol's normal response would have been to lie in ambush until the trackers were in their kill zone, then blow them all away, including the dog. But the team's mission was to find out what was happening in their AO. Opening the operation with a fireworks display would only make further "snooping and pooping" a moot endeavor. So, with all the acumen at their disposal, the six Rangers made preparations to "slip" their tail. Quickly prying open a canister of CS gas, the Rangers dusted their back trail with liberal amounts of the white powder. Tossing the empty can into a nearby thicket, the team formed up on the high-speed and moved out, risking all the perils of running trails in the middle of Indian country. Even though they were taught not to do that, they were intent on putting some major distance between themselves and the enemy trackers.

The patrol had gone nearly a hundred meters, when suddenly from behind them came the most horrible sound. At first, none of the Rangers could identify it; then Dunham realized that it was the dog trying to exorcise a nose full of CS crystals. Seconds later, the forest carried the most horrible howling sounds that the six Rangers had ever heard. They could barely contain their laughter as each man formed his own mental image of the scene that was unfolding a couple hundred meters behind them. However, there was little doubt among them that their friendly neighborhood trackers now numbered one less.

By then, it was growing dark, and the patrol knew it had to find a safe place on high ground to harbor up for the night. The point man angled off the trail, moving straight up the hillside through the brushy single-canopy jungle. The climb was not difficult, and the team soon found itself edging along cautiously in the dim light of an early moon.

Finally, they reached the top of the hill and slipped quickly over the crest. But it was darker on the reverse slope, and the Rangers had a difficult time moving without bumping into everything in their path. Freeland whispered to the point man to look for a place to set up an NDP. A few minutes later, they were clearing a spot in a patch of thick undergrowth and setting out a ring of claymores around their position.

They hadn't been settled in for long when a series of eerie, alien noises began emanating from down in the valley below the patrol. They sounded almost human but were totally unidentifiable, which made their effect on the six Rangers even more pronounced. Somewhere down below them, the VC were showing that this was still their domain. They remained active throughout the night, forcing the long-range patrol to remain on full alert, forgoing much-needed sleep.

The night passed very slowly. The enemy had tried his best to throw a scare into the American recon patrol they knew was hiding somewhere nearby, but that was not a normal patrol; the team of crusty eighteen- to twenty-year-old Rangers had been through riskier situations than that; they knew that only cool heads would keep them alive and help to ensure the success of their mission.

Shortly before dawn, the enemy forces in the valley had either given up on the idea of scaring the American recon team away or believed they had succeeded. Up on the hill, the Rangers decided to move out before the faint illumination of the false dawn made them visible to enemy troops who might be waiting to hit them at dawn. Cautiously, they gathered in the claymores, sanitized the NDP, then moved out of the perimeter while it was still quite dark. Each man following closely the LRRP to his front, the six Rangers slipped silently along the slope toward their final objective.

It was nearly noon when they reached their designated OP, a spot high above the valley on an ancient man-made terrace. Years ago, maybe in more peaceful times, Vietnamese farmers had harvested rice there high above sea level. The unused rice paddies had stood fallow long enough for the hillside jungles to reclaim them. There the patrol established its OP. From their vantage point, they could observe two villages at the edge of the jungle down on the valley floor.

The valley itself was a place of beauty, right off the cover of an Indochina travel guide. The two villages, neither of them large, lay facing each other at opposite ends of the valley. They were separated by an extensive grid of rich rice paddies running along both flanks of a stream that meandered down the center of the valley. At the foot of the mountain, a network of interlocking footpaths connected the two villages.

Freeland set up one-man watches to observe the valley, gave the first one to Dunham, and told the rest of his teammates to grab some sleep until it was their turn to pull a shift. Everything was quiet until midafternoon, when Freeland was on watch. Everything seemed peaceful down below until he suddenly spotted an armed NVA patrol passing by on a trail two hundred meters directly below the team's OP. As he was busy counting them, he hissed loudly back over his shoulder to awaken and alert the rest of his teammates. Soon, Grossman, the team's ATL, had moved up to his side and was busy confirming Freeland's count.

Observing the enemy unit through his binoculars, Freeland's attention was drawn to the last man in the patrol. He was much taller and stockier than the other enemy soldiers who preceded him. The man, who wore a shoulder holster and carried no other weapon, bore facial features that seemed far too broad and too round to be Vietnamese.

The two Rangers watched the NVA until they disappeared into the nearest village. Then Freeland left Grossman on watch and moved back to brief the rest of his patrol. He and Grossman had counted thirty uniformed NVA carrying heavy packs and weapons. Each man was wearing similar olive-drab uniforms and pith helmets bearing bright red stars on the front. These well-equipped and well-armed soldiers were undoubtedly hard-core NVA troops. Freeland ventured a guess that their tail-end Charlie was a Chinese Communist adviser.

While the rest of the team cleared the cobwebs from their brains and saw to their weapons and gear, Freeland called the company TOC and reported the sighting. While he waited for a reply, the four Rangers squatting around him began discussing their options. One of them wanted to go right down there and capture that "Chinese son of a bitch." It sounded like a hell of an idea to the rest of the team, and before long, they had taken a vote among themselves that that was exactly what they were going to do. They spent the next ten minutes planning a strategy, and when they were satisfied with the results, Freeland had them pull in their claymores and check their gear. When everyone was ready, he told Dunham to move out and get the team in position on the outside of the village where the NVA had disappeared.

A half hour later, the patrol reached the edge of the village, and Dunham led them quickly into the heaviest cover he could find. Ahead of them, the trail curved around the base of a low hill and disappeared from sight. Dunham signaled for the team to drop down on all fours and begin low-crawling behind him toward the bend in the trail. He had reasoned that the low hill to their front would keep the enemy from spotting them. Unfortunately, it would also keep them from observing the enemy.

Dunham was about ten meters from the bend in the trail when a small Vietnamese boy suddenly appeared at the edge of the hill. Immediately, the Ranger point man rose to his knees and drew down on the frightened lad. However, he stopped just short of squeezing the trigger when he saw that the boy was standing frozen in place, staring horrified at the six terrifying apparitions kneeling on the trail in front of him. No doubt he had been told many bloodcurdling tales about the "men with painted faces" who came silently in the night and devoured small children who didn't obey their parents. Well, sure enough, here were six of them right before him. He had just become a meal.

The boy's look of abject fear changed quickly to one of total surprise. Realizing that he had not yet been devoured, he suddenly pivoted 180 degrees and disappeared back around the bend in the trail.

Jumping to his feet and advancing to the spot where the boy's skid marks still lay smoking on the hard-packed earthen trail, Dunham spotted him standing just around the bend next to an ancient crone. She was squatting idly in front of a hootch nestled back in the trees and was preoccupied peeling some kind of sweet potato. The boy was standing at her shoulder talking rapidly and pointing back behind him down the trail. For some reason, he seemed to be having difficulty getting his message across, because the old woman continued peeling the potato, totally unconcerned about his rantings. Seconds later, the boy turned back up the trail and locked gazes with the short, but deadly looking Ranger point man. This time he remained where he was, saying nothing to the old woman. Maybe it was his sudden silence that made the old lady turn her head and look down the trail. When she finally spotted the six frightfully painted soldiers standing over pointed weapons, she merely turned back to the front and continued peeling that damned yam, not missing a stroke in the process. However, Dunham thought her strokes suddenly became stronger and more deliberate. But the old woman was cool under pressure. She would have made an outstanding Ranger.

Unfortunately, Team Arkansas was not there on a recruiting mission. Their mission hinged on the element of surprise, and that element had just been compromised.

Dunham moved slowly up to where the boy and the old woman waited in abject fear. He squatted facing them while the rest of his teammates set up security and checked the hootch to see if anyone else was inside. A few minutes later, two of them reappeared and signaled Dunham that it was clear, no one else was home. The Ranger point man rose to his feet and prodded the old woman with the short barrel of his CAR-15. She recoiled in horror and started to panic, but Dunham quickly lowered his weapon to show her that he did not mean her any harm. After some confusing hand signals, he finally convinced her that he wanted her to drop the knife and take the boy into the hootch.

No longer plagued with the possibility of the boy and his grandmother alerting the rest of the village, the patrol re-grouped outside the hootch and began creeping back down the trail. Fifty meters farther on, they heard voices coming from another hootch set back among a cluster of trees out in the area of the rice paddies.

Unable to continue their approach to the village without securing the ground to their rear and flanks, the patrol stopped in place while Dunham stepped over a low fence to get a better look at who was in the tiny structure. Little more than a thatched roof over an open bamboo frame, the hootch was occupied by a young Vietnamese couple, sitting on a tablelike platform, deeply engaged in the throes of love-making. Unaware of the danger lurking nearby, the young lovers continued passionately kissing and stroking each other. In spite of himself, Dunham broke into an involuntary grin, then turned and waved to Schreiber and Grossman to move up. The two Rangers carefully stepped over the fence and dropped to one knee on either side of Dunham. Soon, they, too, were grinning from ear to ear.

While the three Peeping Toms were enjoying the carnal pleasures of the young Vietnamese couple, their teammates, not having seen the three Rangers leave the trail, moved past them and entered the village undetected. This happened at the same time the woman sensed that she was being watched and looked up to see three hideously painted Americans grinning at her from a few feet away. She let out an earsplitting scream and tried to cover herself, as her boyfriend, now completely unfettered, leaped headlong out the backside of the open hootch and lit out across the nearest rice paddy.

Dunham was the first Ranger to recover. He quickly thumbed his selector switch to rock 'n' roll and sent a short burst after the fleeing VC. Grossman, stepping to Dunham's right front to take an aimed shot, caught his teammate's muzzle blast six inches from his right ear. Screaming in pain, the deafened Ranger grabbed his ear and fell to the ground, shouting, *"You son of a bitch, you shot me!"*

Forgetting the fleeing enemy soldier for a moment, Dunham had just bent over to apologize to his teammate and inquire as to his condition when he heard a dull *TOOOP* to his right. He looked up just in time to see the VC, now a hundred meters away, disappear in an eruption of dirt and vegetation as Schreiber's M-79 HE round exploded directly at the man's feet.

Back in the village, the resident NVA platoon had been peacefully enjoying an afternoon nap. Believing that there were probably no American soldiers within a hundred miles, they had failed to post sentries around the village. At the moment, the other three Rangers, standing at the edge of the village looking for the rest of their patrol, suddenly heard a woman's scream, followed in quick succession by a short burst from a CAR-15, Grossman's cursing, and then the distant explosion of an M-79 round. Their only logical reaction was to hit the village hard and fast. So that's what they did.

Freeland, Reamy, and Sedlemeyer split up and ran from hootch to hootch, firing up the NVA, who were just waking up. As the enemy soldiers stumbled around trying to secure their weapons and wiping the sleep from their eyes, many of them fell before the vicious attack by the American Rangers.

Freeland suddenly met head-on the tall Chinese officer as the man ran from the structure where he had been sleeping. Realizing that he and his teammates would soon be high-tailing it out of the village with the surviving NVA hot on their rears, Freeland threw up his weapon and drilled the big Chicom as the man was going for his pistol.

In the confusion that ensued immediately thereafter, the three Rangers pivoted 180 degrees and fled back through the mayhem they had just created. They had only seconds to find the rest of their teammates and get out of Dodge.

Back out on the trail, Dunham, Schreiber, and the rapidly

recovering Grossman were preparing to charge into the village to rescue their comrades when the three missing Rangers nearly ran them down. Not far behind them, the first of the surviving NVA were already coming in hot pursuit. Dunham, Schreiber, and Grossman immediately put down a strong base of fire to cover their teammates, until the two elements had linked up again. Once that was accomplished, the six Rangers turned and ran out along a paddy dike that extended past the hootch that had been occupied by the two lovers. Unbelievably, the girl was still there. Realizing an opportunity when they saw one, Dunham and Sedlemeyer broke off from the team, dashed inside the structure, snatched up the girl, and ran back to rejoin their comrades.

At this point in the action, the team began drawing heavy small-arms fire from the fully recovered NVA. Dunham dragged the female captive behind him as the party of seven sprinted across the narrow dike.

The entire time they were running, the young prisoner kept screaming, "Me no VC . . . me no VC!" and trying to break loose. Dunham didn't speak enough Vietnamese to argue the point with her, and he knew that she was probably maxed out on her English, so he did the only thing left for him to do. He put the still-hot barrel of his CAR-15 along the side of her neck and then pointed to the opposite side of the flooded rice paddy. She got the message! From that point on she shut her mouth and ran as hard as the rest of the Rangers out in front. By the time they reached the stream, Dunham and the woman had caught up with them.

One by one, they jumped into the waist-deep water and began moving away from the village. The high banks gave the team some protection from the accurate enemy rounds now snapping viciously over their heads. However, the stream was not the apparent escape route the Rangers had hoped for. It was flanked on both sides by wide, open paddies, and at the far end of the valley, in the direction they were heading, lay the second village, which by then was crawling with more

NVA soldiers who were also beginning to fire at the fleeing Americans. They had managed to get themselves into one helluva fix, a fix that they were not going to get out of without some outside help.

Freeland shouted for the team to stop, and as his team-mates began placing quick, accurate fire in both directions, he told Schreiber to "light up" both villages with his M-79. Schreiber's aim was predictably deadly, and much of the small-arms fire from both villages quickly subsided. Black smoke and flames were pouring from several hootches in each village, but Freeland knew that their respite would not last for long. He grabbed the radio handset and called the TOC to give the team's sitrep, the first since they had come off the mountain, three long "years" ago. He reported that they were pinned down in the open by a large number of NVA, and they had a live prisoner with them. Freeland knew the word "prisoner" would get an immediate response. The TOC responded by telling them to hold on, slicks and gun-ships were being scrambled as he spoke.

While the team waited patiently for the arrival of the cav-alry, they decided to take a quick look over the edge of the stream to see what the NVA were up to. To their surprise, they spotted a solitary NVA soldier following the trail they had made across the rice paddy. Amazingly, he was walking along nonchalantly without a care in the world, carrying his AK-47 casually across his shoulder. The Rangers didn't understand if this guy thought they had left the province, or if the NVA were sending out a new second lieutenant as a sacrifice for their stupidity in not posting better security. Whatever the reason, the Rangers had a real live pop-up target heading their way.

The Rangers dropped back down behind the bank of the stream and looked at each other as if to say, "Was this guy for real? Where had he been when all the shooting was going on? With all the gunfire and the explosions that had just occurred, this dude must have been tone deaf!"

Freeland looked around at everybody, then said to Dunham, "You take him out."

Dunham nodded and turned to slither up to the edge of the bank. As he took a long, careful aim, Sedlemeyer whispered, "Hey, let me do it."

Dunham dropped back below the edge of the bank. He had no objection to Sedlemeyer having the honors, since the idea of shooting someone that stupid was really beginning to bother him.

Sedlemeyer stepped up, took careful aim, squeezed off his shot . . . and missed!

The last the team saw of that NVA was his back as he disappeared into the trees on the far side of the rice paddy. Everyone looked at Sedlemeyer and slowly shook their heads.

Freeland looked over the edge, then dropped back down and said, "Ben, sneak out there and see if that NVA dropped his AK-47."

Dunham cocked an eyebrow, turned around and gave his team leader a hard stare, and said, "Right! If you want it, you go out and get it."

At that instant, Grossman shouted that the extraction ships were on their way. There was an immediate sense of relief inside the narrow stretch of stream hiding the six Rangers and their frightened prisoner.

Freeland nodded and told everyone that they needed to tighten up the perimeter a bit. He then sent Dunham and Sedlemeyer downstream about fifty meters to secure a blind spot on a right-hand bend in the streambed. He didn't want the NVA suddenly appearing right in their laps as they were making their dash for the helicopter.

It was late afternoon when the extraction ships finally arrived on station. Freeland signaled Sedlemeyer and Dunham to rejoin the team, then contacted the C & C and told them what they were up against. Although the NVA had been relatively quiet since Schreiber had hit the two villages with his M-79, Freeland knew they were still out there, most likely waiting for darkness before coming in for the kill. Well, if everything went okay, he and his Rangers wouldn't be there.

Freeland got back on the radio and told the escorting Cobra gunships where the enemy was located. He informed them that he would have one of his men move up to the edge of the streambank and flash a panel to mark their position. As the two gunships rolled in, Dunham crawled up the bank and began vigorously popping an orange marker panel.

Finally, the pilot of the lead Cobra radioed back, "We got you." Seconds later, he let loose with his rockets. The two Cobras were so close to the Rangers' perimeter that they could hear the *whhooosh* of each rocket as it left its tube. Dunham rolled down into the streambed to avoid the shrapnel and flying debris.

The Cobras made a number of rocket runs, and on each pass they reported they were taking fire from both villages and from positions back in the surrounding jungle. Then, on the very next pass, the Rangers heard a loud *pop*, and saw a puff of smoke pouring from the engine of the closest gunship. The pilot radioed that he had just taken a hit and was going to attempt to get his aircraft home.

The Rangers' C & C aircraft radioed to confirm the changing situation, and quickly added that he had more bad news. The other Cobra had just reported that it was nearly out of ordnance and would also be heading back. Then the pilot of the extraction ship joined in to add that he, too, was nearly out of fuel and would have to return to base.

At that point, the Rangers were looking at each other in open disbelief. That's when the C & C came back up on the push and told them that he would remain overhead until the extraction ship returned with another flight of gunships. He then signed off.

Ten minutes later, he was back on the net with some good news. A flight of fast movers had just arrived on station. They did not have a FAC with them to mark targets, but with the villages still smoking heavily, a spotter aircraft was not necessary. Relaying between the C & C and the F-4 Phantoms, Freeland coordinated the air strikes like a conductor directing an orchestra. The fast movers hit the villages and the surrounding jungle, making repeated passes, ripping the targets apart with their cannon while the Rangers enjoyed the show from ringside seats. Eventually the fast movers used up their ordnance and signed off with a dip of their wings. Once again the patrol was alone.

By then, the LRRPs had been in the stream for nearly five hours, and the sun was beginning to sink over the horizon. The Rangers knew that if they didn't get out of the stream by dark, the odds would suddenly go over to the enemy.

Finally, the patrol received the long-awaited word that the helicopters were once again on station. However, the good-news balloon was punctured by the second part of the message, which left them staring at each other in disbelief. "Be advised, we are going to make one attempt and one attempt only to get you out. If it fails, you are on your own."

The message hit with all the force of an Arc Light strike. If they didn't get out, where in the hell were they supposed to E & E to? They had NVA on all sides of them, with a lot of open ground in between. If they didn't make their aircraft, they were dead men.

Freeland grabbed the radio and coordinated the final approach of the extraction aircraft as the rest of the team readied themselves to sprint for it as soon as it touched down. Schreiber and Dunham each grabbed the prisoner by an arm and positioned her just below the lip of the streambank. If she resisted during the extraction, they would leave her behind—dead.

The Huey slick suddenly appeared out over the muddy rice paddy, coming in at full throttle. The Rangers looked up in horror as the aircraft overshot their position and set down two hundred meters out in the rice paddy. But without hesitating, the six Rangers and their prisoner were up and running for the waiting slick. As they fought their way through the muck and mire, two Cobra gunships roared overhead and began suppressing the NVA fire that was just beginning to flicker from inside the villages and along the tree lines.

Halfway to the aircraft, Schreiber, Dunham, and the female prisoner tripped and fell facedown into the stinking muck of the rice paddy. However, in the same motion they were up and running again, looking like freshly tarred carpetbaggers—minus the feathers.

As they neared the helicopter from the rear, the two door gunners stopped firing their M-60s long enough to let them climb into the open cabin. The team piled aboard, shouting, *"Go! Go! Go!"* at the top of their lungs, not wanting to spend any more time on the ground than they had to.

The aircraft commander lifted the heavily laden ship out of the open rice paddy and struggled forward to pick up the necessary airspeed to clear the approaching jungle.

As they sped away from the valley and its deadly inhabitants, the Rangers broke into broad grins, laughing, shouting, and pounding each others' backs, their recent fear of being left behind already forgotten. Once again, they had cheated death.

The Huey landed a short time later at LZ Baldy, and was met by a pair of MPs who took the female prisoner into custody without a word to her captors. The next day, the brigade S-2 told the Rangers at the team debriefing that the prisoner had admitted being an NVA nurse and had provided them with top-notch intelligence on the NVA units in the area before she died. The Rangers thought at first they had misunderstood him, and asked him what he had meant by that last statement. The S-2 major simply nodded his head sadly and told the team that she had died during interrogation at the hands of the ARVN intelligence people. . . .

LRRP Detachment, 1st Brigade, 101st Airborne Division

One of the first provisional LRRP units formed during the Vietnam War was the 1st Brigade LRRP Detachment of the 1st Brigade, 101st Airborne Division. They quickly earned a reputation for their ability to adapt to a multitude of assignments in a wide variety of AOs. From the very first, MACV's "fire brigade"—the name given to the 1st Brigade, 101st Airborne Division, the nomads of the Vietnam War—was sent anywhere a brushfire ignited throughout the country. It was always the 1st Brigade Screaming Eagles who got the call. And any time they landed, the brigade's LRRP detachment was on hand as the eyes and ears of the brigade.

During the escalation of the war in 1967, U.S. military forces conducted a number of successful operations in the II Corps and III Corps tactical zones. Unable to swing the momentum around in the central part of the country, the NVA and VC decided to focus their attention on the more distant northern provinces. They began exerting intensive pressure on the U.S. Army and Marine forces operating in the I Corps area. Unable to send additional divisions north to take some of the pressure off the beleaguered U.S. troops, MACV put together a collection of units under the name of Task Force Oregon and sent it north to lend a hand to the hard-pressed U.S. Marines and the 1st Air Cavalry Division. Comprised of the 196th Light Infantry Brigade, the 3d Brigade of the

25th Infantry Division, and the 1st Brigade of the 101st Airborne Division, along with attached support units, Task Force Oregon arrived just in time.

The 1st Brigade of the 101st Airborne Division settled into the area around Duc Pho. In the southern part of Quang Ngai Province, the area had long been under the control of the enemy. It quickly earned a reputation as a bad place to be. As the paratroopers combed the mountainous countryside and swept up the wide fertile valleys, looking to mix it up with the enemy, the brigade's provisional LRRP detachment began sending six-man reconnaissance patrols to locate the enemy units for the line doggies.

On 11 May 1967, the 1st Brigade launched phase one of Operation Malheur, a three-battalion incursion into the mountains west of Duc Pho that was designed to destroy the NVA/VC base camps hidden there. The day before the operation was slated to kick off, the brigade LRRP detachment received a warning order for three six-man recon teams to be inserted into the Song Ve Valley, just north of where Operation Malheur was going in the next day. The primary mission of the teams would be to look for NVA/VC base camps, trails, and caches in their recon zone, and to be on the lookout for enemy forces infiltrating or exfiltrating through the area in response to Operation Malheur.

The warning order from brigade S-2 called for two recon teams under the command of staff sergeants Larry Beauchamp and Pappy Lynch to be inserted on the evening of 13 May, and a third, led by S.Sgt. Vincente Cruz, to go in at first light on the morning of 14 May. Cruz's team had a couple of last-minute changes, which always make a team leader nervous just before a mission. His senior RTO, Sp4. Rey Martinez, had to report to Cam Ranh Bay to take the written test for warrant officer flight training. Sp4. Elmer Kolarik was assigned to take Martinez's spot, and a new man to the LRRPs, PFC Sid Tolson, a seventeen-year-old U.S. Army paratrooper, was assigned the junior RTO slot. With a full third of his team—both RTOs—an unknown factor, Cruz was a bit worried. However, with S.Sgt. Larry Christian as senior scout, Sgt. Derby Jones as junior scout, and Sp4. David "Fireball" Dixon as the team medic, he still had a strong mix of veterans he could rely on in a pinch.

On the afternoon of the thirteenth, Cruz, Jones, and Christian flew out to the team's AO. After selecting primary and secondary LZs and PZs, the three LRRPs returned to Duc Pho to get ready for the mission going in the next morning. During the premission briefing, they had been told to keep an eye out for three missing LRRPs from the 3/25th. A Tropic Lightning long-range recon patrol had disappeared in the area six weeks before, and the reaction force that had gone into their RZ the next day had found only two bodies. That bit of news caused some worries among the veteran members of Cruz's patrol.

The "Minute Men" of the 176th Aviation Company were assigned to insert the three long-range recon patrols. The missions would be supported by UH-1Cs from the "Muskets," the gunship troop of the same aviation company.

At last light on the evening of the thirteenth, the first two LRRP teams were inserted. Within minutes, Larry Beauchamp's team was in contact, killing two NVA, and had to be extracted. By the time they were resupplied with ammo, it was too late to reinsert the patrol, so it was decided to reinsert the team the next morning at a different spot right after Cruz's insertion went in.

Pappy Lynch's patrol also inserted on the thirteenth. They immediately moved into cover and went to ground for the night. Their AO had proved cold to that point in the mission.

The sun was just breaking over the eastern horizon when the slick bearing Cruz's team dropped from twenty-five hundred feet down to the treetops. The rest of the way into the AO would be nap of the earth, riding the contour of the rugged terrain.

Suddenly, the LZ was rushing up to meet them, and the six

LRRPs were bailing out of the Huey and sprinting for the trees less than thirty meters away. As the Huey lifted out of the clearing and continued on, the sounds of its turbine fading in the distance, and the quick rush of the two gunships passed overhead on either side of the clearing, the LRRPs were alone.

However, the lonely feeling didn't last long. The sounds of voices shouting in Vietnamese, followed by a number of signal shots from not far away, alerted the LRRPs to the fact that their insertion had not gone unnoticed. They had landed in the center of an enemy base complex of unknown size.

Without waiting for instructions from Cruz, Kolarik was already on the horn to the C & C aircraft reporting that their LZ was full of "little people." At the edge of the trees in a poor defensive position, Cruz quickly realized that they couldn't stay where they were. With a large number of enemy soldiers around them, the LRRPs had to find a more defensible position quickly. They couldn't let the enemy get organized and come after them; the momentary advantage the LRRPs had gained through the element of surprise was already rapidly eroding.

Before moving out, Cruz sent Jones and Christian to conduct a short, circular recon around the team. The two men returned quickly to report that they had found a number of high-speed trails nearby, a large communications cable, and they had spotted a number of enemy soldiers working on bunkers not far away. Cruz realized instantly that they had only seconds to get out of the area. It was even too late to call for an extraction from the same LZ.

The helicopter had dropped them off in a large clearing on the floor of the valley. They would have to reach high ground to get out; low spots could be a deadly funnel for extraction aircraft if the enemy hidden in the hills around them was ready.

Cruz signaled for Derby Jones to lead the team to high ground. The heavily laden LRRPs broke brush straight up the side of the mountain. They climbed for two hours, stopping only briefly to watch and to listen. The sounds of periodic signal shots behind them and the distant shouts in Vietnamese told them they were being pursued.

It was almost 0900 hours when the team received a quick message from the LRRP commo chief back at the TOC telling them that they were in the wrong AO. He was emphatic that they get to an LZ immediately, reiterating several times that the team needed to be extracted as soon as possible. The NCO then suggested that the team return to its original insertion LZ, but Cruz quickly nixed that idea. There was no way he was going to lead his team back into that death trap. He told the TOC that by then all of the suitable LZs in the area were probably covered, and the only choice was to climb to high ground. Cruz signed off, then instructed his point man to continue toward the top of the mountain.

The LRRP CO, 1st Lt. Dan McIsaac, who had been circling in the distance in the C & C aircraft, had discovered right after the insertion that the patrol had inadvertently been put down in the wrong LZ. The valley that the team had gone into had been slated for a massive B-52 Arc Light strike at 1300 hours, less than four hours away. Unfortunately, there was nothing he could do to divert or abort the bombing mission. The B-52s could not be turned back or diverted that late in their mission. With that in mind, he told the aircraft commander of the C & C ship to head back to the LRRP compound at Duc Pho. Once on the ground, he grabbed up a thick coil of half-inch hemp rope and leaped back aboard the chopper.

When McIsaac was back out over the team's AO, he instructed the pilot to get down on the deck and circle the area ahead of the team. He soon found what he was looking for. Quickly, he radioed the team and told Cruz that there appeared to be a bomb crater on a knoll not far from the patrol's present location. The officer then gave the patrol leader a bearing and told him not to waste time getting there.

When the team broke out of the jungle thirty minutes later, they found that the bomb crater was blocked by a single tree rising up from its center. Dixon quickly set a charge of C-4 explosives around the base of the tree and blew it down, opening up the crater. However, when the slick came in, it was immediately discovered that the hillside was too steep for the slick to get close enough to touch down. After several futile attempts to reach the patrol, some of which resulted in serious blade strikes, the aircraft was forced to pull away.

McIsaac quickly rigged the rope he had secured at Duc Pho to one of the D rings mounted in the floor of the chopper. Ordering the crew chief to hold on to his belt, McIsaac then wrapped the rope a single twist around his waist, then stepped out on the skid and lowered the remainder of the rope down to where the team was waiting in the bomb crater. Cruz selected Fireball Dixon to go out first.

The Huey rose up slowly with the LRRP medic hanging precariously from the end of the rope. Radioing ahead to Staff Sergeant Beauchamp's team, which had been reinserted into its AO right after Cruz's team had gone in, McIsaac instructed him to return to his LZ and secure it. He was going to drop off Cruz's team one by one at that location.

Fifteen minutes later, the Huey lowered the first LRRP to the LZ where Sgt. Larry Beauchamp's team waited. Soon, the helicopter returned and picked up PFC Tolson and headed back to Beauchamp's LZ.

In the meantime, a second slick rigged with a rope with a sling harness attached arrived on the scene and lifted out a third LRRP. In that fashion, the two aircraft soon had Cruz's entire team out of the danger area and linked up with Beauchamp's team. The job was completed with two hours to spare.

But the men of Beauchamp's team were upset with the whole situation because they felt that every NVA in their AO knew exactly where they were.

Meanwhile, another slick arrived with a pair of water bladders and some new maps. Cruz was instructed to load his team back aboard, switch maps, and prepare to insert into the same AO, but at a different LZ, one outside the B-52 strike zone.

McIsaac was furious. He requested that both teams be allowed to return to Duc Pho, regroup, and then be reoriented for new AOs. Their missions had been compromised and needed to be scrubbed. But instead of scrubbing the missions, brigade S-2 made the decision to keep both teams in. Beauchamp was ordered to move out of the LZ while Cruz's team was still on the ground drawing attention to themselves. A short time later, Cruz's team would be lifted out and reinserted at their original secondary LZ, where they would refill their canteens, bury the empty bladders, then begin their normally scheduled patrol. It was the recipe for a royal cluster fuck.

Beauchamp was anxious to put some distance between himself and his busy LZ. When, finally, he was given the okay to move out, he told his point man to "haul ass."

While Beauchamp's patrol was leaving contrails in the brush while moving away from the clearing, Cruz was orienting himself to the maps of his new AO. He was already feeling negative vibes about the amended patrol; they were having the kind of poor preparation that violated every tenet of long-range reconnaissance patrolling and usually got good people killed.

Finally, Cruz's helicopter lifted off the LZ and climbed for altitude, then leveled out and headed for a new LZ a kilometer away on the same ridgeline. Coming in far too high, the pilot corkscrewed the aircraft down into an open meadow on the side of the mountain. Cruz knew immediately that every NVA in the area had just pinpointed their insertion.

The LRRPs should have remained aboard and aborted the mission, but someone was out of the chopper as soon as it touched down, and true to their code, everyone else followed close behind.

The team was on a slight, grass-covered knoll on the side

of the mountain. Their only concealment was four- to six-foot-high kunai grass, and there was no cover anywhere around them. In the distance, perhaps 250 or 300 meters away, Cruz could just make out a shallow, timbered rill that trailed down across the open slope of the mountain, eventually widening out into a deeper, narrow valley. The slopes on both sides of the valley were covered with chest-high kunai grass, and the only concealment at all was in the trees along the dry runoff channel.

The smaller valley eventually opened out into a wider valley, and at their junction was a small village. All of that was easily visible from the team's vantage point. And if the LRRPs could see everything down below, anyone down below could easily have spotted the American helicopter that had just dropped off six people on the high ground above.

By then, it was already growing late in the afternoon. According to their instructions, they were to drink their fill of water, top off their canteens, then bury the water bladders. Cruz had assumed that they would do all of this after they ran off the LZ and lay dog in the first cover they came to. Unfortunately, the only cover around was three hundred meters away. Signaling Jones to move out, the six-man patrol broke into a ground-eating trot toward the distant gully, lugging the water bladders with them.

When they finally reached it, panting and soaked with sweat, they set up a security-wheel defensive position while Cruz established radio contact. He wasted little time telling McIsaac that their recon zone was a bad place to pull a reconnaissance patrol.

For the first time, Cruz had the opportunity to study his map, and what little faith he still had in the mission plan was erased by what he saw: if they were approached by enemy forces from any direction, they had absolutely no place to go. Someone in the rear who had never been out in the bush before had made a series of decisions that had just put his team in great jeopardy. Cruz wanted out.

But the morning's activities had cost the LRRPs. The air crews were frazzled, and the aircraft were back at Duc Pho being serviced and refueled. There were no other aircraft available at the time, and it was far too late in the day to do anything about it. McIsaac told Cruz to find a place to base up for the night, and he would be back at first light to pull the team. Cruz had no choice but to comply.

Cruz looked around to find the best place with cover and concealment, where they could hole up for the night. But it didn't take long to realize that they had no place to go. They were already in the dry creek bed, and it was the only place within fifteen hundred meters where there was any conceal-ment at all. Unfortunately, there was no cover. Cruz suddenly felt like a flea on an elephant's ass.

Cruz had Jones lead them a little farther down the dry creek bed, where the vegetation was a little thicker. There, the team crawled up against one side of the bank and set up their defensive perimeter, leaning the two radios against the base of the single tree growing out of the weeds.

Cruz knew that they hadn't fooled anyone watching from down below. They were in a very bad situation that was most likely going to get worse. They would not even be able to move out after dark to another location to throw off the enemy because there was simply no place else to go. Cruz was certain they had already been pinpointed by the enemy. Their only hope would depend on how badly the enemy forces in the area wanted to take them down.

At 2200 hours, a slow, steady rain began to fall, and it con-tinued to fall until just before daybreak. It didn't keep anyone from sleeping, because under those conditions no one got much sleep. Cruz kept two men on at a time all night long, and had everyone awake thirty minutes before daybreak. They had heard nothing unusual during the night.

In the eerie silence of the false dawn, Cruz whispered for each patrol member to take turns easing the "night round" out of the chamber of his weapon and replacing it with a fresh one—just in case the first one had sweated and frozen in the chamber during the night.

When it was light enough to see, the LRRPs breathed a collective sigh of relief. They had passed the danger time. The NVA had not hit them at first light. It wouldn't be long before the choppers arrived and pulled them out, and the stupid fiasco would come to an end.

The LRRPs had scattered out in the brush, not wanting to make a tempting target if they were hit during the night or at first light. Tolson was seated high up on the bank, with Kolarik sitting to his front and slightly below him. Cruz was to Tolson's right and a little farther back in the grass.

To his right were Christian and Jones, in that order. Dixon was down level with the creek bed and fidgeting around a little. Everyone was sitting with their backs to the grass-covered creek bank.

Suddenly, Dixon stood up and signaled Cruz that he was going out of the perimeter to answer nature's call. Cruz signaled back for him to do a short area recon while he was out there. Taking only his weapon and his LBE, Dixon slipped outside the perimeter and moved slowly away to the left.

The rain had stopped a short time before, and everything was still and deathly quiet. The metallic sound of a rifle bolt being racked back, then pushed deliberately forward, suddenly broke the silence. Everyone froze. After what seemed like minutes, but was probably only seconds, Derby Jones shouted, "Hit it," at the same time rolling hard to his left.

The deafening, ripping sounds of two dozen automatic weapons filled the shallow creek bed with stinging lead. The grass and scattered trees were pulverized amid the madly blinking muzzle flashes and choking smoke. Jones continued rolling until he came up at the base of a thick shrub with a natural shield of large rocks around it. The rocks saved his life. A dozen rounds followed him under the bush but bounced harmlessly off the mantle of rocks.

At the sound of the bolt sliding home, Cruz was rolling and

bringing up his rifle even before Jones hollered, "Hit it!" But before he could fire a round, a bullet slammed into the right side of his chest, collapsed his lung, and blew out an even larger hole exiting his back. Flat on his back without a weapon, Cruz flipped over and began crawling rapidly through the grass, reaching cover but not before taking two more rounds in the back.

Somehow, Kolarik survived the opening volley. He had actually managed to grab a frag from his LBE, pull the pin, and toss it down into the creek bed where the enemy fire was coming from. As he released the grenade and twisted around to hit the deck, he caught a round through the back of his right shoulder that shattered the joint, then tore down through his arm before exiting. With his right arm useless, he, too, crawled clumsily through the grass trying to escape the withering fire.

Tolson had been sitting up high when he heard the bolt let go. He froze until the shooting started and was reaching to the right for his weapon when he felt the sledgehammer blow of a round hitting him in the face. The bullet smashed into the young LRRP just below the right eye, went through the roof of his mouth, down through his tongue, and blew out the left side of his jaw. Mercifully, the impact of the bullet to his head knocked him out. Unfortunately, his unconsciousness didn't last long. Tolson came to a minute later, just as a grenade went off right next to him, perforating him with shrapnel. A fragment pierced the cornea of his right eye. His head was swelling from the hydrostatic shock of the bullet, and he was struggling to keep from choking on the bone and blood he was swallowing. Using what little vision he still had from his left eye, he began to crawl through the grass to get away from the enemy fire.

Dixon was already thirty feet outside the perimeter looking for a place to "do his business." He was facing down into the ravine when he spotted the enemy soldiers set up in an

L-shaped ambush along the dry creek bed. He was trying to turn to warn the rest of the team when he heard the bolt rack back in the AK-47. Before he could utter a sound, two rounds slammed into his head, killing him instantly.

Amazingly, Christian and Jones were not hit in the opening volley. While the NVA were reloading, the two LRRPs began putting out a tremendous amount of fire, trying to suppress the enemy ambush. Each man emptied ten full magazines apiece into the creek bed and followed it up with a hail of grenades. It bought them time.

While Jones and Christian fought for their lives, Kolarik, Tolson, and Cruz lay moaning back in the grass. Cruz could barely draw a breath, but he had enough composure to shout for Kolarik to get the radio. He knew that it was their only chance of salvation.

Kolarik had only the use of one arm, but it was enough for him to grab a Prick-25 radio. He crawled out to where he had left his ruck and saw that the spot was right in the middle of the impact area for all the incoming rounds. Without giving it any more thought than that, he crawled out amid the devastation and destruction to retrieve the radio.

Back in the grass, he quickly discovered that the handset had been shot through, rendering the radio useless. With the handset cord severed, he could not transmit an outgoing message.

Leaving his radio behind, Kolarik once again crawled out into the grass and recovered Tolson's bullet-riddled radio. He made it back to his spot in the grass to the sound of bullets pinging off the ground around him. As quickly as he could with a single usable arm, Kolarik changed Tolson's handset to his own radio, then called the rear to report the contact and beg for help.

Cruz's moaning had attracted additional enemy fire. Soon he was hit twice more in the legs. In horrible pain, he waited helplessly to die.

About ten minutes into the fight, the NVA began regrouping, forming up in a horseshoe to try to close in. During a particularly savage exchange of fire, Tolson took two more rounds, in the back.

Kolarik, exposing himself to use the radio, drew heavy fire from several enemy weapons, catching a round in his one good arm, but not before he reached the rear and reported their predicament. Help was on the way.

The enemy had successfully maneuvered around until they were on the three uphill sides of the LRRP perimeter. They were now trying to push them down the creek bed. Jones and Christian were together on the right side of the perimeter, and they had a good angle on the creek bed where the base of the NVA's L-shaped ambush lay. The two LRRPs were making the NVA pay a hell of a price for the trap they had set.

Suddenly, a Chicom grenade arced out of the creek bed and landed at Jones's feet. He rolled to his left and tucked into a tight ball, but it wasn't enough to protect him from the deadly shrapnel that pierced his crotch area and his thighs.

Man, I can't get hurt, he thought, that will leave only Christian!

Pulling a white-phosphorous grenade from his rucksack, he pulled the pin, let it cook off for a two-count, then tossed it at the spot in the grass where the Chicom frag had just come from. The hollow explosion resulted in a series of screams and moans coming from the spot where the frag exploded.

Jones and Christian continued to fire and maneuver as they struggled to make the NVA believe that more than two of them had survived the ambush. Tossing out frags and firing their weapons, the two LRRPs fought like a dozen men. Jones secured his cut-down M-79 and began popping the deadly HE rounds directly into the ambush site, frequently shooting into the trees above the creek trying to get air bursts. It worked!

After about ten minutes, the NVA fire began to die down. Jones knew that they had taken some heavy licks, and they were running very low on ammo. But if they could only hang on a little longer!

Suddenly, he heard someone screaming for Fireball, the team medic. He knew that if Fireball wasn't taking care of the wounded then he must have also been hit. For the first time, Jones realized that most of the teammates were down and needed emergency medical help immediately. Leaving the remainder of the NVA temporarily to Christian's gentle touch, Jones crawled back down to what had once been the team's perimeter and recovered Dixon's aid bag. Only twenty-five feet away, the surviving NVA picked up their fire when they spotted the LRRP scrambling back into the grass, but he made it back without being hit.

While Christian continued to hold the enemy at bay, Jones worked frantically to keep his comrades alive. Using nearly everything in the aid bag, he tried his best to dress the multitude of terrible wounds. There was very little he could do for Tolson's shattered face. If he'd tried to bind the broken jaw, the young LRRP would have suffocated. During the time Jones worked over the wounded, enemy rounds continued to pour in, but there was far less fire than before, and its accuracy had gone to hell.

After exhausting the rest of the medical supplies, Jones gave the three men what encouragement he could, then turned and crawled out into the grass to look for Dixon. Slipping up the creek toward the end of the ambush, Jones quickly located Dixon's body stretched out in the grass. Ducking enemy fire, he struggled to drag his dead friend back into the shattered perimeter.

Reaching the spot where he had left the wounded, he draped Dixon's body around the sole surviving radio. During the remainder of the battle, the slain LRRP absorbed several rounds that would have destroyed the radio.

While Kolarik continued monitoring the radio, Jones collected the rest of the ammo and grenades from the rucksacks and web gear of the wounded and tossed them over to Christian, who had just about run dry himself.

The gunships arrived a short time later. Jones had stretched an orange panel out in the grass to mark the edge of the team's perimeter. Guiding in on the fluorescent panel, the gunship attacked the remaining NVA, forcing them to break contact and flee for cover.

For all practical purposes, the battle was over. The NVA had failed to finish off a very successful ambush. They had not counted on the ferocity of the small American recon team. Jones and Christian, and the three critically wounded LRRPs hung on until a reaction force from Charlie Company 1/327th arrived. With them was the LRRP detachment commanding officer, 1st Lt. Dan McIsaac. He had joined the reaction force up on the ridgeline after it had touched down.

After the battle, Sgt. Derby Jones was put in for a Distinguished Service Cross for his actions that day. By some cruel twist of military politics and basic incompetence, the award was downgraded to a Silver Star. S.Sgt. Larry Christian also received a Silver Star. Somehow, the awards just didn't seem appropriate to the jobs they had done.

☆　☆　☆　☆　☆

Company E, 51st Infantry (LRP), 23d (Americal) Division

January 1968 leaves a bad taste in the mouth of every veteran of the Vietnam War who had the misfortune of being in country at that time. It was the month of the infamous Tet Offensive. It was a time of shock, fear, uncertainty, confusion, and bitter personal trauma. It changed forever the lives of many soldiers from both sides fighting in the perpetual conflict that was Vietnam.

For the Americal Division based at Chu Lai in southern I Corps, it was the birth of a division. With the arrival of the 198th Light Infantry Brigade, the reconstituted 23d (Americal) Infantry Division was complete. The new brigade had a lot to prove. January 1968 would become a terrible playing field for the untested and inexperienced unit.

On 19 January 1968, a warning order came down from the brigade's S-2 requesting a long-range recon patrol from Company E, 51st Infantry (LRP) to perform a ground reconnaissance. The area was a four-grid-square section of Vietnam situated at the base of Nui Lao Son, twenty-five kilometers northwest of Chu Lai. Brigade S-2 had been receiving reports from a radio intercept detachment that had been monitoring a clandestine NVA mobile radio transmitter operating from somewhere in the vicinity of Nui Lao Son, a large mountain west of Highway 1. The radio had been broadcasting from the area for several weeks, and brigade wanted it found and eliminated.

Captain Bjork, Echo 51's commanding officer, had received the warning order early in the morning for the mission scheduled to go in at last light. He immediately alerted Team Sandy's veteran team leader, Sgt. Vic Valeriano, to prepare his team for the mission. Sergeant Valeriano's team was a little understaffed just then, but he accepted the mission without hesitation.

The reshuffling of teams was a long-accepted practice in the LRPs. Although in principle it violated the well-established tenet of team integrity espoused by special operations units everywhere, that basic classroom ideal was rarely achievable in the field during the Vietnam War. In Vietnam, the one-year standard combat tour, promotions, reassignment, judicial and nonjudicial punishment, emergency leave, extension leave, R & R, in-country training, sickness, injury, wounds—and death—all contributed to the impracticality of maintaining team integrity. So it was with no great reluctance that Valeriano accepted the mission even though he had four empty slots to fill on his team.

Valeriano and his best friend and longtime teammate, Sgt. Daniel McLaughlin, quickly recruited the four men they needed for the mission. Valeriano and McLaughlin were so compatible in skill and experience that they often traded roles on missions. Sometimes McLaughlin ran the team with Valeriano at ATL, and other times they reversed the roles. However, neither combination had been found lacking in leadership. McLaughlin's younger brother was also a member of the same long-range patrol company.

With time at a premium for the mission, the two LRRPs recruited Cpl. Solomon Kalua, Sp4. Ron Pepping, Sp4. John Bronson, and Vang, a Vietnamese PRU, who would serve as the team's point man. Bronson, a qualified medic, was an especially welcome addition to the team.

While their new teammates were preparing for the mission, Valeriano and McLaughlin conducted a last-minute overflight of the AO. Flying northwest out of Chu Lai, the helicopter swung out over Highway 1 and approached the recon zone from the east. The Huey slick made two passes at high altitude over the area while Valeriano and McLaughlin studied it closely through their binoculars. The only spot in their entire recon zone suitable for an insertion was a large open rice paddy situated between the V formed by two secondary ridges running down from the east face of Nui Lao Son. Neither LRRP wanted to go in low and visible from anywhere in their recon box, but there was nowhere else from which to infiltrate without walking in from outside the box. And with only three days to accomplish their mission, they did not have the luxury of that kind of time.

Except for the rice paddy, the recon zone consisted of the east face of the mountain and the two secondary ridges. The eastern slope of the mountain was a mixture of single- and double-canopy jungle. The secondary ridges were covered in single-canopy forest with a lot of dense underbrush beneath the trees. The rice paddy had been abandoned for a number of years and was dotted with low weeds and scattered brush.

Returning to the LRP compound at Chu Lai, Valeriano performed a last-minute check of his team. Satisfied that the men were ready for the patrol, he had them load their gear into one of the company's unauthorized three-quarter-ton trucks, then climb aboard the truck or the accompanying jeep for the three-mile drive out to the 1st Marine Division's helipad.

The LRRPs boarded a single Huey slick and hunkered down as the pilot lifted the aircraft off the ground and moved slowly forward to gain airspeed. A pair of Huey gunships soon joined up to escort the insertion ship out to the LZ. The flight took twenty-five minutes, giving the LRRPs time to collect their thoughts.

As the aircraft entered the valley, it banked around and came in to the designated LZ not far from the brush belt running between the paddy and the tree line. It was 1500 hours, and the long shadows cast by the peak towering to their west were already extending out into the rice paddy. As the chopper was approaching the LZ, a few of the LRRPs thought they heard firing in the distance, but couldn't be sure of the direction, nor for that matter if it was being directed at them. Valeriano thought immediately about aborting the mission, but before he could decide, the Huey flared to a hover near the end of the abandoned rice paddy, its skids only four feet from the ground. Valeriano's teammates were already bailing out both sides of the aircraft and sprinting for the sparse brush between the edge of the paddy and the tree line thirty meters away. Valeriano didn't want to go to ground in such thin cover, but the shots they had heard coming in had him worried.

Wanting to sit and assess the situation before committing to the forest just ahead, he held up the patrol a few feet into the brush. Almost immediately they heard voices that appeared to be coming from somewhere between the edge of the brush and the tree line twenty meters to their left. With his teammates circled up around him facing outward, Valeriano whispered to Vang, "What are they saying?"

Vang listened for several minutes, then nodded his head and turned back to Valeriano. He looked at his team leader and said, "They sound like farmers."

Valeriano listened some more, not yet convinced. What should he do? The voices of the Vietnamese didn't seem unduly frightened or alarmed. Maybe they were only farmers. Still on call, the choppers were orbiting in the distance, so it would be no problem to claim that he was compromised and call for an abort. But it was getting dark, and there was an enemy radio transmitter out there. It was a tough call.

Because Sgt. Vic Valeriano wasn't the type of team leader who threw in the towel at the first sign of danger, he made the decision to release the helicopters and Charlie Mike (continue the mission).

Ten minutes later, Valeriano hand-signaled for Vang to move the patrol out to the right. The voices, which by then had stopped, had been coming from the team's left. They moved fifteen meters into the tree line, where they stumbled into a network of freshly excavated spider holes. The holes were still uncovered and had not yet been camouflaged.

Since it was almost dark, Valeriano decided they might as well take advantage of the convenient cover and concealment the enemy had provided, and remain there for the night. Calling the radio-relay team, Valeriano gave the patrol's position, then reported the voices and the spider holes. Relay confirmed the information and signed off to pass it along to the LRRP TOC back at Chu Lai.

Valeriano then instructed his men to form a perimeter among the enemy emplacements, each man occupying a separate hole five to ten feet apart. He set them up in a rough circle with three men facing upslope, and the other three facing the open rice paddy. When that was completed, the LRRPs slipped outside the perimeter to set up their claymores, keeping them in as close as possible. Fortunately, the spider holes eliminated the normal risks from the claymore's deadly backblast.

The LRRP team leader whispered for everyone to remain awake until midnight; then each man would pull an hour of watch during the remainder of the night.

During the night, they heard single rifle shots fired at random intervals from a distance of one thousand to two thousand meters. Most of the shots seemed to be coming from somewhere up on the secondary ridgelines above them. Vang didn't seem overly concerned about the signal shots, but Valeriano was beginning to worry that he might have made a mistake not calling an abort.

The next day, 20 January, the patrol ate an early breakfast, bagged and stored their trash in their rucks, then attempted to cover up as much of the sign they had left in the fresh dirt as possible. With that finally accomplished, they moved out at first light heading north-northwest around the base of the ridge and along the edge of the rice paddy. It wasn't long before they discovered a well-used trail paralleling the edge of the woods.

Around 0900, a C & C chopper from the 198th Light Infantry Brigade flew over the team's AO at an altitude of less than two hundred feet, sending the LRRPs scrambling for cover. Flying low out over the valley, it seemed to be looking for someone. But there weren't supposed to be any other Americans in the area.

Suddenly, there was the sound of static on the team's radio; then a voice broke in requesting a situation report. It was the C & C up in the Huey slick, and he was calling Valeriano.

Valeriano controlled his outrage over the stupidity of this idiot circling out over the rice paddy. The fool did not even realize that he was drawing the attention of every NVA soldier in the area to the fact that there was something going on in their neighborhood. Valeriano snarled over the radio to the C & C aircraft that the situation report was the same as the sitrep he had given the night before, reporting the spider holes and the farmers they had spotted at the edge of the tree line during their insertion.

The young officer aboard the aircraft responded immediately. "There are no friendlies in the area—grease 'em."

Valeriano had heard enough. He signed off, thoroughly disgusted. The mission was beginning to take on all the outward appearances of a classic cluster fuck.

Not wanting to remain close to the edge of the paddy, the team leader signaled for Vang to move the patrol up the slope into the woods along the side of the ridge. It was nearing midday and already getting hot, and Valeriano decided it was a good time to give his team a break. The woods around them were primarily single canopy with a lot of secondary growth that provided denser cover at ground level.

Finding a nearly level spot in a slight fold on the hillside, the patrol quickly set up a circular defensive perimeter. Valeriano picked out a spot for himself in the center.

At 1230, the patrol was still resting on the side of the ridge. A couple of the LRRPs had taken the opportunity to wolf down a cornflake bar or a can of fruit. Others had decided to catch a quick nap; you never got enough sleep on a long-range patrol. Even Valeriano found himself nodding off, so he decided that it was time to get back on the road. The last thing he wanted was for his teammates to begin to let down. He was still having bad vibes about the mission; far too many things had been going wrong on the patrol. His basic instincts were telling him to find a way to get them out of there.

Suddenly, a tremendous ripping sound exploded from below their position down near the rice paddy. Simultaneously, the leaves and limbs above the team began to disintegrate as hundreds of enemy bullets shattered the midday calm. Valeriano realized immediately that they were on the wrong end of an ambush. His team was being hammered, and there was nothing he could do to stop it.

The NVA were firing full-automatic from less than fifteen meters away, up the slope from their ten o'clock position. And more enemy fire was coming up from below from his three o'clock. Valeriano knew they were caught in a terrible cross fire that was chewing his team to pieces.

Valeriano screamed for his teammates to stay down and not to return fire unless they had a target. He could tell from the vegetation and debris still falling into the perimeter from just overhead that the enemy soldiers were firing blind. But terrible damage had already been done; two thirds of his team was already out of the fight. Danny McLaughlin had taken a round through the upper left quadrant of his chest. The bullet had come from below, striking him just above his heart. He was still alive only because of the angle of the bullet.

Pepping, also hit from below, had a grazing round strike him low in the thigh. However, the bullet continued upward, plowing a furrow and opening up his leg from knee to crotch. He was conscious but in great pain.

Vang was slightly higher up the slope when the NVA initiated the ambush. He reacted by getting to his feet to return fire, but a long burst from a nearby AK-47 stitched him across the knees and cut his legs out from under him.

Bronson, the team medic, had also been hit in the opening volley, taking multiple rounds through the torso, one of them entering just below his right armpit. At a time when the team needed a medic in the worst way, the medic was unable to treat even himself.

Seconds after the opening volley, Valeriano grabbed the radio and screamed into the handset, "*This is Sandy, this is Sandy.* Contact! Contact! We're hit! We're hit."

As the enemy fire finally began to subside, a hail of grenades landed inside the perimeter from both above and below. Valeriano and Kalua began grabbing them and throwing them back as fast as they could. However, there was no way they could get to them all. As the grenades began exploding around them, the two men ignored the flying shrapnel and continued to return the frags. Fortunately, the low-powered Chicom fragmentation grenades were more of a nuisance than a danger. However, only a fool would willingly take this kind of punishment.

As the two LRRPs kept hurling frags back at the enemy, Bronson lay back and squeezed a morphine Syrette into his leg.

McLaughlin was already going in and out of shock. He was still conscious but unable to tend to his wounds or help with the team's defense.

Pepping's wound was also painful, but he managed to recover enough to hurl a couple of incoming grenades back at the enemy.

Kalua stood up to throw one of his own frags at the NVA hidden in the dense cover above the patrol. As Valeriano shouted for him to stay down, the grenade hit a tree and bounced back into the perimeter, rolling to a stop between Valeriano and Bronson. Knowing a U.S. frag was a hell of a lot more powerful than a Chicom, Valeriano dove for the grenade and tossed it downhill before it could cook off. Just as he looked back at Kalua to tell him to get down, the scrappy Hawaiian took a single enemy round through the head. He died instantly.

After the grenade attack ceased, there was an eerie lull in the fighting. The surviving LRRPs could hear commands being shouted back and forth in Vietnamese from both above and below them. The NVA leaders were probably coordinating the two elements for a final assault against their position.

At that moment, Valeriano spotted a number of NVA moving below him at the base of the ridge just along the edge of the rice paddy. All of them were wearing gray shorts, khaki shirts, and boonie caps. Each was armed with what looked like a brand-new AK-47.

Suddenly, a single NVA soldier detached himself from the group and began advancing up the slope toward Valeriano, holding his weapon above his head and firing it into the team's perimeter. Before the surprised Valeriano could react, he was hit in the right bicep by a single round as another bullet shattered the hand guard and the stock of his M-16. Momentarily stunned by the force of the blow, Valeriano recovered in time to grab his damaged rifle and empty the full magazine into the NVA at a distance of ten feet, killing him instantly.

Another NVA soldier suddenly appeared to Valeriano's right. The man was attempting to move in above Bronson. Valeriano didn't have time to reload, so he reached for a frag. Pulling the pin, he let the lever fly and held the grenade in his fist as it cooked off, then pitched it at the feet of the startled NVA. The enemy soldier died in the blinding explosion.

The remaining NVA seemed to lose heart after their two comrades had died assaulting the recon patrol's perimeter. Suddenly, the small-arms fire began to lessen, with only an occasional short burst or single round being fired at the LRRP perimeter. It was almost as if the enemy soldiers were content to let the surviving LRRPs know that they were still out there, without risking the lives of any more of their troops.

Besides Sergeant Valeriano, the seriously wounded Pepping was the only LRRP still able to return fire.

During the entire time the battle had been raging, Valeriano had been on the radio trying to get artillery and gunships, or anyone else who could help.

Suddenly appearing over the ridgeline, a single Huey slick was the first to respond. When Valeriano failed to reach the aircraft on his radio, he told the radio-relay team to ask the slick pilot to buzz the area to see if he drew fire.

When the chopper arrived on the scene, the remaining enemy fire immediately ceased. Valeriano took advantage of the sudden lull in the action to stand up and throw a smoke grenade downhill into the rice paddy. He then radioed the relay team and told them to ask the chopper pilot to land out in the rice paddy directly on the smoke if he was still not taking fire. He didn't think about the risk to the air crew. At that time, all he could think about was getting the NVA off his ass and getting some help for his wounded.

The relay team radioed back that the pilot reported that he was not receiving fire. They added that they did not know whom the aircraft belonged to, but it was not one of the regular LRRP lift ships.

Suddenly, Valeriano saw the Huey slick flare out over the rice paddy and settle down twenty-five meters away. Whoever was flying that aircraft was not short *cojones*.

At that moment, Valeriano knew that Team Sandy was finished as a fighting force. It had one dead and five seriously wounded, including Valeriano. Kalua was dead. Bronson, McLaughlin, and Vang were unconscious. Valeriano and Pepping were both wounded but still mobile, even though Pepping could barely hobble. Valeriano was unable to carry anyone but himself.

Knowing that the helicopter could help them only if they were able to reach it, Valeriano ran down through the trees and out into the paddy.

When he reached the helicopter, he grabbed the crew chief by the hand and pulled him out of the chopper. His bicep wound was still bleeding badly, and the crew chief tried to pull away at the sight of all the blood. Valeriano would not let him go. Leading the soldier around the nose of the aircraft to the other side of the ship, he reached in and pulled the door gunner out of his "hellhole," then led the two men back up through the trees to the team's position.

At the sight of the terrible carnage around the tiny perimeter, the two crewmen simply freaked out. Valeriano ordered them to grab McLaughlin and get him down to the chopper. His decision was not based on the seriousness of his wounds, but on the fact that Mac was his best friend, and he couldn't bear to lose him now. Escorted by Valeriano, the two stunned crewmen carried the unconscious LRRP down to the waiting Huey and placed him gently aboard the aircraft.

They returned quickly to the site of the battle, where Valeriano did a quick check of his teammates to see who needed to go out next, selecting Vang in the process. As the two crewmen carried the little PRU down to the open rice paddy, Valeriano got Pepping up and moving on his own, sending him on his way down to the chopper. The team leader told him when he got there to cover the rest of them if they began to take fire. Pepping nodded that he understood.

When Valeriano checked Kalua, he discovered that there was no longer anything he could do for the man. Kalua's brains were seeping from the bullet wounds in his head, and Valeriano knew he was gone. As badly as he hated to do it, he still had living teammates to worry about. He knew that Solomon would understand. He moved on.

Down in the rice paddy, the pilot was getting a little edgy. He was lifting the Huey a foot or two off the ground, then setting it back down again. The two crewmen were also getting nervous. Looking over their shoulders at the ridgeline behind them, they grabbed Valeriano and pushed him inside the aircraft. As soon as he was safely aboard, the pilot pulled back on the collective and began lifting the aircraft out of the rice paddy.

Back in the chopper's bloody cabin, Valeriano did a quick head count and realized that Bronson was missing. My God, they had left one of his men behind! The crewmen had ignored Bronson because they thought he was dead. The morphine had knocked him out, and he did not respond when the men had tried to move him.

When Valeriano realized Bronson was missing, he screamed at the chopper pilot that they had left someone behind. The pilot shook his head and refused to go back. Valeriano went nuts. Pointing the captured AK-47 he had picked up to replace his damaged M-16, the LRRP team leader told the aircraft commander that he would blow his brains out if he didn't go back. The pilot got the message. Going into a sharp left turn, the pilot flew back to the rice paddy and landed once again.

Valeriano and the two crewmen left the aircraft and went back up to get Bronson. When they reached him, they discovered that he was indeed still alive. Bronson was a big, well-built guy, six foot four and over two hundred pounds. However, he was unconscious and dead weight, making it almost impossible to get him back down to the field and aboard the ship. But they finally managed.

The aircraft made the long flight back to Chu Lai, where the pilot set it down on the medevac pad at the 2d Surgical Hospital. Medics were waiting to whisk the wounded LRRPs into surgery. Sometime during the flight back to Chu Lai, Dan McLaughlin had died in Valeriano's arms. Back at the scene of the battle, there had been no time, nor anyone capable, to properly dress McLaughlin's sucking chest wound. He had slowly bled to death internally.

McLaughlin's brother had already left for the rear for a well-deserved R & R. The next day, the unit operations NCO pulled him off the waiting airliner to give him the news about his brother. Ironically, Dan McLaughlin's body had just been loaded into the cargo bay of that same aircraft.

As the wounded were removed from the helicopter, they were quickly rushed into triage. There it was discovered that John Bronson had nine holes in him. He was treated in country, then medevacked back to the States, where, after a lengthy hospitalization, he fully recovered.

Ron Pepping was also medevacked back to the States and fully recovered.

Sgt. Vic Valeriano was shipped to the 106th Army Hospital in Japan for skin grafts, reconstructive surgery, and extensive physical therapy, then sent to Valley Forge Hospital near his home. He would later return to duty.

The PRU, Vang, died later in the hospital. His body was returned to his family for burial.

The next day, a reaction force from the 198th Light Infantry Brigade combat assaulted into the valley and recovered Solomon Kalua's body. They found the bodies of seven dead NVA left where they had fallen. Intelligence reports indicated that the patrol had been tracked from their original LZ by an NVA counterreconnaissance platoon. While the patrol had moved along the edge of the wood line, the NVA had trailed them, while another element moved ahead to set up an ambush in front of the recon team. Fortunately, the team had gone to ground just before they reached the kill zone, forcing the NVA to come after them.

Sgt. Victor Valeriano was awarded his second Silver Star for his actions that day. His best friend, Sgt. Dan McLaughlin, was posthumously awarded a Bronze Star with V device. Vic Valeriano still blames himself for his friend's death. You be the judge.

☆ ☆ ☆ ☆ ☆

Company H,
75th Infantry (Ranger),
1st Cavalry Division

In late May 1970, the U.S. Army and its South Vietnamese allies were well into their famous raid against the NVA sanctuaries in Cambodia. The raid had gone well at first, with the surprised NVA forces reeling before the fast-moving allied units. Virtual warehouses of enemy armaments, munitions, military stores, and equipment were being captured en masse. The enemy's base sanctuaries and supply depots in Parrot's Beak, Angel's Wing, Fishhook, and across the border in Cambodia were a shambles.

However, the sheer weight and numbers of captured NVA equipment were slowing down the operation. It took days to go through and inventory some of the larger enemy facilities, then remove or destroy everything that was found. As the raid began to lose momentum, there was a growing fear among the operation's planners that enemy forces would try to move back in to recover some of their threatened supply dumps and warehouses before the Americans could find and destroy them. This forced the U.S. commanders to concentrate their forces for safety's sake, thereby playing right into the hands of the enemy.

To continue the momentum of the raid, the general staff decided to utilize small Ranger reconnaissance patrols as force multipliers who would surreptitiously infiltrate some of the areas skipped over by the larger forces to look for enemy weapons and supply caches missed by the raiders. It was a dangerous assignment, but one well suited to the long-range patrols of Hotel Company, 75th Infantry (Ranger), 1st Cavalry Division.

On 21 May, a five-man long-range patrol, led by Ranger Sp4. Lee "Shorty" Comstock, inserted into an open grassy meadow sixteen klicks outside Fire Support Base David. FSB David was the 1st Cavalry Division's most forward firebase, and was little more than a makeshift perimeter occupied by an artillery battery with an infantry company for security. It had not been established as a permanent base, but as a temporary forward base to support the incursion. Past operations had taught the Cav that it was best to build a forward firebase up close to an operation, then shut it down and get out before the enemy could put together plans for a well-organized assault against it. The NVA/VC were meticulous planners. They always took the time to observe their enemy's weaknesses before striking. Getting in and out again in a week to ten days was the safest way to prevent being overrun, without spending the time and effort to permanently fortify the base.

The Cav long-range patrol had gone in on a seven-day reconnaissance mission a few klicks from the border. They had spent the entire mission patrolling through the rugged, double-canopy terrain looking for enemy base camps. But except for a few fresh trails, newly built bunkers, and recently tended vegetable plots, the patrol had been uneventful. However, the fact that everything they did find proved to be relatively new and unused indicated that there had to be enemy forces nearby. It was possible that the NVA and VC had merely withdrawn deeper into Cambodia to await the eventual departure of the American forces, especially since the date of the U.S. withdrawal had already been announced by the American media. The enemy knew he had only to bide his time until that day arrived; then he would be able to move back in and pick up where he had left off.

A long history of warfare had taught the Vietnamese many

valuable lessons, especially patience. However, there were enemy units that had been caught behind the lightning-fast allied invasion. And it was very likely that if any of those units remained in the area, they would be looking to deal out a little payback.

On the last day of its mission, the long-range patrol was sitting just inside the forest on a heavily wooded hilltop overlooking a number of broad, grassy fields nestled among the rolling hills. They were less than an hour from their extraction. They had chosen the hilltop to wait for their pickup because it afforded an excellent view of their primary PZ. A major high-speed trail, running north to south, crossed the rolling meadow just below them. A narrow secondary trail came out of a wood line on the other side of the meadow, intersected the first trail, then came up the hill where the patrol was situated.

The team was sitting in a tight defensive circle, patiently waiting for the magic moment to arrive when they would be lifted out and flown back to base for a hot shower, a good meal, and some cold beer. They could almost taste the beer. Suddenly, the patrol's assistant team leader, Sgt. Erwin "Skip" Thessin, spotted three enemy soldiers coming out of the wood line across the meadow below them. He raised his rifle and took aim, then nudged Shorty Comstock as the three men started up the hill toward the team. Comstock took one look, then slowly brought his own rifle to bear on the approaching enemy soldiers. The rest of the Rangers followed Comstock's lead as they scanned the jungle around them to make sure there were no others moving up through the surrounding cover.

"Those guys aren't fucking farmers," Comstock whispered to Thessin as they waited for the enemy soldiers to draw nearer. From their dark-green uniforms, pith helmets, and heavy rucks, the Ranger team leader knew that the targets were NVA.

The three soldiers were moving slowly, weapons at the

ready, and they were carefully scanning the sky above them for American helicopters as they crossed the open meadow. If the three NVA had any idea that there were five U.S. Army LRRPs waiting for them on top of the hill, they gave no visible indication.

As previously decided, Comstock would initiate the contact. He waited until the enemy soldiers were well up the hill and within the patrol's kill zone before he opened fire. Two of the three NVA soldiers went down instantly. The third NVA surprised the Rangers by quickly and accurately returning fire, forcing the Rangers to dive for cover. This gave the man's badly wounded comrades the opportunity to crawl back down the hill. Using the lay of the land and their rucksacks as cover, the three NVA withdrew.

It was over in minutes. The firing had been fast and furious, but an awkward silence immediately settled over the battleground. Comstock waited for several minutes to give the NVA a chance to make another mistake, and when nothing happened, he signaled the team's medic to move over to the south side of the hill to provide cover, then sent Sgt. Chuck Donahoo across to the north side to do the same there. With the team's RTO covering their backside, Comstock and Thessin stepped out into the trail and moved down toward the kill zone.

When they reached the spot where Comstock had taken the NVA under fire, they discovered that, except for a lot of blood covering the area, there was no sign of the enemy soldiers. However, they could see three rucksacks lying close together farther down the hill, so the two Rangers continued advancing side by side, reconning by fire and making sure they hit every place large enough to hide an enemy soldier.

When they reached the rucksacks, Comstock knelt and tied their Swiss seat ropes together while Thessin covered him. Comstock was certain that the enemy soldiers had not had time to booby-trap their packs, but he wasn't going to take any unnecessary chances. He looped the rope around the first rucksack; then he and Thessin got down behind some nearby cover. Comstock took the tail end of the rope and gave it a hard yank. To his great relief there was no explosion. The Ranger team leader repeated the performance with the two remaining packs, and his anxiety was mitigated when again there was no explosion. However, his relief didn't last long, for the main body of NVA soldiers had picked that very time to arrive at the edge of the woods across the clearing. Firing from several different directions, the NVA immediately opened up on the two Rangers. Comstock realized at once that the three NVA they had fired upon had been the point element for at least a full company. The team's hasty ambush had taken a dramatic turn.

Up on top of the hill, Chuck Donahoo was lying prone covering the path to the north, when the sudden burst of fire from the NVA across the meadow caught him by surprise. As he turned back to see what was happening and to cover Comstock and Thessin, to his immediate front, he spotted two enemy soldiers running out of the wood line in a crouch, only twenty-five meters away. It was apparent that the two NVA were attempting to flank Comstock and Thessin. Then he saw a few more NVA at the edge of the trees behind them.

Donahoo swung around to confront the NVA, but opened fire a second too late to hit them. Although he successfully shortstopped the assault on his two teammates, the enemy soldiers now concentrated their fire directly on him.

Rounds from one or both of the two AK-47s knocked the rifle from Donahoo's hands, then lifted him up, spun him around 180 degrees, and slammed him back to earth in the center of the trail. Donahoo, his breath knocked out of him, squirmed around on the ground trying to locate his weapon, only to discover that it was lying a good three feet away. His first thought was that the enemy soldiers had missed him altogether, instead hitting the hollow stock of his M-16. But the sudden realization that he was bleeding badly from his right side caused him to momentarily panic. However, Donahoo was not the kind of soldier who made it a practice to panic. He took a deep breath and told himself that now was not the time for this shit.

The two NVA soldiers, thinking they had killed the lone American soldier who had just spotted them, suddenly broke from cover and ran forward again. Donahoo saw them coming, and in spite of his great pain, he reached back and pulled his rucksack up over his head and dropped it in front of him for protection. Still lying prone, he quickly retrieved his backup weapon, a sawed-off M-79 grenade launcher, and snapped off a canister round at the two approaching NVA. He was relieved when he saw them tumble over backward.

Instantly, he broke open the grenade launcher, shoved home an HE round, then turned and fired into the tree line to his front. An M-79 HE round arms itself during the first few revolutions after leaving the barrel. Even if it doesn't explode, it can still make a rather large hole through a man. But this time, Donahoo was relieved when the round went off. Taking advantage of the confusion caused by the grenade's blast, Donahoo quickly loaded and fired again. Only when the NVA to his front had all disappeared did Donahoo stop to realize how badly he had been hit. It felt like someone had knocked all the air out of him. But at least he could still breathe. His right side seemed heavy and was growing numb, but the numbness kept the pain away. "Shit!" he said to himself, then put the situation in the back of his mind. They weren't out of the woods yet; there would be time to worry about the small stuff later.

Donahoo opened the blooper, ejected the empty casing, and inserted another round. Then, propping the grenade launcher over his rucksack, he pointed it in the general area where he had last seen the NVA. Holding the weapon with his left hand, he took his right hand and reached inside his camouflaged fatigue shirt. Any hopes he had previously entertained that his injury was only a flesh wound were dashed when he discovered the entry wound of a bullet in his right side just below the ribs. There was a thumb-size hole there where the bullet had entered. His fingers quickly located a second, then a third wound a few inches above the first. Like the first wound, the second was seeping blood; the third was hardly bleeding at all. Donahoo quickly felt around his back but there were no exit wounds that he could locate. The young Ranger knew that he was in big trouble; he was already sweating, and his face felt flushed.

Then Donahoo remembered something he had learned in AIT about chest wounds with no exit points. If there wasn't heavy bleeding from the wounds, it usually meant that there was most likely a lot of internal bleeding going on. This could explain the heaviness in his side and lower chest. He was surprised that he wasn't feeling much pain, but he rationalized that maybe there wasn't a lot of pain when you were dying. He decided that there was no time to properly bandage the wounds, so he used the large field dressing from his first-aid pouch to cover the holes and hopefully stop the bleeding. That seemed better than doing nothing at all.

Suddenly there was another burst of automatic-weapons fire from out in front of his position, the bullets slamming into his rucksack and web belt, shattering his canteen. He squirmed back up to his damaged rucksack and fired his M-79 in the direction where he thought the enemy fire had come from. He followed this up quickly with five more rounds. It felt good to be fighting back.

Out on the exposed slope, Comstock and Thessin were having their own troubles. The enemy in the tree line across the meadow were keeping the two Rangers pinned down, unable to make it back to their teammates. Seeing this, Donahoo turned his M-79 to the front and began dropping HE rounds into the edge of the forest where the enemy fire was coming from. While the NVA were down trying to avoid the accurate grenade fire, Comstock and Thessin slipped back into the perimeter at the top of the hill. Donahoo kept up the fire on both tree lines until he finally ran out of ammo.

Realizing that Donahoo was also exposed, Comstock tried to get the grenadier's attention to get him to move back inside the perimeter, but Donahoo was still concentrating on the enemy below. Comstock did not realize that the young Ranger had been badly hit. When Thessin finally yelled at him, "Come on, Donahoo!" the scout only nodded, but said nothing.

Donahoo began to experience a sharp burning sensation in his right side as the numbness began to wear off. He turned to look back at the distance to the team's perimeter, and knew he couldn't reach it in a single sprint. If he could make it at all, it would take him a couple of attempts. By that time the pain in his side was so bad that even walking presented a major problem. He knew he would have to come up with another plan.

Looking around, he spotted an anthill ten meters behind him. It was just a couple of feet high and a meter or so in diameter, but if he could get to it, it would shield him from fire until he could make it back to the team.

Dragging his rucksack behind him, he crawled as quickly as he could. Each lunge made him feel as if his chest were on fire. But he had to keep going. If any of his teammates tried to reach him, the enemy soldiers hidden in the woods would have easy targets.

Somehow he reached the cover of the mound. His teammates were still exchanging fire with the enemy. A thick haze lay over the team's perimeter, and the hilltop reeked of burned gunpowder and shredded vegetation. Donahoo rolled onto his side and tried to get to his knees, but when he attempted to rise, the pain in his side was unbearable. He dropped back to the ground and lay helpless for a few minutes to let the fireworks in his brain die down.

Meanwhile, enemy rounds were grinding down the anthill, threatening to destroy what little protection it offered. So Donahoo once again tried to rise. But that time he felt someone at his side, helping him to his feet. Sure as hell, it was Skip Thessin, Donahoo's ATL.

Thessin quickly got Donahoo up on his feet and moving, but he could only prop up the wounded Ranger with his left arm. Firing at the NVA closing in on them with his right arm, Thessin watched in horror as the enemy soldiers began tossing grenades at them. Donahoo was only vaguely aware of the nearby explosions, but he saw darkening red rosettes growing on the back of Thessin's shirt. Somewhere in the recesses of his pained mind, he knew that Thessin had been hit.

Then Comstock was there, and the NVA couldn't cross the open field below their position. With the radio between his legs, the team leader began directing the gunships just arriving on station to the target-rich tree line across the meadow. While he continued to work the Cobras, his teammates continued to put accurate fire on the encircling NVA.

As the team medic began treating Donahoo's wounds, Comstock took a look at Thessin. His condition wasn't good. He shouted for the medic to work on Thessin as soon as he was done with Donahoo, but Thessin blew him off, saying that his wounds weren't that bad.

Donahoo was in pretty poor shape. His face was no longer hot and flushed; it was drawn, drained of color, and clammy to the touch. The medic knew that the lifeless look in his eyes was the beginning sign of shock. Donahoo would have to reach help quickly if he was going to make it.

"Can you walk?" Comstock asked, expecting a negative reply.

"I can try," Donahoo answered.

"Good, 'cause we're moving down the back side of the hill to reach an LZ and get a medevac in for you and Skip. If we stay here, they'll only be able to drop a jungle penetrator to us," Comstock explained. The Ranger team leader didn't have to point out the implications of that to Donahoo. A helicopter hovering over the team would be an easy target for the company of NVA soldiers less than a hundred meters away.

Comstock got back on the radio and told the gunships to continue working over the enemy positions while the team moved down through the trees to the clearing to their south. In spite of their wounded slowing them down, it didn't take them long to reach their secondary pickup zone. Up over the top of the hill, the Cobras continued plastering the enemy positions with rockets and miniguns, preventing the NVA from interfering with the extraction.

Minutes later, the Rangers heard the unmistakable sounds of an approaching Huey helicopter. Soon they spotted the medevac inbound toward their PZ.

Comstock turned to Donahoo and Thessin and said, "Get ready! You're going out first . . . both of you!"

One of the Rangers suddenly tossed out a yellow smoke grenade to mark the team's position. The medevac swung around and made its final approach, touching down less than twenty meters from the team. Just as the Huey settled in the grass, the NVA ignored the gunships and launched another assault on the Rangers. They were after the medevac.

The three unwounded Rangers turned to face the enemy attack. They had to cover the extraction or Thessin and Donahoo would never get out alive. Suddenly, Thessin broke out of the cover and raced for the medevac with Donahoo draped over his shoulder. When he reached the aircraft, he tossed Donahoo aboard, then jumped in beside him. It was a courageous, superhuman effort for the badly wounded ATL.

With the three remaining Rangers now battling to hold back the NVA, the aircraft commander lifted the Huey off the ground, dipped its nose as he developed transitional lift, then sped away from the clearing. The dull, metallic *ticks* of incoming rounds passing through the thin aluminum skin of the Huey confirmed how close their escape had been.

Airborne and out of range of the NVA gunners, the flight medic inspected the shrapnel wounds in Thessin's back, bandaging them quickly before turning back to work on Donahoo. Cutting open the Ranger scout's shirt, the medic grimaced when he saw the extent of the LRRP's wounds. He had a life-threatening situation on his hands, and he had to act quickly. Without hesitation, he reached into his aid pack and brought out a morphine syringe.

"This will help," he shouted over the roar of the Huey's turbine engine, then plunged the syringe into Donahoo's arm.

Donahoo had already lost a lot of blood, and with the help of the morphine was soon drifting in and out of reality. Finally, the merciful shroud of unconsciousness closed out the chapter of his life titled, "Nightmare."

When he awoke some time later, he was lying on a table in a field hospital. Nurses and medics were hovering over him, cutting away his boots and jungle fatigues.

"Gunshot wound to the right lung!" a voice yelled to his immediate right. Someone tried to get a long tube down his throat and into his collapsed lung. The badly wounded Ranger immediately panicked and began fighting for his life, until others stepped in around him and physically restrained him. Donahoo was too weak to resist for long. Soon he lay helplessly while the medical staff continued their trauma procedures to try to save his young life.

In and out of consciousness, he heard a voice say, "Lacerated liver," then someone else quickly add, "and blood in the abdominal cavity."

Minutes later, softer now, the first voice said, "Broken ribs and bone fragments, too." With that, Donahoo dropped off into a deep, drugged sleep, no longer aware of the probing fingers reaching deep into his chest.

When Donahoo came to again, he was being loaded aboard another helicopter. A nurse who looked like she had just been through a battle was telling the flight medic that Donahoo was stable enough to travel. It didn't feel that way to Donahoo, but no one had asked him.

"Three in the chest, huh?" the medic asked as he read Donahoo's chart. "Don't worry, man, you'll be okay."

Donahoo drifted in and out of consciousness during the

flight to the evac hospital at Long Binh. But he was awake again when he was wheeled into triage and subjected to another round of probing, this time by a tall, thin doctor who talked very little. Finally, he was taken off to a surgical ward, where he was left alone for the rest of the night. It was a night of constant, horrible pain. The young Ranger thought that it would never end.

The next morning Donahoo was prepped, given anesthesia, then wheeled into surgery, where a team of surgeons repaired the tremendous damage caused by the three NVA bullets. Two hours later, he awoke in recovery, dry and groggy from the anesthesia.

Several days later, Maj. Gen. George W. Casey, the 1st Air Cavalry Division commander, presented Sgt. Chuck Donahoo a Silver Star for gallantry in action, along with an Army Commendation Medal and a Purple Heart. Rather than spending the obligatory few minutes at the wounded man's bedside reciting the rote litany of overused pap so common to senior officers visiting the sick and wounded, General Casey remained with the young Ranger buck sergeant twenty minutes, asking about his background and family. He also asked him some questions about Hotel Company and the mission that had caused his wounds. When he finally stood to leave, he bent down and thanked Donahoo and told him he was proud to have had him in his division.

The general's visit never lessened his pain, nor made his recovery any easier, but the officer's genuine sincerity and fatherly concern meant a lot to Chuck Donahoo. General Casey's words, and the courage and loyalty that inspired the actions of Shorty Comstock and Skip Thessin, made Donahoo's long recovery bearable. It taught him that Rangers may indeed lead the way, but it's often how they are led that really makes all the difference.

☆　☆　☆　☆　☆

Company O, 75th Infantry (Ranger), 82d Airborne Division

When the 82d Airborne Division sent a brigade to Vietnam to meet the crisis of the 1968 Tet Offensive, the brigade quickly discovered that it needed long-range patrol capabilities to deal with an elusive enemy that spent most of its time hiding from combat units only to surface with deadly resolve when the odds dictated favorable results. It was a lesson learned the hard way many times over by all U.S. military formations operating in Vietnam. The 82d would find it no easier than its predecessors.

Company O, 75th Infantry (Ranger) was the successor to the 82d's 78th Infantry (LRP) company, but unlike its sister Ranger companies, Company O had very little support from its higher command. Assigned to the populated area south and southwest of Saigon, many of their patrols were conducted along the fast-flowing Saigon River, which was bordered on both sides by expansive rice paddies that surrounded villages and hamlets that were broken up only by an occasional tree line. It was not an area suited to conventional long-range reconnaissance patrol operations. Without the cover and concealment provided by the dense vegetation typical of most parts of South Vietnam, and with numerous civilians living within their areas of operation, the Company O Rangers were constantly exposed and unable to operate as they were trained to do. It was a very unsatisfactory situation that resulted in a greater degree of stress and anxiety than even that usually generated by long-range patrols.

On 13 April, 1969, a Company O heavy team was given the impossible mission of running a five-day reconnaissance patrol in an area along the south side of the Saigon River, approximately twenty klicks outside the capital city. The ten-man team, led by veteran Ranger Sgt. Don Harris, received a warning order to take his patrol in at first light on the following day. The team would be inserted by a U.S. Army aluminum engineer boat at low tide. Harris was upset that there would be no overflight of the recon zone prior to the insertion, but such glaring omissions were rapidly becoming the norm in Company O. Not surprisingly, he also received word that their patrol box was located in the middle of a restricted fire zone, which meant that he would have to get clearance before calling for air or artillery support—clearance that usually took over an hour to get. When you're a ten-man recon team up to your armpits in hostiles, an hour can be an eternity.

To make matters worse, in the middle of a very "brief" briefing, Harris was told that the team's area of operations was in an agricultural belt with little or no cover to speak of, and there was a village approximately fifteen hundred to eighteen hundred meters east of the team's infiltration point. Unfortunately, no one knew for certain if its inhabitants were friendly or hostile. Harris came to the conclusion that if the locals who called this place home were friendly, they probably wouldn't have been targeted for a reconnaissance patrol. The idea of going in to watch a village sitting in the middle of the world's largest continuous rice paddy wasn't comforting. It was even less comforting when Company O's commander and briefing officer ordered the team to use night movement to "muck about" near the village to see if anyone was moving around after curfew. This was like volunteering a man to swim into the Amazon River to find out if there were any piranha in the area.

Harris and his teammates didn't like anything about the

mission. Before arriving at Company O, Harris had served as
a LRP with the 101st Airborne Division and also with II Field
Force. Running missions with two of the finest LRP units in
country, he had learned how to conduct long-range patrols
properly. Many of his teammates had also put in some time
with F/51st LRP and had experienced support at its very
finest. But the assignments they were receiving from the
82d Airborne's S-2 betrayed a total lack of understanding
about how to use the long-range patrol assets attached to the
brigade. Harris and his teammates began to sense that their
value to the 82d ran somewhere between "acceptable loss"
and "cut bait" in the usefulness table. Although their professionalism remained exceptionally high, their morale was
somewhere below sea level.

Before daylight on the morning of 14 April 1969, the ten
Rangers were trucked from their base camp to a docking facility on the Saigon River. They loaded onto the waiting patrol boat and took up positions along the outer gunwales,
trying their best to avoid interfering with the crews' move-
ments. To a man, the Rangers couldn't help but notice that the
boat had a stern ramp. This meant that the craft would likely
have to back up to the shore to drop them off—a maneuver
that would violate noise discipline and take a lot of time to
accomplish.

The run up the river seemed to take forever, and looking
over the gunwales, Harris could see that the only cover along
the shoreline was a narrow band of tall grass and low shrubs.
The river was at low tide, which meant that the muddy river
bottom would have to be crossed to reach the shoreline cover,
and no one knew for certain what they would find on the
backside of the grass. From what Harris and his teammates
could observe, trees seemed to be as rare as friendly faces in
that part of South Vietnam.

Finally the trip was over, and the army engineer craft
swung about and backed in to the shore. Harris and his ATL,
S.Sgt. John LaPolla, both wondered how the boat crew knew

where to drop off the team. There were no terrain features, structures, or indicators along that stretch of the river that would distinguish it from any other stretch of shoreline for ten miles in either direction. But by then it was too late to second-guess anyone. With a silent nod to the crew, Harris led his teammates down the stern ramp and into the gumbo mud along the shore. Fighting the muck that sucked at their boots, the ten Rangers struggled noisily across the mud flats and into the grass and scrub brush lining the river. The ground was no drier in the razor grass, but the concealment gave Harris's team a moment to catch their breath while they lay dog and listened for sounds that would indicate they weren't alone.

After fifteen minutes, Harris signaled for Sp4. Bailey Stauffer, the team's point man, to move out toward a narrow tree line about one hundred meters to the north of their position. The tree line was little more than a two-meter-wide hedge of sparse single-canopy growth, but it offered more cover than the flat, barren, dried rice paddies that spread to the east and south as far as they could see.

The tree line ran, perpendicular, away from the river a hundred meters or so until it intersected a second, longer and denser tree line that paralleled the river, running north and south. From where Harris had squatted at the edge of the grass, he could see that the larger tree line quickly petered out directly across the open paddy from their insertion point. However, it did appear to extend several thousand meters to the north. The village they were supposed to observe lay over a mile away across an open rice paddy to the southeast.

Harris's options were severely limited by terrain, but he would attempt to complete his mission. So, with Stauffer in the lead, the team moved along the edge of the grass until they reached the first tree line. After waiting there for twenty or thirty minutes to observe the second tree line, a hundred meters away, the team spaced out at proper intervals and

moved along as silently as possible through the sparse cover
toward their target.

When they finally reached the second tree line they quickly
discovered that the overgrowth was about twelve feet across,
the only real cover coming from the fact that the ground in the
center of the tree line was a foot or two below the surface of
the surrounding terrain. Apparently, at one time the tree line
had been an old roadbed, or perhaps an old drainage ditch that
had silted in from poor maintenance. Whatever the reason, it
was the only cover the Rangers had for miles around.

Not wanting to remain upright in the tree line for too long,
Harris ordered Stauffer to move south toward the end of the
cover, which also happened to be the closest point of cover to
the village. Just before they reached their goal, they crossed
an old roadbed that ran into the tree line from the east. It appeared to have been unused for years, so its discovery did not
overly alarm the Ranger team leader.

When they finally reached the end of the tree line, Harris
ordered the team to set up in an elliptical perimeter with flank
security on both sides of the tree line. He then placed a single
Ranger out on each end as an observer while he and his RTO,
Sp4. Lambert, set up in the center of the perimeter. It was
close to noon, and the day would be a hot one, so Harris
ordered his teammates to lie low and avoid moving around
until after dark. Any movement above ground level would
most likely be visible to anyone watching from the area of the
village.

When the night finally fell along with the heat of the day,
Harris made ready to send out a six-man patrol to check out
the countryside. It wasn't his choice, but a direct order from
higher command.

At 2100 hours, Harris led the team out into the open rice
paddies while the four-man security force remained behind
in the tree line. It didn't take them long to realize the futility
of their effort. Maintaining noise discipline was impossible
in the dry rice-plant stubble, and in the stygian darkness the

Rangers had a difficult time following each other, let alone trying to locate the enemy. The hair on the back of the team leader's neck was standing at rigid attention.

One hour and 150 meters later, Harris had the team circling back to the tree line. Orders or not, he wasn't going to lead his team into an ambush while stumbling around in total darkness. From past experience in Company O, he knew that a contact in the middle of the night would likely generate nothing more than a "break contact, continue mission" from the gang back at the TOC, with no attempt at rescue until daylight. It was a bad situation even when your patrol wasn't already divided into two separate elements.

The remainder of the night was quiet. Harris kept two men on guard at all times while the rest of the patrol tried to get a little shut-eye. He had already made the decision that at the close of the second day, he would move his team to the north up the tree line away from the village, and then set up another OP. Moving farther away from the village didn't make recon sense, but remaining in the same place at the end of the tree line for two days was a foolish risk he wasn't about to take.

The next morning saw the Rangers awake and alert at first light. Harris kept them in place while he called in a sitrep and ordered part of the team to down their morning LRRP ration breakfast. While they waited for the heat of the day to arrive and bake them and their surroundings, Harris had the team keep vigil. They would wait for the hottest part of the day, sometime during the early afternoon, before they moved again. That would be when the enemy would be least likely to be moving about. When the heat was at its greatest during the middle of the day, the Vietnamese called "time out" and crawled off to enjoy a quiet, cool spot of shade and maybe a short nap—sort of an Indochinese siesta.

Around 1000 hours, the north security man spotted a single APC (armored personnel carrier) coming across the deserted rice field from the east. It was heading right for their position. As the APC drew nearer, Harris grew nervous and radioed in a sitrep to his "higher-higher" to let them know that a serious situation was pending. No friendlies were supposed to be in the area, so someone owed him an explanation as to why they were about to be fired upon by a South Vietnamese armored vehicle. It was bad for morale and would undoubtedly compromise their patrol.

An old roadbed crossed the field from the east and ran directly into the tree line where Harris's team lay hidden, and the APC was fast approaching the roadbed. It continued coming until it reached the tree line and ground to a sudden halt. With the ARVN track commander looking right at them, Harris did the only thing he could do under the circumstances—he stood up and raised his hands in the air. Amazingly, the ARVNs didn't seem at all surprised to discover ten rather large, heavily camouflaged soldiers lying up in a tree line in their AO. In turn, Harris wasn't really surprised that no one had been notified of their arrival. After a short round of worthless pig Latin, punctuated by some wild gestures and arm waving, the ARVNs seemed to accept the fact that everything was normal, and the Rangers could get back to whatever they were doing. Unfortunately, by then the village people must surely have become aware that an unusual amount of activity was going on in that long, thin tree line over by the river. With a final wave and salute, the ARVN APC turned on a dime and went back out on the same path it had come in on.

This was enough for Harris. He immediately ordered his teammates to retrieve their claymores and form up in patrol file. It was time to blow the AO. There were no other options, but even a short relocation a hundred meters north up the tree line made more sense than remaining where they were. Harris stopped the patrol in the center of the ditch not far from where the east-west hedgerow met the north-south tree line. As relocations go, it wasn't much of a relocation, but it was better than remaining at a spot every Vietnamese in III Corps could pinpoint by then.

While checking the area around their new OP, the Rangers'

scouts stumbled across a boneyard at the corner of the paddy in the southwest part of the intersecting tree lines. There were eight to twelve bleached-out skulls and enough assorted bones to reconstruct that many full skeletons. They had obviously been there for a while. There were no visible signs of a violent death, but seldom did that many people pick the same location for simultaneous natural deaths. Just after discovering the scattered bones, Harris and his teammates began an earnest discussion about their chances of finishing off this mission with any degree of success. Once again, he radioed the company TOC and reported a negative sitrep. Once again, he was told to Charlie Mike.

Harris had had enough of that particular brand of rear echelon game playing, especially when he and his teammates were the pawns. He made a unilateral decision that, regardless of orders, there would be no more insane night patrolling during the mission. Reassuring his teammates that they would be playing it safe, the Ranger team leader ordered them to set out claymores and get comfortable for the night.

Around 2300 hours, one of the team's two security men noticed a long string of low-intensity lights moving horizontally from east to west some distance to their north. He immediately woke Harris, who in turn woke up the rest of the Rangers. Satisfied that the lights weren't fireflies or UFOs, Harris reported the sighting, stating that the lights appeared to be people moving about with flashlights a good distance off. Someone at the TOC radioed back and suggested that the lights were aerial flares. Harris immediately nixed that idea. Flares were much brighter and floated down to the ground from high up in the sky. The night crew at the TOC came back and said that it had no reports of any friendly activity in that area, nor did it have any reports of enemy activity at that location. As usual, their suggestion was to continue the mission.

The "aerial flares" continued to move back and forth, from east to west, then west to east, until midnight, when they finally went out for good.

By that time, Harris and his teammates were beginning to get a little nervous. They knew that the lights represented enemy troops moving about the countryside. And enemy troops were always a risk for a long-range patrol.

Unknown to the rest of the team, Sergeant Smith, a recent transfer into the company from the 1st Cav, was handling his nervousness in a much different way. He had earlier popped a couple of dextroamphetamine pills to fight off the sudden sleepiness he was feeling. Now the pills were beginning to work on him, forcing him to be wide awake, but also increasing his sense of anxiety.

Harris knew that the lights were actually flashlights, held in the hands of enemy soldiers moving into position to block off the only cover the Rangers had left. Or maybe they were VC soldiers getting on line to sweep the tree line up to the area where the Ranger team lay hidden. Harris whispered for everyone to stay low along the lip of the shallow depression that ran down the length of the tree line and remain alert.

A short time later the lights came back on for the second time. At that moment, S.Sgt. John LaPolla raised up from his position on the east side of the tree line, almost directly across from Harris and his RTO. No one knows why LaPolla raised up, but the LRRPs believe he was trying to get a better view of the lights.

Sergeant Smith, feeling the full effects of the dex, was also looking back at the lights. When he spotted a shadowy figure rising up on the far side of the team's perimeter, he violated a long-established LRRP principle—always secure your assigned area of responsibility. He immediately violated a second principle. He opened fire directly across the team's perimeter at the darkened form outlined against the open rice paddy, holding the trigger back until the bolt locked open on an empty chamber.

Harris and his RTO had gone down as the first rounds passed over them. By the time the gunfire stopped, Harris was already on the radio hollering, *"Contact! Contact!"* It was at that moment that the Ranger just to the north of Staff Sergeant LaPolla said, "That was no gook, it's LaPolla."

Harris tossed the radio handset to Lambert and crawled the short distance to where LaPolla lay faceup. The team leader ran his hands back and forth over his ATL from head to foot looking for a wound. He found nothing. Grabbing him around his shoulders, Harris pulled LaPolla to him in an attempt to turn him over, only to have the rear half of his skull come off against his chest. John LaPolla was dead.

Looking out to the north, Harris saw that the mysterious string of lights had once again gone out. They would remain out for the rest of the night.

Back in the tree line, holding his teammate's dead body in his arms, Harris heard Smith, behind him, drop his magazine and load a fresh one. The sound was enough to jolt the shaken team leader back to his senses. Gently, he laid LaPolla's body back down on the ground where he had died, then turned and attempted to calm everyone. No one seemed to know for certain what had happened, and there was an immediate danger that the overcharged Rangers would respond with force to the next strange sound or movement. Only Harris realized at the time what had happened for sure, and for that reason he calmly ordered Smith to lay his weapon down.

Smith responded by saying, "No, I'm not going to do it." Harris sensed immediately that to push the issue would only force a confrontation, and a confrontation would only get someone else killed. Gently but firmly, he told Smith to turn around and pull security facing the river to their west.

Since they were fully compromised, Harris decided to take a chance and fire off a white aerial flare. He had to assess their situation and he couldn't do that without illumination. He pointed the flare out at an angle toward the east so that it wouldn't drift down directly over their position.

By then, everyone was wound as tight as a drum and wanted to kill something, anything. Let the enemy come if they wanted to. Company O had just lost a Ranger, and somebody needed to pay for it!

After calling in another sitrep and reporting his ATL had just been killed in action, Harris requested a medevac to recover the body. HQ denied the medevac, telling the team leader to wait for daylight—medevacs don't pick up dead bodies at night. Harris was outraged by this and in shocked disbelief. Dead bodies? John LaPolla was a teammate—a brother, not a "dead body."

Harris kept the team on 100 percent alert the remainder of the night. LaPolla's friends on the team knew he was Catholic, so Sp4. Tortice—a full-blooded Apache and a Catholic—said a prayer over the dead Ranger. Then they rolled him up in his poncho to protect him from the insects. Smith remained silent during the entire ritual.

Early the next morning, a medevac arrived on the scene and requested that the patrol pop a smoke grenade and toss it out into the dry paddy past the boneyard to mark an LZ. When the Rangers complied, the aircraft landed and picked up LaPolla's body. An hour later the rest of the patrol was extracted and flew directly back to the 82d Airborne Division helipad. A deuce-and-a-half was there to pick them up for the long ride back to their company area. When they finally arrived, Harris jumped down from the truck and went directly to see Captain Peters in the orderly room to explain what had happened on the mission. Sp4. Bailey Stauffer soon joined them and wrote up the after-action report.

By the next morning, the company commander had cut orders reassigning Smith, and Captain Peters asked Sergeant Harris to take Sergeant Smith up to Saigon and drop him off with another unit. His days as a Ranger with Company O, 75th Infantry, were finished.

In November 1969, Company O stood down after a short but bloody existence, when the brigade returned to Fort Bragg, North Carolina, and rejoined its parent unit, the 82d Airborne Division. The company's history had been short, shorter than any other Ranger company but Company D. But its LRRPs still carried out their mission with courage and loyalty despite appalling conditions and very meager support. They were Rangers first, and that was all that mattered.

74th LRRP Detachment, 173d Airborne Brigade (Separate)

By mid-December 1967, the 173d Airborne Brigade had nearly completed its withdrawal from the Dak To area. The 3d Battalion, 503d Infantry, D Troop 16th Armor (APCs), and the brigade's LRRP detachment, had moved to Tuy Hoa, while the remaining battalions in the brigade, the 1st, 2d, and 4th, had already deployed, or were in the process of deploying, to the brigade base camp at An Khe. Unbeknownst to them, the brigade's old LRRP detachment had been officially renamed the 74th LRRP Detachment shortly after arriving at Tuy Hoa, and immediately thereafter began pulling missions in its new area of operations.

Around the middle of January 1968, Team Delta, led by S.Sgt. Patrick Tadina, received a warning order for a reconnaissance mission to be launched three days later. The designated RZ was an area on the far side of the river that ran north of Tuy Hoa.

S.Sgt. Patrick "Tad" Tadina, already a legend among the 173d LRRPs, took his ATL, Sgt. Lazlo Rabel, on the overflight the following day. They found that their RZ consisted of vast areas of abandoned fields and overgrown rice paddies and gently rising foothills that sloped upward toward the north-northwest, where they merged with the rugged mountains of the Central Highlands. The foothills wore a covering of thin brush and single-canopy forest on their lower slopes, and light-to-medium double canopy along ridge crests.

At their briefing later that day, the team was told to expect excellent weather during the five-day mission. S-2 said that it had received reports of light-to-medium NVA/VC activity scattered through the area, and told the patrol to be on the lookout for an NVA regiment reportedly moving into the area. Elements of the 3/503d Infantry Battalion were running company-size sweeps in the general vicinity of the LRRPs' recon zone. A few small villages remained in that part of the province, but most of the area's residents had already been re-located elsewhere.

The formation of three slicks and four Delta-model Huey gunships left Tuy Hoa and headed west, then looped back north to deceive watchful eyes. The aircraft crossed the river near the Highway 1 bridge just downstream from where the half-submerged dropped spans of a single-gauge railroad bridge lay. From there, it was still another fifteen minutes to their recon zone.

As the aircraft approached the patrol's AO, the chase ship and the extraction ship dropped out of formation and began the leapfrog maneuvers that were designed to deceive the enemy as to which insertion was the real one. As the two Hueys hedgehopped over the low terrain, the lead aircraft suddenly dropped into a likely looking LZ, while the second aircraft continued flying on until it, too, located a suitable clearing, where the scenario was repeated. If everything went according to plan, enemy observers would have a difficult time ascertaining which of the insertions had actually been the real one.

The two Hueys made five such "insertions," the patrol slipping in on the third. The infil was textbook, with the helicopter touching down briefly along the northwest edge of a narrow, overgrown rice paddy surrounded by brush, which soon gave way to sparse, single-canopy forest. The team had exited simultaneously from both sides of the aircraft, then sprinted into the nearby woods on the northeast side of the paddy.

As the insertion aircraft departed the AO, the team covered a full fifty meters into the trees before dropping to the ground and facing outward in a wagon-wheel defensive perimeter. Sp4. Brooks quickly established commo with the platoon TOC and gave the team's sitrep.

After lying dog for a full half hour, Tadina signaled that it was time to move out. He took the point behind his captured CZ .58, and headed upslope to the northwest. PFC Greg "Olie" Olson, heavily overarmed with a .45 cal. World War II–era M-3 grease gun, a .45 pistol, a Smith & Wesson .357 revolver, and a cutdown Model 1897 shotgun tied across his chest with a couple of pieces of cotton webbing, followed five meters back at the slack position. Even though Olson overburdened himself with extra ordnance, it was good to know that that kind of firepower was along on the patrol.

Once the two lead men were a full ten meters in front of the patrol, Peterson and Brooks moved out of the cover behind them. Recently busted PFC Fletcher Ruckman, also heavily armed with a CAR-15 and a .45 auto, and carrying a chopped Model 1897 in his pack, turned to make sure Sgt. Lazlo Rabel was bringing up the rear, then turned to follow close behind Peterson.

The ground rose gently as the patrol moved slowly to the northwest. Tadina took them nearly three hundred meters from the LZ before impending darkness forced him to hold up the team. They had found no fresh sign of the enemy, but they had cut a couple of old footpaths within the first hundred meters of the clearing. Even though there were old sandal tracks in the trails, there was nothing that looked military or caused them any undue concern.

Tadina stopped the team and signaled for them to set up security. In the fading light, he took Ruckman and Olson with him and went out to conduct a thorough point reconnaissance of the area that lay just ahead. He wanted to find out if there were any enemy troops nearby, and scout the area for a suitable NDP. When they finally located an adequate RON site, the three LRRPs returned to pick up the rest of their patrol and lead them back to the site they had just selected. The thin jungle covering the slope didn't offer a lot of cover, but as long as they remained low to the ground, they had adequate concealment. Uphill to the northwest, they could just make out the spot where the ridge crest met the skyline, but all around them on the other sides the ground fell gently away.

Tadina quietly instructed his teammates to set out five or six claymores, two facing uphill to the northwest, with the rest scattered evenly around the team. He designated the first place they had stopped coming off the LZ as their rally point. Tadina then set the night security watch, one man on, one-hour shifts, two shifts each. That completed, everyone settled down to what they hoped would be a long, uneventful night.

Around 2130 hours, the team began to hear movement above them near the crest of the ridge. It sounded like a large number of people were moving about in the brush looking for someone. Believing they had somehow been spotted on the infil and were compromised, Tadina got on the radio and requested an extraction, briefly outlining his reasons. The TOC listened patiently, then denied the team leader's request, telling him to Charlie Mike. Tadina reluctantly accepted the officer's decision, but to himself, he questioned the judgment of someone who would make such a decision without being there on the ground with them.

After a while, the movement died down and finally disappeared altogether, so Tadina decided to put the team back on 50 percent alert. Sleep was always at a premium on patrol; you had to take it when you could get it.

However, during the next three hours the team had to wake up and go back on full alert two more times. Whoever was out there had evidently not given up the search, and was still looking for the patrol.

Sometime around midnight the sounds seemed to fade away to the northwest, then die out completely. They did not return. Tadina waited a little to make sure, then put the team back on its original security watch.

At the team's regularly scheduled midnight sitrep, the RTO had a problem getting the message through. The signal was strong enough, but the transmission kept breaking up. After several minutes of hit and miss, he was finally able to get the sitrep through to the TOC, but the commo problem only added to everyone's nervousness and anxiety.

Around 0200 hours, Ruckman and Peterson were exchanging guard when the sounds of movement began again, and it seemed to be coming directly toward the team. The two LRRPs were trying to decide whether to wake the rest of the patrol when they saw dim lights flickering on and off in the underbrush just uphill of their position. When the lights began to move directly toward them, they became alarmed. Just as they reached out to awaken their sleeping teammates, someone or something began crashing through the brush and set off one of their trip flares. A split second later, the intruder was charging headlong into the team's perimeter.

Peterson and Ruckman, still down on their knees, looked up in time to open fire on full auto in the direction of the noise. Everything was happening in rapid motion. The two LRRPs could make out only silhouettes and darting shadows, but they could tell their shots were hitting home. They kept firing until a large, dark form suddenly leaped over them, shattering the stock of Peterson's AK-47 in the process, then ran five to six feet beyond them and fell over dead.

When his shaking had quieted down Ruckman realized that he had emptied a full magazine from his CAR-15 into the target, and Peterson reported that he had less than a half dozen rounds left in the magazine of his AK-47.

By that time, the rest of the team was up and frantically searching for targets. When it became apparent that the "battle" was already over and the enemy gone, Tadina switched on his shielded red-lens flashlight and quickly spotted what had attacked his patrol—a large, quite dead wild boar. Tadina was visibly upset, and in strong but hushed tones voiced his displeasure at what had just occurred. There was no longer any doubt that the team had been compromised. The burning flare and the subsequent mini–"Boar" War had seen to that. There was nothing left to do but get back on the radio and once more request an extraction. However, when he called the TOC, he discovered that this time he couldn't even get through. Tadina quickly switched to the alternate frequency, but still had no luck. He switched back to his primary "freak" and continued trying to reach base. That time he picked up someone speaking rapidly in broken English. After a minute or two, he figured out that someone from the ROK White-horse Division was on the team's push, offering his help. Tadina listened for a moment and finally figured out that the radio operator was saying, "I speak little English. I help. Coca-Cola . . . Pepsi . . . Budweiser."

Not wanting to pursue the helpful Korean's strange line of thought, Tadina told him to get off the push; however, the soldier remained insistent that he be allowed to help and wouldn't sign off.

Finally, after several threats and quiet reasoning failed to work, Tadina gave up. He secured the SOI (signal operating instructions) from his RTO, and spent the next several minutes flipping through the code book trying to locate a unit close enough that it could relay his message to the TOC. Finally, after he'd switched back and forth through a number of frequencies, a distant "leg" (that is, non–airborne qualified) artillery battery responded. The signal was not strong, but it was good enough to pass on his message to the TOC. The artillery FDO readily agreed to act as the team's radio relay, and they were soon in contact with the LRRP platoon leader. Tadina gave the team's current sitrep and asked for an extraction, but the message came back quickly, once again denying the extraction.

Tadina was furious, and he demanded that they be picked up. The TOC flatly refused, then signed off the net. The angry

LRRP team leader knew now that they were on their own. Tadina immediately resigned himself to the situation, and ordered his teammates to pull in their claymores and prepare to move out.

Under cover of darkness, the team worked its way upslope another hundred meters. Still heading northwest, they stopped just below the military crest of the ridge in a shallow depression they had discovered during their earlier point recon. As quietly as possible, the six men slipped into the low spot in the jungle floor and formed up in a tight defensive circle, feet toward the center of the perimeter. Tadina decided that it was best not to risk the additional noise they might make putting out their claymores in the dark. Instead, he hoped that the dark of night and the team's stealth in moving into their new position would protect them through the remaining hours of darkness. It was by then 0300 hours, and with the excitement of the past hour, no one slept for the rest of the night.

The patrol moved out again at first light, still heading northwest. They immediately spotted lots of fresh sign on the floor of the jungle, indicating that a large number of pigs had been rooting around and feeding in the area. That explained the noises they had heard upslope of their original NDP the night before. It also explained the 150-pound boar that had overrun their position. It didn't account for the dim lights they'd seen, and they remained a mystery.

The patrol soon reached the top of the ridge and discovered that it leveled out onto a wide, flat plateau. The team moved out, zigzagging another six hundred or seven hundred meters, during which they discovered a number of small trails, some of them quite fresh.

Ninety minutes later, they swung around and were moving to the west when they walked up on an immense clearing. It was the last thing they expected to find right in the middle of the jungle.

After observing it quietly for ten or fifteen minutes, Tadina decided that, at three hundred meters wide, the clearing was too wide and too open to traverse at that point. He decided to send out a couple of scouts to the north in hope of finding a way around the large open area.

After covering nearly two hundred meters and still not discovering a suitable place to cross, the two LRRPs returned to the patrol to report their findings. It was not good news for Tadina. He then sent the two scouts to the south to see if they could locate a safe crossing in that direction.

The recon element encountered a dense hedgerow two hundred or three hundred meters south of where the team had reached the clearing. The natural barrier seemed to run all the way across the base of the clearing and peter out back in the sparse brush on the opposite side. Satisfied that they had discovered a secure place to cross, the two scouts returned quickly to the team, anxious to report their findings.

After listening to their report, Tadina led the patrol back to the base of the hedgerow, then held them up at the edge of the jungle while they observed the area they had to cross. After fifteen minutes, satisfied that there were no enemy troops lying in wait for them, Tadina moved the patrol into the shadows cast by the hedgerow and led them safely across the clearing.

At the end of the hedgerow, they found a trail running north and south just inside the trees. They moved a few meters past the trail and set up in the thin concealment of brush and trees on the west side of the clearing. The jungle thickened considerably another fifty meters in, but Tadina's plan was to remain out in the scanty cover closer to the clearing and the trail, and work their way back to the north, circling the expansive field.

A short time later, they had reached a point directly across from where the team had originally encountered the open area, when Tadina spotted a bottleneck in the clearing another three hundred meters to the north. He decided to head toward that point and use it to recross the open area back to the east side.

The team had just begun to string out in patrol file and was about to continue north when Rabel, following immediately behind Ruckman, heard Vietnamese voices on their back trail. Before turning back to face the threat, Rabel sent Ruckman forward to the head of the column to warn Tadina.

After alerting Tadina, Ruckman was returning to his position next to Rabel when he suddenly heard Tadina's nearly inaudible danger signal behind him. Simultaneously, Ruckman spotted five VC moving parallel to the team, but out near the edge of the clearing.

Tadina quickly gave the hand signal for hasty ambush. The team turned to face the clearing, then went slowly to ground. Ruckman, unable to reach his original position in the column, had to drop in place next to Brooks. There had not been enough time for him to make it back to support Rabel. He didn't like that, but he could only freeze and hope the enemy passed them by.

The VC soon pulled even with the hidden LRRPs lying frozen behind a thin screen of brush. Carrying their weapons at sling arms, it was apparent from their easy conversation and their relaxed gait that the VC were not aware of the presence of the long-range patrol lying hidden along their flank. But it was also obvious that there were more enemy soldiers than the original five they had spotted.

The VC column was now passing less than three meters from where the patrol lay hidden. The LRRPs held their breath, not fully understanding how or why the enemy soldiers had not yet spotted them lying motionless in the thin cover. One of the VC, a female, glanced to her left and looked directly at the bush concealing Ruckman and Brooks, then looked away again without reacting.

As the VC point man walked up to within three meters of Tadina's position, the LRRP team leader, weapon at ease, stepped boldly out in front of him, blocking the trail, and said, *"Dung lai"* (stop).

The VC paused for a moment, then casually said something back in Vietnamese to Tadina. When Tadina failed to respond immediately, the VC realized that something was wrong and shouted a command, whereupon the enemy soldiers behind him went for their weapons, prompting the LRRPs to open fire.

Brooks and Ruckman had three targets to their immediate front. Ruckman fired at the center target, then shifted toward the front of the column, while Brooks fired at the same target and shifted fire to the rear of the column. Two of the VC dropped to the ground dead, and a third, the woman, lay badly wounded in the trail.

Tadina, still standing out in front of the lead VC, who had immediately dropped his weapon and thrown up his hands, shoved him aside, opening fire down the length of the enemy column and hitting several more VC.

Olson, to the left of Brooks and Ruckman, fired up a number of enemy soldiers standing directly in front of him, while Peterson, to his right, did the same.

Alone at the rear of the patrol, Rabel emptied a full magazine into what he thought was the end of the enemy column and then followed up with a single fragmentation grenade.

It was over as quickly as it started. Tadina yelled, "Cease fire," and immediately put Ruckman and Olson out on security, Ruckman in the clearing facing south and Olson back at the edge of the jungle facing north. As soon as security was in place, the rest of the team moved out onto the trail to search the bodies and secure the weapons. The LRRPs quickly discovered five dead VC, two badly wounded, two lightly wounded, and two more uninjured. While Peterson, Rabel, and Brooks guarded the prisoners, Tadina walked over to the radio and contacted the LRRP TOC. When he got them on the net, he gave a quick sitrep, then asked for an immediate extraction, reiterating that this time he had six prisoners and a number of enemy weapons.

Unbelievably, the LRRP platoon leader told Tadina that he was unable to provide assets at this time. Tadina was speechless.

At that point, the commanding officer of the 3/503d cut in and reported that he was en route to the LRRPs' location and would be on station in two minutes.

Minutes later, an unescorted C & C slick arrived overhead and set down in the clearing right along the edge of the trail where the successful ambush had just occurred. As the aircraft was coming in, two VC who had been following up the enemy column, and unseen by the LRRPs during the ambush, broke from cover and disappeared over the hedgerow. Ruckman was able to snap off a couple of quick rounds as they vanished, and Rabel fired a short burst to back him up, but the enemy soldiers escaped.

Colonel Cleland, accompanied by a bug-eyed major, stepped down from the helicopter and walked up to Tadina. After a short conversation, he gave Tadina the option of "taking care" of the prisoners and climbing aboard the helicopter, or loading the prisoners aboard the aircraft and remaining behind to go after a rocket launcher that the colonel had just spotted on the way in.

Tadina turned to his teammates and repeated the colonel's "generous" offer, but he prefaced his statement by admitting that if the colonel had the balls to land and give them this option, he was all for going after the launcher. Well, that was the end of the democratic part of the discussion! The rest of the LRRPs knew that when "the legend"—and Pat Tadina *was* a legend among the 173d LRRPs—gave his personal opinion, no one in his right mind would choose to disagree.

By then, the two badly wounded VC had expired. Tadina, Peterson, and Brooks finished securing the four remaining VC and began loading them along with their weapons and gear aboard the aircraft. Colonel Cleland stepped forward to lend a hand, while the REMF major, garbed in starched fatigues and spit-shined jungle boots, yelled at Ruckman to pick up the wounded VC female and put her aboard. Ruckman sneered at the man and refused, stating that he was pulling security because they had just had two very live VC disappear to the south.

The REMF major wouldn't accept any excuses at all, and immediately began to berate the heavily armed LRRP.

Colonel Cleland, hearing the discussion, turned to the major and said, "Get her in the ship, now." The senior officer turned to Ruckman, smiled and gave him a thumbs-up, then went back to loading the chopper. Ten meters away, a thoroughly humbled but still spiffy major attempted to load the badly bleeding VC onto the helicopter without staining his uniform. Needless to say, his efforts were unsuccessful.

After the chopper was loaded, Cleland commended Tadina, then turned and climbed aboard. The aircraft lifted out of the clearing and began climbing for altitude. The colonel quickly confirmed the location of the enemy rocket launcher and radioed a back azimuth to the LRRPs still on the ground. Tadina shot a compass heading to the southeast, put Olson at point, and moved the team out in the direction of the enemy position.

About forty-five minutes later, Olson broke through the scrub and found a second clearing, much smaller than the first one. Staying to the left side of the clearing, the team moved two hundred meters to another small hedgerow, which they quickly but carefully crossed. About seventy-five meters to their right front, Olson spotted what appeared to be a large, metal, olive drab–colored tripod.

As the patrol cautiously approached, they noticed there was no sign that anyone had been around the object. When they reached it they saw that it was one of the bomb racks the U.S. Air Force used on its fixed-wing aircraft. Tadina set up security around the object and radioed the TOC, identifying the device they had just discovered, then requested an extraction from their present location. Once again, the TOC radioed back that they had no air assets available at that time. Before

Tadina could respond in an appropriate fashion, Colonel Cleland broke in and informed the LRRPs that he was inserting a company-size element into the clearing the patrol had just left. He advised the LRRP team leader to take his team back to that point and join up with the infantry element. He asked Tadina if it would be feasible to bring out the bomb rack or destroy it in place.

Tadina quickly informed him that neither option was possible. The rack was too heavy and the LRRPs did not have explosives with them. Tadina then took out his compass and shot a new azimuth laying out a different route back to the clearing.

When the patrol reached the clearing a half hour later, the infantry company had just landed and was preparing to move out as soon as the recon unit arrived. Tadina approached the infantry commander and was informed that the company was preparing to pursue the two VC who had escaped the team's ambush. He told Tadina that the LRRPs were now op con to him and would be pulling point during the operation.

Tadina (expletives omitted) declined. The LRRP team leader immediately contacted his TOC and was told that the patrol was *not* op con to the infantry company. At that point, Colonel Cleland's chopper landed back in the clearing. The colonel joined the discussion and stated that he had believed that the patrol was under his control, but Tadina explained that brigade LRRPs didn't operate for any particular battalion command, but for the brigade. Once again, Tadina contacted the TOC and that time was told that extraction ships would be on the way as soon as they inserted another team, approximately five minutes.

The infantry company had already begun to move out in column, when the extraction slick, escorted by two Delta-model gunships, arrived on station. The slick quickly landed and picked up the LRRP patrol, which happily waved good-bye to the colonel and his boys.

After the team returned to its compound and was debriefed, they were told that the infantry company, A/3/503d, had just discovered a recently evacuated fortified enemy village only seven hundred meters from the clearing. It was thought that the thirteen-man enemy element that the LRRPs had destroyed had been a resupply column heading from the village to a nearby enemy base camp.

As the team members were walking away from the debriefing room, Peterson turned toward Ruckman and waved what appeared to be a shiny boar's tusk at him. Ruckman, failing to see the humor in it, only frowned.

☆　　☆　　☆　　☆　　☆

Company D, 75th Infantry (Ranger), II Field Force

On 20 March 1970, Company D, 75th Infantry (Ranger) received notice from II Field Force that the unit was being deactivated. The company, originally activated to replace Company D, 151st Infantry (Ranger) of the Indiana National Guard, had been in existence for only five months. However, as II Field Force was also being dismantled, there was no longer a need for it to maintain a long-range reconnaissance company. The Rangers in the unit who still had time remaining in Vietnam were given the option of transferring to other Ranger companies or to any other unit they desired, and as an added incentive of uncharacteristic generosity, Lieutenant General Ewell, commander of II Field Force, announced that he was more than willing to transfer intact teams to other Ranger units, if they so chose, provided that each man on the team wanted to go.

Accepting their fate and waiting for their orders to arrive, the Rangers of D Company stood down and relaxed, their war at least temporarily on hold.

Around 1030 that night, the CQ runner stepped into Sp4. Thomas Delaney's hootch and told him to report to the company TOC immediately. Delaney, the team leader of Ranger Team Three-five, did not expect anything important, so he was quite shocked when Maj. Richard Drisko told him that II Field Force had just requested a Ranger heavy team for a mission into an area of the Parrot's Beak in Hau Nghia

177

Province. The team's AO, an area of dense jungle along the Cambodian border, was very likely to be hot, and the patrol was instructed to go in heavily armed. The 5th NVA Regiment, the 101st NVA Battalion, and elements of other units were thought to be operating in the immediate area, and for some reason, II Field Force wanted to verify their presence. Documents and prisoners were always the best sources of available intelligence, and Delaney's team would have to initiate contact with the enemy to acquire either; that is, it was not going to be a recon mission, but a contact mission, and it was scheduled to go in early the next morning without benefit of an overflight or even a good night's sleep.

Tom Delaney, although only a specialist fourth class, was a very dedicated and competent soldier. He had served an earlier hitch in the army from 1964 to 1966, attaining the rank of sergeant. Delaney put in another three years in the Reserves before making the decision to go back on active duty. Unfortunately, the army would only allow him to come back in at his permanent rank at time of discharge, that of Private First Class.

However, Delaney's maturity, skill, and experience impressed his superiors and soon earned him a team leader slot in Delta Company. So it was no surprise to anyone when he had been selected to lead the heavy team, Three-five/Three-one Hotel, on what was to be Delta Company's last mission.

Delaney left the TOC and went directly to his team barracks, where he found Sp4. Richard "Bear" Papp and Sp4. Dick Badmilk. He quickly informed the two Rangers that Team Three-five had a mission scheduled for the next morning. Since everyone had already turned in their gear, he told them to alert the rest of the patrol, Sp4. Richard "Herd" Nelson and Sp4. Richard "Fitz" Fitzgerald, and draw new equipment from Supply. Delaney then went to locate Sgt. Wallace "Wally" Hawkins, the team leader of Team Three-one. When he found him, he described their mission and told Hawkins that his team had been designated to make up the other half of the patrol. After discussing the actual composition of the heavy team and the equipment they would need to take, the two team leaders separated to rejoin their patrols. They still had a lot to do before the sun rose the next morning.

Hawkins quickly rounded up the rest of his team—Sp4. Ken Dern, Sgt. Richard R. Momce, Sgt. Marc Lampheer, Sgt. Bruce Mohn, and a "cherry" private first class, junior RTO, who had just come into the company. He sent them scrambling to draw new gear and prepare for the mission the next day.

Delaney was still short a man on Team Three-five, so he was not totally surprised when 1st Lt. Jim Kaireski showed up and volunteered to fill the slot. The popular platoon leader had been out on other patrols and had already earned his CIB. In addition, he fully understood that if he was acting as a member of the team, his rank would mean nothing and he would be the low man in the food chain.

Drisko had told Delaney that the patrol would be out "pretty damned far," and a radio-relay site was being established at an ARVN Ranger compound located less than two klicks away from the team's AO. It would be manned by three Delta Company Rangers, S.Sgt. Ed Phillips, Sp4. Fernando Delacruz, and Sp4. Rusty "Captain Zigzag" Hawk. The relay team's job would be to pass radio transmissions from Team Three-five/Three-one Hotel to the company commo section in the Ranger TOC, where Sp4. Kaiser "The Professor" Sebensky would jot down everything on paper before reading it back for confirmation.

The next morning at first light, the twelve Rangers went down to the chopper pad to board their aircraft. The mission would incude five Huey slicks from the "Annie Fannies" of the 117th Assault Helicopter Company—two chase ships, two insertion aircraft, and a C & C chopper carrying Major Drisko. In addition, a brace of Cobras from the "Playboys," 334th Armed Helicopter Company, had been designated to fly escort during the mission and would link up with them on the way.

At 0730, the five aircraft lifted off and proceeded south-southwest from Long Binh. It was a new experience for the Rangers, who had always operated up near Song Be, north-northwest of Long Binh.

The weather that day was scheduled to be hot and clear, and it was already well on its way there by 0815 when the two Hueys finally approached their AO. As the lead helicopter bearing Team Three-five moved in and hovered over the LZ, the six Rangers looked down and quickly discovered that there was no LZ beneath them, only a dense bamboo thicket with a scattering of single-canopy trees. They knew immediately that something was seriously wrong. Surely, they were not expected to go in there! There was simply no place to land, and the aircraft was still hovering fifteen to twenty feet above the ground.

Suddenly, the crew chief began screaming for them to go, and one by one, the heavily laden Rangers stepped out on the skids and began dropping from the aircraft.

As the first six men hit the ground hard, the second chopper moved in over the LZ and discharged its cargo in the same manner. As the twelve Rangers tried to assess the damage incurred on the insertion, the aircraft lifted out of the LZ and departed the AO. In the silence that followed, Delaney discovered that two of his teammates had suffered crippling injuries during the insertion. Nelson had broken his kneecap, and the junior RTO from Hawkins's team had broken his ankle. Neither man was capable of continuing on the mission.

Delaney immediately called for an extraction. There was no doubt in his mind that his patrol had been compromised during the insertion. The helicopters had remained far too long in the same place while getting them in, thus giving any enemy soldiers in the vicinity plenty of time to pinpoint their exact location.

Major Drisko radioed back that the insertion aircraft were all low on fuel and would have to return to base. He said that he would medevac the two injured Rangers in his C & C aircraft, but the rest of the team would have to cut an LZ first.

Delaney took four of the Rangers and set up security while the remainder of his team began hacking out a hole in the middle of the bamboo and small trees. Believing that the entire patrol was going to be extracted, the Rangers made little effort to keep their noise level down to a minimum. When Major Drisko's aircraft finally touched down in the LZ to lift out Nelson and the new man, the rest of the patrol got the shock of their lives when their CO ordered them to Charlie Mike.

Delaney realized they had to get out of the area immediately, before the enemy had time to react. Delaney's only hope was that when the enemy finally arrived on the scene, he would assume that the entire recon team had been extracted. But for the enemy to believe that, the patrol would have to put a lot of distance between it and the LZ, and make sure it left no sign of its passage in doing so.

Delaney hurriedly assigned the new man's radio to Dern and told Mohn to carry Nelson's M-60, then put Bear Papp up on point. Giving him an azimuth of forty-five degrees, Delaney waited for Papp to move out, then stepped in behind him at slack. Delaney always carried his own radio, so the five-foot-four, 120-pound Ranger was packing quite a load as he followed quickly after his stocky point man. With Lieutenant Kaireski walking the third slot and Sergeant Wally Hawkins bringing up the tail end of the patrol, the ten Rangers moved quickly away from the LZ.

Three hundred meters later, Delaney whispered for Papp to locate a place to hole up and lay dog. Papp moved a little farther, then led the team off its original line of march at a sharp angle before crawling into some thick underbrush, where they would be able to hear anyone following them.

Forty-five minutes later, satisfied that no one was pursuing them, at least not for the moment, Delaney gave Papp a new azimuth and sent him off on a different heading. Easing along cautiously through the jungle, the Ranger point man soon

began noticing that select trees had been systematically removed from the surrounding jungle, opening up the forest
without destroying the overhead canopy. Some of the trees
had been freshly cut, within the last two days or so.

Growing more nervous by the minute, Papp had covered
less than 150 meters when he encountered a narrow footpath
stretching in front of him. It didn't take a rocket scientist or a
native tracker to tell him that the trail was well used. Then,
barely fifteen feet away, he spotted a freshly built machine-
gun emplacement. It was facing down the narrow trail, but
was empty at the time. Whoever had constructed the bunker
had not yet taken the time to camouflage it.

Papp stepped out on the narrow trail and began to follow it.
It was not something they usually did, but the team was attempting to avoid leaving a discernible back trail while
putting distance between it and the original LZ. Unfortunately, running a trail was the best way to accomplish that.

Papp hadn't moved fifty meters when the footpath ran into
a major high-speed trail. He could easily see that the high-
speed was heavily used and covered in fresh sign. He wasted
no time standing there in this exposed position. Turning
around, he gave the hand signal to back slowly away.

Twenty meters back from the trail, Papp had a quick conference with Delaney. The two men decided to wait where
they were until dark, then move into some nearby cover and
set up their RON. The ten Rangers formed up in a tight circle
and sat silently, listening to the sounds of the jungle.

The rest of the afternoon was uneventful, and when it finally grew dark, Papp led the patrol back up to the main trail.
Hesitating there for a few minutes to make sure no one was
coming from either direction, the point man stepped out into
the trail. Once again, he remained on the high-speed, cautiously leading the patrol another twenty meters around a
sharp bend in the trail, before cutting sharply to his left and
then backtracking through the jungle parallel to the trail until
he reached a spot just across from the intersection they had

just left. At that point, he cut left again and moved the patrol into a dense stand of bamboo ten meters back from the trail intersection. It was a good spot for an OP/RON. They had a good view of the trail, coming and going, and plenty of cover to conceal them from prying eyes. For the first time since the beginning of the mission, the team felt secure.

The Rangers took turns slipping out into the darkness to set up claymores around their perimeter. Then a few of them took the last opportunity to eat their evening meal.

Everyone was soon wondering what the next day would bring. With all the fresh sign they had seen during the day, they knew that the enemy had to be close at hand.

At 2005 hours, the Rangers suddenly heard the *karuuumph . . . karuuumph . . . karuuumph* of mortar rounds impacting not too far away. The rounds hit out in the jungle, not really close to the hidden Rangers, but near enough that it still made them feel a little uneasy. Delaney picked up the radio handset and called the radio-relay team at the nearby ARVN base to see if they were firing the mortars. The relay team reported back that no fire missions were going from their location. The Rangers realized the NVA were probing blindly for them. There was no longer any doubt that the enemy knew they were in there somewhere.

The mortaring continued intermittently until about 2130 hours, then stopped completely. But for the hour and a half that the enemy had walked the rounds blindly through the jungle around the Rangers, the patrol had been forced to hug the ground and eat dirt.

After the mortar fire finally ended, Delaney put everyone on 100 percent alert for the remainder of the night. They remained that way until the first gray illumination of the false dawn began to lighten the jungle around them.

At 0600 hours, when it was light enough for the Rangers to see around them, they cut tiny balls of C-4 and used them to heat cups of boiling water for hot cocoa and coffee. The C-4 gave off no discernible scent and burned so intensely that it boiled the water in seconds. A cup of hot liquid was always a good way to start out a long day, that is if there were no enemy soldiers in the vicinity.

At 0630 hours, the patrol began to hear roosters crowing three hundred to four hundred meters away. In the damp chill of the morning, the Rangers began looking at each other with grins on their faces. The roosters reminded them that they were indeed not alone out there. It was once again time to assume their role as hunters, and hunting was beginning to look pretty good.

An hour later, Delaney cocked his head, then held his fingers to his lips to silence the rest of his patrol. Less than fifteen meters away, back in the direction of the trail, the sound of voices speaking Vietnamese could be heard. They were talking in low tones and making every effort not to be heard.

Everyone on the patrol reached slowly for their weapons, then sat ready to wait and see what developed. After a while, the sounds passed, and everything was quiet again. The enemy soldiers had left the area, but would they be back?

At 0800 hours, Delaney called in his morning sitrep to Lobster Four-eight, the radio-relay team stationed at the nearby ARVN Ranger compound, reporting the enemy voices they had heard nearby a half hour before.

When Delaney had finished the sitrep, he decided to lead a four-man recon patrol out to see what was in their recon zone. He selected Bear Papp, Lieutenant Kaireski, and Wally Hawkins. With Papp at point, followed by Delaney, Kaireski, and Hawkins, the recon patrol slipped out of the perimeter and edged out to the main trail.

The Rangers waited in the trees at the edge of the high-speed for a full five minutes, listening to the sounds of the jungle. When they felt that it was safe to continue, they stepped out onto the open trail and started to move cautiously down it. They hadn't gone more than thirty meters when they came to a Y in the trail. Papp conferred briefly with Delaney, and they decided to take the left branch. It was twelve inches wide and heavily used. Papp also noticed that a ditch ran along the right side of the trail. A three-foot-high berm paralleled it on the back side of the ditch. It was definitely man-made.

Papp eased forward another twenty meters until he spotted a booby-trapped 105mm artillery round along the left side of the trail. The trip wire leading to it was rusted and had broken in two. He motioned Delaney up to show him his discovery. Delaney nodded and signaled for him to continue on.

Thirty meters farther along, lying in the ditch next to the trail, Papp spotted a USAF five-hundred-pound bomb. He wasn't certain if the giant bomb was booby-trapped or if the poor saps who had been trying to move it had just given up and left it there in the ditch.

By then, the hair on Papp's neck was standing on end. He was fully alert, senses keenly attuned to his surroundings. Any little sound, any minute movement, any faint smell in the air could mean instant death.

Suddenly, the path turned hard to the left and disappeared around a bend in the trail. At that point, there appeared to be a tiny small-game trail leading off to the right, running across the ditch and up over the berm. The recon patrol was now nearly a hundred meters away from the rest of the team and was facing a major decision about what to do next. They could continue up the main trail, follow the footpath over the berm to see where it led, or turn around and go back the way they had come to rejoin their comrades. A hundred meters could easily become a thousand miles if they walked into an enemy ambush. Papp and Delaney conferred briefly, then decided to cross the ditch and follow the game trail.

Ten meters beyond the ditch, they encountered a cache of monstrous proportions. There were stacked crates of AK-47s, SKSs, RPGs, B-40s, 82mm mortars; case after case of ammo for those weapons; and dozens of two-hundred-pound sacks of rice. Everything was unguarded and covered with green tarps, but it appeared that the enemy was already in the process of moving everything out of the cache.

Delaney decided that they had seen enough; it was time to go back the way they had come. However, he told Papp that when he got to the Y back down the trail, he wanted him to take the other leg. The point man nodded that he understood.

When Papp reached the Y, he proceeded forty meters down the unexplored trail when all of a sudden the trail expanded from a foot wide to nearly six feet across. There in the middle of the widest part of the trail were the deep ruts caused by the passage of iron wheels—lots of iron wheels.

Papp's sixth sense went haywire. He sniffed the air and strained to listen to the strange silence that was now blaring loudly around him. Something was terribly wrong. Delaney motioned for him to continue, and the big point man moved cautiously up the trail. Fifty meters ahead, he once again signaled for everyone to stop. There, just ahead of him in the trail, was a letter written in Vietnamese. When he stooped to pick it up, he saw that the letter was dated March 22, 1970—that morning.

Delaney came up to see what was holding up the patrol. When Papp handed him the letter, Delaney looked at it, nodded his head, then sent his point man back up the trail. He sensed they were close to something big.

Forty meters away, just around a bend in the trail, Papp once more signaled a halt. He again motioned for Delaney to move up to the front. There, lying directly in the middle of the hard-packed earthen trail, was a crudely drawn map. Papp reached down and picked it up, then handed it to his team leader. While Delaney studied the rough map, Papp commented, "Tom, they're baiting us. We're fixing to walk into an ambush, big-time. We've seen enough. Let's call for an extraction and get the fuck out of here. Let higher-up run an Arc Light in here."

Delaney looked up at his point man and shook his head. "Let's go a little farther, Bear," he whispered.

Papp started out once more, moving painstakingly slowly. Soon, the trail straightened out again. Sixty meters from the spot where he had found the map, Papp was just starting to lift his foot to take another step when he heard the faint sounds of chopping to his left. Slowly, he held up his hand to stop the patrol, then dropped to one knee facing the direction of the noise. The chopping sounds stopped as suddenly as they had begun.

He cautiously gave the signal for Delaney to move up to his position. When the team leader reached his side, Papp pointed toward the jungle to his left and whispered that he had heard chopping in there. As if to verify his statement, the chopping started up again.

That was enough for Delaney. He had seen and heard all he wanted to see and hear. The team leader whispered to Papp that it was time to pull back and call for an extraction. It was 0945 hours.

Papp, Delaney, and Kaireski had turned and started back down the trail in the direction they had just come from, reversing their slots in the process, when a long burst of automatic-weapon fire erupted from Hawkins's location behind them. When the three Rangers looked back, they saw Hawkins standing in a crouched position spraying the jungle beside the spot that Papp and Delaney had just vacated. Without waiting for an invitation, the entire recon element turned and fled down the trail back toward the Y intersection.

When they finally reached the rest of the team, they found the six Rangers they had left behind now wide-eyed and fully alert. They had heard the firing but had no idea what had happened. Then everyone realized that no one but Hawkins knew what was going on.

Bear Papp, swigging water from his canteen between gasping for breath, looked up at Hawkins and panted, "What the fuck were you firing at?"

Hawkins shook his head and muttered, "I'm not sure. The guy was wearing camouflage fatigues."

Papp grimaced when he heard this, then added, "Oh shit, we fired up an ARVN Ranger team."

Hawkins shook his head once more, and said, "No, this guy was a gook and had an AK-47."

By then Delaney was on the radio calling in the contact and requesting an extraction. Unfortunately, the Ranger CO, Major Drisko, had not yet had his fill of danger and death. He ordered Delaney to take his entire team and go back up there to check for bodies, weapons, and documents.

Delaney put the handset down and repeated the major's message to his teammates. Then he looked over at his point man and said, "Bear, you going to take point? Drisko wants us to go back up there."

There was little Papp could say or do. Of course the burly point man didn't want to go back up to the point of contact. He had been at the game too long to be a fool; the same could not be said of their commanding officer.

It was 1000 hours when the sounds of heavy movement started up in the jungle around the patrol's perimeter. It was no more than twenty-five or thirty meters away. It stopped just as quickly as it had started. It was particularly unnerving to the ten Rangers waiting frozen in the jungle.

At 1025, Delaney made the decision to take the four-man recon element back up to check out the spot where Hawkins had fired up the enemy soldier. This time, however, as they approached the area, Papp stepped off the trail, crossed the ditch, and slipped into the woods along the opposite side of the berm. He paralleled the trail another seventy-five meters, moving cautiously, then came to an abrupt stop. When Delaney eased up next to him, Papp pointed down at the still-fresh pile of human feces at his feet. Delaney nodded.

The patrol began moving again, looking left and right for any signs of blood trails or signs of battle. Twenty-five meters farther on, the patrol swung around and went on line, with Kaireski to Papp's right, then Delaney and Hawkins. Papp suddenly stopped and dropped down into a low crouch, staring intently at something to his immediate front not more than twelve to fifteen feet away. The object he was watching didn't quite blend in with the rest of the jungle. He couldn't put his finger on it, but something was definitely out of place.

A number of large anthills rose here and there on the flanks of the trail. Some of them were nearly eighteen inches high. Papp stared hard at the object, then looked over at the neighboring anthill, and back to it again. All of a sudden the lights came on! It was a machine-gun bunker so well camouflaged that he still wasn't sure if he was actually seeing it. But it was there, all right, not more than a foot above the surface of the ground.

It suddenly struck Papp that if the bunker was occupied, he was a dead man. He took a quick look to his right and saw that Lieutenant Kaireski, Delaney, and Hawkins were still moving slowly ahead. They hadn't yet spotted the machine-gun emplacement.

Papp tried to get Delaney's attention, finally making a loud hissing noise that sounded like air coming out of a leaking zeppelin. When Delaney stopped and looked over at his point man, he saw that Papp was jabbing his finger at a spot in the jungle just ahead of him. Then, as the point man started sliding quickly to the left, all hell broke loose across the front of the patrol. It was 1038 hours.

The enemy's opening blast caught Papp while he was still in a crouched position, and a bullet took him hard in the right thigh, entering above the knee and coming out through his right buttock. Amazingly, the bullet missed both the femur and the femoral artery. But the impact of the high-velocity round flipped the point man head over heels and spun him around in midair. When he came down again, he was lying flat on his back behind one of the anthills. Papp knew that he had been hit hard, but he had yet to see the extent of his wounds.

Delaney yelled over to where Papp lay bleeding behind the anthill, wanting to know how badly he had been hit. The wounded point man didn't answer at first. Instead he looked down at his leg and saw that his right thigh muscle had been severed and was twitching uncontrollably as it contracted and released, contracted and released. From the size of the hole, he could only guess that he had been hit by something in the range of a 105mm howitzer. But whatever it had been, it sure didn't look good for him now.

The NVA were no longer firing at him, but seemed to be concentrating on the other three Rangers who were busy returning their fire. The enemy soldiers probably thought they had killed the Ranger point man with their opening volley. How wrong they were!

Remaining hidden behind the cover of the anthill, Papp yelled over to Delaney that he had been hit in the leg, but it wasn't broken. Not one to be an alarmist, he told his team leader that he would be all right.

Some of the enemy's initial rounds had torn into the anthill that protected Papp, forcing a mass migration of most of the ants that lived there. They were coming out in droves and crawling all over the wounded Ranger. Fortunately for him, he wasn't so worried about a bunch of harmless, crawling insects running across the ground when the air above him at the moment was still alive with the fast-moving, death-bringing kind.

Papp suddenly realized that he was unarmed. Although he had been badly wounded in the leg, there was sure in hell nothing to keep him from returning the favor and killing a few of the enemy. He looked around to find out what had happened to his weapon and spotted it lying a few feet off to his right. Since the CAR-15 was in the open, directly under the NVA guns, Papp played dead while slowly inching his right arm out from behind the anthill. After several minutes, the weapon was within reach. But as he grabbed the handle, he got a little too anxious and one of the NVA spotted his movement. The enemy soldier opened up on the wounded Ranger's position just as he snatched his weapon back to his side.

Even so, being armed again, Papp felt 100 percent better.

But enemy machine-gun fire began tearing apart the rest of his shelter. He was slowly becoming increasingly exposed to the enemy fire.

Unable to leave his position, Papp began returning fire at the enemy bunker fifteen feet away. At the same time, Delaney was putting out a tremendous amount of suppressing firepower of his own, enabling Lieutenant Kaireski to crawl across the trail to check on the wounded point man. However, that succeeded only in drawing more machine-gun fire from a number of enemy positions.

Seeing the predicament of their two teammates, Delaney and Hawkins laid down a devastating suppressing fire at point-blank range, driving the enemy to cover and enabling Kaireski and Papp to use hand grenades to knock out the NVA machine-gun bunker. As the grenades exploded inside the bunker, Kaireski helped Papp to his feet, and the four Rangers began backing down the trail toward the rest of the team.

As soon as they reached their perimeter, Delaney was on the radio calling for a Dustoff and an emergency extraction while Kaireski and Badmilk worked on Papp's leg, trying to stop the bleeding.

A few minutes later, Major Drisko, flying C & C, got on the horn and reported that the medevac chopper had just been shot down a hundred meters out on its way in to pick up Papp. It was 1140 hours.

Finally, Dragon Three-eight and Dragon Three-nine radioed that they were inbound and fully loaded. The aircraft commander of the lead Cobra asked Delaney to mark his location with smoke. Delaney declined, telling the pilot that he would mark his position by panel. He didn't want to reveal his location with a smoke grenade. The pilot radioed back that he fully understood. The enemy soldiers had moved around the team's position as the choppers roared in, but they still did not know exactly where the Rangers were. Popping a smoke grenade would have had the same effect as sending out party announcements.

The gunships made a number of runs using miniguns to drive the enemy away from the team. The patrol chimed in by blowing the claymores just as the Cobras opened fire. This was a precaution, just in case the NVA tried to move in close to avoid the Cobras. The deadly cross fire between miniguns and claymores proved to be too much for the NVA.

The Cobras pulled out to come around a second time, launching their deadly 2.75-inch rockets and stitching the jungle with 40mm grenades. By the time the Cobras finally expended their ordnance, two more Dragon gunships were already on station, ready to take over. When the lead ship aircraft commander asked Delaney how close his gun run had been from the patrol's perimeter, the team leader responded, "Twelve to fifteen feet, but bring it in closer."

The pilot answered, "Negative, that is danger close," whereupon Delaney came back angrily saying, "They're all around us, bring it in closer, goddamn it!"

The pilot finally got the gist of the Ranger's message. "Roger that. It's your call," he said. Seconds later the rounds tore up the jungle right up to the edge of the team's perimeter. It was close enough to have taken out the Rangers' claymores if they had not already been fired.

The second pair of Cobras soon ran dry and headed back to their compound to rearm and refuel. Things got real quiet outside the patrol's perimeter after the choppers were gone. The next pair of gunships was still ten minutes out and the turnaround time for the Dragons was nearly twenty minutes. The Rangers would have been in real danger if the enemy decided to make his play at that moment.

Just after 1200 hours, Warrant Officer Stalls, one of Delta Company's slick pilots, came up on the Ranger push and told Delaney that he was going to try to get in to medevac Papp. The slick was soon hovering directly over the team as the crew chief kicked out a .50-caliber ammo can at the end of a rappelling rope.

Papp grabbed his weapon, and sat upright while two of his teammates tied him to the end of the rope. Before he had time to say good-bye, he was being pulled up through the thin jungle canopy. He closed his eyes because he was fully exposed to any NVA soldier down below with a yen for a little payback.

The enemy soldiers in the trees below were already directing small-arms fire at the hovering Huey. Papp heard the heavy thumping sounds of an enemy .51-caliber machine gun firing from somewhere back in the jungle, and RPGs and B-40 rockets streaked out of the trees, barely missing the aircraft. Miraculously, the slick pilot kept his cool and gently lifted the badly wounded Ranger out of the jungle. However, his aircraft had taken a number of hits and had to head for the nearest friendly base, the ARVN Ranger compound a couple klicks away, to assess the damage and get the wounded Ranger inside the aircraft.

When they finally reached the compound, Warrant Officer Stalls held the aircraft in a slow descent until the rope holding Papp reached nearly to the ground. S.Sgt. Ed Phillips and Sp4. Fernando Delacruz from the radio-relay team lowered their wounded comrade to the ground. When the slick landed a few minutes later, the two Rangers and one of the door gunners loaded Papp into the Huey's open cabin. In seconds he was on his way to Long Binh and a date with the 24th Evac Hospital's triage unit. He arrived there at 1315 hours.

After Papp had been lifted out, Major Drisko radioed Delaney that a platoon from D Troop, 3/17 Cav, had just been inserted west of the team's perimeter to reinforce the Rangers, but they were already in contact. A full infantry company was at that moment being put in north of the enemy complex to sweep into the area from that direction. He called back a few minutes later to report that the infantry company had also come under heavy fire during its insertion and was pinned down on its LZ. The Rangers would never see either element.

Drisko then told the patrol to prepare to move out in the direction of the Cav troopers, a rather risky situation for the nine Rangers remaining in the enemy complex. If an infantry company and an aerorifle platoon couldn't reach his patrol, what made the major think his Rangers could reach their "rescuers"?

Delaney decided to take three others and try to reach the closest reaction force, then lead them back to the patrol's perimeter. He took Lieutenant Kaireski, Hawkins, and Fitzgerald and slipped out of the RON site heading back into the enemy base complex to the west. They hadn't gone far when a large enemy force hidden in the trees opened fire, severely wounding Hawkins. The patrol's assistant team leader took a .51-caliber round just above the right knee, and was hit in the left leg and ankle by small-arms fire.

Seeing Hawkins go down, Delaney moved away from the other three men to draw fire to himself, shouting for Lieutenant Kaireski to leave his grenades and magazines behind, grab Hawkins, and get the hell out of there while he and Fitzgerald covered them. He yelled that they would meet them back at the RON.

Not long after Kaireski had reached the patrol's perimeter with the badly wounded Hawkins draped over his shoulder, Delaney and Fitzgerald showed up with weapons still smoking. Immediately, the Rangers began taking small-arms fire from several locations.

Delaney was soon back on the radio giving directions to the recently arrived gunships. And the patrol was once again embroiled in a fight for its life.

At 1312 hours, a single RPG round exploded at the feet of Sp4. William Fitzgerald, critically wounding him. Hawkins was also in bad shape by that time, and Delaney knew that if he didn't get the two wounded Rangers out quickly, they would be dead in less than an hour.

The team was also running low on ammo. They still had six claymores but they had not yet been able to put them out. At that moment an approaching Dustoff chopper radioed the team that it was on short final. Soon, the surviving Rangers watched in silence as the jungle penetrator was lowered into the team's perimeter. Within minutes, Fitzgerald and Hawkins were on board and on their way to medical care and safety.

Delaney quickly got the remainder of the patrol up and moving out toward the team's original LZ. Once they reached it, the Rangers used their remaining claymores to blow an even larger landing zone.

At 1520 hours, a Huey slick dropped into the small clearing and took six of the remaining seven Rangers aboard. Tom Delaney alone had remained behind. As the aircraft lifted out of the clearing and banked away to gain airspeed, Sp4. Tom Delaney realized for the first time that he was completely on his own. As the sound of the slick faded in the distance, and the jungle reverted to its normal hostile, unfriendly silence, the young team leader suddenly felt a terrible loneliness come over him.

Delaney had been prepared to leave with the rest of his team, when Major Drisko called to order him to remain behind. The officer wanted Delaney to go back to where the 3/17th Cav was located, link up with them, then lead them back to the enemy cache site. It was an insane order, but Tom Delaney was a soldier.

Delaney took a deep breath and set out on his dangerous assignment. It took the resolute Ranger nearly two hours to work his way back around the enemy base complex and cover the five hundred meters to where the Cav troop was still held up at their LZ. By the time Delaney had completed the linkup, it was too dark for him and the Cav troopers to go stumbling around in the woods to find the cache site. Instead, they decided to spend the night huddled together in a tight defensive perimeter. If they were still alive at dawn, they would try once more to reach the NVA bunker complex.

The night proved uneventful, so when the sun rose high enough to put some light on the subject, Delaney moved up to point for the Cav, and they headed toward the base camp. Inside the complex, they discovered numerous NVA casualties, and soon located a number of tunnels and fighting bunkers. In one of the tunnels, they found a 150-bed underground hospital complete with fully equipped operating rooms. The hospital was filled to the brim with wounded NVA soldiers, and a pair of not so lucky ones lay dead on the two operating tables. There were another forty or fifty dead NVA stacked like cordwood outside the entrance to the hospital. During the search of the hospital, gunfire erupted back near the operating rooms. A short time later, the American forces gave up trying to capture the facility and blew the entrances with explosives, effectively sealing it and entombing anyone left alive inside.

After spending most of the day working through the complex, all the remaining American troops were extracted later that afternoon.

During the subsequent patrol debriefing, Delaney and his remaining Rangers were informed that they had actually been operating across the border inside Cambodia. That bit of new information failed to surprise them.

On 29 April 1970, allied forces launched an unprecedented military incursion into Cambodia. Their target was the enemy sanctuaries and supply dumps hidden deep in the jungles just across the border. Between 29 April and 30 June, thirteen major operations were conducted as part of the incursion. The successes of the Cambodian raid were measured in part by the capture of enough individual weapons to equip fifty-five full-strength NVA infantry battalions, and enough crew-served weapons to equip eighty-two to ninety battalions. They also pulled out enough small-arms ammo to provide a basic load for fifty-two thousand soldiers. In addition, over ten thousand enemy soldiers were killed in the fighting. It was a major blow to the enemy, and would set back their plans to invade Vietnam for another year.

The following medals were awarded to the members of Team 3-5/3-1 Hotel for their actions that day:

Sp4. Thomas E. Delaney—Silver Star
1st Lt. James Kaireski—Silver Star
Sp4. Richard Papp—Bronze Star with V device
Sp4. William Fitzgerald—Bronze Star with V device
Sgt. Wallace Hawkins—Bronze Star with V device
Sp4. Dick Badmilk—Army Commendation Medal with
        V device
Sp4. Ken Dern—Army Commendation Medal with
        V device
Sgt. Marc Lampheer—Army Commendation Medal with
        V device
Sgt. Richard R. Momce—Army Commendation Medal
        with V device
Sgt. Bruce Mohn—Army Commendation Medal with
        V device

Major Drisko was also awarded the Silver Star for gallantry in action.

Company E,
52d Infantry (LRP),
1st Cavalry Division

When the North Vietnamese and Viet Cong launched the Tet Offensive on 30 January 1968, most U.S. forces were caught by surprise. However, their response was both quick and deadly. Everywhere, enemy forces were rapidly swept from the battlefield, and the survivors were driven back into sanctuaries in Cambodia and Laos. Only in I Corps were the North Vietnamese able to hold out for any length of time. It was there, in and around the Imperial City of Hue, that U.S. forces had to face their greatest threat. And it was there that a number of long-range patrols from the 1st Cavalry Division had to face their greatest challenge.

In early March 1968, five LRRP teams from Company E, 52d Infantry (LRP) were stationed at the Cav brigade compound at Camp Evans, an old Marine base northwest of Hue. The recon teams had been pulling patrols in and around the foothills along the base of the Chaine Annamatique west-northwest of the Imperial City of Hue on the Perfume River. NVA battalions had occupied Hue from the onset of the Tet Offensive, and were holed up in the Citadel, the emperor's fortress. They were being slowly but systematically destroyed by elements of the 1st Marine Division in vicious house-to-house fighting.

Outside the city, units from the 1st Cavalry Division and the 101st Airborne Division were preventing enemy reinforcements from reaching the city and at the same time hunting down NVA units attempting to escape back into the mountains. Much of the Cav's operations were being conducted in the piedmont country lying between the heavily occupied coastal plains and the rugged mountains to the west.

Sgt. Rick Tedder was in his tent at the LRP compound at Camp Evans on 10 March when the warning order came down for a reconnaissance mission across the Bo River (Song Bo) southwest of Camp Evans. Intel reports indicated increasingly heavy enemy activity in the area, and brigade S-2 suspected that NVA troops were massing to strike the brigade forward support base at Camp Evans. Tedder's team had been back from its last patrol for only three days, and it was not yet their turn for a new mission. But the team ahead of them had a number of personnel sick and was not fully operational. Tedder's team was next in line and drew the patrol. When he tried to complain to his CO, Major Gooding, Gooding didn't want to hear anything about it.

At the patrol briefing conducted by Gooding and the company operations officer, 1st Lt. George B. Udder, Tedder was informed that his team was to insert near a small village nestled in the grasslands about two kilometers east of the mountains. Intel had information that the inhabitants of a number of small villages in the area were supplying enemy forces back in the mountains, not far away. Tedder's team was to set up an OP outside one village and watch for any suspicious activity in the area.

No specific length of time had been assigned to the mission, but the LRRPs were told to take rations for a four-day patrol. The length of the mission would be decided once the team was on the ground; no one felt that it would last very long.

Tedder went out on the overflight the next day at last light. Escorted by a single gunship, the overflight was designed to fool the enemy into believing that it was a long-range patrol insertion. At low level, the single aircraft staged three false insertions while Tedder gathered the information that he needed to put the patrol together. After the third false insertion, the slick returned to the site of the first one to see if it had stirred up any activity. There were plenty of open areas among the grass-covered hills around the village suitable for insertions and extractions, and the young NCO quickly decided on a number of spots for his primary and secondary LZs and PZs, none of which were far from each other.

A few tree lines were scattered around the area, but it was a far cry from the type of terrain that LRRPs ordinarily preferred. The weather was supposed to be hot and clear, with almost no chance of precipitation.

The patrol, consisting of Tedder; his ATL, Sp4. Steve Belfiglio; senior RTO, Sp4. Roy Olson; team medic, Sp4. Randy Kurth; point man, PFC Felix Leon; and PFC Don Holcomb at rear security, had been together on a number of patrols.

Tedder, a shake 'n' bake, SF-qualified, Ranger-tabbed NCO, was one of the finest team leaders in the unit. A year of undergraduate school at Portland State University in Oregon attested to his basic intelligence, but the year had provided far too few challenges to keep him enrolled while a war was going on. He enlisted. He would go back and finish his education after he helped defeat his country's enemies.

His assistant team leader, Steve Belfiglio, was a streetwise kid from New Jersey who was as deadly with the CAR-15 as he was with the cutdown M-79 strapped to the side of his rucksack. And he was very good with both.

Roy Olson, a big Swede from Wisconsin, was an excellent radio operator and, like everyone else on the team, carried a CAR-15 as his weapon of choice.

Randy Kurth was the newest man on the team, which probably explained why he was stuck with the medic bag and designated the team doc. He had received no more training in field-expedient medicine than his teammates, but he was the new guy.

Felix Leon had enlisted because he wanted to show his parents that he could make his own decisions. The son of a wealthy Puerto Rican family, Leon had not long before put through papers to adopt a young Vietnamese orphan girl. His father was already pulling strings to see that the adoption happened.

Ron Holcomb was an ex–Golden Gloves boxer who had challenged Tedder to a match back at the division base camp at An Khe. Tedder, a pretty fair pugilist, had not known of Holcomb's skills in the ring, and had walked into a vicious right hook early in the match. When he woke up several minutes later, he learned the truth about his opponent.

Because of the open terrain, Tedder decided to carry a starlight scope along on the patrol. The bulky night-vision device would come in handy for observing the village at night. As an added precaution, he instructed Leon and Holcomb each to pack a LAW antitank rocket, just in case their small arms and Belfiglio's blooper proved too light to hold back an enemy assault. Even when close to air and artillery support, when you had to party, there was nothing as reassuring as providing your own band.

The patrol went in at 1500 hours on the twelfth. The helicopter made a single false insertion, then put the team in on the second touchdown. It hovered briefly over the grassy clearing at the edge of the tree line, while the six LRRPs exited both sides of the aircraft and dropped the final four feet to the ground. They immediately headed for the nearest tree line, where they ran another ten meters into the woods and lay dog for two hours. Once on the ground, Olson got a quick commo check and gave their sitrep; then he passed on the Delta Tango preplots that Tedder had just given him.

By 1700 hours, the team had seen and heard nothing unusual, so Tedder gave the signal to begin moving slowly toward the village, hugging the tree line and making use of the sparse brushy cover. Staying in the long shadows cast by the nearby mountains to its west, the patrol moved twenty-five to fifty meters, then stopped to watch and listen again.

The poor cover and concealment was not to Tedder's

liking, and he was anxious to find something more suitable to hide in. Around 1900 hours, the team moved into a small thicket and established a tight wagon-wheel perimeter. Cautiously, the LRRPs took turns setting out six claymore mines in a horseshoe pattern around the team. They left the back door open for a quick E & E route. They were only a half klick away from the base of the mountains.

Tedder's patrol hadn't been set up for more than thirty minutes when the Rangers heard the sounds of movement coming from two or three locations around them. Tedder immediately suspected that enemy troops were looking for them. However, the LRRP team leader didn't want to move the team from its defensive position without knowing the exact location of the enemy. To be safe, he had Holcomb call in the movement to their TOC. He then told his teammates that if the enemy got too close, they would blow their claymores, toss out a couple of grenades apiece, then E & E toward the designated rendezvous point in a large clearing near the village.

The team lay quiet for a while and listened to the sounds of men walking about around them. Soon they heard Vietnamese talking in the distance. Figuring the NVA would settle down soon, this was confirmed a short time later when they heard the dull sounds of metal pots and pans banging around. Soon, they could smell lit cigarettes and cooking food.

Tedder put his team on 100 percent alert. Around 2230, the enemy troops seemed to quiet down. At about 2330 hours, the team heard two quick shots from the direction of the enemy. At first the LRRPs didn't know if the enemy soldiers were reconning by fire, or just trying to keep the patrol on its toes.

At 2345 hours, the LRRPs heard fifteen to twenty single shots, fired in rapid succession. The shots were fired by a number of weapons. It sounded almost like a squad of men enjoying a single-shot "mad minute." Tedder had to make the decision whether to blow the claymores and E & E or ride it out for a little longer. After a few minutes' deliberation, he signaled for his teammates to blow the claymores and run.

The six LRRPs escaped and evaded toward the village four hundred to five hundred meters away. At about the halfway point, the patrol stopped to listen for the sounds of pursuit. Sure as hell, they could hear enemy troops coming on like a pack of bloodhounds. They were shouting orders back and forth and talking among themselves. At that time, none of the enemy had yet fired a shot.

Olson radioed in the contact and requested an immediate extraction. Then Tedder got on the radio and requested the DTs he had called in on their last position. He walked the 105mm rounds, coming out of LZ Uplift, from the team's NDP up toward their present location. When he knew the rounds were hitting among the enemy soldiers, he walked them in within thirty meters of their perimeter. It was terrifying for the six LRRPs to lie there with no cover or concealment to protect them from shells impacting a spitting distance away.

Finally, after calling a cease-fire, Tedder kept his team in place for the next fifteen minutes to listen for the sounds of any movement. It didn't take long. Soon they heard movement not more than fifty meters away. It was coming from the patrol's back trail.

Tedder ordered his team to open fire with small arms and the M-79 grenade launcher. The enemy soldiers responded by returning fire. Judging from the rate of return fire, Tedder assumed that they were facing at least a full platoon. Fortunately, the enemy fire was hitting nowhere near the team, nor were the enemy forces using RPGs or RPDs. As usual, when the NVA could not locate their enemy, they fired high, and their rounds passed harmlessly overhead.

The LZ was still two hundred meters away, and the patrol had to cross an open area to reach it. When the team heard the sounds of choppers approaching, they jumped up and boogied for the LZ. As they ran across the wide, grassy expanse, the team leader radioed the pilot and told him he was preparing to throw out a smoke grenade. The slick pilot turned on his searchlights when he got close and verified the location and color of the smoke. The team leader then told him that the rounds coming out of the smoke would be "friendly" rounds.

The aircraft commander of the extraction slick spotted the team hiding in the grass, and directed the gunships onto the enemy positions. While the gunships worked over the area, the extraction ship came in out of the night and set down in the clearing thirty to forty meters away from the team. On Tedder's command, the six LRRPs leaped to their feet and ran out toward the waiting aircraft. In seconds, everyone was safe on board and on their way back to Camp Evans. It was nearly 0200 hours.

When the patrol returned to Evans they were told to catch a few hours' sleep because they were going back out the next day! On 14 March, the members of the patrol cleaned their weapons and reoutfitted, then prepared to reinsert into the same AO at last light, but this time from the opposite side of the village.

That afternoon, Tedder went out on a second overflight to take another peek at his AO. At 1600 hours, the team boarded the slick; the mission was a go.

Once again the chopper came in low over the rolling hills, flying contour lines just above the chest-high kunai grass. As the Huey approached the LZ, it flared to a hover four feet above the ground, and the LRRPs quickly exited both sides of the aircraft, jumping the final few feet into the grass. They spread out, quickly going to ground in the LZ as the sounds of the chopper faded in the distance.

The six LRRPs spent fifteen minutes frozen in place on the LZ, watching and listening. It appeared that they had gotten in without being seen. While the gunship and extraction slick moved farther away from the team, they faked two additional insertions before finally pulling back up into the evening sky. The aircraft circled around and climbed into a high orbit three to four miles to the east of the AO, well out of the sight and hearing of the team.

Once again, Olson announced that he had established good commo with the rear. Tedder kept the team there for another fifteen or twenty minutes, then gave Olson the nod to release the choppers to return to base. The patrol was only five hundred meters from the target village.

It was soon fully dark. Tedder silently gathered up his patrol and moved it one hundred meters, into the taller grass that covered a nearby knoll. Once safely ensconced on the higher ground, the LRRPs set up a cold NDP, put out their claymores, and posted guards—two men on, two hours per shift. The rest of the night was spent uneventfully watching the stars, except for the occasional interruption of a wood rat scurrying through the perimeter.

At around 0300 hours, Tedder roused the patrol and told them to get ready to move out. Then, after checking his map and compass with a penlight and shooting an azimuth to a point within a hundred meters of the village, he whispered to his teammates that they were going to attempt to infiltrate to a spot overlooking the village, out on the end of the low ridgeline they were already occupying.

Thirty minutes later, the patrol slipped silently off the grassy knoll and moved cautiously in leaps and bounds toward their OP, 200 or 250 meters away. When they finally reached the spot Tedder had selected, it was still too dark to see anything, so they sat back in the grass to wait for first light.

During the early minutes of the false dawn, Tedder realized that the location he had picked for an OP left a lot to be desired. He whispered to his teammates that they would have to crawl another twenty-five to thirty meters through the grass, then set up a new OP at another spot less than a hundred meters from the village.

The new location proved to be an excellent choice, for they could clearly see everything that went on in the village. The site was still in the chest-high grass, but on elevated ground overlooking the village a hundred meters away.

By 0630 hours, everyone on the team was ravenous, but Tedder cautioned them to put off eating until later. The village would be waking up, and he didn't want any unnecessary movement in the OP. One member of the team had actually asked if he could light up a cigarette. Tedder's hard look in the man's general direction had ended that nonsense.

The patrol was set up in a very tight group where Tedder could account for each man at all times. Below, the village was just beginning to come to life, and by 0800 hours, its inhabitants were moving about their everyday tasks.

It wasn't long before a group of five young girls, perhaps thirteen to sixteen years of age, carrying long baskets on their backs, began moving away through the brush behind the village and soon disappeared into a small patch of trees fifty meters away. Thirty minutes later, they returned without their baskets. Tedder suspected that a contingent of enemy troops was hidden in the trees behind the village. Tedder recorded his observations in his notebook.

About 0930 hours, a thirteen- or fourteen-year-old girl left the village and headed straight for where the team lay hidden. She seemed to be out for just a leisurely stroll and gave no indication that she suspected anyone was hidden in the grass to her front.

To the LRRPs' alarm, the young woman walked until she was within fifteen meters of the team. Peering cautiously through the grass, Tedder eased out his K-bar and indicated to his ATL that if she got any closer, they would have to quietly take her out. It was not something either man looked forward to, but if they didn't and she spotted them, she would quickly alert the village.

Finally stopping ten meters away from the hidden LRRPs, the young girl stood for a few minutes looking back down toward the village. Finally she moved slightly to the right, then slowly turned around and strolled back down to the village, never realizing just how close she had come to dying. It was 1000 hours.

By noon, the LRRPs had counted approximately thirty people moving about the village. All appeared to be local inhabitants, and no one seemed up to anything out of the ordinary. Except for the five young women who had taken their baskets into the nearby woods, there had been absolutely no sign of anything unusual.

Tedder's teammates had still not eaten since the day before, and they were beginning to grumble and look upon him as the Antichrist. Just as he was about to relent and let them chow down, he spotted three VC wearing black pajamas and carrying AKs step out of the grass seventy-five to eighty meters to the right of their position. The enemy soldiers looked around for a moment, then started to move down toward the village. Unnoticed by Tedder and his comrades, a small, well-used trail came out of the grass and ran down across the front of the team and entered the village. The three VC were on the trail.

Tedder noticed that the enemy soldiers seemed very alert and were carrying their weapons at port arms. The three men were wearing no web gear, and the rucksacks on their backs looked nearly empty. They wore Ho Chi Minh sandals. Tedder also noticed that the three soldiers were moving in single file and maintaining proper interval; obviously they were not local village militiamen out for a stroll.

At that moment, Tedder kicked himself about the claymores. The open grassland where they were hiding didn't provide any terrain features suitable for stopping a claymore's deadly backblast, so Tedder had decided against using them. But he was kicking himself in the ass over that decision.

Down in the village, the locals were by then in the middle of their siesta and no one was stirring inside. Tedder secured the radio from Holcomb and quickly called in the sightings. By that time the VC were moving directly across the team's front sixty meters away.

Tedder got Lieutenant Udder on the radio and asked for instructions. Udder went off the air for thirty seconds, then came back on line and told Tedder to engage the VC. He added that they should also attempt to take a prisoner. Tedder didn't have to guess that the thirty-second pause in Udder's transmission had occurred because he was relaying his report to Major Gooding.

Using hand signals, Tedder quickly designated targets to shooters and motioned for them to open fire on his initiation. Contact was imminent and company SOP was for the TOC to crank up the choppers. So Tedder knew without asking that he didn't have to worry about calling for an extraction.

By that time, everyone had moved up on line where they could get a clear shot. When the three VC reached the point nearest the team, the team leader initiated contact. A second later, everyone else opened fire.

Just as the team commenced firing, the VC were passing behind a cluster of thick brush standing just outside the village. After the volley had ended, it appeared that all three of the enemy soldiers had dropped from view down into the brush. No one could tell for certain if the three men had been hit or if they had merely dived into the nearest cover.

The six-man long-range patrol now stood up in the grass while each member put at least four or five mags apiece directly into the brush. There was no return fire.

Down in the village, everything remained quiet. After Tedder called for a cease-fire, the team quieted down and listened for a full ten minutes. Hearing nothing, they called in and reported the contact, stating that they believed that all targets were down.

Taking orders directly from Major Gooding, Udder now instructed the team to move cautiously down to the kill zone to check for a prisoner.

As the five LRRPs got on line, they routinely spread out in a concave formation, the men five to eight meters apart as they moved down toward the brush from their position on the high ground. When they were only thirty meters away, Tedder held up his hand to stop the team, and then told two of his teammates to toss CS grenades into the brush. The thicket was only about thirty feet in diameter, but it was very thick and choked with brush that was six feet high. When the two men tossed out the CS grenades, the team hit the ground and lay prone while they watched for anyone who might run out of the brush.

When no one emerged, they took off their masks and waited until the CS had cleared before moving forward again. Tedder had already decided that no one had survived the ambush, but that still had to be confirmed to satisfy Major Gooding.

The team stood up and moved forward again, wrapping itself three-fourths of the way around the thicket. The mouth of their horseshoe-shaped formation opened directly toward the village.

The team leader moved to the left side of the cover with Private First Class Leon out ahead of him. Tedder intended to circle around the brush far enough so that they weren't directly exposed to the village, then move in to check out the bodies.

Allowing Tedder to pass him and move beyond, Leon finally stopped no more than a couple of feet away from the cover. Tedder was standing to one side less than ten feet away. By that time, the rest of the LRRPs were spread out at different points around the thicket.

As Tedder once more started to circle the brush, he suddenly heard a quick burst of fire from an AK-47, and yelled, "Who shot?"

No one answered. Then the team leader looked to his right and saw Private First Class Leon on the ground, halfway sitting up, reaching down to feel one of his legs. As Tedder started toward his wounded point man, another single round fired, and he knew then that it had come from the thicket.

Tedder immediately opened fire into the thick brush at the

spot from where he suspected the gunfire had come. Receiving no fire in return, he asked if everyone was okay. When a couple of LRRPs answered yes, he quickly told them that Leon had been hit. Tedder then went down on his knees to treat the wounded LRRP's injuries.

From the look of Leon's wounds he had caught a six-to-eight-round burst across both legs, breaking the femurs at midthigh, but missing the femoral arteries. However, he was bleeding badly, so Tedder removed his neckerchief and tied it tightly above the wound on Leon's right leg to serve as a tourniquet.

Suddenly, he heard movement in the brush to his left. When he looked up, he saw a Viet Cong soldier lying on the ground less than six feet away, trying to raise his weapon to fire once again.

Tedder quickly swung up his CAR-15 and popped the wounded enemy soldier with a short burst through the top of his head.

Satisfied that the threat had been eliminated, Tedder immediately returned to the task at hand, securing the tourniquet around Leon's leg. Now realizing that Leon's left leg was also in need of constriction, Leon pulled off his own neckerchief and handed it to his team leader. He didn't seem to be in a lot of pain at the time, but Tedder knew *that* would not last. The tourniquets were effective in slowing down the bleeding, but the LRRP point man still needed to be medevacked immediately if he was to survive.

A few minutes later, Olson came around to help, moving up to cover Tedder as he continued treating Leon's wounds. Tedder was busy starting a serum albumin IV drip to keep Leon from going into shock from blood loss. There was little else he could do for the wounded LRRP.

After a while, Leon looked up and, through clenched teeth, told his team leader that he was beginning to feel a lot of pain, so Tedder pulled out a morphine Syrette and jabbed it into Leon's thigh, just above the wounds.

Then one of the LRRPs on the other side of the thicket shouted that he still heard movement in the brush. Tedder stood up, pointed his weapon at the thicket, and began hollering, "*Lai dai! Lai dai!* (Come here! Come here!)"

No one answered at first, but suddenly a VC showed his face through an opening in the vegetation. Tedder and Olson covered the enemy soldier, who was sticking his hands through the brush to show they were empty. Tedder motioned with his rifle for the man to come out. The VC finally stood and stepped out of the thicket. He was unarmed.

The team leader tried to persuade the enemy soldier to drop to his knees and fold his hands behind his head, but the VC would neither go down nor fold his hands behind his head. Instead, he just stood there grinning a big toothy grin at Tedder as if he thought the whole affair was just a big joke.

Outraged by this unexpected and irrational reaction, Tedder stepped up and clubbed the VC to the ground with his CAR-15, leaving him lying flat on his back, groggy from the force of the blow.

Olson, still standing guard over Tedder, told the team leader that he had already called in the contact and requested a medevac. With the VC secured, Olson handed his weapon to Kurth, who had just come around from the back side of the thicket.

Tedder dragged Leon ten feet back from the thicket, then shouted for everyone to come around to his side of the brush. It was at that moment Delfiglio discovered that Holcomb had been hit by the single shot fired after Leon was wounded. The round had caught Holcomb in the shin just below the knee. The wound, while not mortal, was causing him a lot of pain. Delfiglio gently removed Holcomb's ruck, lifted him in his arms, and carried him around to where the rest of their teammates were gathered.

Tedder saw that Holcomb was in agonizing pain, but there wasn't a lot he could do other than to apply a tourniquet above the knee and jab a morphine Syrette into the wounded man's thigh. But at least Tedder had his team together again.

Suddenly, four ARA gunships swooped in over the low grassy ridge, and immediately spotted the patrol in the open. Tedder quickly threw a smoke grenade into the thicket and got on Olson's radio to request rockets on the target. The gunship pilot came back and told him that one of the gunships had just reported that it was taking fire. He told Tedder to move his people back from the thicket and take cover.

At that time, the team received a radio call that both a medevac and the patrol's lift ship were inbound and on a short string. While the gunships continued working back and forth over the surrounding countryside looking for targets, the two slicks appeared over the area and circled around to come in over the LRRP patrol. Suddenly, both the gunships and the door gunners on the two slicks opened up on a target they spotted back in the brush. At the same time, one of the gunships moved in and fired up the thicket fifteen to twenty meters from the team. If the last VC still in the thicket had survived the LRRPs' earlier fire, the gunship had just trashed any hopes he still had of surviving the affair.

As the gunship opened fire on the thicket, the LRRPs dove for cover, putting their hands over their heads to protect themselves. They hugged the ground while the 2.75-inch aerial rockets did their thing.

The lead gunship radioed Tedder that they had taken fire from at least a platoon of NVA moving up through the grass. They had killed a large number of them, and had succeeded in running off the rest. The NVA had been approaching the village from the same direction the three VC had come.

While the gunships continued working over the grass, the medevac and the slick landed together twenty or thirty meters away from the thicket, which was now burning merrily away. Tedder picked up his badly wounded point man and carried him to the waiting medevac. Leon's legs were dangling uncontrollably where they had been broken at midthigh. It made him very difficult to carry.

Tedder got the wounded man aboard the Huey just as Belfiglio and Kurth arrived with Holcomb. As soon as both wounded LRRPs were safely aboard, the medevac went light on its skids and lifted out of the LZ. Tedder and his comrades returned to where Olson was still securing the prisoner.

The remaining LRRPs recovered their gear, grabbed the prisoner, and boarded the waiting slick. Once they were in the air and on their way back to Camp Evans, the crew chief leaned over and shouted for Tedder to "lighten their load," suggesting they toss out the captured VC. Tedder smiled and shouted back that he had almost killed the man earlier, but brigade S-2 needed a prisoner.

When they landed at Camp Evans twenty minutes later, the chopper dropped off everyone at the LRRP compound except Tedder and the prisoner. Tedder stayed aboard, sitting across the open cabin from the enemy soldier with his weapon trained on the man's chest. The slick pilot lifted off the chopper pad and made the short hop over to the brigade POW compound on the other side of Camp Evans. There Tedder turned the POW over to the MPs.

Two days later, the 1st Cavalry LRRP Detachment received official word that Private First Class Leon had died aboard the hospital ship, USS *Hope*, anchored in Da Nang harbor. Unknown to his teammates, when Leon had been shot across the legs and was falling forward, one of the rounds had entered his body from the top of his shoulder. It had not left an exit wound, nor had it caused any external bleeding. But the damage to the LRRP's organs and the severe internal hemorrhaging had proven mortal.

Holcomb's wound ended his days as a soldier, and he was soon medevacked back to the States for extensive treatment.

Tedder expressed his great displeasure to both Major Gooding and Lieutenant Udder that obtaining a lousy prisoner had cost him two of his men. His venting made Tedder feel a little better, but made no impression on the senior officer.

Later, Sgt. Rick Tedder was awarded the first of his two Silver Stars for the action that day. PFC Felix Leon was posthumously awarded the Bronze Star medal with V device and the Purple Heart. Sp4. Ron Holcomb was awarded a Bronze Star with V and a Purple Heart. Everyone else on the team also received Bronze Stars with V.

After the war, Rick Tedder discovered that Felix Leon's parents had carried through with the adoption process of the little Vietnamese girl. It was a legacy to their fallen son.

☆　　☆　　☆　　☆　　☆

Company P, 75th Infantry (Ranger), 5th Infantry Division (Mechanized)

By May 1971, the Vietnamization program was in full swing. In northern I Corps the commander of XXIV Corps and his ARVN counterpart collaborated on a decision to combine a U.S. Ranger unit and an ARVN Ranger unit to run a joint operation in the spirit of cooperation. Company P, 75th Infantry (Ranger) from the 5th Infantry Division (Mechanized) was selected as the participating American Ranger company.

Papa Company was still recovering from heavy losses suffered during Lam Son 719, the failed ARVN invasion of Laos, where the company went from nine operational long-range patrol teams to two and a half operational teams in a period of thirty days. However, the company still managed to put together a special ten-man "scratch" team for the joint operation. It was commanded by Capt. Charles Funderburke and consisted of S.Sgt. James Hussey, S.Sgt. Don Hughes, Sgt. Phil McCoy, Sp4. Steve Loggins, Sgt. Gregg Gain, Sgt. Thomas Perry, and three other Rangers whose names have since been forgotten.

The ten-man ARVN component was also commanded by a captain, or *dai uy*, who liked to flash around a photo of President Lyndon B. Johnson pinning a Silver Star on his chest.

The Americans thought that the ARVN Rangers had to be pretty good troops, and looked forward to serving with them; no one was sure what the ARVNs thought of the Americans.

The mission was scheduled for the final week in May and would last six days. During their briefing, the personnel of the combined patrol discovered that their mission was unlike any other LRRP patrol they had ever pulled before. They would be going in to secure an old U.S. Marine firebase on the Khe Sanh plateau overlooking the abandoned Khe Sanh Marine forward combat base. Using the hilltop as a patrol base, the Rangers would then run joint reconnaissance patrols into the surrounding countryside.

Neither Captain Funderburke nor anyone else on the operation believed for a minute that the combined twenty-man patrol had enough people to secure the firebase *and* field a number of reconnaissance patrols. They would be fully exposed on the crest of the mountain, and with teams running patrols into the jungle below there would be little more than a skeleton crew left behind to secure the base. It was a fool's plan, and fool's plans too often killed the wrong people, leaving only the fools behind to blame the failures on the dead.

Captain Funderburke made his thoughts known after the briefing, but his protests fell on deaf ears. The mission would go in as planned. The Rangers were told that this was a "high visibility" mission that would be under the scrutiny of some very high-ranking people. It *had* to succeed! The Rangers were unimpressed by that line of reasoning and muttered among themselves that it was the high visibility they would present to the surrounding NVA that they were worried about. They cared little about what some distant American and ARVN generals thought. The brass wouldn't be around when the shit hit the fan.

The morning of the mission found everyone at the company chopper pad. With all the players gathered together waiting to lift off, it looked like Grand Central Station. Tiny Papa Company—at full strength little more than a reinforced platoon—hadn't been able to field more than a couple of teams since the end of the ARVN invasion of Laos. But that morning the pad was full of helicopters. There were four Huey slicks to handle the twenty Rangers, a fifth bird for command and control, and two pairs of Cobra gunships with accompanying LOHs. To the complete disgust of the Papa Company Rangers, there was even a special slick for the ARVN *dai uy*.

The operational plan called for the two Hueys bearing the Americans to go in first to sweep the firebase and set up security. Then the two slicks carrying the ARVN Rangers would land to drop off their loads. Finally, the *dai uy*'s helicopter would bring him in when everything was secure.

The insertion went off without a hitch, and the Rangers quickly began to consolidate a defensive perimeter for the coming patrols. The firebase was located on the top of a flattened hill large enough to support a full artillery battery and its accompanying infantry security force, so it was obviously much too large an area to be secured by a mere ten to twenty Rangers. But the Rangers were not the ones calling the shots there—that was being done by some tactical incompetent from a desk in an underground bunker over at XXIV Corps headquarters.

The team quickly established a 360-degree defensive perimeter on the western end of the firebase because the Rangers understood that there was nothing they could do to keep an enemy assault from ascending unimpeded to the unprotected eastern end of the hilltop. If the neighboring NVA commander figured out the hill was occupied by just a twenty-man recon element, the Rangers would be overrun quicker than it would take them to get a last radio message off to the brigade TOC.

It was easy to see why the Marines had abandoned the firebase; higher hills dominated the base on three sides. If the enemy occupied any of them and directed heavy-weapons fire down on the Rangers, the operation would come to a quick and fatal end. Even if the NVA failed to bring up their big stuff, a few observers with radios could easily track every move the Rangers made. Patrols leaving the hilltop would run directly into well-planned and well-laid ambushes.

While Staff Sergeant Hughes's team cleared the bunkers and checked the immediate area for booby traps, Staff Sergeant Hussey and Sergeant Gain went out on a brief area recon to take a closer look at all the likely avenues of approach to the firebase. The two Rangers went out about five hundred meters, where they quickly discovered a number of recently used sleeping positions and a fresh, heavily traveled trail. They continued to scope out the area during the afternoon, finally returning to their teammates at the top of the hill at dusk. In their opinion, chances of surviving the next six days weren't all that promising.

The two men stopped to set up some trip flares as they reentered the patrol base. By that time, everyone had been assigned a two-man fighting position and was instructed to rotate security with their holemates, each man pulling two hours on, two hours off, for the remainder of the night. Even though it was a 50 percent alert, none of the Papa Company Rangers thought it was too tough. Their anticipation of a quick encounter with the enemy was overpowering.

The first part of the night passed peacefully enough, but between 0200 and 0300 hours the enemy closed in and began to probe the Rangers' positions not far from where Hughes's team was located. Without warning, a vicious firefight erupted. Gunfire broke out, followed by explosions, and green and red tracers were soon crisscrossing through the darkness. Enemy movement continued at the northern sector of the firebase. After ten to fifteen minutes of hostilities, the enemy decided he had discovered what he came for and withdrew. In the darkness outside their perimeter, the Rangers could just make out the forms of three enemy bodies lying at the edge of the gently sloping hill. Captain Funderburke refused to send anyone down to check out the bodies, as he was not sure how large an NVA element they had engaged, nor was he willing to expose any of his Rangers out in the open.

Funderburke then called in a sitrep on the contact and reported that the team had been compromised. He also requested an extraction. He realized that since the enemy had felt them out, it would not take them long to mount a stronger assault on the Rangers' position, and with men out on patrol, there would be even fewer people left to defend the perimeter. But the word soon came back that due to the bad weather and the fact that the Rangers had suffered no casualties in dealing with the enemy probe, there would be no extraction.

At first light, Funderburke sent out a four-man patrol to search the dead NVA and recover any weapons left on the battlefield. However, they returned quickly, saying they had found no sign of any enemy bodies. Somehow, without detection by any of the Rangers standing watch, the enemy had come in during the night and policed the battlefield. The ramifications were sobering.

Finally, "higher" called to inform Captain Funderburke that it had been decided to resupply the team and then reinsert it not far away, on another abandoned Marine firebase. While the Rangers waited for the resupply bird, they went over the action of the previous night among themselves. It was soon determined that not one ARVN Ranger had fired his weapon during the fighting. That did little to inspire confidence in the ability of their counterparts, nor did it enhance the spirit of Vietnamization.

The resupply ship finally arrived to replenish their water and ammo. As it lifted off the LZ, it began receiving intense small-arms fire from one of the nearby hills, taking a number of hits, which wounded some of the crew.

The Rangers immediately returned fire in an attempt to suppress the enemy guns, then directed gunships in to work over the area thoroughly. Once again, the ARVN Rangers did not fire a shot.

A short time later, the extraction aircraft arrived and began to take out the patrol in reverse order of their insertion—first the *dai uy*, then the ARVN Rangers, and finally the Papa Company Rangers.

As the first aircraft landed on the new hilltop, an enemy mortar round impacted nearby, showering the chopper with shrapnel. The five Rangers jumped out and ran for cover as the Huey slick lifted away from the abandoned firebase. No one had been hit, and the chopper had not sustained any damage, but five Rangers were on the ground, and mortar rounds were bracketing the LZ.

The Ranger commander on the ground radioed the remaining aircraft to abort the insertion, but orders from higher overrode them. Soon the remaining aircraft came in under fire and deposited their loads.

While most of the Rangers sought cover, a few maneuvered around to the other side of the perimeter to try to locate the mortar tubes. When they finally spotted one, they directed the gunships in on the target, and began to lay down suppressing fire of their own. In spite of the air support, the mortar rounds continued falling, soon wounding Sergeant McCoy in the neck.

When Staff Sergeant Hussey went over to treat McCoy's wound, to his great relief, he discovered that the wound was only superficial.

Suddenly, several ARVN Rangers arrived at the position held by the Papa Company Rangers and began speaking loudly in Vietnamese and pointing back in the direction they had just come from. Loggins and Gain went back to see what the commotion was all about. They quickly discovered that one of the ARVNs had taken a direct hit from a mortar round and was dead. After the ARVNs refused to lend a hand, the two Papa Company Rangers wrapped his remains in his poncho and carried him back to the American position. When the two Rangers reported the incident to Captain Funderburke, he decided that enough was enough and got on the radio to higher. After a little persuasion, he convinced them that the patrol should be extracted.

Hussey and Funderburke decided that the best course of action was for the team to withdraw to the backside of the hill, and then run parallel along the crest to the opposite end, where an old Marine helipad was located. That would better serve as an LZ and, if they could get there without being observed, they might be able to get out before the NVA mortar crews had time to readjust their tubes.

When the ARVN Rangers were informed of the plan, they immediately began running for the pad, leaving behind the body of their dead comrade. The Americans began to withdraw in pairs, the entire time keeping up the pretext that they were still in their original positions, so the enemy wouldn't shift fire to the other LZ. Two of Staff Sergeant Hughes's men grabbed the dead ARVN Ranger and carried him to the helipad.

The first two helicopters were able to land, load, and get away again without any trouble. But just as the third aircraft was taking off, mortar rounds began walking toward the LZ. Finally, the last bird arrived and Captain Funderburke and two Rangers jumped aboard. As Gain and another Ranger arrived carrying the dead ARVN, Funderburke and Perry jumped off the aircraft to make room for them. As the two Rangers got aboard with the body, a mortar round impacted right in front of the helicopter. In a reflex motion, the pilot lifted off, leaving Captain Funderburke and Perry still on the ground. The remaining Ranger aboard the lift ship saw to it that the situation was reported, and the other bird with the American Rangers aboard quickly went back in to recover the two men.

But still the mission was not scrapped. Higher command once again decided to reinsert the team on another abandoned Marine firebase, this time on Hill 1015 just outside the Khe Sanh Combat Base, and not far from the peak that had housed TELSTAR—a recently abandoned U.S. communications outpost. Papa Company Rangers had reconned that outpost prior to Lam Son 719 for a special army unit that had set up a secret commo base on its peak.

As a Cobra/LOH Pink team flew low over the mountaintop to check out the situation, an enemy soldier on the ground popped a red smoke grenade. The slick pilots mistakenly assumed that one of our LOHs had dropped it to mark wind direction. As the first slick, carrying Captain Funderburke, set down on the ground, the officer stepped off the aircraft and was immediately hit by enemy small-arms fire. One of the door gunners was also wounded as enemy machine guns swept the LZ. As the last members of the patrol landed and tried to set up a defensive perimeter around the wounded officer, they realized that they were caught in a cross fire coming from two bunkers just off the LZ.

The Rangers quickly formed up in a circular perimeter; the ARVNs occupied the center, once again avoiding participation in the firefight. Loggins and Gain took up a defensive position behind a freshly dug grave, the mound of dirt serving as a protective berm.

Hussey was busy patching up Captain Funderburke, who had been hit seriously enough that Hussey was certain his war was over. Staff Sergeant Hughes's team was busy putting down suppressing fire on both bunkers, which were extremely well concealed and dug in. Loggins soon moved to another position to put more effective fire on one of the bunkers.

After he finished treating Funderburke, Hussey crawled up and was placing extremely effective single-shot fire into the other bunker when an enemy round creased his thumb. The NCO calmly looked down and said, "Damn!" then he smiled and began returning fire.

Suddenly the M-60 gunner took a direct hit that wounded him and destroyed his weapon. The remainder of the Papa Company Rangers continued putting down a steady base of fire until the gunships were finally able to line up for rocket runs against the NVA bunkers.

After the Cobras made four passes firing 2.75-inch rockets dangerously close and destroying both enemy bunkers, Loggins and Hughes leaped to their feet and charged downhill to clear out the emplacements. Gain then got on the radio and requested a medevac extraction for the wounded Rangers. Finally higher agreed to extract the entire team and call off the mission. The subsequent extraction of the patrol proved uneventful, and everyone was finally accounted for.

As the Rangers flew back toward their base camp, each man's expression revealed his disgust for the entire operation. It had indeed been an ill-advised and ill-fated mission from its inception. Higher command had put the Rangers in a lethal situation that was incompatible with the basic concepts of long-range patrolling. When the Papa Company Rangers were not given the necessary opportunity to train and work with their ARVN Ranger counterparts, it had resulted in a potentially fatal situation; the ARVNs were not familiar with American Ranger standards and SOPs, and not one member of the U.S. team had been able to assess the combat readiness of their South Vietnamese counterparts.

The consensus was that they should not have been repeatedly reinserted once it had been established that the enemy knew of their mission. And to make matters worse, it was later discovered that the ARVN Ranger radio operator, who had open and total access to all friendly intel, coordinates, and radio frequencies concerning the mission, was an enemy agent.

The final cost of the operation was relatively light, with three Company P Rangers and two U.S. helicopter crewmen wounded in action, and one ARVN Ranger killed in action. Seven NVA soldiers were confirmed killed by actual body count.

71st LRP Detachment, 199th Light Infantry Brigade

In mid-December 1967, American forces throughout Vietnam were told to stand down from Christmas Eve through New Year's Day. It was the same story as the bilateral ceasefire that preceded the previous year's holiday season and, of course, had never managed to live up to its supposed bilateral status. No one really expected 1967 to be any different. Many of the long-range patrol units in and around the Saigon area sent recon teams out into the field with instructions to keep their eyes open but to avoid contact. Naturally, that didn't mean that you couldn't open fire and kill a few people if the situation got "delicate" on you—at least that's what the LRRPs believed.

So, it was no great surprise when two of the six teams that made up the 199th Light Infantry Brigade's 71st LRP Detachment received warning orders on 18 December to prepare for a five-day patrol east of the Parrot's Beak. Two five-man long-range patrols were selected for the mission. The two teams were to insert at last light on the evening of 20 December, going in five minutes and five hundred meters apart. They were to patrol through their AOs, searching for enemy units coming out of their sanctuaries in Cambodia and moving toward Saigon.

The overflight conducted on the nineteenth with the team leaders and their ATLs aboard indicated that the terrain the recon teams would have to cover consisted of level-to-rolling hills, covered with scrub brush, bamboo, and single and double canopy up near the crests of the hills. The weather forecast was hot and clear, with no sign of precipitation.

When the aircraft landed at the 199th Light Infantry Brigade's helipad at Long Binh, Sgt. Tom Files, the team leader of Cobra One-three, and Sp4. Doug Berry, his ATL, stepped down to the ground and into the waiting three-quarter-ton truck for the ten-minute ride back to Camp Frenzel-Jones, located on the north side of the huge Long Binh military complex. Files hadn't been too pleased with what he had seen of the AO; it didn't appear to be the kind of terrain that would hold NVA or VC Main Force units of any great size. However, that didn't mean that there might not be a thousand enemy soldiers double-timing across the area every night.

That's why the brass wanted the 199th's long-range patrols to go in for a thorough look-see.

Around 1700 hours on 20 December, the patrols' two lift ships and a C & C slick took off from the 199th's helipad and joined up quickly with a pair of orbiting Huey gunships.

The flight out to the recon zone took less than a half hour, and when the five-ship formation reached the mission area, the lead ship carrying Cobra One-three went in first. There was no time for the usual contour flying, tree hopping, and false insertions. Cobra One-three was running low on daylight, and the other team still had to get in.

The Huey crossed a sluggish, muddy river twenty meters wide and flared out over a low-lying clearing just large enough to handle a single aircraft. Not wanting to risk a touchdown in the chest-high elephant grass whipping about in the chopper's rotor wash, the pilot looked back and signaled for the patrol to go. The five heavily armed LRRPs were already outside the aircraft riding its skids when they leaped the final eight to ten feet and disappeared into the blowing grass.

As the Huey lifted out, the five camouflaged recon men broke for the protection of the nearby tree line, a scant twenty meters away. Dropping into the first available cover, Files, who carried his own radio, immediately made a commo check and gave the team's first sitrep. There had been no sign of enemy troops in and around the LZ or anything else that appeared unduly dangerous, so Files quickly released the aircraft to allow them to get the other team in on the opposite side of the river.

The plan was for the two teams to divide up the recon zone, making sure they kept a prominent terrain feature between them at all times. When one team was on high ground, the other team would stay low, and vice versa. It was always risky working two teams so close together, but if both teams knew what they were doing, then it wasn't so dangerous. Besides, there was an unquestionable comfort in having five more comrades only half a klick away. At noon on the fourth day, the two teams were scheduled to link up at a point where a tributary stream ran into the river. The combined patrol would then NDP together and move to their designated PZ the next morning.

Files listened over his radio as the second team made it safely into its LZ. He got a quick commo check from the other patrol's RTO, confirmed their immediate direction of march, then signed off the net. Nodding to his four teammates that everything was fine, he motioned for Sp4. Greg Callahan to take the point and move the team out.

Callahan had been in country for only a few months, but the young LRRP had grown up hunting and fishing and running the river bottoms outside Davenport, Iowa, and he proved to be a natural in the bush. Files felt comfortable with the Hawkeye up in front.

Berry, swinging his M-60 out to his left, stepped up behind Callahan to walk his slack. Up front, Callahan had to suppress a quick grin; it was always a comfort to him knowing that he had a one-hundred-round belt of 7.62mm backing him up if the shit hit the fan.

Files was next. The burly team leader looked more like a

noseguard than a LRRP. He was as wide as a double barn door with shoulders that looked like a fireplace mantel. Files had a deep Southern accent that usually tickled the people on the other end of his radio transmissions. And speaking of radios—the bruising team leader always carried his own. He liked the idea of having his own commo with him at all times. It eliminated the need for keeping an RTO at arm's length. Two people standing together drew proportionately twice as much fire as one person standing alone. And Files's great strength made the added weight of a PRC-25 radio seem like little more than an extra LRRP ration.

The fourth spot in the patrol was allocated to the junior RTO, a new man who had not been around long enough to be called by name. Not trained to operate the PRC-25 that he carried, for the moment, the cherry was nothing more than a beast of burden for the team's artillery radio. But that unpopular role would keep him alive and out of danger long enough to learn. And learning was the best way to earn your way home in the passenger compartment of a Freedom Bird instead of in its cargo hold.

Sp4. Bob "Oh Toothless One" Devlin brought up the rear. Armed with his favorite weapon, an M-79 grenade launcher, and a .45-caliber pistol for backup, the streetwise New Yorker carried enough HE rounds to sink Manhattan Island.

Each team moved about five hundred meters from its LZ before setting up in false NDPs until darkness swallowed them up. Then each carefully moved another 150 meters before setting up in its real NDP. Silently, they set up in wagon-wheel perimeters and put out their claymores. Each team leader then established his security watches, one man on, one hour each shift, beginning at 2200 hours. Except for the normal first-night jitters, the evening proved uneventful.

Both teams were up and awake at the first signs of the false dawn. Those who had an appetite ate a cold LRRP ration or a cornflake bar for breakfast and prepared to break camp. Cobra One-three moved out around 0700, coordinating its actions with the other team so that they would not accidentally stumble into each other. The two teams remained on opposite sides of the river for the time being. Although the river was a good twenty meters wide, its average depth of three to four feet and its sluggish current made it a poor natural barrier. Before the mission was over, both teams would cross and recross the meandering waterway, but just then it was the border between their AOs.

Files stopped his patrol occasionally for fifteen-minute breaks, not only to rest his men but also to test the air and listen for sounds that didn't belong. After a while, he would nod to Callahan to move out again on the predetermined azimuth. Experienced LRRPs always avoided haste because impetuosity would kill a LRRP as quickly as a VC ambush.

The patrol moved all day but found no sign that the enemy had ever set foot in the area. Just before dark, Files contacted the other team leader to coordinate their NDPs. The second night was also uneventful.

Day three was much more of the same, with Cobra One-three continuing its cautious patrol through the rolling hills. Although it did encounter a few old trails, there was no indication that they had been used in the past few months. The weather remained oppressively hot, and every member of the patrol was already running low on water.

During the fourth day of the mission, Files established radio contact with the team leader of the other patrol and told him to begin moving to the rendezvous point for their linkup. The two teams were scheduled to spend their final night together within a couple hundred meters of their PZ, then extract at the same time the next morning.

At around 1100 hours, each team was closing on the mouth of a small, fast-moving stream, where it emptied into the river. During that part of their mission, they remained in constant contact with each other; linkups were always dangerous.

The other team reached the rendezvous point thirty minutes before Cobra One-three. The Rangers secured the area and notified Files that they were already in place and set up in a defensive perimeter.

Cobra One-three approached the designated meeting place from the opposite side of the river and had to cross it above the point where the tributary emptied into it. Toward noon, Callahan spotted the other team and began moving toward them. After the linkup was safely completed, everyone took an extended break and filled their canteens from the nearby tributary. The atmosphere was very relaxed. Neither team had found any fresh sign.

The two team leaders quietly warned their teammates not to fill all their canteens, since they were extracting the next morning. There was no point in carrying excess water back to Long Binh. Each man filled only two canteens.

A short time later, the two teams filed out of their perimeter with Cobra One-three bringing up the rear. They angled away from the small stream and climbed a shallow ridge to get a better view of the terrain ahead of them. Files wanted to get a look at their PZ before dark.

By the time they had covered two hundred meters, they realized that they had made a big mistake. They should have filled all their canteens; the heat was still on the uphill side of hot out in the open terrain, and the LRRPs were going through their water very quickly.

The patrol had covered nearly five hundred meters by 1500 hours. Files, who had taken over control of the combined teams, continued pushing them down the crest of the low ridge. According to his map, the PZ couldn't be too far ahead.

Around 1530 hours, Callahan was leading the patrol down the descending finger of the ridgeline when he spotted the PZ about 150 meters away, a large field surrounded by woods. Even though the small stream had angled away from the river at its union, the river's serpentine meanderings had brought it back around to within a hundred meters of its more freely flowing tributary. It was in that narrow pocket of land that the patrol had located its PZ.

The PZ was nearly the size of a football field, eighty meters down its length and with a width of nearly sixty meters. Two-thirds of the way down the field, right where it cut back along the tributary stream, there was a slight dogleg in its path.

Files stopped the patrol at that point and set up a defensive perimeter on the slope overlooking the PZ. He then sent out a pair of two-man recon elements to scout out the entire perimeter of the field. An hour later the recon patrols were back. Both patrols reported that the field had been burned off in the past two to three weeks and was covered in two to three inches of powdery black ash. One of the patrols had also spotted fresh footprints in the ash along the far edge of the field and had discovered a well-used trail that crossed the small stream.

At that point, Files pulled the patrol back away from the PZ and moved it down closer to the small stream, where they could once again replenish their scanty water supply. It was almost 1630 hours.

When the patrol reached the stream, they found an earthen ledge or shelf that dropped away from the higher ground about five feet, and there formed a second ledge, which then dropped down once again to the streambed. Files instructed the patrol to set up their NDP on the upper ledge. He intended to spend the night there; then early the next morning they would move down the embankment and across the stream to their PZ on the other side.

But it wasn't long before Files began to notice the thick scrub brush and bamboo around them. The bamboo thicket to their right was especially of concern; it offered an excellent avenue of approach to an enemy unit trying to move up on the patrol. After pointing that out to his teammates, a quick discussion ensued as to which side of the stream they should spend their final night on.

By 1700 hours, a number of the LRRPs had run completely out of water. Callahan and a man from the other team volunteered to take some canteens down to the stream to refill them. The small stream was only about fifteen meters away, just down below the lower embankment. At that point the stream was only three or four feet wide, and no more than six inches deep. Files okayed the resupply, and the two LRRPs gathered up a number of empty canteens and slid down the embankment to the edge of the stream.

Once in the streambed, they located a deeper hole where it would be a little easier to fill the canteens. With a last look around them, they squatted in the open next to the stream and pushed the first of the empty canteens beneath the surface of the water.

Dusk was setting in by then. In the silence of the coming night, the gurgling sounds of the water flowing into the canteens seemed to carry for miles. The two LRRPs grew more and more nervous as the minutes slowly passed. Suddenly, the other LRRP stood up and looked around. He whispered to Callahan that someone was watching them. Callahan had the same feeling. Finally, he stood up and joined his comrade as they scanned the area around them. The hairs on the backs of their necks were standing at rigid attention. They didn't see anything, but they sensed that something was not right. After a while, they dropped back down to the water, anxious to be done with the job and back in the company of their teammates. They finally finished their task, but as they attempted to climb up the cutbank back to the team, they made a lot more noise than they wanted to.

Still nervous, the two soldiers rejoined the patrol and distributed the canteens, telling the rest of the team that they had a feeling they were being watched. Files, too, had sensed something. Alerted by the anxiety of his teammates, the veteran team leader decided to keep the patrol where it was for the remainder of the night. They were already set up in sort of an L-shaped perimeter, with good cover and elevation in their favor.

Files ordered his teammates to put out eight claymores,

zigzagging the wires back and forth into the perimeter to deceive any VC who might stumble upon them in the darkness. The claymores were out far enough that there was no extra wire left on the spools. When the LRRPs were done with the job, the mines covered every likely avenue of approach, and Files began to relax.

It was late when the LRRPs finished their evening meal. Everyone had settled down by then, but no one was really tired. Each team leader posted a one-man guard detail from his team on watch for one hour at a time.

Around 2200 hours, the LRRPs heard movement upstream, about forty to sixty meters from their perimeter. It sounded as if a number of people were moving through the brush. They seemed to be moving slowly and deliberately, almost as if they were trying to avoid making any noise, but not really aware that anyone was listening. Files recalled that the official cease-fire was still in effect, and made up his mind that he would not initiate contact unless the enemy stumbled into their perimeter.

After a while, the sounds seemed to fade away. Then suddenly, they began hearing more noises seemingly from everywhere at once. Files couldn't be positive that the latter sounds were not just the result of an overactive imagination and the stress of the mission. However, he had no choice but to assume they had been compromised. Reluctantly, he woke up the entire team and put them on full alert for the rest of the night.

Sometime around 2330 hours, the movement began once again, this time coming from thirty meters upstream, right at the point where the trail crossed the stream. Suddenly, the other team, set up on the foot of the L, opened up with intense small-arms fire, then set off a couple of their claymores. There had been no warning, just the sudden response to something Cobra One-three had not seen.

The patrol immediately began taking sporadic small-arms

fire from somewhere across the creek, forty to fifty meters away. The enemy fire was very inaccurate, but the LRRPs responded anyway, firing at the muzzle flashes. They couldn't tell for certain just how many enemy soldiers were out there, but the other team had already reported that it had seen several of them moving down through the stream crossing.

Files radioed in the contact, but did not immediately ask for an extraction. The patrol was more than holding its own for the moment, and there was still a question as to the size and commitment of the enemy force they were facing.

Files told his men to stop firing and to use hand grenades. This seemed to quiet down the enemy fire. During lulls in the shooting, however, the patrol could still hear movement up the stream near the trail crossing and on the far side of the water.

During one of the lulls, Callahan heard movement out to his front. Grabbing for his claymore detonator, he squeezed the trigger and nothing happened. He did it again and again, still nothing. It was almost midnight.

At that time, the team was informed that extraction ships were on the way. By then the enemy fire had died to almost nothing. There was still some occasional fire, but it was passing high overhead.

After a while, Files told his teammates to retrieve any claymores that had not yet been blown. Each man who went outside his perimeter to recover his claymore was covered by another LRRP watching from the edge of the shelf. Finally, after all the mines had been recovered, it was discovered that the wire to Callahan's had been cut cleanly in two.

Files instructed everyone to prepare to move out toward the PZ. After they crossed the creek, the ten LRRPs moved in file along the edge of the PZ weaving in and out among the trees to avoid making targets of themselves.

Suddenly, a pair of Huey gunships arrived on station and radioed the patrol to mark their position with a strobe light.

As soon as the patrol had circled up and complied, the gunships began prepping the tree line around the PZ. There was no return fire from the enemy. It was 0030 hours.

The first slick that arrived on the scene landed twenty meters from the team. The aircraft's rotor wash immediately raised a blinding black cloud of ash that reduced the patrol's visibility to three or four feet. Files shouted for his team to provide security while the other team ran across the open field and struggled aboard the waiting chopper, which quickly turned toward the river and lifted out. It drew no enemy fire.

Soon the second chopper came over the trees, about fifty meters to the right of Cobra One-three. It was about fifty feet above the ground, and just beginning to suck up clouds of dark ash into its rotor wash, when something that looked like a giant sparkler rose out of the woods away from the edge of the clearing, and flew straight up at the aircraft.

The RPG rocket hit the chopper in the nose bubble but failed to explode. However, the impact still managed to do its share of damage. The patrol had been up and moving as the chopper was flaring in. They had been on a dead run out into the clearing when they had spotted the RPG round. The first noise they heard was the sound of something huge displacing air as it whirled back over the top of them. They didn't realize that the Huey's rotor blade had just missed them.

At the same time, Callahan was suddenly hit hard in the chest and hurled backward. Thinking he had been shot, he lay there trying to gather his thoughts when Berry stopped next to him and said, "Are you okay?"

Callahan looked up but didn't answer. The Huey's turbine was still whining thirty meters away. Berry suddenly chuckled and said, "It's a radio. You got hit by a damn radio. Are you okay?"

Callahan answered, "I think so," then got back to his feet and started moving again.

The LRRPs still couldn't see anything, but now they knew

something was definitely wrong. Files yelled, "The chopper's down. Form up a perimeter around the chopper."

There was no small-arms fire coming from the enemy at that time. The two gunships, seeing that the chase ship had gone down, moved in close and pasted the woods until they were out of ordnance.

The blinding ash cloud finally began to clear, and everyone began to smell the unmistakable odor of JP-4. The chopper's fuel tank was leaking, and the revving turbine could ignite it at any minute.

The team was still trying to form up in a perimeter, when suddenly, a broken specterlike figure emerged from out of the ashy cloud, stumbling around in a daze. As one, the LRRPs raised their weapons to fire, only to recognize the one-piece flight suit of an army aviator. It was the pilot, and he was missing his left arm just below the elbow.

One of the LRRPs quickly grabbed him and pulled him down to the ground, where he could attempt to stop the bleeding.

Files shouted, "There are people in the chopper. We've got to get them out."

Callahan and Berry rushed to the chopper and tried in vain to get the unconscious copilot out. They managed to get his harness off and were pulling him out when suddenly someone was standing behind them waving a pistol and screaming, "Get away from him! Get away from him!" The two LRRPs froze in place.

Files materialized behind the man and quickly got him in a rear headlock, then grabbed the pistol away. Wasting no time in argument, he dragged the dazed door gunner back toward where the pilot was being treated.

By then everyone was trying to get away from the chopper because of the leaking fuel. Berry and Callahan were dragging the copilot back to where the rest of the team was set up thirty or forty feet away. At that point, the door gunner recovered enough to shout, "We're missing a man."

Moments later, they could hear someone back in the vicinity of the wreck moaning; then the sound started building until the man was screaming and pleading for someone to get him out of there.

At about that time the patrol began taking sporadic small-arms fire from seventy meters away. Some of the rounds were hitting the chopper.

More gunships finally arrived and began firing up the surrounding tree lines. Under the protection of the cover fire, Files and Berry leaped to their feet and ran back to the wreckage to look for the crew chief. The chopper was lying on its left side, and they soon located the badly wounded man pinned beneath the helicopter. The bottom edge of the cabin floor had badly broken both of the crewman's legs.

The two LRRPs yelled back that they needed a shovel to dig him out. Miraculously, someone came up with an entrenching tool from the wreckage. Files began digging madly while Berry struggled to pull the wounded man free. The two men somehow managed to drag the crew chief—by then unconscious—back to the perimeter that the rest of the team had formed in the open clearing. Drifting in and out of consciousness, he was in bad shape and still in a great deal of pain. It was nearly 0130 hours.

About the same time that Files and Berry were rescuing the crew chief, the sky above them was suddenly full of helicopters. As many as six gunships, including a pair of newly arrived Cobras, were firing up the perimeter of the PZ, including the shallow ridge back across the river. There was no return fire.

Suddenly, a Cobra landed out in the middle of the pickup zone about sixty meters away. Once again, the cloud of ash destroyed visibility. Undaunted by his temporary blindness, the Cobra pilot fired a three-second burst from his minigun directly into the trees across the field at ground level. Satisfied with his handiwork, the pilot then lifted back into the night sky and disappeared.

Files was now in radio contact with the commander of the aviation assets circling over the crash site. He quickly gave the colonel a sitrep and called for an emergency medevac. Seconds later, the C & C aircraft set down forty meters back from the wrecked Huey, and the colonel radioed Files and ordered him to strip the downed chopper of its machine guns, radios, and SOI code book and put the stuff aboard his helicopter.

While four of the LRRPs were following the colonel's orders, a single medevac landed in the middle of the field. In seconds, the medic and crew chief got out of the aircraft and ran over to where Devlin was still treating the wounded, and with his help they loaded the injured on board.

The team took a full five minutes to accomplish their mission. By that time the wrecked aircraft's turbine had stopped running. Without a word of thanks or appreciation, the colonel signaled his pilot to get him out of there.

Several minutes later, another slick landed to pick up the team. By then, most of the ash had been sucked out of the area and visibility immediately after the landing was much better. It was now 0200 hours.

When Cobra One-three landed back at Long Binh, the detachment first sergeant was waiting with a driver and a three-quarter-ton truck to pick up the team. In the back of the truck was a full cooler of ice-cold beer. Top never forgot anything! The TOC and the LRRPs back at the compound had heard that the second chopper had gone down after picking up the team. Naturally they had assumed that everyone had died. There would be rejoicing at the LRRP compound over Cobra One-three's sudden resurrection.

The patrol tried to unwind during the short ten-minute trip back to their compound. The beer helped, but it wasn't enough. When they finally reached it, they dropped their gear and were met briefly by their CO, First Lieutenant White, who welcomed them back and complimented them on the job they had done. The officer then told the first sergeant to take them to the mess hall, where the cooks had been alerted to have sandwiches ready.

Lieutenant White and the detachment XO, Lieutenant Brown, debriefed Files at that time. When they had finished, they notified the rest of the team to get cleaned up and get some sleep. There would be a full briefing at the S-2 first thing in the morning.

During the briefing the next morning, the aviation staff were there and quickly got involved in the investigation, trying to claim that the pilot had been at fault and was responsible for the crash of the Huey the night before. The LRRPs present were outraged at their callous attempt to railroad the courageous pilot and his crew. To a man, the LRRPs stood their ground and stated that they had seen the aircraft take a direct hit from an RPG rocket just prior to the crash. The aviation officers, frustrated by the LRRPs' attempt to counter their own findings, demanded that the LRRPs put their statements in writing, which they quickly did.

Every LRRP on Team Cobra One-three filed a written affidavit to support and exonerate the pilot. It was a well-established fact that LRRPs loved and respected their pilots. They knew to whom they owed their allegiance and their lives.

LRRP, B-36,
5th Special Forces
Group (Airborne)

Utilizing six-man LRRP teams from the army's 1st, 9th, and 25th divisions, 11th Armored Cavalry Regiment, and 199th Light Infantry Brigade, Detachment B-36 had been conducting recon and prisoner snatch missions throughout western III Corps since 5 September 1967. Calling the venture Rapid Fire I, B-36 worked these army recon teams alone or in conjunction with twenty-man hatchet teams made up of Cambodian Khmer Serei volunteers led by Special Forces personnel. The operation was under direct command of II Field Force and was to provide direct intelligence on enemy units operating in the III Corps Tactical Zone to II Field Force and to any other U.S. commands in the area.

The 25th Infantry Division had recently sent down a request to B-36 for a special reconnaissance patrol to check out Recon Zone I-99, an expanse of high ground that overlooked the Saigon River. The enemy had launched a series of 140mm rocket attacks against the division's base camp at Tay Ninh, and the Tropic Lightning G-2 suspected that the rockets were being fired from somewhere inside RZ I-99; the recon team was to find out.

S.Sgt. Dallas Pridemore was given the mission on 14 September. Although he was given carte blanche to put together the best six-man team he could find from within the unit, he was not given the usual amount of time to prepare for the mission. He called Sgt. David Spencer into the TOC for a short conference.

Spencer was a veteran LRRP who had been an assistant team leader on a number of hatchet missions under Special Forces sergeant Frank Polk. He was no stranger to combat. Pridemore told Spencer about the mission, then asked him if he would be willing to serve as assistant team leader on the patrol. Spencer had just returned from a hairy hatchet mission during which Sergeant Polk had been medevacked, so the young ATL was looking for something a little "different" to settle his nerves. He quickly accepted Pridemore's offer.

Pridemore also selected Bill Miller, an eighteen-year-old LRRP who was a teenager in spirit; Patrick Wesson, a nineteen-year-old veteran going on thirty; and two Cambodians whom the LRRPs affectionately called Old Man and Big Cowboy. They were older than the Americans they were going out with, but they were completely loyal and could be counted on to perform well in a tight situation.

Pridemore and Spencer sat down over the map overlays of their RZ and preplotted a number of artillery concentrations. One was at a trail junction, another on a loop in a creek, and a third at the intersection of two grid lines on the map. When they finished, Pridemore told his new assistant team leader to meet him down at the chopper pad at 1400 hours to accompany him on the overflight.

The overflight was flown that afternoon high above War Zone C. It was a single, slow pass over the team's AO, but it confirmed that their RZ was a heavily jungled area with but a single LZ where they wanted to go in. That was bad news for the patrol. Isolated LZs in heavily used VC/NVA areas were almost always watched by the enemy; they would probably have to shake trackers right after their insertion.

It was actually a little chilly down on the chopper pad before dawn the next day when Pridemore gave his teammates a last-minute equipment check-over, then ordered everyone to climb aboard the lift ship. The pilot lifted off the tarmac and headed north toward the team's RZ. It wasn't long before the pilot looked back over his shoulder and gave the team leader the signal that they were approaching the LZ.

The aircraft banked sharply, at the same time losing altitude as it neared the clearing. Finally, the helicopter was hovering just above the ground in a thin spot in the middle of the jungle that didn't look nearly as open or nearly as large as it had on the overflight. But it was enough to get the team in and the chopper out.

The six LRRPs were out in seconds and sprinting for the nearest tree line. As the sounds of the departing helicopter faded in the distance, the patrol reached the cover of the trees and dropped to the ground in a tight defensive circle. The six men lay there at the edge of the jungle, watching and listening. If enemy soldiers were in the vicinity of the clearing, the two Cambodians would pick up on it.

Finally, hearing and seeing nothing to alarm them, Pridemore decided that his team had gotten in undetected. He called in a commo check on the radio and reported a negative sitrep to the TOC. Signing off, he signaled his teammates to move out, with Big Cowboy at point and Miller walking his slack. Pridemore moved into the three slot, followed by Old Man carrying the PRC-25 radio, then Wesson, and Spencer back at drag.

Seventy meters from the LZ, Big Cowboy and Old Man began hissing and motioning for the LRRPs to drop down. They had sensed some kind of danger, although the Americans had seen and heard nothing. Squatting in a circle, facing outward, the six LRRPs waited breathlessly, listening and watching.

Within seconds, two VC appeared from the direction of the landing zone. They were only about fifty meters away and moving quickly. The men crossed the patrol's back trail, going diagonally from the team's right rear to their left front. The four Americans and two Cambodians watched as the enemy soldiers disappeared into the thick jungle less than thirty meters away.

Ten minutes later, Pridemore gave the signal to move out again. As one, the six LRRPs rose from the cover they had been hiding in and continued their patrol. But before they could take a step, Old Man looked back at Spencer and silently mouthed VC, then pointed in the direction where the two enemy soldiers had disappeared. When he turned and pointed to the rear and repeated his signal, Spencer understood that there were VC in front of the team and behind it.

Big Cowboy stepped out, leading the patrol gingerly through the jungle. Everything went well for the next two hours, until Old Man informed the rest of the team by sign language that they were still being followed. He indicated that their tracker was a single individual, and he was close.

The team held up and set out security while they held a brief conference to decide the best course of action. After discussing several possibilities, the decision was made for Spencer to hang back as the team moved out in hopes that the VC tracker would blunder into him.

Spencer found a spot in the brush next to the trail and lay prone facing the team's back trail. As he listened to the patrol moving away from him, he felt a momentary pang of fear that he was being abandoned. Thankfully, that passed in a second, and he refocused on the task before him. He had a man to kill, preferably with a single, well-placed shot. He only hoped Old Man had been right about there being only one VC on their tail.

Fifteen minutes later, no one had yet appeared, and Spencer had to give up and rejoin the patrol. He slipped silently out of his ambush site and eased cautiously back up the trail. He knew that the rest of the team would be waiting not far away, yet he was still caught off guard when he pushed aside some brush and found himself looking down the barrel of Old Man's M-16.

After Spencer whispered that he had seen and heard nothing, Old Man indicated that he felt the VC was still back there. He was so certain that the Americans couldn't help but believe him. Spencer realized that the VC trail watcher had to be good. He knew that the VC had not gotten close enough to spot him where he lay in wait, yet somehow the man had sensed that he was there and had intentionally held back. It was going to be tough to shake him.

Pridemore kept the team in position for nearly fifteen minutes more, hoping that the VC would make a mistake and close the distance. It was only when both Big Cowboy and Old Man expressed their views with hand signals and head shakes that Pridemore realized the trail watcher was not taking the bait. It was time to get moving; the longer they waited in one place, the more time additional enemy troops had to close in on them.

As they continued patrolling through the jungle, it soon became apparent that something was missing. There was nowhere in War Zone C where so much ground could be covered without encountering an enemy trail crisscrossing through the jungle. They might not all be in active use, but they were there, just the same. But there were no signs of trails, recent or old, anywhere in their recon zone, even though they knew there were VC all around them.

It was almost noon when they reached a fairly large stream. The waterway was nearly twenty meters wide and bordered on both sides by high muddy banks. The bank on their side and a good portion of the opposite bank were covered with dense stands of bamboo. Much of the bamboo had fallen over into the sluggish stream, choking the area near the shoreline. The LRRPs could see that the fallen bamboo would make crossing the stream difficult. And there was no doubt among them that they had to cross the stream. Their patrol route dictated their passage through the RZ on an azimuth of 130 degrees. Unfortunately, the stream in front of them flowed directly across their path, and if they did not cross the stream they would be unable to cover the southern half of their recon zone.

Big Cowboy and Miller slid down the steep bank into the stream as their teammates provided security behind them and across the stream. They slowly waded across the slow-moving current, getting hung up momentarily in the submerged bamboo, then fought their way through and up the opposite bank. When they were safe on the far side of the stream and providing security, Pridemore and Old Man slipped into the water and followed them across, while Spencer guarded their back trail and Wesson watched both flanks.

After the first four LRRPs had successfully traversed the stream, Pridemore signaled for Spencer and Wesson to cross. Without waiting, Spencer stepped in with Wesson right behind him. The two LRRPs were surprised at how chilly the water was.

As they crossed, they struggled through the bamboo on the near shore as the water reached up to their chests. Spencer noticed that Wesson was having difficulty getting through the bamboo, and soon he was stuck. The assistant team leader turned back to help him, only to have Wesson whisper to him to go on.

"That's not the way it works," Spencer whispered back, as he continued to struggle through the water. He reached out his hand to Wesson, and soon the trapped LRRP was able to extricate himself and continue across the stream. The two men made it to the opposite shore and rejoined their companions.

Pridemore decided that this was a good place to take a break. With the stream at their backs, their pursuers would have to expose themselves to cross it. This would leave them vulnerable to the patrol's fire and also give the LRRPs a running start if they had to escape and evade. Pridemore signaled for Wesson to watch the team's right flank, where the stream disappeared around a bend. He placed Big Cowboy to the patrol's front while Miller watched their left flank. Spencer and Old Man faced the far side of the stream while Pridemore cranked up the radio to call in a sitrep.

After the team leader had finished his commo chores, he

turned around and whispered for his teammates that it was okay to eat. Spencer pulled a dehydrated LRRP ration from his pack and added the appropriate amount of water, then set the meal aside to wait for it to rehydrate. He had just looked up to take another peek at the opposite shore when Old Man's hiss caught his attention. The Cambodian was jabbing at his temple with his right finger and muttering something about VC. He then motioned for Spencer to slide over to one side behind a large tree nearby. When Spencer complied, Old Man seemed both relieved and satisfied.

So that was it! The old Khmer was uncomfortable with the team's ATL sitting out in the open. But from his new location Spencer could no longer see anything across the river unless he shifted around and poked his head out from behind the tree. That bothered him, but not as much as did his noticing that Old Man was staring intently down their back trail, a worried look on his face.

Finally, Spencer's LRRP ration had sat long enough to be palatable. The assistant team leader looked around before chowing down, and saw that the other LRRPs were dividing their time between eating and observing their zones of security—everyone, that is, except Old Man, who was still staring into the jungle on the opposite side of the stream. Spencer nodded, then held out his LRRP ration to him, but the Cambodian only smiled his tight-lipped smile, squinted, then shook his head.

Everyone had just finished eating when Spencer saw Old Man's expression change. A split second later, cursing in Cambodian, he was on his feet charging toward the stream and firing a long burst across the water. As Spencer turned to support Old Man, return fire from the far side of the stream slammed into the tree that he was hiding behind. The ATL slid out to the edge of the tree and tried to open fire, only to discover that his selector switch was frozen on Safe!

He slipped back behind the tree, pulled out a spare maga-zine, and was using it to pound the selector switch over to

Fire, when enemy rounds began coming through the trees from their front. Immediately, Big Cowboy and Pridemore began firing at the muzzle flashes blinking in the bamboo to their southeast. Pausing to jam home a fresh magazine, Pridemore yelled for Old Man to bring him the radio.

Old Man was firing into the jungle across the stream, yet he managed to roll onto his side, grab the handset, and hand it to Pridemore without pausing. It was an incredible example of the Cambodian's coolness under fire, but it would almost go unnoticed in the middle of the raging battle.

Pridemore lay flat on the ground, calling in the contact to the TOC. Because of the heavy firing going on around him, he could hardly hear the voice on the other end of the line. Big Cowboy and Miller were keeping the enemy pinned down in the bamboo to their front as Wesson fired across the creek, to the right of the team.

By then Spencer had freed the selector switch on his weapon and had joined the battle. Raising up on one knee, he began supporting Pridemore and Old Man as they chewed up the jungle on the other side of the stream. Suddenly, two rounds smacked into the tree just above Spencer's head. Old Man shouted something in Cambodian that Spencer failed to understand, then blasted the enemy soldier who had shot at the LRRP assistant team leader.

Spencer rolled hard to the right and came up on the other side of the tree. He spotted a number of shadowy figures flitting through the thick bamboo on the opposite shore and opened fire on them. The figures scattered, then fled to the west along the stream, leaving Spencer unsure if he had managed to hit any of them, or if he had even seen anything. On the other side of the tree, Old Man was still busy hosing down the jungle across the river.

Pridemore was back on the radio, still shouting to make himself heard over the sounds of gunfire. Suddenly, he turned to his teammates and screamed, "We're going to Maguire-rig out." He slapped Spencer's leg and yelled, "You go first."

Spencer shook his head. "Wesson and Miller should go first."

Pridemore disagreed, shouting, "You and Wesson go first."

Spencer knew that it was no time to argue; he quickly agreed.

Pridemore yelled, "Pop smoke!"

Spencer pulled the pin on a yellow smoke grenade and pitched it out along the team's back trail. The sulfur-colored cloud billowed around the team, staying close to the ground because of the dense bamboo.

Soon, the first slick arrived on the scene and spotted the smoke down among the trees. The aircraft commander worked the chopper in over the team, and the crew chief kicked out the weighted rigs as the other door gunner fired down into the jungle to keep the enemy's heads down.

Over the roar of the Huey and the sounds of battle, Spencer screamed for Wesson to get into one of the Maguire slings. Crawling on his belly, the young LRRP slipped his leg through the cargo strap and D-ringed his harness to the rope. Nearby, Spencer discovered that the ropes were tangled in a knot just above the loops. If the aircraft lifted out with the ropes snarled like that, the two LRRPs would be spun out of the rigs and tossed into the jungle.

While Pridemore, Miller, and the two Cambodians fought to hold back the enemy, Spencer worked to untangle the ropes. Ignoring the bullets whizzing past his head, the assistant team leader stood up to untie the final knot.

Above him in the helicopter, the bellyman, Wal Handwerk, was screaming for Spencer to cut the ropes. Spencer couldn't hear him, nor did he realize that the aircraft had been taking intense small-arms fire the entire time that Spencer was trying to untangle the rigs. Suddenly, the enemy found the target and their rounds began striking the chopper. Unable to wait any longer, Handwerk sliced through the ropes, letting them fall around Spencer, tangling him helplessly in their coils.

Spencer struggled free of the snarl just as Wesson was climbing out of his slackened Maguire rig. The two men looked to see what was happening around them, just in time to hear Pridemore shout, "We have to get to an LZ."

The team leader pointed toward the southwest, then looked back at Spencer and said, "You're on point."

Spencer grimaced, then flipped open the cover of his lensatic compass to shoot an azimuth. It led right across the bend in the stream. It was dangerous to try to recross the open stream under fire, but that was their closest route to an LZ. Spencer yelled for Wesson to follow him, then slid down the muddy embankment into the stream.

As he waded away from the shore, he suddenly was aware that Wesson had *not* followed behind him; he was still up on the bank firing across the water. Pridemore and Old Man were behind him, while Miller and Big Cowboy were hosing down the bamboo toward what was now their rear.

Suddenly, a large explosion erupted right at Spencer's feet, slamming him back hard against the mud embankment he had just slid down. Water and debris rained down around him and there was an intense pressure inside his eardrums, almost as if he'd been diving in deep water.

The dazed assistant team leader struggled to his feet, still trying to clear the cobwebs out of his head. With a sudden lunge, he lurched back out into the stream, intent only on reaching the bend fifty feet away. He only half noticed the water spouts kicking up to his right. They failed to have any real significance for him, other than that they didn't seem natural. Then he spotted tiny lights blinking madly on the edge of the jungle on the opposite shore. Instinctively, he raised his weapon and fired at the lights.

Above and behind him, Old Man and Wesson had also spotted the hidden VC and began blasting away at the bamboo that concealed him. Suddenly, a limp form detached itself from the shredded bamboo and tumbled headfirst into the water. Spencer saw the body of the dead VC submerge beneath the surface of the stream, but in his state of mind didn't really recognize it for what it was.

No longer seeing the blinking lights, Spencer continued wading toward the bend in the river. When he finally reached the far shore, he crawled out of the water and lay half submerged at the bottom of the embankment, sucking air into his lungs.

By that time, his head had cleared somewhat, and he was acutely aware that he was taking fire. He raised his weapon and began to fire back as he climbed the slope and struggled to get through the dense bamboo. Seconds later, he broke out of the bamboo and into a large clearing on the other side. He was at the LZ!

Spencer turned to cover the area to the southeast as the first of his teammates began climbing the bank behind him. He hesitated for a moment when he suddenly spotted a strip of tiger-stripe camouflage backing away from the river, thinking it was one of his teammates. Then Big Cowboy blasted the area, and it was gone.

The six LRRPs quickly withdrew to the center of the clearing, where they continued their intense fire into the surrounding jungle. They popped another yellow smoke grenade to mark their new position, and ducked low as a pair of Huey gunships moved in to rake the jungle around them. While the gunships kept the VCs' heads down, the LRRPs' extraction ship slipped in and recovered the patrol.

The team's debriefing back at the TOC didn't take long. They had failed in their mission to locate the enemy rocket launchers, but they had managed to verify that the enemy was there in force and was monitoring potential landing zones. That bit of information alone might save the lives of other recon teams assigned to infiltrate the area in the future.

LRRP Detachment, 196th Light Infantry Brigade

When General Westmoreland gave the final go-ahead for the formation of provisional LRRP units in Vietnam, he failed to provide for the equipping and manning of those units. And most of the parent organizations quickly learned to resent the drain of their best people into the newly formed LRRP units. The commanders of the individual line units began throwing up roadblocks to impede the loss of their superstars.

Likewise, the first recruits in the long-range reconnaissance units quickly discovered that cooperation in obtaining the supplies and equipment they needed to carry out their mission was as hard to come by as qualified personnel.

The 196th Light Infantry Brigade LRRP detachment recruited its first members by posting notices for volunteers on line company bulletin boards. From the initial batch of recruits, twelve men were selected and immediately sent to MACV Recondo School at Nha Trang for training. Among those first graduates was young Sp4. Vic Valeriano, the son of a career U.S. Army intelligence officer who happened to be stationed at the U.S. embassy in Saigon in 1966.

When Valeriano graduated from Recondo School, he wrangled a couple of days in Saigon with two of his buddies before they had to return to the 196th LRRP compound in Tay Ninh. Naturally, the first place Valeriano went was to visit his father. During the course of their conversation, the young LRRP happened to mention the difficulty he and his comrades had obtaining the necessary equipment and supplies needed to run long-range reconnaissance patrols.

Colonel Valeriano was a father before he was an officer, and he listened sympathetically as his son explained the kind of equipment they needed. When young Vic had finished, Colonel Valeriano told him to wait while he made a phone call. A short time later, a middle-aged lieutenant of Cuban ancestry arrived at the embassy. When Colonel Valeriano introduced the officer, he explained that the man had participated in the Bay of Pigs invasion before becoming a supply officer in the U.S. Army. At that time, he was in charge of food items at the docks in Saigon.

Before long, Vic had the vouchers and paperwork needed to "legally" raid every warehouse along the river. Over the next two days, the three LRRPs filled the colonel's jeep and a large number of Saigon taxis with enough gear to outfit four LRRP detachments. All of the "appropriated" items were courtesy of the 1st Infantry Division. In addition, the young LRRPs finagled their way into a "special" Special Forces warehouse and got away with vast quantities of the highly regarded South Vietnamese indigenous rations.

When they finally managed to arrange for shipment of all the "reallocated" items to the LRRP compound, they became the most popular guys in the company. And the 196th LRRPs became the best-equipped long-range recon patrollers in Vietnam.

By early 1967, the 196th LRRP detachment was barely a full platoon. Under the able command of 1st Lt. John Maxwell, the unit had been attached to F Troop, 1/17th Cav, a mechanized reconnaissance unit running APCs and gun jeeps. When the brigade left its permanent base camp at Tay Ninh and deployed to an AO along the Cambodian border during Operation Junction City I, the LRRPs went with them.

On 19 February 1967, S.Sgt. Robert Weber's team was ordered to participate in a battalion-size infantry sweep right up against the Cambodian border near the Parrot's Beak area of South Vietnam. Carrying camouflage clothing and boonie hats inside their rucks, the six-man patrol was to go in with a line company wearing OD fatigues and helmets. When the line unit reached the border, it was to pivot around and return to their jump-off point while the six-man LRRP patrol remained behind, hidden in dense cover nearby.

The mission was scheduled to go in on 20 February, and there was no time for an overflight. During the briefing, Weber learned that the terrain in the area was level to rolling with a lot of single and double canopy. The area along the border was more open, covered in broadleaf plants, high grass, and scrub brush.

Their mission was to monitor the area for enemy units suspected to be infiltrating South Vietnam from across the border. The patrol was scheduled to last three days and would enjoy clear and warm weather the entire time.

On the twentieth, the alert team left the forward fire-support base with the line company as planned. The LRRPs were not used to the OD fatigues and heavy M-1 helmets, and joked about it among themselves. Fortunately, there were no incidents during the sweep. When the line doggies reached the border around 1630 hours, they took their time turning around and sweeping back toward their base. S.Sgt. Earl Twoomey, the LRRPs' acting operations NCO, was along on the sweep with two other LRRPs. During the time it took for the line company to reverse its line of march, Weber and his teammates had dropped off into some thick cover twenty-five meters from the border. Quickly stripping off their OD fatigues and helmets, the six LRRPs passed them over to Twoomey and his two comrades, who shoved them inside their rucksacks and moved out with the rest of the grunts. The six LRRPs quickly applied camouflage face paint to their faces, necks, and hands, then sat back to lay dog. They planned to remain in place for an hour or so until the line company cleared the area, then move out in the gathering dusk to locate a suitable OP.

As the line company neared the border region, the six LRRPs spotted a large number of barely discernible trails scattered throughout the area. The trails crossed back and forth over the border.

The team was set up in a patch of thick scrub brush. As it began to grow dark, they were preparing to move out when they heard voices in Vietnamese on the other side of the border about a hundred meters away. Weber and his assistant team leader, Sp4. Vic Valeriano, discussed the situation and decided to split the team into two separate OPs because of the large number of trails in the area. Selecting two secondary trails that ran along the border and intersected a large primary trail that crossed the border not far from their position, the two men agreed to set up OPs as close to the trail intersections as they could safely get. In case either element needed support, they would be less than twenty-five meters apart. Since the team leader and the assistant team leader each carried his own PRC-25 radio, they would still be able to communicate with each other by radio.

Weber took his point man, Sp4. Bill Connor, and his rear security, PFC Paul Rosselli, with him and set up an OP in the brush five meters back off the intersection farthest from the border. Valeriano moved into the brush near the intersection closest to the border. With him were Sp4. Mike McMahon, the team's slack man, and PFC Mark Brennan.

Weber and Valeriano set up their teams in tight, in a straight line along the main trail, with the secondary trails to their right. Since they were so close to the trail, they decided not to put out their claymores. Their plan was to spend the night in those positions, then move to a new location just after dawn.

Around 1800 hours, it was beginning to grow dark. Valeriano told his two teammates to catch some sleep while he took the first four-hour watch. He promised to wake Brennan at 2200 hours. It didn't take long for the two LRRPs to fall asleep.

However, minutes later, less than five feet away, nine Main Force VC suddenly walked past Valeriano's position. Before he could wake his teammates or signal Weber on the radio, the VC had already passed his site. They were walking rapidly and in total silence. They had approached in the growing darkness without making a sound. It was still light enough that Valeriano could tell that the VC wore soft caps and had weapons slung over their shoulders.

When he was certain that the enemy soldiers were well out of range, he quickly woke his two teammates and told them about the sighting. He decided to signal Weber's element, using the prearranged radio squelch code to communicate. The two men decided to form back up again, setting up in a circle at Valeriano's position, where there was better cover.

Behind Valeriano was a wide area of massive broadleaf plants. The huge plants were hollow around their centers, which made an excellent place to hide. After linking up again, the six LRRPs moved fifteen meters farther back from the trail, and set up in a circular wagon-wheel defensive perimeter inside one of the large bushes. They once again decided not to put out their claymores. With VC on the prowl, Weber kept everyone on 100 percent alert. There would be no sleeping that night.

At about 2130 hours, the recon team heard movement and voices all around them. They could make out the sounds of footsteps out on the trail, brush being moved about, and metal clinking against metal. Before they realized what was happening, a large enemy unit had set up a cold camp in the brush all around the team's position. In minutes, the enemy soldiers had their food out and were busy eating. Weber and Valeriano had no idea how long the enemy soldiers would remain in the area.

The full moon had been slowly rising in the night sky. By 2230 hours, it was nearing its zenith, and the bright moonlight was shining directly down on the LRRPs' perimeter. Inside the bush, the six recon men were uncomfortably aware of just how bright it had become—Weber could read his map without the use of a penlight—and began to worry about being spotted by the enemy troops moving silently around them. He also noticed that the faded jungle boots worn by the LRRPs stood out like white, ankle-length gym shoes. Something had to be done. With a full platoon of Main Force VC scattered around them, some less than five meters away, it was only a matter of time before someone stumbled across the LRRPs.

Weber and Valeriano literally put their heads together to discuss their options. They didn't have many. Valeriano recommended that if they were compromised and had to shoot their way out, their best bet was to escape and evade into Cambodia, in the same direction from which the enemy soldiers had come. The VC would never expect the Americans to do that.

The two long-range patrol leaders decided that at the first sound of gunfire, Weber would take the lead and break for the border, while Valeriano and Rosselli held back to cover the team and make sure everyone got out. Once they were sure no one had been left behind, the two LRRPs would make their own escape. Weber selected a tall tree standing alone about twenty meters on the other side of the border as their initial rally point.

Satisfied that their plan was the best one available to them, they sat back to wait for the inevitable contact. While they were waiting, Weber alerted the TOC about their situation and called in a number of artillery preplots around the immediate area.

About 0330 hours, two VC stood up and began walking toward the bush hiding the Rangers. They approached the thick patch of cover and began to step inside, about to trip over Brennan and Connor, when the two LRRPs opened fire at point-blank range. They fired three rounds each on semi-auto, dropping the two VC.

The team leaped to their feet and went into their immediate-action drill, busting out of the brush and firing all around them on full automatic. As enemy soldiers recoiled from the sudden onslaught, they stumbled around in confusion, not sure of what was happening.

Weber, McMahon, Brennan, and Connor took advantage of the enemy's confusion to dart across the dirt road that ran along the border. Crossing the shallow ditch and running up the fifteen-foot berm on the other side, they made straight for the lone tree standing just ahead.

Behind them, Valeriano and Rosselli were getting ready to bring up the rear, emptying their magazines into the milling enemy soldiers. When the two LRRPs saw that everyone had gotten away, they began lobbing frag grenades into the brush. Each man tossed three frags, making sure that they landed in a 180-degree fan behind them.

As the grenades began detonating in the brush, the two LRRPs broke across the road and followed their teammates. Valeriano and Rosselli leaped the ditch and hit the berm running full tilt, expecting at any moment to hear the sounds of small-arms fire erupting behind them or to feel the impact of enemy bullets striking them in the back. But the VC had been slow to recover, and the two-man rear guard was able to make it into the thick cover back away from the road.

When they reached the tree, they found their teammates already set up in a defensive box, awaiting their arrival.

The ground on the Cambodian side of the border was slightly higher than on the Vietnamese side. In the bright moonlight, the LRRPs could easily observe their old NDP. They waited several minutes, watching and listening, but they could not see or hear any movement coming from the other side. However, they did hear the sounds of men running, but it was fading in the distance as the VC disappeared into the jungles of South Vietnam.

Using the preplotted artillery concentrations, Weber began calling in fire missions, and the first rounds impacted right on target. However, they were also hitting very close to the LRRPs—far too close for comfort. Weber kept raining fire on the enemy for what seemed like forever, but was probably no more than ten or fifteen minutes.

The LRRP team remained around the tree, about twenty meters into Cambodia, for the remainder of the night because the single-canopy trees and lush vegetation were much better concealment than that available on the other side of the border.

About 150 meters away, the Rangers could see an abandoned guard shack at the end of the road. They had spotted it earlier in the mission, but from the Vietnamese point of view. After a while, Weber finally decided that they had successfully broken contact. However, they still had the problem of not being able to extract during the night.

The action ended at 0230 hours. The team remained where they were for the rest of the night. At daylight, the TOC radioed the team that it had decided to pull them out as soon as possible. Weber radioed back that that was fine by him.

At 0530, a slick and a single gunship arrived on the scene and came right in. The patrol had left their PZ and moved twenty-five meters back across the road into Vietnam. As the helicopters approached, Weber held up a strobe light to mark the LZ.

The patrol still had to move another twenty-five meters out into the open scrub brush as the Huey hovered just above the ground. The team broke cover and climbed into the aircraft, boarding on the right side of the helicopter.

A short time later, they returned to the fire-support base where brigade had established its forward HQ. Brigadier General Knowles, the commanding officer of the 196th Light Infantry Brigade, was there and he debriefed the team, then congratulated them for keeping cool in a bad situation.

A *New York Times* news correspondent named Don Oberdorffer was also present. Afterward, he requested permission to interview the team. The *Times* ran the story on the front page a couple of weeks later. Brennan's father happened to read the article and sent a copy to his son. For a little while, Weber's team enjoyed the good-natured harassment that went along with fleeting fame. After all, they were the best-equipped long-range recon patrollers in Vietnam.

☆ ☆ ☆ ☆ ☆

LRRP Detachment, 9th Infantry Division

In the fall of 1966, troops of the 9th Infantry Division, stationed at Fort Riley, Kansas, knew they were Vietnam bound. The arrival in country of the 1st Marine Division, the 173d Airborne Brigade (Separate), the 1st Brigade of the 101st Airborne Division, and the 1st Cavalry Division during 1965 heralded an escalation of U.S. military forces that would continue unabated until 1968.

In preparation for its own combat role in Indochina, the 9th Division responded to Gen. William Westmoreland's call for the formation of long-range reconnaissance patrols within all army brigades and divisions arriving in Vietnam by establishing its own long-range reconnaissance patrol detachment.

The original volunteers for the newly formed unit shipped out to Panama in November 1966 to complete the Jungle Warfare School, at that time the only training outside of Vietnam realistic enough to prepare its graduates for the war in Indochina.

When the 9th Division arrived in Vietnam in January 1967, eleven members of the division LRRP detachment were sent immediately to Nha Trang to attend the recently established MACV Recondo School, conducted by 5th Special Forces Group. Upon graduation from the grueling course three weeks later, the 9th's LRRPs returned to their unit compound at Bearcat to conduct patrols throughout the division's area of operations.

259

On 8 July 1967, the 9th Infantry Division LRRP detachment, originally attached to Troop D, 3d Squadron, 5th Cavalry, was reassigned to HHC, 9th Infantry Division. At that time, the unit roster showed a detachment strength of ninety-five men.

The LRRPs of the 9th Infantry Division were assigned an area of operation unique to that of any other U.S. Army long-range reconnaissance patrol unit. Initially, the unit was assigned to patrol an area of operations southeast of Saigon, an immense expanse of relatively level terrain covered in dense triple-canopy jungle, broken only occasionally by vast rubber plantations and expansive rice paddies.

In that area, in mid-August 1967, a 9th Infantry Division LRRP team successfully conducted what can only be described as the classic long-range reconnaissance patrol.

It all began after a recent number of infrared contacts and positive sensor readings from a number of newly developed and highly sophisticated detection devices indicated the presence of "someone or something" in an area that had been recently "swept clean" by elements of the 9th Infantry Division's 1st Brigade. The area, located near the junction of Bien Hoa, Long Khanh, and Phuoc Toy provinces, was close enough to Saigon that a worried division headquarters decided to send in a long-range reconnaissance patrol to confirm the source of the sensor contacts.

Stretched dangerously thin with most of its assets out on patrol, the division's LRRP detachment had to scramble hard to put together a recon team to conduct the patrol. Led by the unit's first sergeant, M.Sgt. Roy Nelson, the team consisted of Sgt. Howard Munn, assistant team leader, Sp4. Tom Kloack at point, Sp4s. Hilan Jones and Jerry Fairweather as scouts. Given an unusually large AO, twenty-five square kilometers of nearly impenetrable jungle, every man on the team knew that they would have to break a lot of brush to cover their recon zone in the five days allotted for the patrol. To make things even more difficult, on the second day of the mission, heavy monsoon rains moved in over the team's area of operations and showed every intent of hanging around.

On the third day of the mission, 20 August 1967, Sp4. Kloack was moving along easily at point, taking advantage of the torrential monsoon rains that masked the team's noise, scent, and movement. The rains had proved an asset as far as concealment and stealth were concerned, but Kloack was acutely aware that the rains would also drive Charlie to cover, increasing the risk of a sudden, deadly confrontation caused by the team's walking into an enemy encampment without realizing the danger. However, the risk was worth it. The LRRP team still had a lot of tough ground to cover, and they were rapidly running out of time. They had been on the move since early morning. Everyone was soaked, and the skin on their feet was beginning to wrinkle and take on the color and consistency of the flesh of dead fish. Trench foot was becoming a real possibility.

The patrol had just moved across a low area covered with high, thick kunai grass and had started to move up a slight rise on the other side. Suddenly, the point man held up his clenched fist to stop the team, then pointed ahead toward a newly excavated trench system supported by a number of reinforced bunkers. There were signs everywhere indicating the area had been recently occupied. Raw earth and unweathered, fresh-cut logs made the emplacements easy to spot. The enemy complex was so new that it was immediately apparent that the VC had probably moved in right behind the 1st Brigade sweep, beginning construction of the camp even before the grunts had fully cleared the area.

Cautiously, in case they stumbled into something larger than they could handle, the five LRRPs continued moving up the slope. Five pairs of squinting eyes panned back and forth, searching the vegetation for the enemy soldiers they knew had to be somewhere nearby.

Soon the team found more bunkers, including a number of

aboveground equipment-storage caches, and finally they located a couple of tunnel entrances. The tension was building when Master Sergeant Nelson finally halted the team. Quietly, he alerted his people to fan out to provide security 360 degrees around their position, while he sent Kloack into one of the two tunnels. The LRRP point man soon reemerged and reported in hushed tones that he had discovered an underground rice cache big enough to feed one hell of a lot of VC for a very long time.

With the rain drowning out any sounds the team made, the five LRRPs continued to move farther up the gently sloping hill. As they reached the crest, Kloack slowly dropped to one knee and raised his hand, holding up two fingers. The rest of the patrol went to ground as the team leader, M.Sgt. Roy Nelson, moved cautiously up to the point man's side. Just ahead, partially concealed by thick ground fog, were the forms of two VC guards sitting under their ponchos with their backs up tight against a large tree, obviously riding out the pounding rain. The enemy soldiers seemed totally oblivious to the fact that they were being observed by a U.S. long-range reconnaissance patrol crouched less than twenty meters away.

Suddenly Nelson cursed himself under his breath for not realizing what the signs had meant. Uncamouflaged bunkers and trenches, equipment stored out in the open, raw earth and fresh-cut branches and logs, unguarded food caches—they all should have pointed to the fact that they were in the middle of a large enemy base camp currently under construction. And large enemy base camps meant enemy soldiers—large numbers of enemy soldiers somewhere nearby who would not take kindly to having their sanctuary invaded by an American reconnaissance patrol.

Nelson felt like a fool, but there was no time to kick himself at the moment. His patrol was in the middle of a hornets' nest, and its only chance for survival was to find a way out without disturbing the hornets.

But before the team could slip away from the area, the

driving rain began to diminish. It was only then that the five Americans heard the sounds of chopping and hammering coming from just over the crest of the hill. Not only was the camp occupied, but its occupants were active. It would be only a matter of time before the patrol was discovered.

Nelson had to do something immediately, or they would be finished. Slowly, he signaled for the team to withdraw. Moving obliquely away from the crest of the hill, the five soldiers crept cautiously back down the slope, keeping at right angles to their original route of approach. As they slipped carefully through the trees, they encountered more trenches and bunkers that seemed to be an extension of the same defensive perimeter they had penetrated on their way up the hill.

At the bottom of the rise near the southeast edge of the camp, the plot—and the tension—suddenly began to thicken. Just before them stood a wall of waist-high grass so dense that Kloack was certain he would be unable to penetrate it without making noise. Five men moving through it would sound like a marching band at the Rose Bowl parade. To bust through the grass while the rain was diminishing to a drizzle would surely alert every VC in the trees surrounding the grass that their secret base camp was no longer a secret.

At that point the gods of war decided once again to get behind the good guys. The sky suddenly opened up and the monsoon rains returned with unexpected fury. Since the heavy downpour would cover any sound the team made breaking through the grass, and it would also mask their movement from prying eyes above them, Nelson raised his weapon to port arms and pushed off into the grass. He wanted to get his team clear of the huge VC encampment before darkness set in and the camp's inhabitants moved into their night defensive positions.

The LRRPs avoided walking in column; instead they chose to "walk small" to avoid being noticed. With each step they took they expected to hear shouts of alarm raised at the discovery of the five trespassers moving through the VC encampment. Casting furtive glances to their left and right, through the fog and driving rain the Americans could see dim shadows and surreal forms moving back and forth among the trees. Even in the rain, the enemy was up and moving about. Some were as close as thirty to forty meters. It seemed like hours had passed before they were finally out of the grass and clear of the encampment.

After they had put a little distance between themselves and the VC base camp, Nelson stopped to shoot an azimuth toward a large open area known as JFK because of its size. It was still several klicks away, but it was the closest place within walking distance that could accommodate a night extraction without running the risk of having a chopper fly into a tree or the side of a hill.

Three nerve-racking hours later the team arrived at the edge of the immense clear-cut and was extracted without incident.

At the division G-2 debriefing, Master Sergeant Nelson was surprised and outraged to discover that his team's hard-earned intel was not only disputed but openly scoffed at by the division operations officer. The rear echelon major was quick to find fault. "You LRRPs are always bringing in bull-shit like this. There's no one out there. The 1st Brigade just swept through that AO."

Nelson was momentarily taken aback by the obvious insult to his team's integrity, but he was not some green buck sergeant. He was a master sergeant in the United States Army, and no rear echelon pencil pusher was going to challenge his credibility.

"Sir, I'll bet my stripes on it," he said, looking the officer right in the eye.

Smiling, overly sure of himself, the staff officer asked, "How many you got, Sarge?"

Nelson proudly answered, "Six, sir. I'm M.Sgt. Roy Nelson, the LRRP company first sergeant."

The staff officer, even though he now knew he was not dealing with some young recon team leader, was still hesitant to give in. "Sergeant Nelson, how could you be sure of your location when you reached the camp? I know that because of the weather, you had not received a single location fix during the two and a half days your team was in there, nor were there any overflights of your AO."

Nelson grinned. "Sir, I *always* knew where I was. I have never erred on a location during any of the long-range reconnaissance patrols that I have conducted. I consider myself an excellent judge of terrain and an expert map reader." During a previous tour in Germany, Nelson was the only individual to ever max the USAEUR map test.

Drawing detailed sketches of the VC base camp, Nelson smiled as he listened to division staff personnel go all the way to the top to get a B-52 Arc Light—at the time somewhere between Guam and South Vietnam en route to a target in II Corps—diverted to his team's previous recon zone.

Immediately after the subsequent Arc Light, the 2/39th Infantry Battalion and elements of the 11th Armored Cavalry Regiment assaulted back through the target area. During their three-day sweep, the U.S. soldiers made contact with substantial numbers of dazed enemy soldiers at least thirty times. In addition, more than seventy VC bodies were discovered slain outright by the Arc Light. Another thirty-three were killed during the remainder of the operation. In addition, thirteen AK-47 rifles, a number of RPG rocket launchers, a Chicom 7.62mm machine gun, an 82mm mortar tube, seventy-two hand grenades, over eleven thousand rounds of assorted small-arms ammo, miscellaneous rocket and mortar rounds, two base plates for 60mm mortars, a bipod for an 81mm mortar, twenty-three mortar fuses, fifteen cluster bomb units, fifteen homemade claymore mines, two protective masks, a typewriter, a Chicom field radio, two demolition kits, a Soviet flag, and twenty pounds of maps and documents were also recovered.

The enemy documents captured during the joint infantry/armored cavalry operation established that elements of the

1st and 3d Battalions of the 274th VC Regiment had been in the strike area.

The achievement of the 9th Division's long-range reconnaissance patrol in establishing the location of the VC base camp without itself being detected by the enemy was directly responsible for the completion of a very successful military operation. This ultimately resulted in two Main Force VC battalions, units that had just moved into the proximity of the Saigon/Bien Hoa/Long Binh military complex in preparation for the '68 Tet Offensive, being severely mauled while suffering the destruction of their base camp, all with no loss of American lives.

Company M, 75th Infantry (Ranger), 199th Light Infantry Brigade

Company M, 75th Ranger, was one of the smaller Ranger units of the Vietnam War. Never comprised of more than sixty personnel, the undersize company nevertheless performed excellent service protecting the northern approaches to Saigon. Operating with the added handicap of having no dedicated helicopter units to support its teams in the field, its patrols often found themselves stuck out in the bush waiting for a ride. It was an uncomfortable situation, which sometimes proved life threatening.

On 11 July 1970, Company M received a warning order for a three-day mission into a recon zone twenty klicks northwest of Bien Hoa. The company's main base camp was at Bien Hoa, but because of all the "Mickey Mouse BS" that went on in a military complex of that size, most of the teams had moved up to their forward operational base at Xuan Loc, staging for patrols out of there and also Fire Support Base Mace.

The team selected for the patrol consisted of nine men, seven U.S. Rangers and two ex-NVA *chieu hoi*s, a slightly larger team than a typical long-range reconnaissance patrol, but the mission had been scheduled in the middle of the southern monsoon season, and Company M's teams often found themselves extended in the field for additional periods of time. It was generally believed that the added manpower of a "heavy" team was a plus in case the patrol had to ride out the weather without outside support.

The team leader for the patrol was S.Sgt. William Sloyer. Sloyer was an experienced patrol leader, but a situation existed on his team that was highly unusual: two of Sloyer's teammates were career soldiers who, by U.S. Army standards, were long past the age considered acceptable for long-range patrolling. However, a strong application of the Uniform Code of Military Justice had reduced the two soldiers to ranks more befitting the younger men who typically carried out reconnaissance work behind enemy lines.

Sp5. Robert McBride was a thirty-five-year-old former first sergeant who had earned his CIB serving with the 82d Airborne Division in the Dominican Republic. Unfortunately, an unexplained incident in which he crashed a jeep into a senior officers' volleyball game saw him reduced several pay grades to E-5. However, the demotion subtracted nothing from the man's experience and leadership ability, which would prove a strong asset to Sloyer's patrol. McBride was such an outstanding commo man that he volunteered to carry the team's artillery radio and took care of directing their fire missions himself.

Sp4. Haynes was the other "bonus" Ranger on the team. Haynes was also a thirty-five-year-old Special Forces–qualified former first sergeant who had been busted all the way back to private E-2 for punching out an enlisted man. Haynes offered no excuse for the transgression, nor did he let it affect his loyalty and his dedication to his service. The former senior NCO was serving his eighth year in Vietnam and was probably one of the most experienced men ever to step into a set of tiger fatigues.

There was no doubt in anyone's mind that Sloyer's team was the most leadership-heavy long-range patrol in Vietnam. Fortunately for Sloyer, he was sharp enough to recognize his good fortune, often deferring decisions to the two former first-shirts. That prevented disharmony and made excellent use of the leadership glut he faced.

In addition to McBride and Haynes, Sloyer had a full team

of talented recon men. Sp4. Carr, the patrol's point man, had the highest personal body count in the company. Carr was a veritable mountain man in the woods, with a trigger finger as quick as his wit.

Sp4. Rossman walked Carr's slack and was as good in the number-two spot as Carr was at number one. Sloyer would not have to worry about his point element.

PFC Guy Farmer was back at his favorite spot at the rear of the team. Farmer carried an M-14, for its accuracy and its ability—because of its larger bullet—to put someone down and keep him down.

The team's senior RTO was Sp4. Mark Johnston. Johnston carried the patrol's primary radio, a PRC-77, and handled the team's radio traffic. He was a very experienced LRRP.

To round out the team, Sloyer had been assigned a pair of former NVA soldiers. The company had been using *chieu hoi*s off and on for a few months with mixed results. Moc, the older of the two, spoke a little English and had been out on a few missions with Sloyer, and he seemed to be all right. But Tan, the other one, spoke no English at all and was new to the teams, an unknown entity who would remain so until he had proved himself on patrol.

Taking McBride and Haynes with him, Sloyer flew out for an overhead look at the AO the afternoon the warning order came down. Flying well below the thousand-foot ceiling, he could see that the terrain consisted primarily of a low, rugged mountain range covered in thick, triple-canopy jungle. Sloyer spotted small meadows here and there among the hills, and larger open areas down lower in the valleys. He was bothered by the fact that the monsoon weather in that type of terrain caused a lot of ground fog. Combined with the low, unstable ceiling, it would not take much to get the team socked in and unable to be extracted. Although the mission had been scheduled for three days, he made a mental note to himself to tell the members of his team to carry enough meals to last for a week.

Returning from the overflight, Sloyer attended the premission briefing and got the final word on the weather. He was told that it would most likely be touch and go while they were in, with several waves of precipitation moving through the area. However, occasional breaks in the weather would permit the team to be extracted reasonably close to its designated time. In any case, coming out on schedule was not as critical as being able to extract in an emergency if they were compromised. For a few days, they would just have to be exceptionally careful where they stuck their noses.

S-2 had also reported that the AO was probably only a transitory area for NVA units staging out of Cambodia, so any enemy soldiers they happened to encounter would most probably be on the move.

The team flew out to FSB Mace to stage for the mission. It was scheduled to go in at last light on the twelfth, but due to bad weather that day, the mission was scrubbed. The same thing happened again on the thirteenth and fourteenth. The team began to think that the patrol might never go out. Finally, on the afternoon of the fifteenth the weather broke enough that it was decided to attempt to get the team on the ground. So the men of the nine-man patrol donned their gear, applied a final coat of camouflage paint, and walked out to the helipad. It was 1500 hours, earlier in the day than the team normally liked to insert, but they had to go when the helicopters and the right weather were available.

The two insertion slicks landed to pick up the patrol, with Sloyer and four others loading on the first ship, and the four remaining Rangers climbing aboard the second. They lifted off quickly and joined up with the C & C chopper and a pair of Charlie-model Huey gunships. As the five-ship formation climbed above the cloud cover and broke out into clear, bright blue sky on the other side, the Rangers were amazed at the difference they saw. It was almost like being in a new world.

Twenty-five minutes later, as the aircraft neared the Parrot's Beak, the slicks began a slow, steady descent back down through the clouds, finally breaking through less than five hundred meters from their designated LZ. The landing zone was in a long valley surrounded by high, thickly forested hills. There would not be the usual false insertions designed to fool the enemy; the helicopters were needed elsewhere. The patrol would be going straight into their LZ.

The first chopper moved in over the large brushy clearing and came to a hover six to ten feet above the ground. Johnston, the radio operator, noticed how high the skids were from the ground, so he quickly pulled off his rucksack and radio and dropped them into a clump of brush, then jumped behind them. Going in from that height with a rucksack and the added weight of a PRC-25 radio would be asking for an injury. And any kind of an injury at the beginning of a mission was either an abort or a team with a man short.

After the first five patrol members had dropped to the ground, they spread out quickly to allow room for their four teammates coming in on the second aircraft. When everyone was safely on the ground, the patrol moved swiftly uphill, quickly covering the twenty-five or thirty meters to the wood line. There, they set up a wagon-wheel security perimeter while Johnston established radio contact with the TOC back at Xuan Loc. He reported that everything was okay and the patrol was proceeding with its mission. On Sloyer's word, Johnston released the helicopters.

Thirty minutes later, the patrol moved out in single file. Moving slowly and cautiously up through the dense rain forest, the team went seventy-five to one hundred meters before discovering a heavily used high-speed trail, nearly two meters across, running north and south along the side of the ridge. There was no fresh sign on the trail, but the Rangers knew that the recent heavy rains would have washed away any fresh sign. There was a lot of overhead cover above the trail, making it nearly impossible to spot from above.

Sloyer decided to continue climbing the ridge. The trail they had found was halfway up the hill, but the patrol was too close to the LZ to set up an OP or an NDP at that point in the mission; they needed to put more distance behind them.

Just before dark, the team reached the military crest of the ridge. Sloyer circled them up in the thick, leech-infested brush and instructed his men to put out their claymores. However, he cautioned them to keep the mines in close. It was to be a cold camp with no smoking and no boiling water for LRRP rations or coffee.

Because of the seniority of the two hard-core "lifers" on the team, Sloyer usually conceded to their smoking on patrol, but only after he felt sure that no enemy forces were in the area. That was a concession that he was willing to make in exchange for having their expertise on the team.

Sloyer set up his security watches, one man on, one hour at a time, and let everyone else grab some shut-eye. Except for the dampness everywhere, things were comfortable until just before 2200 hours.

Johnston was on guard when he spotted Tan, the new *chieu hoi*, squirting insect repellent on leeches crawling on the ground. While Johnston watched in amazement, the Kit Carson scout pulled out some matches and started lighting them. The RTO quickly shook McBride awake and pointed to the scene now unfolding across the perimeter. Rubbing the sleep out of his eyes, McBride scrambled over to the *chieu hoi*, grabbed him in a choke hold, and stomped out the fire.

Waking up Sloyer, the now irate former first sergeant quickly told him what had just transpired. Sloyer listened then woke Moc and told him to tell his fellow countryman that if he ever did anything like that again he would "cock-adau" (kill) him. Cowering under the Ranger team leader's vicious wrath, the Vietnamese nodded that he understood. The rest of the night passed uneventfully.

The next morning, the entire team was awake and alert by the false dawn. A short time later, Sloyer signaled to his men that it was okay to eat, then had Johnston call in a negative sitrep.

At dawn, the patrol moved out of the NDP and continued south, staying just below the military crest of the ridge. They stopped at 1000 hours and set up a patrol base, while Sloyer sent out a pair of two-man recon elements to check the surrounding terrain. Carr and Haynes dropped straight down toward the valley where they had inserted the previous evening, while McBride and Johnston slipped up over the crest and down the opposite side. Each element was to patrol in a wide circle and return to the patrol base in an hour. Sloyer told them that if they made contact with the enemy and were unable to return to the patrol base, they were to escape and evade back to the team's original LZ.

McBride and Johnston were working their way down the reverse slope of the ridge when they encountered an unusual structure sitting right in the middle of the game trail they were following. It looked like a circular, coil-shaped maze made of four-foot-high bamboo poles embedded side by side into the ground. Neither man had ever before seen anything like it. The only thing they knew for certain was that the damned thing hadn't just grown there—it was definitely man-made. While McBride pulled security, Johnston radioed their discovery in to Sloyer back at the patrol base. Sloyer listened, then told him to back off and set up an OP to monitor the structure. If they didn't see anything in thirty to forty-five minutes, the two Rangers were to return to the patrol base.

Johnston and McBride pulled uphill into thick cover twenty-five meters away and watched. When nothing happened in thirty minutes, the two men rejoined the team. They found that Carr and Haynes had arrived there twenty minutes before them. When the two Rangers described the structure to the rest of the team, Haynes quickly identified it as a Montagnard animal trap. He reported that he had seen them before when he had served up in the Central Highlands with 5th Group. Small animals like pigs and deer would get confused when they moved into the traps, plunging forward until they reached the center. Since there was no room to turn around, they would simply mill about until the owner of the trap showed up to collect his quarry.

While the rest of team had been back at the patrol base, Sloyer had to continually admonish Tan for trying to speak with Moc. Moc realized that his companion was being too noisy and tried to get him to quiet down, but the man simply would not shut up. With the patrol once again intact, Sloyer told Moc to tell him that if he persisted in being so loud, he was going to knock Tan's teeth out.

Tan had already been challenged by Sloyer several times for carrying his weapon slung over his shoulder. Every time Sloyer tried to correct Tan, the man became argumentative and refused to obey. At that point in the patrol, Sloyer was convinced that Tan was a major problem. McBride became outraged over the ex-NVA's refusal to comply with the rules of the game. Tan was endangering the team, and McBride wanted to kill him on the spot. Since killing Tan would only cause more problems back in the rear, Sloyer ruled that out as an option—for the time being.

It was nearly noon when the team resumed its patrolling. They continued north, paralleling the ridge top until 1400 hours, when Sloyer once again called a halt and sent out a two-man recon patrol. This time Farmer and Haynes went, circling in front of the patrol. They returned thirty-five minutes later with nothing new to report. Except for the old trail not far above the LZ and the Montagnard animal trap, the area appeared to be dead.

Sloyer kept the team there until twenty minutes after dark, then pulled them back about seventy-five meters, where they set up an NDP overlooking their back trail. Like the first night, the second proved uneventful.

At dawn on the third day, the patrol climbed the ridge and dropped off down the military crest on the reverse slope, overlooking the valley that had been designated as their primary PZ. When they radioed the TOC to set up their extraction, they were told that Xuan Loc was socked in and the team would have to remain in the field. They were told to Charlie Mike to the northeast toward their designated PZ.

That created a couple of immediate problems for the Rangers: The patrol was almost out of water and would have to find some pretty quick, and they still had the problem of an incompetent *chieu hoi* to deal with. By that point in the patrol, they had all come to the conclusion that Tan had not actually surrendered to the allies but had been kicked out of the North Vietnamese Army.

The water problem would be much easier to correct than the personnel problem. From their position on the military crest of the reverse slope, the men of the team could hear the sound of water running in the valley below. Sloyer instructed Carr to lead them off the slope to a point where they could set up just above the stream.

When they reached that point a short time later, the patrol quickly established a wagon-wheel defensive perimeter, while Sloyer sent them down one at a time to fill their canteens. A heavy fog had settled in above them along the top of the ridge, and ground fog choked the other valley, but the floor of the valley they were in was free of fog.

After they had rested and replenished their water supply, Sloyer conferred with McBride and Haynes and decided to cross the valley and move up the opposite ridgeline. Their reasoning was that they didn't know at the time just how long it would be before they would be extracted, and they didn't want to spend a day or more in the vicinity of their primary PZ before the slicks arrived; that would have provided an excellent opportunity for the enemy to establish a well-organized going-away party.

Quickly crossing the clear, fast-moving stream, the patrol climbed the opposite slope and reached the military crest at approximately 1300 hours. Once again, Sloyer set up a patrol base and sent Carr and Haynes out on a circular recon along the face of the ridge they were on. He sent McBride and Johnston up over the top to check out the reverse slope.

An hour later, everyone was back at the patrol base with nothing new to report. Carr then led the team another two hundred meters along the face of the ridge until Sloyer gave the signal to stop. It was almost 1600 hours, and dark clouds were rolling in. For some reason, each day the team had been on the ground, they had been caught in heavy rainstorms at precisely 1600 hours.

With only minutes to spare, Sloyer told everyone to take shelter on the downwind sides of the large trees growing around them. The daily thunderstorms had saturated the ground, making it extremely wet and muddy. Noticing this, Sloyer was beginning to get concerned about the tracks they were leaving behind. It was true that the next day's rains would erase any sign that they had made the day before, but there was still the problem of the twenty-four-hour wait between the storms and the tracks they had left since the last one. If the enemy happened upon the fresh sign, it wouldn't take them twenty-four hours to find the patrol.

For that reason, Sloyer decided to move higher, into the heavier ground cover along the crest of the ridge. When they finally reached it, it was nearly dark. Carr got down on his hands and knees and led the team into a dense, thorny thicket, where they set up in the usual tight, wagon-wheel perimeter. In the fading light, Sloyer signaled for each man to put out his claymore, then set up the guards, one man on, one-hour shifts. Johnston had erected a field-expedient wire antenna in the overhead cover, enabling the team to enjoy excellent commo throughout the night. Good commo during the dangerous hours of darkness was always an added comfort to a long-range patrol. Just as on the two preceding evenings, the third was peaceful.

The morning of the fourth day dawned bright and sunny. Johnston immediately called in a sitrep reporting that the weather over the team's AO had cleared. He followed this report with a request for an immediate extraction.

The Ranger TOC came back with the disconcerting news

that Xuan Loc was still socked in and all aviation assets were still grounded. They advised the team to Charlie Mike to the northeast, where they would be lifted out as soon as the weather broke back at the rear.

Even though the sky was clear over the team, there was still a lot of ground fog down below in the valley. Sloyer instructed Carr to move down through the jungle slowly and cautiously. Two hundred meters away, Carr broke out of the trees overlooking a large meadow on the slope just above the valley. The fog was just beginning to lift. There in the sunlight before them, the entire meadow was covered with thousands of large, crimson, poinsettia-like flowers. It was a scene meant for a postcard!

It was almost 0900 when the team finally established an OP overlooking a beautiful valley. They observed it for thirty minutes before Sloyer huddled up with Haynes and McBride to discuss their next move. They all agreed that it would be dangerous to cross the open meadow or go down into the valley, so they opted to climb back up over the ridge above them.

When they crested the ridge, they once again heard sounds of water running below. Following the ridgeline to the north-northeast as it dropped down into a large valley that ran across its face, they angled down the side and soon discovered a breathtaking sixty-foot-high waterfall. To one side, highlighted in the condensation from the cascading water, was an eight-sided symmetrical spiderweb, fifteen feet in diameter. Its jewel-like gridwork was picture-book perfect, prompting Rossman to comment, "I bet we're probably the first white men to ever see this place." Twenty feet away they found a number of rusted Budweiser cans, blowing Rossman's supposition all to hell.

The patrol stretched back out and crossed the creek, then climbed back up to the crest of their original ridgeline. They were still two or three klicks from their secondary PZ. The TOC had reported to them during their noon sitrep that the weather back at Xuan Loc was finally breaking and the patrol would be pulled the next day.

Sloyer signaled for the patrol to move into an NDP site up on the ridge. One more uneventful night, and the mission would be history.

During the morning sitrep on the fifth day of the mission, Johnston was instructed to tell Sloyer to move the team out toward the PZ. Their extraction was scheduled for sometime early that afternoon. They still had half a day to cover the twenty-five hundred meters between them and their pickup point, so there was no need to hurry.

At about 1000 hours, Sloyer stopped the patrol for a break. The Ranger team leader told Johnston and two other Rangers to put out claymores to the front, back, and above them as a precautionary measure. At the time, they were less than five hundred meters from their PZ.

Johnston sat down, dropped his ruck, and was reaching for a claymore when a single NVA soldier suddenly materialized out of the heavy cover ten feet away. The man had come up an eighteen-inch-wide footpath from the valley. None of the Rangers had spotted the well-camouflaged trail. McBride had spotted the NVA before the man had seen him, and had quietly alerted the LRRP behind him. The message was being passed around the perimeter, but had not yet reached everyone.

The NVA soldier was carrying an AK-47 slung over his shoulder. He was wearing a khaki uniform, rubber-soled boots, rucksack, and web gear. The man was only four feet away when McBride stepped out into the open and asked him to surrender. Braver than he was smart, the NVA went for his weapon. McBride stitched him from groin to shoulder with half a magazine on rock 'n' roll. Each bullet hit home.

Responding as trained, every LRRP fired a full magazine into his security zone outside the perimeter. As soon as the firing was over and everyone was reloading, Johnston called in the contact.

As soon as the dead NVA hit the ground, Tan ran up to him and began firing into the man's body on full automatic at point-blank range, shouting loudly in Vietnamese that he had killed him. Then he grabbed the dead man's AK-47, waved it in the air over his head, and continued hollering as if he had just scored the winning run in the last game of the World Series.

Sloyer stepped up and angrily grabbed the AK out of Tan's hands at the same instant that McBride stripped him of his M-16. He would never get it back again. With Tan temporarily under control, the rest of the team quickly began setting up security and stripping the body. They recovered the weapon, three magazines, a number of family photos, and several balls of rice. There wasn't a lot in the man's ruck, indicating that he was probably not far from his base camp. When the Rangers finished stripping the body, one of them stood over it and dropped an ace of spades on the body.

When Johnston got hold of the TOC and reported the contact, he was told that gunships were being scrambled. The TOC ordered the team to begin moving toward the PZ. Sloyer instructed his Rangers to pull in the three claymores, then signaled Carr to head northeast, parallel to the crest above them. While they were moving, Johnston took a call from the TOC saying that if the team could be at the PZ in forty-five minutes, the choppers would be waiting for them. With that little bit of good news, the patrol voluntarily picked up the pace. It was almost over. They had only half a klick to go.

Ten minutes later, the gunships reached the area of the pickup ahead of the slicks. Coming up on the team from behind, they were over the spot where McBride had killed the NVA when they called Johnston and asked him for a long count so they could home in on the team's position. The woods around the patrol were beginning to thin, becoming single canopy. When the gunship pilot asked the team to mark its current location with smoke, Johnston said that he would mark his location with an orange signal panel instead.

The helicopter pilot quickly verified the team's panel and told Johnston that the patrol should continue moving north toward the PZ. But five minutes later, he was back on the net requesting a second mark and asking how many were on the team. Johnston slowed up, and replied, "Nine!"

The pilot radioed back and said, "You got some problems. I'm seeing a whole lot more than nine people."

Johnston asked, "How far away are they?"

The pilot came back, "A hundred meters behind you."

The NVA were on the move and coming right up their asses! Suddenly, the pilot ordered the team to get down flat and not look up. He told them he was going to make a gun run on the enemy column.

Johnston set up the first gun run coming in from the front of the team so that the helicopter's guns could fire directly down the enemy column. Before beginning the run, the pilot asked if anyone on the team had a visual on the NVA coming up behind them. Johnston passed the request up and down the column, then answered, "No."

The Ranger team was still moving and strung out in patrol file. To that point, all of Johnston's communication with the gunships had been made on the move. Just before the first gun run, Johnston told everyone to stop and get down on the ground. No one felt it necessary to ask why.

As soon as the first gunship finished its run, the team broke cover and began a sprint for the PZ. As of that moment, they had still not taken any fire.

The gunships made three more gun runs, the team hitting the ground hard before each one, then getting up and running again before the next one came in. After the fourth gun run, which had resulted in Johnston's heel being shot off his right boot, the aircraft commander announced that the NVA were still coming and they were getting close. He wanted to bring his fire in closer.

Johnston answered his transmission by screaming, "You just shot the heel off my boot! Are you shooting at us or the NVA?"

The pilot came back immediately, saying, "No, I can see both of you. They are that close."

By then, the patrol was in thinning cover, scattered brush, and single-canopy trees. At that time, they turned and fired back toward where the NVA were supposed to be. The LZ was only twenty-five meters away. Reloading as they ran, when they reached the edge of the clearing, they turned once again, got on line, and continued to put out suppressing fire. There was still no return fire.

The PZ behind them was big enough to accommodate easily both slicks at the same time, and neither pilot wanted to be the second ship in. They had already spotted the team kneeling and firing from the edge of the clearing, so there was no need to pop smoke grenades. While the Rangers continued pouring fire downrange, the two slicks came in on line and set down quickly in the clearing.

Without waiting for a final signal, everyone broke cover at the same time and sprinted for the waiting aircraft. The first Rangers to reach them boarded quickly, then turned to add their firepower to that of the door gunners, who were already spraying the cover at the edge of the tree line.

Sloyer was still running for the aircraft, holding on to Tan by his LBE; Sloyer wanted to make sure the former NVA didn't seize the opportunity to rejoin his former comrades. As the slicks lifted out of the clearing and began to climb for altitude, the gunships moved in with miniguns and rockets to devastate the jungle where the NVA had last been sighted.

It was 1500 hours and still bright and sunny. The helicopters flew back to the rear, landing at FSB Stinson. There, the Rangers caught a ride on a deuce-and-a-half loaded with cartons of shaving cream. Xuan Loc was still a twenty-minute drive.

On the way to their forward base camp, the tensions and

stresses of another close call got the best of the members of the team. No one will ever admit exactly who started it, or even why it started, but the seven Americans were soon engaged in the wildest shaving-cream fight the world has ever seen. With a deuce-and-a-half truck full of foamy ammo, and twenty minutes in which to use it, the seven Rangers managed to go through half the cartons in the back of the truck. By the time the trip was over, the driver had developed a massive and permanent hard-on against U.S. Army Rangers, and that hard-on failed to subside even when the now foamy white recon team jumped deftly down from the back of the truck outside the Ranger compound.

The only thing that had marred the trip back to the base was Tan. He had stupidly attempted to join in the fun by tossing a CS grenade through the open window of a civilian bus. The bus driver had immediately lost control of the vehicle, allowing it to run off the road and out into a field. While CS gas poured out of the windows, dozens of screaming passengers fought each other to abandon the vehicle.

Tan had made his final blunder in the Ranger company. Sloyer and McBride wanted desperately to kill him on the spot, but saner heads prevailed. Instead, he was sent back to the ARVNs with instructions to smuggle him back into North Vietnam. With Tan back in an NVA uniform, our final victory would be assured. It would be the last time that Sloyer took out a *chieu hoi*.

Company E,
50th Infantry (LRP),
9th Infantry Division

The 9th Infantry Division was the only major U.S. Army unit to conduct operations in the Mekong Delta area of South Vietnam. With most of the terrain in the IV Corps Tactical Zone at or below sea level, the U.S. military units fighting there were forced to conduct a much different type of war from that being fought over the remainder of South Vietnam. Mobility was achieved primarily by helicopter and river patrol craft, and ground actions were usually quick, hard-hitting, deadly affairs.

The 9th Infantry Division's long-range reconnaissance patrols were also handicapped by the "water world" that made up most of their area of operations. The large civilian populations in the area and the limited range of cover and concealment made it extremely difficult to move about unobserved during daylight hours. Recon teams were often forced to move only at night.

No-fire zones, poor cover, and a cagey enemy, who frequently mixed with the local villagers during the day and became Viet Cong guerrillas after dark, made it nearly impossible to conduct covert patrols without extremely high risk of detection. To conduct patrols in that type of environment, the E/50th LRRPs were forced to operate much like their U.S. Navy SEAL counterparts.

Back in the fall of 1968, the LRP company had been operating from the anchored ships of the Mobile Riverine Force, but after they were caught smuggling beer on board—a rule strictly enforced by the MRF commander—they were unceremoniously kicked off the ship. However, when a VC sapper team swam out to the USS *Westchester Country* from nearby Toi San Island with a large amount of plastic explosives and blew a couple of very large holes in it, the LRRPs were quickly forgiven and invited to return to the anchored ships.

They soon found themselves running ambush and interdiction patrols along the trails and canals surrounding the MRF. The overwhelming success of the patrols kept the long-range reconnaissance men smugly satisfied with their new role as the security force for MRF.

Team One-seven had been particularly successful, pulling several very effective ambushes over a three-week period, especially in the vicinity of a major canal intersection known as "The Crossroads," located halfway between My Tho and Ben Tre. The area consisted of a large expanse of dense forest and mangrove swamps bordered by several kilometers of open rice paddies. Nearly half of Team One-seven's ambush patrols had resulted in contact with the very active local Viet Cong force.

On 27 January 1969, Ranger Team One-seven, Company E, 50th Infantry (LRP), prepared for another routine night ambush patrol. Sgt. Richard Ehrler, One-seven's team leader, planned to insert his six-man patrol by helicopter as close as possible to a tree line, then move several hundred meters to the canal, where they would set up their ambush. Ehrler had overflown the area late that afternoon on the way out to drop off a two-man radio-relay team at Ben Tre. The relay team, consisting of George Calabrese and Chuck Semmit, would handle the patrol's communications while it was in the field.

The patrol inserted an hour before dark, and immediately found itself in some very deep shit. Before Ehrler could even get his team off the LZ, a single VC, carrying an AK-47 over his shoulder like a hobo's staff, strolled out of the jungle a hundred meters away. He immediately spotted Ehrler and jumped back into the jungle just as the LRP team leader cut loose with a sustained burst from his M-16. Miffed at himself for missing the easy shot, Ehrler did the only smart thing he could do: he radioed for an immediate extraction and requested a reinsertion into the team's secondary LZ a couple of klicks away.

The helicopters were still in the area, so the request was accepted. The aircraft quickly returned and recovered the ambush patrol. A short time later, they were back on the ground again and ready to move out.

That time the team landed in an open rice paddy near a small abandoned hootch. Ehrler recalled checking it on a previous mission and discovering that it had been used in the past only as a shed for housing water buffalo.

It was already growing dark when Ehrler dropped to one knee by the shed to observe a nearby tree line. He wasn't very happy when he spotted another Vietnamese male just inside the woods staring back at him. When the LRRP team leader reported this through his radio-relay team to his TOC, he was ordered to Charlie Mike. Ehrler was certain they were in for an interesting night.

He kept his team in place near the shed until it was fully dark, then gave the signal for them to move out. About an hour later, they heard a brief burst of automatic-weapons fire coming from the vicinity of the buffalo shed. Clearly they had done the right thing in waiting until after dark to move out. There was no doubt now that the enemy had spotted the patrol coming in and had attempted to take it out.

The burst of gunfire back at the buffalo shed also convinced Ehrler that his team had successfully evaded the enemy, so he decided to move the team into the nearby jungle to get them under cover. Unfortunately, the LRRPs immediately detected the sounds of heavy movement around them. Freezing in place, they soon discovered that it was coming from a group of Vietnamese peasants on their way home from working in the fields all day. Unfortunately, until the peasants departed the area, the patrol would not be able to reach the cover and concealment of the nearby trees.

Finally, the Vietnamese moved on, and the team was able to resume its patrol. It soon ran into a cluster of five hootches scattered over an area the size of a football field. A cursory check revealed that all but one of the structures appeared to be empty at the time. Ehrler, not wanting to be caught out in the open, signaled the patrol to move into the one vacant hootch that appeared to be isolated from the rest. Much to their surprise, the LRRPs discovered that the hut was built like a fortress: from the ground up, almost to a height of four feet, the walls were made of thick, hardened mud, broken only by a narrow doorway. There was also an aboveground bunker built right into the earthen walls of the hut, with an overhead ceiling constructed of compacted dirt over a layer of large mahogany logs. The place was almost impregnable to small-arms fire.

Ehrler quickly deployed his team inside the hootch; it was an excellent spot for an ambush. Given the other huts in the vicinity, someone had to be using the area. They were situated among a number of small rice paddies, and the interconnecting paddy dikes were constantly being used by the VC as footpaths as they moved through the area. It was a natural fortress except for one side, where a heavily thatched wall prevented visibility in that direction. The thatch was dry and very brittle to the touch and would have caused a lot of noise to remove it. Instead, Ehrler posted two of his teammates, Leon Moore and Roman Mason, at the outside corner of the building next to the thatched wall. He instructed the two Rangers to jump over the wall and kick holes through the thatching if they were compromised during the night.

Silently, the LRRPs left the hootch to set up their claymores. When that had been done, and their ambush was in place, they sat back to wait for the enemy to show up. They had completed the active part of an ambush. The rest took only patience and a little luck.

At 2300 hours, Ehrler put the team on 50 percent alert. Richard Thompson, Mark Durham, and Mason immediately went to sleep, while Norman Crabb, Moore, and Ehrler pulled the first guard shift.

It was close to 2320 hours when Ehrler thought he saw movement in the trees 150 meters away. It was a clear night, well lit by starlight. Ehrler slipped quietly over to Moore's position and retrieved the team's starlight scope. When he asked Moore if he had seen anything from his position, the LRRP reported that he hadn't. However, Moore was facing directly away from the tree line.

The LRRP team leader then edged over to Crabb's position, where the two recon men spent the next fifteen minutes watching the wood line. What held their attention for that long was the twenty or so VC who were moving about in the trees across the paddy from their position, far too many to take on with a six-man ambush patrol.

The two LRRPs were not overly concerned about a large number of enemy troops moving about so close to their position; they were in the middle of VC-controlled territory, and spotting enemy units moving about at night was not a rare event. Besides, they had no reason to believe that the VC even knew their patrol was in the area. And just in case, they had a healthy number of claymore mines facing the wood line if the enemy troops there decided to get nosy and wander over to check out the hut on the other side of the paddy.

However, a few minutes later, Ehrler decided to play it safe and wake the rest of the team. With that accomplished, he contacted their radio-relay site and told them to alert the TOC and inform them of the situation they could soon be facing.

Just then he heard the sound of voices coming from somewhere behind him. Thinking it was Mason and Moore, the team leader grabbed his weapon and started around the corner of the hootch to shut them up and tell them to get back inside the building. He had just turned the corner when he realized that the voices were speaking in Vietnamese. And there in front of him, standing four feet away, were five armed enemy soldiers.

The VC were looking directly down at Mason and Moore, Ehrler's rear security element. The five enemy soldiers were so preoccupied watching the two LRRPs that they didn't notice Ehrler standing behind them. Slowly, Ehrler raised his M-16 and was preparing to waste them when he spotted about twenty more VC on the other side of the paddy dike, ten feet away from where Mason and Moore lay sleeping.

Convinced that he had not yet been seen, Ehrler slipped silently back around the corner of the hootch and in hushed tones, quickly apprised Crabb of the situation going down outside the hootch. Telling him to cover the closest VC while he went inside to wake Durham and Thompson, Ehrler said a silent prayer that some miracle would occur to prevent the coming disaster.

After he woke the rest of his teammates, Ehrler got the relay team on the radio and whispered that they needed assistance immediately. While he waited for confirmation, he peered over the wall and saw that Mason and Moore were still asleep, totally unaware of what was happening. There was no way that Ehrler and the rest of his teammates could come up with an idea to distract the VC long enough to warn their men to get out of there. With over twenty weapons trained on them at point-blank range, their salvation was now in the hands of their Maker.

Finally, the radio-relay team called back and reported that division would not send gunships until the team was actually in contact. Knowing that there would not be enough time for the gunships to respond once the shooting began, Ehrler ordered his teammates to open fire at once, hoping to put enough rounds into the VC to force them into momentarily forgetting about the two sleeping LRRPs, affording them the opportunity to escape inside during the resulting confusion.

Unfortunately, the plan failed to work. As soon as the four LRRPs stood up and opened fire, Mason and Moore snapped awake and were immediately cut down by the VC before they had a chance to get to their feet.

Inside the hootch, the mud walls were holding up surprisingly well against the heavy battering they were taking from the enemy AK-47s. The thick thatch roof even managed to absorb the blast of several hand grenades. Fortunately, the enemy soldiers Ehrler had spotted back in the trees had not yet joined in the firefight, thereby keeping the LRRPs out of a potentially deadly cross fire.

Ehrler finally realized that the enemy soldiers in the woods behind them had been quietly waiting for the survivors of the patrol to make a run for the trees. Clearly, the VC *had* known all along that the team was in the area. It was the only thing that could explain what was happening at that very moment. But Ehrler was not about to lead his men in an escape attempt in any direction. They weren't going anywhere.

He knew that Mason and Moore were probably already dead, but the team was still not going to leave them behind. Risking more lives to recover your dead might not have made sense to anyone else, but that was the way that LRRPs operated.

Ehrler took his radio and was crawling around the hootch to a point where he could fire into the right flank of the attacking enemy force when he spotted more VC on the left flank. The team was now completely surrounded and was taking fire from three sides.

At that moment, an RPG round sailed in through the open doorway and detonated on the ground three feet in front of the LRRP team leader. The explosion flipped him fifteen feet across the hootch and slammed him hard into the wall on the far side of the room.

Ehrler never lost consciousness, but for the first few seconds after the explosion he felt as if someone had smacked him across the face with a two-by-four. The intense pain quickly ebbed into a dull, constant throb, and when the wounded LRRP team leader opened his eyes, he realized for the first time that he could no longer see.

Ehrler recalled that before the blast there had been enough light in the hootch to see quite well. The incoming tracers and the muzzle flashes from their own weapons had provided adequate illumination. But now as he squinted and rubbed his eyes, there was absolutely nothing. Ehrler might have been blind, but he realized that he had no time to worry about it.

Ehrler crawled slowly across the floor, arms outspread in front of him, groping desperately for his missing weapon and the team radio. Suddenly, another tremendous blast, to his right, rocked the hootch. Someone yelled that Thompson had been hit, and moments later came a confirmation that he was dead.

Although only five minutes had elapsed since the initial shots had been fired, half of Ehrler's team had already been killed, and he was unable to see.

Somehow in the total darkness, he managed to locate his M-16 and the missing radio. Ehrler quickly got in touch with the radio-relay team and demanded to know where the Cobras were. He was told that the gunships were en route.

Just then, Hotel Volley Two-seven, the 105mm battery on Firebase Claw, came up on the LRRP push and asked if they wanted artillery support. However, with two dozen VC only ten to twenty feet away and the team leader blind, Ehrler had no choice but to refuse. There was no way he could pull one of his remaining two teammates off the wall long enough to adjust artillery fire on their own position.

After an intense fifteen-minute exchange of fire, Crabb shouted to Ehrler that he was out of ammo and Durham was on his last magazine. Ehrler yelled back that he still had most of his basic load remaining, and quickly began passing his magazines up to the two men at the wall. Finally, he tore off his web gear and tossed it over to them, keeping only a grenade for himself—in case the VC overran their position.

Suddenly, Ehrler could tell by the sounds that the VC fire

was beginning to slacken. This had to mean that the enemy, too, was running low on ammunition, or that they were withdrawing from the fight. Ehrler ordered Crabb and Durham to return fire on semiautomatic only to conserve their remaining ammo. He told them not to fire unless they had specific targets.

Ehrler then contacted the relay team again to ask them where the gunships were, and to advise them that if the Cobras didn't arrive in the next few minutes, the TOC would only have to send in Graves Registration for a reaction force.

Ehrler heard the voice of Charger Two-one breaking in on the LRRP tactical push, calmly telling him to mark his position so that the gunships could begin their runs. The blinded team leader located the strobe light in the cargo pocket of his pants, and pitched it across the hootch in Crabb's direction. He told him to turn it on and toss it out the door. With the strobe light flashing outside the hootch, Ehrler reported to Charger Two-one that anything more than ten meters in any direction from the light was all his.

The enemy soldiers who were still able to flee, broke and ran as the rockets and miniguns from the Cobra gunships plowed up the countryside around the hootch. The three surviving LRRPs crouched in terror behind the earthen walls. Outside the walls, everything died. The "friendly" fire from the Cobras came within mere feet of becoming very "unfriendly" fire, but the accuracy of the gunships was uncanny.

Ehrler shouted for Crabb and Durham to be ready to drag their dead comrades to the extraction ship as soon as it landed. If there was no effective sniper fire, they could go back then to retrieve their gear and equipment.

Suddenly, a single Huey slick flared out over the nearby rice paddy and set down amid the carnage surrounding the battered hootch. The aircraft commander waited patiently while the two LRRPs dragged the bodies of their three slain comrades to the waiting helicopter, then quickly returned for their gear. While the gunships continued tearing into the nearby tree line, keeping the enemy there at bay, Crabb returned and grabbed Ehrler by the hand, then personally led the blinded team leader back to the extraction ship.

Ehrler spent the next ten and a half months recovering from his wounds and learning how to live as a blind man. Today, he still remembers the men who died with him that day. And he says he can still see fine—in the darkness where he lives.

☆ ☆ ☆ ☆ ☆

Company F,
75th Infantry (Ranger),
25th Infantry Division

In April 1970, the 3d Brigade of the 25th Infantry Division, based at Cu Chi, was poised to begin operations in a tactical area known as the Renegade Woods. The area, a longtime enemy stronghold, was located west of Saigon in the Hieu Thien District of Tay Ninh Province. The brigade's primary mission was to locate, engage, and destroy VC/NVA forces that were known to be massing in the Renegade Woods. Intelligence reports gathered from captured enemy documents and prisoner interrogations indicated that two VC Main Force battalions were infiltrating into the area and establishing a base complex. The enemy units were trying to rebuild and refit after suffering heavy losses in operations against the 1st Cavalry Division operating to the north. Third Brigade was afraid that once the enemy units were healthy and at full strength again, they would begin conducting offensive operations against the U.S. and allied forces in the area.

The Renegade Woods was a large expanse of double-canopy forest located in the middle of the open grasslands of Tay Ninh Province. The nearly level forested terrain was choked with a thick undergrowth of vines and creepers that restricted movement to existing trails or newly cut pathways. Among the trees there was a small number of clearings where only sparse grass grew. Some of the clearings were large enough for single or multiple ship landings. However, there was seldom enough cover or concealment in the clearings to provide protection during an insertion. Surrounded by dense forests, the clearings proved to be ideal killing zones against anyone attempting to infiltrate into the area.

At 0700 hours on 2 April 1970, just prior to the 3d Brigade ground units' launching their operations, a "yellow jacket" message (an NVA radio transmission) was intercepted. It came from an unspecified area in the Renegade Woods. Almost immediately, the warning order came down from brigade S-2 to Capt. Paul Schierholz, commanding officer of Company F, 75th Infantry (Ranger), requesting that he send in a heavy combat patrol, just ahead of the infantry operation, to take out the radio transmitter. The Rangers were instructed to drop into an open area adjoining the hidden transmitter site, shoot it up, then get out.

At the same time, a light scout team from Troop D, 3/4th Cavalry, flew a visual reconnaissance over the area near the transmitter. They reported no sign of enemy activity in the area, especially around a nearby clearing that appeared suitable for a multiship LZ. However, at another site close by, the scout team pilots did report signs of recent enemy activity, and sighted a number of freshly built structures sitting back under the trees.

The mission was immediately assigned to Ranger Teams Three-eight and Three-nine, consisting of thirteen Rangers under the combined command of 2d Lt. Phillip Norton. Norton was fortunate to have as assistant team leaders veteran sergeants first class Alvin Floyd and Colin Hall.

The remaining members of Norton's patrol were Sgt. Fred Stuckey, Sgt. Michael Thomas, Sgt. Charles Avery, Sgt. Samuel Seay, Sp4. Donald Tinney, Sp4. Donald Purdy, Sp4. Richard Guth, PFC Steven Perez, PFC Raymond Allmon, and PFC Kenneth Langland.

The mission had not been planned ahead, but had come as a hasty, spur-of-the-moment operation. Basically, the patrol had been slapped together from a group of volunteers who had had the misfortune of being congregated at the mess hall when the warning order came down. Second Lieutenant Phillip Norton, the Ranger 2d Platoon leader, had immediately volunteered to lead the operation. Two of the company's three platoon sergeants also volunteered to go along as his assistant patrol leaders. This was not SOP in a Ranger company. It was highly unusual to find "brass and double rockers" on a Ranger combat patrol.

Sgt. Mike Thomas was another Ranger who volunteered for the patrol. Thomas was only four days from his ETS date back to the States, and a number of his comrades challenged his judgment, but he was adamant. No one was going to keep him from one last chance to "kick a little butt" before he returned home to the humdrum civilian world.

Norton hurriedly briefed his teammates on the essentials of the mission, telling them that an enemy radio transmitter was their target. The radio was reported operating somewhere near their insertion LZ.

Lieutenant Norton didn't think there could be anything more than an enemy platoon guarding it. He told his teammates that it would be a "quickie"—get in and out before the enemy had time to react. No one ever got hurt on a quickie. Norton also informed his patrol that they had less than a half hour to grab their gear and weapons and prepare for the mission.

The Ranger officer then ordered Sp4. Tinney and privates first class Allmon and Langland to secure M-60 machine guns from the company armory. This was a combat patrol, and Norton wanted some firepower with him. He also instructed Private First Class Perez to pack an M-79 grenade launcher to add a little fire support to the patrol's war-making capabilities.

Sp4. Richard Guth, a division-trained sniper, took his scoped M-14. Except for Sgt. Mike Thomas's lone CAR-15, everyone else was armed with M-16s.

The patrol members quickly tossed their gear into the trailers towed behind a pair of jeeps from the company motor pool, then jumped aboard. They proceeded out to the Centaur chopper pad at the 3/4th Cavalry Squadron compound a half mile away. The thirteen Rangers then climbed swiftly aboard the two waiting slicks from Delta Troop.

Captain Schierholz, flying command and control during the mission, climbed into the lead helicopter occupied by Ranger Team Three-nine. Lieutenant Norton's Team Three-eight was already aboard the number-two ship.

The helicopter bearing Team Three-nine lifted away first, followed fifteen seconds later by Team Three-eight. Escorted by a light scout team consisting of a LOH scout helicopter and a single Cobra gunship from the Centaurs, the two Hueys departed Cu Chi airspace and settled in for the short flight out to the patrol's AO in the Renegade Woods.

As the aircraft approached the operational area, Lieutenant Norton saw that there were only two possible LZs available for the insertion. The first was in a small clearing next to the forest where the light scout team had spotted enemy structures under the trees earlier that morning. The second clearing was long enough for the two slicks to insert simultaneously. Norton decided to use the larger of the two LZs.

The slicks approached the clearing together and inserted simultaneously. The LZ was a large open field with spotty clusters of dried grass, barely sufficient to hide the barren earth beneath it. The field was totally devoid of cover and concealment.

As soon as the two teams were safely on the ground, they moved toward each other and linked up before moving toward the nearest tree line. Not far from the edge of the woods, the lead element of the patrol discovered a large number of footprints in the dust.

Not far away, they spotted a canvas Lister bag hanging from a post in the open. It was nearly full of water. A short distance from the Lister bag, nestled back at the edge of the trees, was the well that had provided the water.

At that point, the patrol was stretched single file along the edge of the forest. Lieutenant Norton didn't like the looks of things and made a quick decision to get into some cover.

There was a thick hedgerow running out into the clearing about twenty meters away. Norton signaled his point man to move out on a 270-degree azimuth, heading in the general direction of the enemy structures that the light scout team had spotted back in the woods less than ninety minutes before. Stuckey moved out, followed by Norton and Purdy. They headed toward the opening at the end of the hedgerow and the small clearing just beyond it.

As they reached the end of the hedgerow, Stuckey and Norton spotted a deep bomb crater near the center of the clearing. Five meters to the left of the bomb crater was a smaller depression made by an exploding artillery round.

As the two Rangers moved around the end of the hedgerow and into the clearing, an RPD light machine gun opened up on them from a distance of only fifteen meters. Stuckey had stopped just seconds before the gun opened fire and Norton had moved up to his side.

Sp4. Don Purdy was just clearing the opening when the enemy machine gun opened up on Lieutenant Norton and Sergeant Stuckey. Incredibly, the RPD rounds tore past them without hitting either man.

Norton immediately turned to his left and dove into the bomb crater, while Stuckey found shelter from the withering fire in the smaller artillery crater five meters away. While the RPD continued to flay the ground above the two Rangers, Purdy, still standing back by the opening, stepped up to give them cover fire.

Suddenly, an AK-47 opened up farther down the tree line, knocking Purdy's weapon from his hands and damaging the bolt. Hands stinging from the impact of the rounds, he quickly recovered his weapon and opened fire at the chattering machine gun. However, his M-16 was no longer working properly.

The RPD gunner continued working his grazing fire over Stuckey and Norton, and the two Rangers were effectively pinned down, unable even to raise their heads. Not knowing what had happened to his team leader, Stuckey raised his M-16 above the lip of the crater and emptied a full magazine in the direction of the enemy machine gun. Realizing that he was not doing any good with his M-16, Stuckey then rolled over on his back and pulled two frags from his web gear and tossed them in a high arc toward the RPD.

Back at the end of the hedgerow, Purdy was still having troubles with his damaged weapon. Since it was not working properly, he, too, decided to tackle the machine gun with grenades. As Stuckey's frags began detonating in the cover around the enemy machine gun, Purdy followed it up with two "hot potatoes" of his own, silencing the gun.

Down in the bottom of the bomb crater, Lieutenant Norton quickly recovered from the shock of the NVA ambush. He reached for his handset and established radio contact with the LOH scout helicopter circling nearby. He told the scout ship pilot that the patrol was in heavy contact with enemy forces in the trees to his front. The Cobra pilot broke in and asked if the patrol had friendlies to their front.

Norton replied, "No! Fire up the tree line."

The Cobra circled around and came in low, making a lateral pass across Norton's immediate front. The pilot then slowed the gunship to a hover as he raked the wood line with his minigun. Afterward, no more fire came from the trees.

Fifteen seconds later, Norton decided it was time to vacate his bomb crater and get back to the team. He gathered himself and rolled out of the hole in the ground, struggling to regain his feet.

Stuckey saw him coming, leaped out of his own cover, and grabbed Norton by his web gear. Turning in the same motion, he jerked the lieutenant back toward the end of the hedgerow where the rest of the patrol was just moving up.

While the action had been taking place out in the center of the clearing, Purdy had shouted for Allmon to move up to the end of the hedgerow with his M-60, but by the time the young

Ranger had set up the gun and was ready to fire the battle was already over.

Back with the rest of his patrol, Norton now took stock of their options. The patrol had already lost the element of surprise, and the enemy was alert and ready. So it no longer made any sense to continue with their mission. The VC would surely defend their radio transmitter, if in fact it was still in the neighborhood. Nevertheless, Lieutenant Norton was not willing to risk the lives of his Rangers assaulting dug-in positions, especially when there was probably no longer any purpose to it. Instead, he did the right thing by making the decision to escape and evade.

With enemy troops in the woods on the other side of the hedgerow, it would now be folly to attempt an extraction from the LZ they had just used. To the right of their LZ was a clearing just big enough to handle a couple of slicks, but it was still in range of the enemy gunners on the other side of the hedgerow. Norton decided to move the patrol to the east, to put some distance between themselves and the enemy soldiers back in the woods. He recalled from his maps that there was another large clearing not too far to the east, well out of range of the enemy machine gun.

Norton radioed Floyd to face the west and cover his team from the enemy in the trees while he took them across the clearing on the other side of the field. Once his team was under cover, they would provide security while Floyd moved his team across the open area to join them.

As Norton's team passed through the narrow opening in the trees and moved out into the adjoining clearing, a large number of enemy troops hidden in the trees on the opposite side of the clearing suddenly opened fire from a distance of twenty-five meters. The Rangers immediately went on line and assaulted across the open field.

When Norton and the rest of the Rangers from Team Three-eight finally fought their way across the open field and up to the edge of the woods, they discovered numerous well-camouflaged bunkers hidden five meters back in the dense tangle of brush.

Seay and Purdy ran into a well-disguised enemy machine-gun bunker housing another RPD. Purdy was so close to the gun port that he could have reached down and grabbed the smoking barrel. As if rehearsed, Seay moved to one side, Purdy to the other, and the two Rangers began alternating between firing and throwing hand grenades into the enemy bunker until the weapon went silent.

Out in the open clearing, Sergeant Floyd had moved Team Three-nine up to where they could lend a hand. They began putting out a tremendous volume of suppressing fire in an attempt to cover the assault team.

Suddenly, from the far end of the clearing, a number of enemy troops appeared and began firing at both Ranger teams. They were apparently maneuvering around the edge of the field in an attempt to flank the Rangers, but for some reason they had opened fire while they were still in the open. One VC, standing out in the clear less than thirty-five meters away with a sandbag full of HE rounds, was busy plopping 40mm grenades over the heads of the Rangers with an M-79. Stuckey spotted the VC after he had gotten off his second round and killed him with a well-placed burst before the man could adjust his aim. Stuckey then fired at the man's ammo bag until it began to smoke. The Ranger point man wanted to make sure no one else moved up to reclaim the weapon and turn it against his teammates.

Norton realized that Floyd's team was now coming across the clearing to join Team Three-eight. The officer tried unsuccessfully to establish radio contact with Three-nine before realizing that his radio was no longer functioning. He quickly turned to look at Floyd's team just as they moved out into the open field. He couldn't understand why they were in a staggered file instead of on line. Before Norton could warn them, a B-40 rocket sailed out of the wood line from a spot fifteen meters to the left of Team Three-eight. As Norton watched in horror, the round hit Sergeant Floyd head-on, killing him instantly. The resulting blast also killed Sergeant Thomas, who was standing just behind Floyd, and wounded Sp4. Tinney, who was moving up behind Thomas. The bodies of Floyd and Thomas were horribly shredded by the force of the blast. Tinney fell, draped across his M-60, not moving. Norton could not tell for certain if he was still alive or not, and there was no time at the moment to make sure.

Seeing the damage done to Team Three-nine by the B-40 rocket, Norton shouted for Team Three-eight to withdraw from the woods and move back toward the protection of a large bomb crater in the middle of the clearing behind them. Norton could not get any help with his radio not working, so he ran to where Floyd's mangled body lay bleeding in the open and stripped the PRC-25 from his corpse. Dodging enemy small-arms fire, he zigzagged back to the edge of the crater and jumped into it. He was soon joined there by the three remaining survivors of Team Three-nine.

Squatting in the bottom of the crater, Norton worked feverishly to replace the severed handset from his radio with the good handset from Floyd's. He made the switch in record time but discovered that he still had difficulty raising anyone. Norton checked everything and came to the conclusion that there had to be dirt in the handset cord connections. During the next few minutes, Norton detached the handset cord from the female fitting three times, each time wiping the threads with his shirt and blowing on the points to clean them; without commo they were doomed.

In the meantime, both the Cobra and the LOH from the light scout team were pounding the wood line. The helicopters could easily see where the enemy fire was coming from even without having the Rangers on the ground marking their targets. The Cobra gunship stood off away from the trees putting 2.75-inch rockets, 40mm grenades, and 7.62 rounds from its minigun directly into the tree line. As the Cobra rolled out to come around on another run, the LOH pilot darted in and held his aircraft so that his M-60 gunner could sweep the tree line. Both aircraft were risking themselves to save the trapped patrol.

The rest of the surviving patrol members had managed to reach the temporary safety of the bomb crater, but they were in a box, and it would soon become their grave if help did not arrive in the next few minutes. The ten Rangers did what they could to keep the NVA off their backs, but they were soon running low on ammo.

A large number of B-40 rockets and hand grenades exploded along the lip of the crater, wounding almost everyone inside. Then, sixty meters to their north, a sniper began firing from an elevated position somewhere back in the trees. Occasionally, one of his rounds snapped into the side of the crater. Amazingly, he kept missing. But even if he was the worst sniper in Vietnam, it would be only a matter of time before he got lucky and hit someone.

At that time, a number of enemy soldiers broke out of the wood line and began moving up on the patrol. It was a particularly bad time for Sp4. Don Purdy, whose damaged M-16 had finally fallen apart, leaving him without a weapon.

Now, seeing a large number of VC attempting to crawl across the open field to close with the Rangers, Purdy began moving about the perimeter distributing his magazines among the surviving Rangers who could still shoot. Not satisfied only to help, Purdy picked up the patrol's two LAWs and fired them into the trees on the far side of the clearing. The first rocket detonated in the woods, causing a noticeable decrease of fire from the VC.

But when Purdy zeroed in on another target with the second LAW and squeezed the firing button, nothing happened. He repeated the process two more times, and still got misfires. Purdy threw the weapon out of the crater and began grabbing up all the loose grenades he could find. When he had an armload, he began heaving them out among the VC crawling toward the team.

Off to one side, a finger of brush extended from the tree line into the field, to within five meters of the bomb crater. Ten meters back in the thick cover of the brushy finger, the VC had infiltrated in another RPD light machine gun under the cover of the firefight. That weapon was playing hell with the Rangers. Every time one of them tried to look over the edge of the crater for a target, the enemy machine gun opened up and drove him back down again.

Suddenly, Sergeant Hall stood straight up in the bottom of the crater and said, "Enough of this shit!" With those words of battlefield wisdom still ringing off the sloping walls of their fortress, the burly senior NCO jumped out of the bomb crater and charged straight at the VC machine gun nest. The three VC manning the RPD panicked when they saw the massive Ranger storming their position. Without waiting for an invitation, they rose as one and turned to flee. Sergeant Hall was not having any of that at the moment, so he leveled his M-16 and dropped all three of them before they could escape.

As soon as Sergeant First Class Hall returned to the crater, the enemy sniper made that "one in a thousand" shot and hit the senior NCO hard in the left side. Hall put his hand to the wound, grunted, and muttered, "Shit," then continued to fight.

Seconds later, a Ranger on the far side of the perimeter spotted the sniper as he moved to take another shot. It was the sniper's last move.

Down in the crater, Norton finally managed to get the radio working, but his transmissions kept breaking up, making it necessary to repeat each message several times. However, he soon managed to contact Captain Schierholz flying on station in the C & C helicopter. Lieutenant Norton requested an immediate extraction.

When Schierholz came back seconds later and told him that they had to hold tight, as they would not be getting an extraction for a while, Norton changed his request to an ammunition resupply as soon as possible. But once again Schierholz replied that he could promise nothing at that time.

A short time later, the C & C radioed Norton back and told him that the light scout team was going off station. They were out of ordnance and low on fuel, and would have to get back to Cu Chi to rearm and refuel. But before the two aircraft left, they made a number of dry runs over the tree line to keep the enemy on their toes. From the temporary reduction in the volume of fire that occurred as the two helicopters made their dry runs, every man on the patrol realized that even the empty helicopters had a positive effect on their survival.

The two slicks were still in the area, and after the light scout team had departed for the rear, the Hueys began buzzing the tree line, attempting to distract the VC. The combined firepower of their four M-60s once again sent the VC scrambling for cover.

During the ensuing battle, Purdy continued moving about the perimeter tossing the last of his unused magazines in front of each man. Suddenly, Sergeant First Class Hall picked up one of the mags and exclaimed, "You got dirt in it."

Purdy put his hands on his hips, stared down at the senior NCO, and said, "Well, don't use the fucking thing then." Everyone in the crater snickered at first, then broke out laughing as they were suddenly struck by the humor of the exchange. It was a brief but welcome moment of levity in the Ranger patrol's fight for survival.

The two slicks continued passing back and forth overhead, using their machine guns to support the team. Their M-60 fire was a tremendous help, but it was not enough. Finally, the C & C radioed Norton that the slicks, too, would have to return to base. Their fuel level had reached the critical point.

Down on the ground, the Rangers understood that without air support, the surrounding VC would quickly leave their bunkers and overrun the Ranger position. They were nearly out of ammo and grenades, and they were virtually surrounded. Even escape and evasion was out of the question.

Aboard Centaur Two-three, the door gunner, Sp4. Richard Adams was an ex-Company F Ranger. The aircraft commander was WO James "D.R." Tonelli, who had gone to basic training with Sp4. Don Purdy. The two soldiers had been good friends there. As the C & C called to inform Lieutenant Norton that he and his Rangers were about to be abandoned, Tonelli decided that it was time to take matters into his own hands.

Banking the Huey around to come in from the east, Tonelli radioed the Ranger patrol leader. "Suppress your fire . . . suppress your fire, I'm coming in . . . I'm coming in."

Suddenly, the Rangers down in the bomb crater heard the unmistakable sounds of an approaching Huey slick. Peering cautiously over the edge of the crater, the Rangers watched as the solitary Huey came in over the tree line where the enemy bunkers were located. While Centaur Two-four with Captain Schierholz on board continued flying high cover, Centaur Two-three came in under fire and set down at the lip of the bomb crater that held the ten Rangers. The aircraft flared to a landing on the right side of the crater with its tail boom facing the wood line where the heavy enemy fire was coming from.

By that time, a number of VC had maneuvered all the way around to the other side of the woods so the helicopter and the Rangers were in a deadly cross fire. While the Huey slick sat waiting for the Rangers to climb aboard through the left side of the aircraft, Captain Tocco, the peter pilot, reached outside the cockpit through an open side window and began firing at the wood line to his front with a .38-caliber revolver.

Lieutenant Norton remained in the crater communicating with the helicopters while the rest of the Rangers scrambled aboard. Only when nearly everyone was on the Huey did Norton leave the crater and run for the crowded helicopter. On the way to the aircraft, he passed Tinney's body still draped over his machine gun. Suddenly, he noticed that the dead soldier didn't appear to have been hit as hard as Thomas and Floyd. Norton slid alongside Tinney and quickly checked

for a pulse. Amazingly, he detected a faint heartbeat. Tinney
was alive!

Norton turned and grabbed the unconscious man and
began dragging him across the open field to the waiting
chopper. When Stuckey and Purdy saw Norton struggling
with the body, they turned back to help. Adams, the door
gunner on the left side of the helicopter, also witnessed the
difficulty Norton was having, and leaped from his hellhole to
help his old comrades. The four men quickly lifted Tinney's
limp body and placed it on the edge of the cabin floor. Purdy
leaped aboard and cradled Tinney's head in his lap, while
Adams returned to his place in the starboard hellhole.

There was no room aboard the helicopter for Norton and
Stuckey, so the two Rangers stepped up on the skid and
draped themselves over Tinney's body to hold him in. From
inside the crowded Huey, Purdy and Guth reached out and
grabbed hold of their web gear to keep the Rangers from slipping off as the chopper went light on its skids and struggled
for transitional lift to get out of the clearing. As the Huey
began to pick up speed, it finally began to gain altitude. Just
as it seemed on the verge of escape, the aircraft took a large
number of hits through the rotor blades and the cabin floor,
causing it to vibrate and shudder. With its hydraulics affected
by the enemy rounds, Tonelli fought the helicopter into the
sky and out of reach of the enemy gunners.

The laboring Huey flew out of the area and headed for the
25th Division's base camp at Cu Chi. Tonelli realized that
Norton and Stuckey would never survive the twenty-minute
flight out on the skids. So two klicks away from the PZ, he located a large field, then horsed the shot-up aircraft to the
ground and set it down in the center of the open field. While
he kept the engine revved at full power, the Rangers quickly
rearranged their seating to allow Stuckey and Lieutenant
Norton to climb inside.

Stuckey and Norton had been attempting to get a serum albumin IV into Tinney's arm during the short flight from the

battleground to the open field, but they were having a difficult time finding a vein. But once on the ground, Stuckey managed to get in a needle, as Lieutenant Norton rigged the albumin drip.

As the Rangers finished their work and scrambled aboard, the pilot once again struggled aloft, then set off again for the final leg of his flight. A short time later Tonelli fought to land at the 12th Evac Hospital at Cu Chi, where medics and nurses were waiting for the overloaded helicopter.

As the first two medics approached the aircraft, the lead man looked inside the chopper and promptly passed out. The remaining medics began placing Tinney, Avery, Perez, Allmon, and Stuckey on gurneys and wheeled them into triage. However, when they approached Sergeant Hall, he would have none of that. He shook off the medics trying to get him on a gurney, and walked into the hospital on his own.

Stuckey still had a piece of OD metal from either Lieutenant Norton's PRC-25 radio or his pack frame embedded in his left cheek. While the orderlies were cutting off his clothes, Stuckey reached up and pulled out the shrapnel himself. Holding it out for them to see, he told the medics that he was okay and needed only a bandage, but they ordered him to remain there until they had a chance to check him over for other wounds.

As the medical staff worked over Tinney and Avery, Stuckey climbed down off the gurney and slipped back outside. He quickly secured a pair of cutoff fatigue pants, pulled them on, and rejoined the rest of his teammates.

By that time, in the usual large assortment of unauthorized vehicles, the entire company had arrived at the evac hospital to pick up the survivors of the mission. Tinney, Avery, Perez, Hall, and Allmon remained behind at the 12th Evac, though Perez, Hall, and Allmon would return to the company later that day. Avery's knee wound was serious and would send him back to the States. Sp4. Donald Tinney died ten days later without ever regaining consciousness. No one on the patrol had noticed that a tiny, eraser-size hole at the base of his skull had been caused by a sliver of shrapnel from the B-40 rocket that had killed Floyd and Thomas. That tiny sliver had caused hemorrhaging and tissue damage to Tinney's brain. Mercifully, he did not survive the wound.

The rest of the patrol were debriefed as soon as they reached the company area, and a large number of brass from every level of command throughout the division attended.

Back in the Renegade Woods, the fighting continued for five more days. Before it was finished, five infantry companies would be fed into the battle. U.S. artillery batteries would fire 741 rounds in support of the operation. Three flights of Cobra gunships, three air force AC-119 Shadow gunships, and eighteen fighter-bomber air strikes would be used to pound the two enemy battalions trapped in the Renegade Woods. A large inventory of enemy weapons, munitions, ordnance, supplies, and equipment was captured intact or destroyed at the scene of the fighting. Enemy dead on the battlefield numbered 101 confirmed, with one enemy soldier captured, and two more choosing to surrender. U.S. casualties numbered twelve killed and thirty-four wounded.

SFC Alvin W. Floyd was posthumously awarded the Distinguished Service Cross. Sgt. Michael Thomas and Sp4. Donald Tinney were posthumously awarded the Silver Star medal. First Lieutenant Phillip Norton, SFC Colin Hall, Sgt. Fred Stuckey, and Sgt. Charles Avery also received Silver Stars. The remaining six Rangers were awarded Bronze Stars with V device.

LRRP Detachment,
11th Armored Cavalry Regiment

☆   ☆   ☆   ☆   ☆

The LRRP detachment of the 11th Armored Cavalry Regiment was formed in April 1967 and placed under the command of the air cav troop. The first recruits were volunteers from line companies within the regiment. Recognizing the value of formal training, the detachment commander made sure that nearly every volunteer was sent to the MACV Recondo School at Nha Trang as soon as a slot was available. Although the detachment never numbered more than twenty-five or thirty men, its value to the regiment far surpassed its numbers.

Based at Xuan Loc, the LRRP detachment ran numerous missions in support of regimental operations. Operating in four- to seven-man teams, the LRRPs quickly made a reputation for themselves within the regiment.

On 9 May 1968, the military intelligence company at regiment sent a warning order to the detachment requesting a long-range recon patrol to go into an area just south of the village of Xa Bien Hoa, twenty kilometers southeast of Xuan Loc, to locate and observe an enemy base camp that was suspected to be in the area. The three-day mission was given to Sgt. Bob Bowman's five-man recon team.

As soon as he was notified of the mission, Bowman ran down his teammates and told them to meet him at the TOC. After they'd all sat through the intel briefing, Bowman told his men to start packing for the patrol while he and his assistant team leader, Staff Sergeant Chambers, flew out to take a look at the area of operations.

When they returned to the LRRP compound an hour later, Bowman told his teammates that their recon zone looked good. There was plenty of cover and concealment and several suitable LZs. The terrain in the AO was level to rolling, broken only by a number of long, deep ravines. The weather forecast was for clear and hot; they would be using a lot of water. However, a number of clear streams flowed through the recon zone, so the team would have no problem keeping water in their canteens. That meant they could carry more ammo and grenades and fewer canteens.

Bowman told them that he would be carrying the radio himself on the patrol. Their call sign would be Bullet Six-two. Staff Sergeant Chambers would carry a starlight scope, while everyone else wore their standard patrol load.

The team awoke well before daylight the next morning. Bowman and Chambers dressed quickly and checked on their teammates. Sgt. Sam Roller, an experienced Arkansas woodsman, would take point on the patrol and rotate with Sp4. Frank Teixiera. Sp4. Kenny "K-bar" Barr would bring up the tail end of the patrol.

Thirty minutes later, the five LRRPs were walking out to the air cav troop's helipad, two hundred meters from the LRRP detachment compound. Before long, the first rays of the sun began to creep over the eastern horizon; it was time to go. The men quickly overcame the usual premission jitters and climbed aboard the waiting Huey. Finally, the ship went light on its skids, then lifted off from the chopper pad. Swinging around to the south, the Huey joined up with the two chase ships and the C & C aircraft before heading out toward the area of operations.

In twenty minutes, they were out over their target area. Immediately, the insertion slick and the two chase ships slipped down on the deck and began popping in and out of every clearing in the area. On the third pop-in, the chopper flared over a large rectangular field measuring two hundred by three hundred meters. A large number of six- to eight-foot anthills rose out of the sparse cover. The ground between the anthills was covered with scrub brush and grass three to four feet high. There was an occasional bald spot where nothing grew at all. As the aircraft slowed a few feet above the ground, the five-man recon team quietly dropped from the skids and disappeared into the trees thirty meters away.

Fifteen meters into the single-canopy forest, the LRRPs, still in file, eased to the ground and set up a herringbone security pattern—the point man observing the front, the three men in the center alternating the flanks, and the last man covering the rear. Bowman quietly called for a commo check, gave a negative sitrep, and released the helicopters. The patrol remained at that location for fifteen minutes, listening and watching. Finally, Bowman signaled for Roller to move out. They still had nearly two klicks to travel to reach the area where the suspected enemy base camp was located.

They patrolled slowly and cautiously through the trees until they reached a thick, mature bamboo grove at approximately 0930 hours. While easing through the bamboo, they discovered a large open field about the size of a football field. It was covered with scattered waist-high shrubs, and a number of trails crossed the field, coming together in a crow's-foot configuration at the opposite corner.

Bowman decided to stop and set up a day-halt position in the bamboo to monitor the area. Setting up a tight perimeter a few meters back from the edge of the field, he told Barr and Teixiera to drop their rucks and LBE and make a thorough recon of the perimeter of the field. He instructed each man to take his weapons, a bandolier of ammo, a couple of frags, and a squad radio to communicate with the patrol base. Bowman reminded them that the radios worked only line of sight.

Barr and Teixiera slipped out of the bamboo and skirted the field, following a clear, shallow stream that ran down its west side. Eventually, they approached the edge of a deep ravine and immediately heard voices coming from it. Stopping, the two men slowly dropped to the ground and disappeared into the thin vegetation. After a while, when nothing else happened, they sat up in the grass. They could still hear the voices ahead. They seemed to be coming from the same area.

Cautiously, the LRRPs crawled to the edge of the ravine, which they were surprised to discover was much larger than they had originally thought. Forty meters wide, and forty feet deep, the ravine ran on as far as they could see. They were amazed when they discovered that the top of the ravine was actually at a lower elevation than the nearby stream. They quickly radioed back to the patrol base and reported what they had found, then told Bowman that they were going to crawl part of the way down into the ravine for a closer look.

A few minutes later, Bowman lost radio contact with his recon element. There had been no shots fired, nor any calls for help, but he could no longer reach them with his radio. He continued calling for the team, fearing that something had happened to them. Just when he was ready to go out to find them, the two men crawled back out of the ravine and returned the two hundred meters back to the team. Bowman listened quietly as the two men reported that they had seen tables made of bamboo, and a number of bamboo hootches. They had also spotted eight or ten VC, and could hear a number of others talking and carrying on just a few meters away. They'd heard the distinct sound of pots and pans banging together as if someone were cooking.

Bowman called in the information to the LRRP TOC, then decided to set up an RON back in the bamboo. The LRRPs established a circular perimeter without claymores, and sat back to wait. They were seventy-five meters from the main trail, and far enough back in the bamboo that they couldn't see what was going on out in the field, but they could hear, and the enemy soldiers down in the ravine gave them plenty to listen to.

Bowman plotted and called in a series of artillery concentrations to the 8-inch howitzer battery at the firebase supporting the patrol. He designated their original LZ, a number of points along the perimeter of the field to their front, the trail junctions, and the ravine as primary targets. Then he set up a two-man security watch, beginning at 1900 hours, and sat back to wait.

Unfortunately, no one was able to sleep with that many VC so close. From the time they set up in the bamboo until two hours after dark, the team listened to the constant sounds of pots and pans banging together and a large number of people laughing and talking. The VC in the ravine must have been pretty sure of their security, because they did not seem remotely concerned about noise discipline. However, the LRRPs could see no sign of illumination against the trees along the ravine, indicating that the enemy was at least practicing light discipline. From the sounds of their voices and the laughter, the LRRPs could tell that there were a number of women down in the ravine among the VC.

While the LRRPs were listening, they noticed a small wildcat that would watch them intently for a few minutes, then run back up and disappear into the bamboo. Each time it returned, it would come a little closer. Finally, it got to within arm's length of Sergeant Roller, who reached up and poked it lightly with his K-bar. The surprised cat disappeared into the night without making a sound. They never saw it again.

The next morning, the team ate and called in a sitrep, reporting that things had been quiet in the ravine since 2200 hours the previous night. At that point, Bowman decided to move the team to the opposite end of the field. He wanted to get closer to the spot where the main trail broke out of the woods and ran the length of the field. He pointed out that it was also closer to the team's pickup zone.

When they reached the area, they set up another day-halt back in the trees and posted security. Before long, Bowman decided to ambush the trail thirty meters out in front of them. He sent Barr crawling out into the field to a little rise off to one side, and told him to hide a claymore mine there, facing down one side of the trail. When Barr had made it safely back to the protection of the trees, Bowman told Roller to crawl out about thirty feet into the field, and set up a second claymore near a large anthill covering the other side of the trail.

Ten minutes later, Roller was hiding the claymore in the middle of the anthill, two feet above the ground, and making sure it was well camouflaged. When he was satisfied that no one could see it from the trail, he turned and started low-crawling back toward the woods where Chambers and the others were covering him. It was 0800 hours.

Roller, still twenty feet from reaching the cover of the woods next to Chambers, suddenly saw Chambers's eyes go wide. Roller froze instantly and watched while Chambers told him by means of hand signals that five VC had just come out of the woods near the ravine and were coming up the trail across the open field right at them.

The VC were walking along like they didn't have a care in the world. They were carrying their weapons slung upside down and had no security out. They were armed with AK-47s and SKS rifles. They were wearing light khaki uniforms and Ho Chi Minh sandals, and two of them wore rucksacks on their backs.

Roller was lying in the open under some low shrubs with his back to the approaching enemy. He was faced with a horrible dilemma. He couldn't get back to cover without being seen, and he couldn't see the five VC coming up his backside. And to make matters even worse, the detonator for his claymore was disconnected from the electrical cord and was still in the cargo pocket of his pants.

While Roller lay there wondering what to do, Chambers, still hiding back in the brush, continued signaling Roller to keep him up on what the enemy soldiers were doing. He told Roller that they had stopped, and three of the VC were now moving back toward the woods where they had come from, while the first two continued moving directly up the trail in the direction of the Rangers.

Ever so cautiously, Roller slipped the detonator from his pants pocket and hooked it up to his claymore wire. Finally, he was able to turn halfway around to where he could look back over his shoulder at the approaching VC. He could just see the two enemy soldiers approaching, barely making out the three others disappearing into the woods.

The nearest VC was only ten meters away from Roller and three feet from the anthill when Roller detonated the claymore. The two VC disappeared in a fine red mist, splashing blood on Barr, hidden seventy feet away.

As the smoke began to settle, Roller screamed at Barr to blow his claymore, but the LRRP had already yanked it free and was pulling it in hand over hand. After Barr had recovered the antipersonnel mine, Bowman regrouped the team back at the day-halt position, then told them to get ready to escape and evade toward their PZ one hundred meters away. Bowman had already been on the radio calling in the contact and requesting an extraction. At the same time, he had called for the artillery fire on the preplots on the ravine. The first volley of two rounds impacted just as the LRRPs were beginning to move out for the PZ. The first round was a smoke and the second was HE. Unfortunately, they missed the ravine and landed within thirty meters of the team.

Shouting at Bowman, Roller told him to add 150 meters and fire for effect. Bowman complied immediately. The next salvo impacted right in the middle of the ravine.

Back in the trees around the ravine, the LRRPs heard shouting, screaming, and the loud sounds of pans banging around. The next salvo landed right on target.

Bowman called in a few adjustments, then turned and told his point man to head for the PZ and not waste any time getting there. Five minutes later, they were at the edge of the woods next to the PZ, hiding behind a large anthill while waiting for choppers, when the TOC called back and ordered the team to go back to the ravine and assess the damage to the enemy base camp. The five LRRPs only shook their heads in disbelief at the stupidity of the command, but had no choice but to comply.

The team quickly reformed with Teixiera at point. Roller

moved up to take slack. The patrol moved out sharply and proceeded down the trail toward the ravine. In the distance, they could still hear people shouting and yelling back in the woods near the ravine.

The LRRP patrol made it back to the opening at the edge of the field near where they had just blown the ambush. Teixiera was up at point cautiously looking straight ahead across the field. Behind him at slack, Sam Roller was scanning the right side of the trail, while Barr at the number-three slot was observing the left side.

Teixiera, hyper by nature, was walking point for the very first time, and he was highly nervous. Bowman was back at the number-four slot, still working the 8-inchers back and forth over the ravine.

Suddenly, Roller spotted the barrel of an AK-47 assault rifle sticking out from behind a tree twenty feet off the right side of the trail. Realizing that it was aimed directly at their point man, Roller yelled, "Tex, get down!" and at the same time dove to the right of the trail. As he hit the ground, Roller could see that the enemy soldier's entire left side was exposed. Flipping his selector switch to rock 'n' roll, Roller stitched the NVA soldier from his crotch to his shoulders, emptying an entire magazine into the man.

When there was no return fire, the LRRPs slowly got back to their feet and pulled off the trail to the right. Setting up a quick perimeter around the dead soldier, the rest of the team watched and listened as Bowman called in the contact and reported that they had been on their way to check out the artillery impact area but had met resistance. The TOC told them to strip the body and return to the PZ for extraction.

The LRRPs checked to make sure there were no other enemy soldiers hiding among the trees, then began to collect the dead soldier's gear and his weapon. There was no doubt among the LRRPs that the man was not a VC. His close-cut hair, his clean, well-manicured fingernails, full rucksack, pith helmet, and brand new AK-47 (still full of cosmoline) had NVA written all over it.

They cut off the dead man's rucksack and his shirt, then took his helmet and weapon. Inside his rucksack, they found a Chicom mess kit, a Czech compass, two foreign-made miniature pineapple grenades, two rice tubes made from pant legs tied off at both ends, one AK magazine (in his weapon), and sixty loose rounds. The patrol gathered up all the captured gear and headed back to the PZ at a run.

Before the patrol had gotten twenty meters away from the edge of the field, regimental S-2 radioed and told them to go back and recover the body. The LRRPs shook their heads in utter disbelief, then turned around and went back to get it. They couldn't understand the need for bringing the body out. If S-2 wanted to know if the guy was NVA or VC, the LRRPs could tell them that.

Finally, dragging it back through the woods nearly a hundred meters, they reached the PZ and set up security around the base of a giant (and still very active) anthill. The TOC radioed that the lift ships were on the way. Bowman radioed the artillery FDO and told him to cease fire and stand by, then called the incoming aircraft and told them that the area was secure and the PZ was cold.

It was 1100 hours when the Huey slick finally flared out and landed a short distance away. The team left its position around the base of one of the giant anthills and tossed the dead NVA soldier into the open cabin. Scrambling in behind it, Bowman screamed "Clear!" to the aircraft commander.

As the Huey lifted out of the clearing, ARA gunships from the air cav troop arrived and began pounding the ravine with rockets. On the way out of the area, the crew chief shouted to the LRRPs that the ARA pilots were reporting that they had groups of people running around the ravine everywhere. Once again, the regiment's LRRP detachment had accomplished its mission.

Company D, 151st Infantry (Ranger), Indiana National Guard

Company D, 151st Infantry (LRP), Indiana National Guard, had arrived in South Vietnam on 28 December 1968. It had been selected to replace Company F, 51st Infantry (LRP) (Abn), as the long-range patrol element of II Field Force. Company F, 51st, had recently been deactivated, and its four platoons had been utilized to staff the newly formed 78th Infantry LRP detachment assigned to the 3d Brigade of the 82d Airborne Division, and the 79th Infantry LRP detachment assigned to the 1st Brigade of the 5th Infantry Division (Mech).

After Company D's activation, most of the company had traveled down to Panama to complete the U.S. Army Jungle Warfare School, while those who were not yet airborne-qualified attended jump school at Fort Benning, Georgia.

Based at Long Binh, the new LRP company began conducting operations immediately upon arrival in South Vietnam. However, just over a month later, Company D, 151st Infantry (LRP) lost its "LRP" status when the Department of the Army decided to bring all the U.S. Army long-range patrol companies and detachments under the common heritage of the 75th Infantry (Ranger) regimental designation. That action went into effect on 1 February 1969.

A week later, the new Ranger company received a warning order from II Field Force G-2 for a recon team to go into an area twenty miles northwest of Saigon on a five-day recon/ambush patrol. No overflight was made, but aerial photos were used to locate trails, streams, and other prominent terrain features throughout the area, and also to pinpoint a number of suitable LZs and PZs.

SFC Pappy Hayes, the company operations NCO, assigned the mission to Sgt. Jack Jarvis's Team Two-seven. When Jarvis found out that his team had won the lottery, he quickly notified his ATL, Sp4. Terry MacDonald, and told him to round up the rest of the team. After the briefing, the team RTO, Sp4. John Mason, went off to grab a couple of extra batteries for his radio, while Sp4. Walt Hasty and Private First Class Schwartz headed for the ammo bunker to pick up grenades, claymores, and some belted ammo for Hasty's M-60. The sixth man on the team, a *chieu hoi* named Ty, would show up later.

Since its arrival and in-country acclimatization, the company had been running full tilt, with most teams working a grueling five-day-out/two-day-in patrol schedule. It was a tough way to break into the dangerous business of long-range patrolling, but Delta Company, 151st Infantry (Ranger) was probably the best-trained long-range patrol company to enter the war. The necessary experience would come with time.

The insertion went in at 1030 hours the next morning. With two Huey gunships in trail on the rear flanks of the insertion slick, the pilot flew right into the LZ and flared to a low hover in the north corner of an abandoned field covered with twelve-inch-high grass and scattered scrub brush.

High overhead, the C & C aircraft circled in a wide, lazy orbit, watching the insertion go in down below.

As the lift ship hovered four feet over the open clearing, the six-man recon team exited both sides of the aircraft and ran the last twenty-five meters into the wood line. Pushing inside the trees fifteen meters, they dropped to the ground in a tight circle and lay dog for another thirty to forty-five minutes while Mason established commo and called in a negative sitrep. Just before Jarvis signaled Ty to move out, Mason radioed the C & C to release the choppers.

Maintaining a regular five-meter interval, the patrol moved west beneath single canopy. They moved slowly, staying in thick cover as much as possible. After two hundred meters or so, the team encountered a three-foot ditch, twelve to eighteen inches deep, running north to south. It looked like a runoff ditch, but it was bone dry at the time.

The patrol halted for a few minutes, then crossed the ditch and moved fifteen meters beyond it. There, under the trees, they discovered a major high-speed trail twelve to eighteen inches wide and running northeast to southwest. While the team set up security in the fairly open area around them, Ty and Jarvis checked out the trail. It wasn't long before Ty, who spoke reasonably good English, told Jarvis that he was familiar with the trail. He quickly added that there would be three enemy soldiers coming by at approximately 1700 hours.

Jarvis decided to pull back into the nearest cover to set up an ambush. Unfortunately, the nearest suitable cover near the trail was back at the ditch, fifteen meters away.

Quickly, the patrol dropped back to the ditch and set up a linear ambush. With four claymores facing the trail—one up and one down the ditch, and two more on their back trail—the six Rangers were loaded for bear. It was nearly 1230 hours.

Hasty took up a position watching the north end of the trail with MacDonald, while Ty and Schwartz set up on the south end. Jarvis and Mason were in the center with the radio. The six Rangers took turns pulling security and downing cold LRRP rations. Relying on Ty's knowledge of the local VC, MacDonald told Hasty he was going to cut some Z's, and asked Hasty to wake him at 1600.

At 1750 hours, everyone was awake and fully alert. Just like clockwork, the team heard voices coming down the trail from the north. Unknown to them at the time, the trail crossed the dry ditch just thirty meters north of the team. The voices sounded as if they were in the far end of the ditch when they first heard them. Suddenly, three VC stepped out of the brush on the trail and began moving down it to the south. They were talking easily among themselves and looking down at the ground as if they knew there was no one within a hundred miles. Each had an AK-47 slung over his shoulder. They wore black pajamas, Ho Chi Minh sandals, and were bareheaded.

As the three enemy soldiers advanced down the trail, the Rangers secured their claymore detonators and held their breath while they watched the VC enter the kill zone. When Jarvis initiated the ambush, all four claymores facing the trail detonated in a millisecond. The Rangers immediately followed up the claymores with small-arms fire, expending multiple magazines into the kill zone.

As MacDonald ran a full magazine through his CAR-15, the last man in the enemy patrol unexpectedly broke out of the smoke and ran back up the trail to the north. MacDonald was caught unprepared by the maneuver, and was unable to reload and fire his empty weapon in time to stop him.

Grabbing the M-79, he put the sights on the spot up the ditch where the trail crossed it thirty meters away. Trying to time the shot to coincide with the fleeing VC's arrival, MacDonald fired the HE round and saw it detonate just as the VC hit the opening. Turning back to the trail, he recovered his CAR-15, reloaded, and joined his teammates in raking the kill zone. As he fired long bursts out on the trail, he was remotely aware that Hasty was, once again, melting the barrel on the M-60 to his left.

The Ranger machine gunner had previously earned a reputation in the company for his love of the weapon. The only problem was that once he started working out with the "hog," he forgot to let up on the trigger and fired until the final piece of brass kicked out of the chamber. He had warped more than one barrel in the short time the company had been in country.

Suddenly, MacDonald felt a searing pain in his back. He knew in a minute that he'd been hit. He'd always been told that if you were shot, you either felt nothing at all or you experienced a painful burning sensation. Just his luck that he got the painful burning sensation! He stopped firing and looked up at Hasty, who was still sweeping the trail with the M-60. Over the loud chatter of the light machine gun, Mac-Donald shouted, "Look at my back . . . my back is on fire!"

Without breaking stride on the M-60, Hasty looked down and snarled, "Man, I don't see no blood. You ain't hit!"

With that, MacDonald could only respond meekly, "Okay," then continue his firing. He would discover later that you should never stand on the right side of a maniac working out with an M-60. The hot brass has to go somewhere.

By the time each man had gone through three to four mags, and Hasty had burned up the two-hundred-round belt in his M-60, there was no longer any movement out on the trail. Jarvis immediately called a cease-fire.

The five Rangers and their Kit Carson scout waited in silence for nearly two minutes, watching and listening for any signs of life from out on the trail. There was no return fire. Jarvis and Schwartz stood up and stepped into the open to check the kill zone. At the same time, Ty slipped out to the right to check farther down the trail to the southwest. Back in the ditch, Hasty pulled out a Marlboro and lit it off the warped, red-hot barrel of his M-60. Kneeling beside him, rubbing his back, MacDonald said nothing.

Out in the kill zone, Jarvis and Schwartz found a single Ho Chi Minh sandal and a couple of major blood trails headed due west, where the two VC had crawled away from the trail. The two Rangers rejoined their comrades while Mason got on the radio and called in the contact. Jarvis told him to request an extraction.

By that time, it was getting late in the day. The patrol was two hundred meters from its designated PZ, and Jarvis wanted to get out of the area before dark. By then, every VC in the province knew an American recon team was in the area, and the VC could be counted on to try getting even.

The TOC soon radioed back and told Mason that the choppers were cranking up and would soon be on the way. They would reach the team in "three zero mikes." Thirty minutes is a long time when you're sitting on the bull's-eye with sirens going off all around.

Ten minutes passed before the patrol began to hear signal shots fired to the south. The firing was coming from a number of individual weapons firing two single rounds in a row. They heard the two-shot signal two more times over the next five minutes. The second time, they were markedly closer. It didn't take a rocket scientist to realize what was happening. The LRRPs were about to have some company.

Jarvis instructed his men to take up positions in the trench and be ready to open fire on his command. Thirty seconds later, they heard the sounds of movement coming from down the trail about forty meters away. Jarvis thumbed the selector switch on his weapon to full auto and opened fire. As the rest of the patrol joined in, the enemy began returning fire. The rounds from the enemy weapons were snapping through the trees above the Rangers, sending a cascade of branches and debris raining down on them. Jarvis muttered a silent prayer, giving thanks for the shallow ditch they were in.

The two sides exchanged fire for thirty seconds; then Jarvis called for a cease-fire. As things quieted down they no longer heard firing from the VC to their south. However, seconds later, the team began receiving fire from the west, thirty-five to forty meters away. Jarvis couldn't be sure, but it sounded like two to three AKs firing short bursts. And their aim was improving.

As the Rangers began to return fire, Schwartz was shooting from his position in the ditch between Jarvis and Ty. Suddenly, the two men heard him shouting, "I'm hit . . . I'm hit."

Jarvis emptied his magazine toward the enemy, then looked down and shouted, "Where?"

Kneeling in the bottom of the ditch, cradling his arm, Schwartz looked up and held out his hand. From the look and the location of the tiny cut on his little finger, Jarvis quickly realized that the young Ranger had only sliced himself on the magazine release on the side of his receiver. Frowning and shaking his head, Jarvis turned and slugged Schwartz on the side of his head, taking the young Ranger's mind immediately off the pain in his finger and causing the wound to heal in record time. Combat-expedient first aid! Seconds later, the fully recovered Schwartz was once again firing into the trees across the trail.

Mason suddenly looked up and said, "The helicopters just radioed that they are five mikes out and closing."

Jarvis responded to the good news by reaching into the side pouch on his rucksack and pulling out a smoke grenade. Removing the safety pin, he casually tossed it out toward the trail. Seconds later, the customary *pop* was followed by a dense cloud of yellow smoke.

It was getting pretty close to dark by that time, and the prospects for a clean extraction were growing dimmer by the minute. Suddenly, two Huey gunships roared over the trees and identified the patrol's smoke. Mason reached the pilots on the radio and instructed them to make their runs south to north just west of the smoke.

Over the next five minutes the two gunships made two or three runs each, tearing apart the jungle on the other side of the trail with miniguns and rockets. The enemy small-arms fire immediately ceased.

Taking advantage of the momentary lull in the firing, Jarvis told Mason to call the gunships back and tell them that the team was going to blow their remaining claymores and head east. Seconds later, with four staggered blasts, the remaining claymores detonated north and south of the ditch and back toward the team's PZ. Before the smoke and dust had time to settle, the Rangers were up and running through the woods toward the PZ. They neared the edge of the clearing much quicker than they had anticipated, nearly charging right out into it without realizing that it was there.

By then the gunships had finished hitting the woods on the other side of the trail, and were over the PZ to cover the extraction. Without hesitating, the lead ship made a quick gun run down the tree line on the east side of the PZ just as the team arrived.

As the gunship broke away over the top of the team, a Huey slick reported that it was on short final a hundred meters out and closing. Five seconds later, the chopper began receiving heavy small-arms fire from five or six AK-47s shooting from somewhere in the trees to the north. With a quick burst of acceleration, the Huey pulled out of the PZ and aborted the extraction.

One of the gunships came in immediately after the Huey had departed the area and made two more runs against the VC to the north. By that time, it was growing too dark to read. The C & C notified the Rangers down at the edge of the clearing that they would make one more attempt to pick up the team. If that didn't work, the Rangers would have to find a place to hole up for the night or escape and evade out of the area.

That time, as the slick approached the pickup zone, the two gunships, out on the flanks and slightly in trail, escorted the Huey in, firing up the surrounding woods as they came. Only a fool, or a fool's commanding officer, would step out in the open and face a deadly minigun. Even the door gunners on the slicks were firing.

As the Huey flared to a hover just above the clearing, the patrol broke cover five meters back at the edge of the woods and sprinted for the waiting chopper. Almost as one, the six men dove through the open doorway and took up firing positions from inside the open cabin. The slick pulled pitch and fought its way up and out of the tiny clearing, then struggled for altitude.

The team returned to the Ranger compound well after dark. The debriefing by their operations officer was thorough but short. It was Team Two-seven's first contact. Five broken cherries on a single patrol! As for Ty, well the South Vietnamese hadn't been a cherry for a long, long time.

2d Brigade LRRP Detachment, 4th Infantry Division

When the 4th Infantry Division moved into the Central Highlands of Vietnam in 1966, it took over the largest divisional area of operations in country. It was also the most remote and one of the deadliest. As the three brigades separated and moved out to secure their individual tactical areas of responsibility, they quickly realized the need for long-range reconnaissance patrols. Unlike the other divisions serving in Vietnam, the 4th Infantry Division's commander authorized each brigade to form its own long-range patrol detachment. Those early LRRPs were to become some of the finest long-range patrollers in the Vietnam War.

The 2d Brigade of the 4th Infantry Division was based at the Oasis, thirty miles west of Pleiku. At the end of May 1967, the entire brigade, and especially its LRRP detachment, was experiencing major problems with personnel turnover. The soldiers who had deployed in country with the division a year earlier were now rotating back to the States.

The LRRP detachment's operational teams found themselves in a major state of fluctuation, and team integrity had gone to hell. No LRRP ever knew who he would be going out with on his next mission. And every member of every team that went out into the field did so not knowing for certain just who on his team he could count on in a bad situation.

When a warning order came down from brigade S-2 on the last day of May 1967 for a BDA mission along the path of an

Arc Light along the Cambodian border, the unit's first sergeant found himself in a quandary. He had no team leaders left in the detachment compound to take the mission. Looking around for someone capable of handling the four-day patrol, he was forced to go against the established detachment SOP and ask Sgt. Ronald Bonert to take it.

Bonert, a native of the Chicago area, had already served his year in Vietnam and was due to DEROS in six days. He had already packed his bags and had stood down. However, as a favor to the first sergeant and not wanting to let his unit or his buddies down, Sergeant Bonert accepted the mission.

Since Bonert no longer had a team of his own, he was forced to slap one together from the sparse collection of unattached LRRPs still in the company area. In a stroke of luck, he discovered that Sp4. Dan Harmon, a Native American Indian from Kodiak, Alaska, was still in the area and asked him to serve as assistant team leader.

Bonert and Harmon had a lot in common, especially since they were both scheduled to catch a C-130 down to Cam Ranh Bay on the same day. Like Bonert, Harmon was due to DEROS on 5 June. And like Bonert, his sense of loyalty and pride would not allow him to sit idly by when his unit needed him. Unlike Bonert, Dan Harmon had just returned to the detachment from a lengthy stay in the hospital. He had been wounded in both legs during an earlier mission, and his teammates had been forced to leave him behind. However, the courageous young LRRP had refused to give up and had crawled out at night on his own. Bonert knew that Harmon was a man he could count on.

The two leaders went slowly through the LRRP compound, weighing their alternatives before recruiting the rest of their team, finally selecting Sp4. Ron Coon and a new man, Sp4. Jim Sommers, to fill out the patrol. Coon had gone out with Bonert before and was steady in the field, but it was to be Sommers's first patrol.

Around noon on the thirty-first, a few hours after the Arc

Light had gone in, Bonert and Harmon flew out for a closer look at their LZ. They became a little concerned when they discovered the AO's proximity to the Cambodian border. There was always a lot of heavy enemy activity that close to the border, and neither LRRP had an overwhelming desire to make his last mission his most memorable one.

At 1330 hours on 1 June, the four LRRPs walked slowly down to the brigade chopper pad, 150 meters from the LRRP compound. They quickly climbed aboard the Huey slick, took off, and picked up the rest of their helicopters on the way—a pair of Huey gunships, a C & C slick, and a chase ship. The five-ship formation flew west to the team's AO, then dropped down low into the foothills west of the mountains and north of Highway 19.

The chase ship and the insertion slick went into the AO with the chase ship in trail. When the insertion ship suddenly dropped into a clearing to make a false insertion, the chase ship shot past it and continued on, while the insertion chopper popped back up behind it. The two aircraft made two more leapfrog exchanges until, on the fourth one, the insertion slick hovered a couple of seconds longer than usual over a small cul-de-sac on the side of a hill, and the four LRRPs dropped ten or fifteen feet from the chopper's skids into the thick grass. As the slick popped back up behind the chase ship, both aircraft, followed closely by the two gunships, continued on as if nothing had happened.

Once on the ground, the LRRPs quickly gathered themselves together and ran uphill toward the wood line to their north. Even though the direction of their march was to the south, they headed north for a hundred meters or so to mislead anyone who might have been watching the insertion.

They hit the trees twenty-five meters off the LZ and went another fifteen to twenty meters into the woods before going to ground. There, just in front of them, was a major high-speed trail, wide enough to handle vehicular traffic. Everywhere there were fresh footprints in the dirt, and a few feet back in the brush a large number of freshly dug spider holes lined both sides of the trail. The trees overhead had even been tied together to camouflage the trail from the ever-present American aircraft.

Five minutes into the mission, the patrol had already located a major artery of the Ho Chi Minh trail. Unfortunately, their mission was a BDA, so monitoring the trail would have to be left for the next patrol sent into the area.

While Bonert and Sommers pulled security, Harmon and Coon moved in for a closer look at the trail and found tracks in the moist dirt that could only have been made during the previous fifteen to thirty minutes. The tracks in the trail had been made by NVA rubber boots, not the Ho Chi Minh sandals of the Viet Cong.

The patrol pulled back away from the trail and lay dog for fifteen minutes, making a commo check and reporting on the trail. When they failed to see or hear anything in the area, they called in and released the helicopters.

Finally, Bonert signaled for Coon to move out. The Recondo School– and sniper-trained point man slipped through the double-canopy jungle, skirting the trail as he led the team on a wide, swinging hook back around the open LZ and eventually to the south-southwest. The patrol needed to reach the area where Highway 19 had been cut off at the border. The Arc Light had gone into an area just south of where the highway ended against a large timber and earthen berm that had been bulldozed across the roadbed to cut off the highway. The LRRPs thought some air force flyboy might have gotten a hot infrared reading or spotted smoke drifting up from some Montagnard's cookfire, and decided to spend a few million of Uncle Sam's dollars on the chance there might be someone down there. More likely, the strike was planned as the result of hard intelligence from the comint people.

Bonert had noticed on the overflight that two-thirds of the strike zone was across the border inside Cambodia, a direct violation of the Geneva Convention and official U.S. policy in Southeast Asia. However, it was close enough for government work, and no one would be the wiser if the four LRRPs slipped across the imaginary line forty or fifty meters to see what the air force had bought for its money.

Still heading south, the four-man patrol eventually moved out of the jungle and into a large open area full of ten-foot-high brush and thick masses of wait-a-minute vines. This brushy area occupied nearly two-thirds of a grid square and extended all the way to the north of Highway 19. There were no trails through the maze so, to avoid making excessive noise, the patrol had to take its time covering the fifteen hundred meters to the highway. Unfortunately, their passage left a trail that even Ray Charles could have followed.

The patrol reached a point three hundred meters north of the highway by 1700 hours that evening. They were only four hundred meters east of the Cambodian border, and they knew that they were in an area of heavy enemy traffic. Moving into the densest cover they could find, the patrol set up a box formation in a cold NDP and put out their four claymores facing north, south, east, and west. Bonert posted a guard immediately after dark, one man on at a time, one-and-a-half-hour shifts.

Just after dark, NVA forces across the border suddenly opened fire with an RPD machine gun, sending a long one-hundred-round string of white tracers directly over the patrol's NDP. This happened every hour on the hour until first light. The first time it happened, everyone on the team simply freaked, but they soon realized that the fire was far too high to be directed specifically at them. It was coming from a long distance away and seemed more likely a beacon and a time mark for NVA troops moving about the area at night.

Sometime around 0130 hours, the LRRP on watch heard several single shots fired in quick succession back in the direction from where the patrol had inserted earlier that day. The patrol had covered nearly twelve hundred meters before dark, just about the same distance as the shots they had just heard.

The guard woke up the rest of the team a short time later when he began hearing voices shouting to the northeast. Bonert and the remainder of the LRRPs felt pretty sure that the NVA had just discovered their back trail.

They had left a rather noticeable trail in the grass, moving south, but that couldn't be helped. Now they were going to pay the price for it. Since they were still in the thick brush, the trail led right up to where they had set up their NDP. Luckily, as a precaution, Coon had buttonhooked fifty meters back along their trail, and that might give them a little warning if the NVA came before daylight.

The remainder of the night passed rather quietly, considering the earlier activity. At first light, the LRRPs quietly picked up their gear, sanitized their campsite, and slipped quietly away through the brush in the direction of Highway 19. According to Bonert's map, they should cut the highway right where it met the border.

When they broke out of the brush ninety minutes later, right before them was the large berm of brush and downed trees that had been used to interdict traffic on the highway. If their maps were correct, the border was 150 meters to the west.

When they got a little closer, they could just make out the border area, where the brush had been thinned a little. The team followed that trace about five hundred meters to the beginning of the Arc Light strike zone. But while working toward it, they encountered another major high-speed trail very similar to the earlier one—wide, well camouflaged, and full of fresh tracks.

Bonert stopped the team and signaled the men to set up on the near side of the trail for a few minutes to monitor the high-speed for any foot traffic before attempting to cross it. There was none.

Finally, he signaled Coon to lead them across the trail, where they immediately encountered the northwest end of the Arc Light strike zone. Setting up security, Bonert took pictures of some of the bomb craters—just run-of-the-mill, general bullshit photos that didn't amount to anything for intelligence purposes, but meant a lot to the brass; it gave them a chance to see firsthand just what good planning and an open-ended budget could accomplish.

As the patrol continued to follow the Arc Light farther into the strike zone, they soon discovered that it was far too tangled to move in. From his spot at the rear of the patrol, Bonert signaled for Coon to stop, and then turned around and backed them out of the deadfalls and shattered earth. He planned to skirt the worst of the mess, then come back into it about halfway through. For the time being, they were still on the Vietnamese side of the border.

When they finally managed to back out of the Arc Light zone, they had to turn back and recross the high-speed trail to get around the edge of the damage. When they reached the trail, they paralleled it for two hundred meters, since it was going in the same general direction they wanted to move. They weren't pleased with that, but they had no choice in the matter.

Before long, they reached a point where they were forced to recross the trail once again. Coon was just coming up to cross the trail, when he suddenly froze in his tracks. Behind him, Harmon came up slowly and, placing his hand on the young point man's left shoulder, gently shoved him to the ground.

From where the two men lay, Harmon pointed out four NVA set up in ambush positions up along the trail. They had their backs to the team, and hadn't seen them approach, but there was no doubt between either of them that the ambush had been put together just for them.

The LRRPs had walked up on the back side of the ambush, and that had saved their lives. They were less than twenty meters away from the NVA, and had no idea how many more were still hidden in the brush around the trail.

Slowly, the two men stood up and began backing out of the area. When they were clear, they moved fifty meters back out to Highway 19, jumped in an old bomb crater, and set up a defensive perimeter. They remained there for nearly twenty minutes, calling in the report and trying to get their hearts out of their throats. Then, weighing their options, Bonert decided to circle around and recross Highway 19 to get back on the north side.

They quickly left the questionable safety of the bomb crater, moved up to within ten meters of the edge of the highway, and were just getting ready to cross. They were standing there deliberating for a few minutes about what to do next, when two NVA soldiers ran out of the brush ten to fifteen meters to their left, crossed the highway, and jumped into the ditch on the opposite side. No one had time to react or to fire a shot. One minute there was no one there, and the next minute the two enemy soldiers were running across the highway and jumping into the ditch.

Without waiting for Bonert to say anything, Harmon and Coon pulled out M-26 frags and threw them high into the air toward the ditch on the other side of the road. As the two frags were at the zenith of their arc, they met two Chicom stick grenades coming back the other way. The LRRPs immediately dove for the nearest cover. Fortunately, the LRRPs' grenades functioned just like the directions said, while the Made-in-China grenades performed more like castanets, and failed to explode.

Flinching at the sound of the explosions, the entire patrol leaped to their feet and moved two hundred meters to the east as fast as they could run. Of course, Bonert realized that their BDA mission had just been canceled, and the only thing left to do at that point was to get out of Dodge on the fastest pony they could find.

On the north side of the road, to their east, was the dilapidated remains of an old triangular border outpost from the French colonial days. Originally constructed of compacted earth and reinforced with logs, the three-sided fortress was nearly seventy-five meters on a side. There had been a large bunker in each corner made from the same materials, and a fourth one in the center of the compound.

Over the years, the timbers had rotted away to dust, and the earthen berm was not far from once again becoming a part of the surrounding countryside. The roofs of the bunkers had caved in, but the depressions were still there, and the one at the western end of the fortress made a suitable place for the LRRPs to seek cover. As soon as they were set up, Bonert got on the radio and called the TOC to report that they were compromised and requested an extraction.

The commander of the battalion that the LRRPs were op con to heard the call and broke in to say that he had had a company in that same area a week before and there was nothing out there. Then he told Bonert that he couldn't spare any birds.

Bonert then called for a fire mission. He soon got a 155mm battery to fire a few HE rounds in the vicinity of the ambush and a couple more on the north side of the road where the two NVA had jumped into the ditch. It was about 0930 hours.

A short time later, the TOC radioed back and said that the battalion commander had just authorized three tanks and an infantry platoon to run down Highway 19 to the border and extract the patrol. By that time, the team was watching a squad of NVA as they moved out into the cover and set up in the brush three hundred meters to the west of the French fort and right along the border close to the team's last NDP.

A few minutes later, Harmon spotted more movement along Highway 19 on the south side of the road, 150 to 200 meters west of the team. Once again, Bonert called in a fire mission on the enemy targets.

At 1330 hours, the patrol was told that one of the tanks had thrown a track and that they would be out to get them as soon as it was fixed. That was good news for the LRRPs, as the nearest friendlies were twenty klicks away.

At about 1430 hours, three M-48 tanks with a platoon of infantry in two columns behind them came rolling down the middle of Highway 19 from the east. The LRRPs watched them draw closer until the lead tank pulled to a stop out on the highway just even with the patrol. In the turret, a helmeted first lieutenant rose up and hollered, "What in the hell are you doing in there? Don't you know you're in the middle of a minefield?"

At that point the LRRPs were just happy to see the tanks. They weren't too worried about a goddamn minefield.

The officer shouted, "Get down." Then slowly but deliberately, the lead M-48 backed off the road and out through the twelve-to-eighteen-inch grass to where the LRRPs sat waiting inside the collapsed bunker. When they saw the tank coming, they crawled out of the hole and moved up on the highest remaining section of the berm. When the tank finally reached them, the four LRRPs climbed gratefully aboard. While Harmon, Sommers, and Coon found places to sit on the top of the tank, Bonert moved up next to the tank commander and began pointing out to the lieutenant the enemy situation as they knew it, at which point the officer drove his tank back out onto the highway and right up the road into the middle of the NVA.

When they saw what the tankers were up to, the LRRPs wanted to get off the fast-moving steel giant, but they never got the chance. Following closely behind the other two tanks, the lieutenant left the infantry struggling to catch up and raced up the road to the spot where the NVA had set up their ambush.

When they reached the area where the LRRPs had reported all the NVA activity, the three tanks turned off the road and out into the brush on the north side of the road. As they sat there with their powerful engines running, the number-two and number-three tanks lowered their cannons and fired canister rounds into the brush. Then without even stopping to assess the damage, the three tanks backed up to the highway and pivoted back to the east. Once again, the lieutenant's tank became the lead tank. The poor infantry had just caught up and were now forced once again to fall in behind the last tank.

The small-armor/infantry force had moved about a hundred meters down the road when the NVA exploded a command-detonated mine under the track of the lead tank, blowing off the tread. Five seconds later, a similar explosion occurred at the rear of the column, and the third tank found itself disabled from a thrown tread. The center tank was now unable to pass to the front or retreat to the rear on the narrow highway, effectively trapping it between the two disabled tanks.

At the first sounds of combat, the infantry platoon bailed into the ditch along the south side of the road. They would remain there until the shooting came to an end.

Suddenly, two RPG rounds *whooshed* out of the cover along the road and hit the lead tank on the turret. One of the rounds exploded at Coon's feet, blowing off one of his combat boots and perforating him with shrapnel.

The other round went off between Bonert's feet, shredding his legs and throwing red-hot shrapnel everywhere. The second round had detonated about eighteen inches from Coon's head; however, Bonert saved his life by absorbing most of the blast.

Sommers had been on the back side of the tank when the RPGs had hit the turret near the front. He had taken a small fragment in the back but had missed the main force of the blasts.

When the RPGs had exploded, Harmon had been at the rear of the turret, with Coon at the center, and Bonert toward the front. Coon had been knocked senseless, but remembers someone grabbing his web gear and dragging him off the turret. He found out later that Harmon had managed to pull him off the exposed tank. He ended up in the ditch, where he promptly passed out.

Harmon had then climbed back up on top of the tank and was trying to get Bonert over the edge, when he took two

AK-47 rounds through the heart from very close range. One of the rounds had hit him squarely in the chest, while the second round had gone in under his right armpit and had come out the other side.

Harmon was knocked off the tank by the force of the rounds, landing fifteen feet out in the hard-packed dirt road. He lay there for a moment or two, calling for his mom. He was still calling for her when he died.

Bonert was still up on the tank. Sommers had managed to get down after the explosions and make it to the ditch. He was there next to Coon when Coon finally came to. The ambush was still going on, and Coon could hear the tanks firing canister rounds into the brush at point-blank range. He was on his stomach and feeling pretty uncomfortable, when he realized that he was lying on his CAR-15. Blood was dripping on his weapon, and he could feel warm blood gushing down his back. He was more worried about the wound in his back, and when he reached back to check it he discovered much to his relief that it wasn't blood—one of his canteens had been punctured.

Bleeding from his eyes and ears, Coon found that his right eyelid had been pinned open by a piece of shrapnel. As he checked over his body, he discovered that he had shrapnel wounds everywhere. Pulling himself together, Coon sat up and heard Bonert screaming for help up on the tank. Coon looked over at Sommers and said, "Where's Harmon?"

Sommers looked up and pointed to a body out on the road. Reacting immediately, Coon crawled out in the road and started moving to where Harmon lay dead. At that moment, out of the corner of his eye he spotted an NVA soldier stand up and take aim at him. Coon moved to fire him up, but his first round hit the road right in front of him, throwing up a geyser of dirt. When he brought the weapon back up again, it wouldn't fire at all. Fortunately for Coon, when he first fired, the NVA had dropped out of sight and never showed himself again.

Coon continued, crawling out to where Harmon lay in the road. When he finally reached him and rolled him over, he saw that Harmon was already dead. Coon was devastated. He grabbed Harmon's weapon to replace his own jammed one; then Coon crawled back into the ditch with Sommers.

Not long after that, he tried to go out and help Bonert, but he kept blacking out. Through the entire battle, no one from the infantry platoon left the ditch to come up to help. The tank crews stayed buttoned up inside the tanks, but kept up a base of fire with their cannons and their coaxial machine guns to keep the NVA away from the road. The lieutenant had lost an arm during the initial ambush and had remained inside the tank. One of the lead tank's canister rounds had taken out the two NVA who had fired the RPGs.

Bonert was still alive on top of the tank and he was screaming in pain, but the NVA left him alone; they were using him as bait, hoping that the Americans would go to his aid. However, the only person who came up to assist the tankers and the LRRPs was a South Vietnamese interpreter by the name of Tam. He had been with the infantry when the battle started, and had come forward alone to offer his help.

Coon and Sommers began to worry about their rear. Immediately behind them was the area where their patrol had walked up behind the enemy ambush earlier that day. They couldn't understand why the NVA had not already attacked them from behind.

Around 1600 hours, someone called a cease-fire. Not long after that, the infantry came up to where the tanks sat idling in the road. A few of the grunts managed to get Bonert down off the tank and treat his wounds. Someone called for a medevac, and it wasn't long before two Dustoff helicopters were sitting out on the road. Bonert and the tanker lieutenant, along with Harmon's body, went out on the first medevac. Coon and Sommers caught a lift on the second ship.

Shortly before the medevacs had arrived, an M-88 tank retriever and another M-48 tank came around a curve in the highway one thousand meters to the east. Right after negotiating the curve, the tank hit a command-detonated mine and threw a track in the middle of the highway. It was Charlie's day to score big.

Meanwhile, the grunts swept through the ambush site and dragged the dead bodies of four NVA soldiers out of the brush along the side of the road.

The second medevac, carrying Sommers and Coon, landed at a nearby firebase, where another Dustoff was waiting to pick them up and ferry them back to the Oasis. It was dark by the time the aircraft landed at the field hospital, where medics put them on gurneys and wheeled them inside to triage. As a masked doctor started to work on Coon, the man's eyes suddenly grew wide, and he turned around and left the operating room. Soon a medic came in and told Coon that he had to take off his gear. Coon sat up and removed his LBE, then handed it to the medic. That's when he discovered what had so unnerved the doctor. One of the LRRP's M-26 fragmentation grenades had been blown in two by the force of the RPG, and the blasting cap was now hanging down, fully exposed.

The doctor returned a short time later and spent the next two hours picking shrapnel out of Coon's head and body. After most of the shrapnel had been removed, Coon was medevacked to the evacuation hospital at Pleiku the next morning, where he found Bonert sitting up in bed. The doctors were doing everything in their power to save his legs. Coon told him about feeling guilty for not getting him off the tank. Bonert told him that he'd done the best he could.

They treated the flash burns in Coon's eyes and took out more shrapnel while he was at Pleiku, then medevacked him again to the hospital at Qui Nhon. He was there a day or two, then flown down to the navy hospital at Subic Bay. From there he was sent to the U.S. Army hospital on Okinawa. He left there the first week in July and returned to the platoon.

Coon found a lot of new faces back at the detachment. He also learned that his friend and team leader, Ron Bonert, didn't make it after all. The tough Chicago kid had died twelve days after being hit. Ron Coon still grieves for Ron Bonert and Dan Harmon. He feels he could have done more.

Company C,
75th Infantry (Ranger),
I Field Force

Company C, 75th Infantry (Ranger), I Field Force, was one of three Field Force Ranger companies to serve during the Vietnam War. Headquartered at the Oasis, near An Khe, the four-platoon company was nearly twice the size of most other U.S. Army Ranger companies, the "other" being Delta Company, 151st Infantry, Indiana National Guard, the long-range patrol element of II Field Force.

By 1970, Charlie Company was working out of Task Force South headquarters at Landing Zone Betty just outside of Phan Thiet. The Charlie Company Rangers ran patrols over large areas of Vietnam, extending from the South China Sea to the Cambodian border.

On 2 February 1970, Capt. Gerald Colvin, the company operations officer, notified 1st Lt. Richard Grimes that a number of teams from his platoon were slated for long-range reconnaissance patrols into an AO near the Cambodian border. One of the team leaders Grimes contacted was S.Sgt. Chester Golden. Golden was a very experienced long-range patrol leader, and at eighteen years old was one of the youngest E-6s to serve during the Vietnam War. His Ranger Team Two-two was an experienced one that knew what it was doing in the bush. When Golden reported to Grimes a short time later, he was told that the mission involved a saturation reconnaissance operation involving six teams.

Golden and his assistant team leader, Sp4. Henderson

341

Carter, flew out the next afternoon for a single pass, high-altitude overflight of the area. Henderson, an ex-Michigan State football player, was the son of a retired black Marine colonel, and the third son to serve in Vietnam. Carter's two brothers had served previous tours as officers in the United States Marine Corps. One of them, a Marine aviator, had been killed in action. The southern California native had dropped out of college in his third year looking for some action. He found it in a prior tour with the 173d Airborne Brigade.

The remainder of Team Two-two consisted of Sp4. Jack R. Arnold, the patrol's highly experienced RTO. Arnold knew his way around both the PRC-25 and the PRC-77 that he was carrying on that patrol. Arnold was also a well-trained medic, which made him a double-plus on any long-range recon patrol.

The team's point man was Sp4. Javier "Sam" Sarmienta. Sarmienta was a natural in the woods, possessing the uncanny ability not so much to blend in as to be "assimilated" into his surroundings. His was a gift that only a few had.

If the point man was a critical slot on the team, so was slack. It was the slack man who corrected the point man's mistakes and watched his flanks. Mistakes were intolerable and unforgivable on a long-range recon patrol. They killed more Rangers than all the booby traps in South Vietnam, Laos, and Cambodia put together. And you couldn't ask for a more experienced slack man than Sp4. Thomas "OD" O'Doughteraty. O'Doughteraty was on his third tour in country. The first two, with the Screaming Eagles of the 101st Airborne Division and the Third Herd of the 173d Airborne Brigade, had prepared him well for the demanding job.

The team's rear security was ably handled by Sp4. Patrick White, another Ranger with a lot of patrols under his belt.

The overflight had revealed very little useful information other than confirming the fact that their recon zone consisted of heavily timbered steep hills. Golden and Carter had patrolled that kind of terrain before, and they knew it would be a nightmare to move through. The thick double- and triple-canopy jungle could hide an NVA division, and the LRRPs wouldn't know it until they stumbled over the bunkers. To make matters worse, in that type of terrain, LZs were as rare as in country R & Rs.

Just after daylight on the morning of 8 June, Team Two-two linked up with three more Charlie Company recon teams as they ambled aboard the waiting Chinook helicopter for the fifty-minute flight out to the battalion-size 173d Airborne Brigade fire-support base that would serve as their jump-off point for the mission. The Chinook was scheduled to drop them off at the firebase, then return to Phan Thiet to pick up two more Ranger recon patrols. Their radio-relay team had gone out to the FSB the day before and were ready to handle the commo for the six recon teams for the next five days.

The Chinook flew west-northwest out of Phan Thiet and arrived at the battalion fire-support base in just under an hour. Team Two-two was there nearly an hour and a half before its turn to go in. Finally, they boarded a Huey for a fifteen- to twenty-minute flight to the recon zone.

It was a straight-in insertion, the lift ship touching down in a tiny LZ situated at the bottom of a shallow basin at the foot of a heavily forested hillside. As the helicopter settled in, the Rangers exited both sides of the aircraft and dashed around to the front of the chopper. The ground to the port, starboard, and front of the Huey sloped uphill from the LZ, forcing the team to duck their heads to avoid the whirling rotor blades. The team met at the front of the aircraft as the chopper lifted out of the clearing and flew off in the distance.

Heading uphill, they immediately disappeared into the dense single canopy surrounding the LZ. Lying dog in the cover for the next ten minutes, Arnold called in a commo check, reporting a negative sitrep to the relay team back at the fire-support base. Sure that their insertion had gone unnoticed, Golden signaled for Arnold to release the choppers.

The patrol moved out, working uphill into the thicker

double-canopy jungle, spaced out no more than two meters apart. Three minutes later, they heard a single rifle shot from their left rear on the far side of the LZ. Golden realized that his original assessment had been wrong. The enemy had indeed observed their insertion. Arnold called back to the relay team to report the change in their status.

Undaunted by the fact that news of their arrival would most likely precede them, they continued the patrol uphill toward the ridge above them. Their intensity level was by then at 110 percent. About forty-five minutes into the patrol, Carter suddenly sensed that something around them was not right. He couldn't quite put his finger on what it was, but alarm bells were going off. It didn't take long for the rest of the team to pick up on the negative vibes.

Directly in front of him at waist-high level was a thick layer of broadleaf vegetation overshadowed by a dense stand of ten-foot-high bamboo. Carter raised a clenched fist, then dropped to one knee as the rest of the team went to ground behind him. They were still stretched out in file, so they immediately set up a herringbone security formation, each man facing out in alternating directions.

Just as Carter went down, he noticed that there was a cleared space in the jungle to his left front. He had seen that before, the well-camouflaged approach into an enemy base camp, and someone was at home. He could smell, feel, hear, and even taste their presence. Rising up a little to take a second look, he was finally able to penetrate the shadows enough to see an entire enemy platoon moving about under the heavy double canopy. It took him only one glance to know that it was a Main Force VC unit. They were dressed in dark blue and black pajamas. He had also spotted a sprinkling of khaki uniforms among the darker ones, probably indicating the presence of NVA cadre.

Over the next few minutes, the Rangers silently observed twenty-five to thirty enemy soldiers in bivouac, going about their normal routine without any suspicion that they were being watched from less than ten meters away.

Imperceptibly, the six Rangers slowly melted into the jungle floor. Not one of them could understand how their approach had gone unnoticed, or how the Viet Cong platoon had failed to hear the sounds of their insertion. The enemy soldiers were so sure of their own security that an NVA senior lieutenant had what appeared to be his wife and five- or six-year-old daughter sitting there with him. The Rangers could hear the voices and laughter of other women and children in the background.

The Rangers could also make out a number of shelters erected at ground level and heavily camouflaged with leaves and branches, invisible from aerial detection. From the looks of the encampment, it seemed to run into the jungle, indicating to the Rangers that there might be far more than just a platoon back under the trees. A number of RPD light machine guns and RPG grenade launchers were sitting about the edge of the perimeter, but the patrol observed no crew-served weapons.

The six Rangers lay frozen in place for five to ten minutes, quietly discussing the situation among themselves. Arnold cranked the radio down to silence any unexpected squelch, then reported the situation to the relay team. Seconds later, he was advised that Delta Troop, 2d of the 1st Cav, was on pad alert back at the firebase and cranking up their aircraft. Help was only fifteen minutes away.

At that time, the patrol began to sense that the enemy soldiers were becoming rather nervous. They had clearly become aware that something was wrong. On Golden's signal, the six Rangers slowly pulled out half their fragmentation grenades and placed them on the ground in front of them. There was no longer any time for deliberation. Their cover was about to be blown, and they knew that if they didn't act first, they had only seconds to live.

On the second signal from Carter, the six men rose up on

one knee and began tossing frags into the milling enemy soldiers who were just beginning to respond to the threat. While the grenades cooked off among the stunned soldiers, the Rangers put down a heavy base of fire at point-blank range, spraying the enemy encampment.

The surprise had been complete; they had to maintain the edge to keep the VC off balance. As they continued rapid fire for five minutes, they understood that they would be out of ammunition before the helicopters arrived on station. If that happened, they would never make it back to the LZ.

Inside the base camp, everything was in pandemonium. The Rangers were killing everything in sight, including a number of civilians who had been trapped inside. Few of those in sight escaped. But as the team wound down its level of fire to conserve its final magazines, the enemy quickly recovered and began returning fire of their own.

Arnold was on the radio calling *"Contact! Contact!"* There was no longer any reason for silence. Every enemy soldier still alive in the trees to their front knew exactly where they were.

Minutes later, the first gunships and scout helicopters arrived overhead and began firing up the enemy encampment. Golden popped a smoke grenade to mark the patrol's location, but the aircraft had already spotted his men through the trees. By that time, the Rangers were out of frags and nearly out of ammo, and Golden yelled for them to put on their gas masks and throw out their CS grenades as the enemy return fire continued.

The Rangers were getting desperate now, and Arnold radioed for an immediate ammo resupply. Suddenly, two Delta Troop LOH scout helicopters arrived overhead and began dropping loose belts of unusable 7.62mm ammo down through the trees.

Arnold immediately radioed the aircraft and screamed, "There is no fucking '60 down here!"

By then, the CS gas had begun to dissipate. The Rangers

pulled off their gas masks, and continued to lay down a heavy suppressing fire. The LOHs swung back around and came down among the trees firing their M-60s into the base camp. The surviving enemy soldiers, just seven to ten, continued to return fire, and as the Rangers began to run out of ammo, the VC fire began to increase in intensity.

Sensing the change in pitch, the LOH pilots moved back and forth just above the trees and continued plastering the area. Soon, they, too, were taking fire from enemy gunners hiding among the trees.

The scout ship pilots were soon back on the radio reporting enemy dead and wounded everywhere. They spotted a large number of blood trails and described them as standing out in the jungle like shiny new pennies. The pilots also reported that they had spotted a number of enemy soldiers trying to outflank the team.

At that point the gunship and LOH pilots also began to run out of both ammo and fuel. They radioed the team that they were going back to the firebase to rearm and refuel, and promised that they would be back in thirty minutes. Thirty minutes was a long time to wait in a one-sided firefight.

At that moment, the grenades and rockets ignited a brush fire down among the trees. It quickly picked up speed and began sweeping toward the embattled Rangers. Totally out of ammo, they literally jumped out of the frying pan and into the fire. Golden shouted to his teammates to break contact and run for the LZ.

Unknown to the Rangers, the Cav aerorifle platoon had just been inserted into the same LZ the patrol had used earlier. They were roughly two hundred meters from where the action was still taking place. They had taken no fire coming in, but the tiny LZ limited the choppers to dropping off the Blues no more than one ship at a time.

Up on the hillside, the Rangers were still racing the flames down toward the LZ. They moved into a steep ravine and climbed up a small berm on the other side that offered little in the way of cover and concealment, but did manage to get them out of the way of the fire.

Almost out of water, and completely stressed out by their harrowing flight, the team met up with the aerorifle platoon halfway between the LZ and the enemy bivouac area. Relatively safe, the Rangers gratefully accepted a few bandoliers of ammo and extra canteens of water from the Blues.

Shortly afterward, the combined force moved back up to where the battle had raged a short time before. Team Two-two was out in the lead. Golden moved up to take over point, and they soon reached the spot where the Rangers had made their stand.

Arnold and O'Doughteraty had remained behind a short distance with the command element. Within twenty to twenty-five meters of the encampment, Arnold and O'Doughteraty spotted movement in a ravine with overhead cover fifteen meters away. As they approached the ravine, the two Rangers opened up, emptying several magazines apiece down into it. There was no return fire.

Covered by a number of Blues, they slipped down into the ravine to investigate, and quickly discovered an earthen dugout excavated into the bank. It was large enough for three or more people. The shelter was well concealed and could not be seen from above.

Weapons at the ready, the two Rangers moved closer to get a better look and discovered the bodies of the NVA officer, his wife, and their little girl. The man and his wife were facing each other, eyes fully open, a look of great fear frozen on their faces. The little girl was lying to the inside of the dugout, and had died looking up at her parents, killed by bullets that had gone through her father.

The two Rangers were devastated. That was not what their war was about. They had been too efficient in their shooting. Not one of the family had survived. Aching inside, they moved slowly forward and checked the bodies. They found nothing of value.

The remainder of Team Two-two entered the base camp just before the Blues arrived. This time there was no return fire. It was obvious that the VC had paid little attention to basic security. If they had, the outcome might have been tragically different—tragically for the Rangers. They had been very lucky. But even with their great luck, they would still have been overrun if the VC had pressed their attack, especially after the team had run out of ammunition and grenades. The only explanation for what had happened was that the Viet Cong had pulled back to protect their dependents trapped inside the encampment at the time of the attack.

When Arnold and O'Doughteraty climbed back up out of the ravine and moved over to where the Blues were waiting, a senior NCO asked his commanding officer for permission to empty a belt from his M-60 into the dead officer and his family. When the captain failed to respond, and the NCO lifted his machine gun, Arnold pulled his revolver and put it to the man's ear and said, "If you squeeze off one round, I'll blow your fucking head off." Standing beside the captain a few feet away, his RTO turned pasty white.

This brought an immediate response from the officer, who said, "Sergeant, I think perhaps you shouldn't fire the machine gun." The NCO slowly took his finger off the trigger, the matter ended for the time being.

The Blues and the Rangers continued checking out the base camp, recovering weapons and equipment, and picking up documents strewn here and there. Bodies were everywhere. Blood, bone, and body parts littered the hillside, attesting to the savagery of the battle. While they finished sweeping through the camp, scout helicopters and Cobra gunships flying back and forth, searching for survivors, kept reporting blood trails leading off in every direction. They were still encountering small numbers of VC firing up through the trees at the LOHs.

The enemy appeared to be fighting a rear-guard action as

they retreated from the area. However, they were obviously still confused and disorganized.

Finally, it was getting late in the day, and everyone started pulling back toward the LZ. The Hueys began landing in the LZ, extracting Team Two-two on the initial lift. Team Two-two had been the first of the saturation recon teams to make contact and be pulled out of the field.

The Rangers were flown straight back to LZ Betty at Phan Thiet, where they were debriefed about the events leading up to the firefight. The very next day, Team Two-two was once again alerted to go back out in the field. They were ordered to return to the site of the previous day's battle, but they would be accompanied by a full dismounted mechanized infantry company from the 173d battalion that was based out of the fire-support base. The team went back into the LZ late in the morning, landing in the same exact place as the day before.

Golden and his teammates were on the ground fifteen minutes before the infantry company combat assaulted into the area. It didn't take the team long to discover that this particular company had never operated with a Ranger element before. Arnold learned to his displeasure that the company commander wasn't used to a spec four RTO telling a line captain what to do. The West Point officer was highly offended by Arnold's forwardness and made sure that he and the rest of the Rangers understood that this was his operation.

Once again the Rangers led the infantry sweep back through the area of the contact. But this time they moved well beyond the previous search area, and soon discovered the reason for the bivouac—lots of good, clear water throughout the area. They also discovered a major trail network running through the jungle.

After-action reports estimated that Team Two-two had hit at least a full Main Force VC company, if not a battalion. They were indeed lucky to be alive. The carnage caused by the six heavily armed Rangers amazed even the infantry commander. Although the VC had returned during the night to police up their dead and sanitize the battleground, the evidence of the incredible devastation was still there for anyone to see.

They remained in the area for the rest of the day, but found nothing of any consequence. At 1600 hours, Team Two-two was extracted from the LZ. The line company remained behind to continue running patrols.

Stopping off briefly at the battalion fire-support base, the Rangers returned to Phan Thiet. It was a mission that all of them would not soon forget. Patrick White and Jack Arnold were awarded Bronze Star medals with V device nearly a year after the battle. They never found out if the others had received medals for their heroic actions that day.

Appendix 1

The Honor Roll of LRRPs, LRPs, and Rangers
Killed or Missing in Action

173D AIRBORNE BRIGADE

1.	SGT Raymond Hoyt Hudson	173d LRRP	06-15-66
2.	SP/4 William Elice Collins Jr.	173d LRRP	01-23-67
3.	CPL James Elliott Dewey	173d LRRP	04-04-67
4.	SP/4 Clifford W. Leathers Jr.	173d LRRP	06-21-67
5.	SFC Charles James Holland	173d LRRP	08-18-67
6.	SSG John Walter Thompson	74th LRP	01-03-68
7.	SGT Wayne Lynn Harland	74th LRP	05-01-68
8.	SGT Michael Anthony Gerome	74th LRP	05-07-68
9.	SSG Donald Giles Waide	74th LRP	05-07-68
10.	SFC Alain Joseph Tremblay	74th LRP	07-07-68
11.	SSG Laszlo Rabel	74th LRP	11-13-68
12.	SGT Raymond Stanley Reeves Jr.	74th LRP	11-19-68
13.	CPL Arthur Frederick Bell	N/75 RGR	05-12-69
14.	PFC Ronald Steven Holeman	N/75 RGR	07-13-69
15.	SSG Theodore Mendez Sr.	N/75 RGR	07-14-69
16.	PFC Ronald Gene Thomas	N/75 RGR	07-14-69
17.	SSG Cameron Trent McAllister	N/75 RGR	09-07-69
18.	SP/4 Steven Thomas Schooler	N/75 RGR	01-13-70
19.	CPL John William S. G. Kelly	N/75 RGR	02-15-70
20.	SGT Victor Del Greco Jr.	N/75 RGR	03-02-70
21.	SGT John Richard Knaus	N/75 RGR	05-07-70
22.	SGT Paul Lajada Ramos Jr.	N/75 RGR	05-13-70
23.	SGT Bruce Charles Candri	N/75 RGR	07-14-70
24.	SGT Roberto Lerma Patino	N/75 RGR	10-22-70
25.	SSG Juan Santos Borja	N/75 RGR	04-28-71
26.	SP/4 Lawrence Ray Peel	N/75 RGR	04-28-71
27.	CPL Joseph Edward Sweeney	N/75 RGR	05-29-71
28.	SP/4 Joseph D. Hayes	N/75 RGR	06-13-71

199TH LIGHT INFANTRY BRIGADE

1.	SSG Robert J. Carmody	71st LRRP	10-27-67
2.	CPL Linden Brook Dixon	71st LRRP	10-27-67
3.	SGT Stephen Perry Jones	71st LRRP	10-27-67
4.	CPL John Peter Turk	71st LRRP	10-27-67
5.	SSG Robert Alton Williams	71st LRRP	10-27-67
6.	SP/4 Ronald Roy Hammerstrom	71st LRRP	12-07-67
7.	SP/4 Neal Arthur Smith	M/75 RGR	09-06-69
8.	SSG Robert Larry Oaks	M/75 RGR	11-11-69

INDIANA NATIONAL GUARD

1.	SP/4 Charles Kenneth Larkins	D/151 RGR	02-11-69
2.	SGT Robert T. Smith	D/151 RGR	04-12-69
3.	SP/4 Peter Frank Fegatelli	D/151 RGR	05-10-69
4.	SP/4 Bishop Skip Baranowski	D/151 RGR	07-08-69
5.	1LT Kenneth Thomas Cummings	D/151 RGR	09-04-69
6.	1LT George L. Kleiber Jr.	D/151 RGR	09-04-69

82D AIRBORNE DIVISION

1.	SSG Jerry Don Beck	O/75 RGR	04-06-69
2.	SGT Daren Lee Koenig	O/75 RGR	04-06-69
3.	SSG John Anthony LaPolla	O/75 RGR	04-15-69
4.	CPL Michael Joseph Kelly Jr.	O/75 RGR	04-25-69
5.	CPL Charles Herman Wright	O/75 RGR	09-19-69

5TH INFANTRY DIVISION (MECHANIZED)

1.	SFC David Edward Carter	P/75 RGR	08-10-69
2.	SGT David Leon Barber	P/75 RGR	12-21-69
3.	SP/4 Roy Jeffrey Burke	P/75 RGR	12-21-69
4.	SP/4 James Howard Dean	P/75 RGR	12-21-69
5.	SSG Thomas Joseph Dowd	P/75 RGR	12-21-69
6.	PFC Gary Phillip Sinclair	P/75 RGR	12-21-69
7.	SP/4 Ronald Lee Biegert	P/75 RGR	03-15-70
8.	SP/4 William Peter Kastendiect	P/75 RGR	04-01-70
9.	SP/4 Vernon Ray Riley	P/75 RGR	04-28-70
10.	SSG Rodney Kenneth Mills	P/75 RGR	05-05-70
11.	SP/4 Raymond Hugh Apellido	P/75 RGR	09-20-70
12.	SP/4 Anthony Joseph Gallina	P/75 RGR	09-20-70
13.	SP/4 Dale Alan Gray	P/75 RGR	09-20-70
14.	PFC Glenn Garland Ritchie Jr.	P/75 RGR	09-20-70
15.	SGT Harold Erwin Sides	P/75 RGR	09-20-70
16.	PFC Stephen Lee Smith	P/75 RGR	03-01-71
17.	SP/4 James Thomas Williams Jr.	P/75 RGR	03-01-71
18.	SGT Michael Edward Koschke	P/75 RGR	03-20-71

19.	SGT James Daniel Schooley	P/75 RGR	03-20-71
20.	SP/4 Steven Charles Wray	P/75 RGR	04-01-71
21.	SSG Johnny Harold Lawrence	P/75 RGR	04-04-71

23D (AMERICAL) INFANTRY DIVISION

1.	PFC Alex James Hernandez	E/51 LRP	01-10-68
2.	SP/4 Jim Daniel Martinez	E/51 LRP	01-10-68
3.	CPL Solomon Kalua Jr.	E/51 LRP	01-20-68
4.	SGT Daniel P. McLaughlin Jr.	E/51 LRP	01-20-68
5.	SP/4 Terry Ernest Allen	E/51 LRP	03-04-68
6.	SGT James Richard Davidson	E/51 LRP	03-04-68
7.	SP/4 Ramon Sanchez Hernandez	E/51 LRP	03-04-68
8.	SGT Ronald Bryniel Johnson	E/51 LRP	03-04-68
9.	SSG Edward Martin Lentz	E/51 LRP	03-04-68
10.	SP/4 Jose Enrique Torres	E/51 LRP	03-04-68
11.	CPL James Edward Kesselhon	E/51 LRP	03-21-68
12.	SGT Raymond Charles Garcia	E/51 LRP	07-03-68
13.	SGT Alan Francis Angell	E/51 LRP	07-20-68
14.	SGT David James Ohm	E/51 LRP	07-20-68
15.	PFC Bradley Keith Watts	E/51 LRP	09-15-68
16.	SP/4 Joseph Jess Gavia	G/75 RGR	04-24-69
17.	SGT Arthur Edward Scott	G/75 RGR	05-12-69
18.	SP/4 Joel Wayne Forrester	G/75 RGR	05-19-69
19.	CPL Larry Joe White	G/75 RGR	06-30-69
20.	CPL John Willie Bennett	G/75 RGR	10-14-69
21.	SSG Robert Joseph Pruden	G/75 RGR	11-20-69
22.	SP/4 George Thomas Olsen	G/75 RGR	03-03-70
23.	1LT Harold Edward Basehore Jr.	G/75 RGR	04-23-70
24.	PFC Edward Gerard Mathem	G/75 RGR	08-03-70
25.	SP/4 Larry Allen Mackey	G/75 RGR	10-13-70
26.	PFC Barry Howard Berger	G/75 RGR	01-10-71
27.	SSG David Lee Meyer	G/75 RGR	01-11-71
28.	SGT Thomas Edward Snowden	G/75 RGR	05-15-71
29.	SGT Danny Gerald Studdard	G/75 RGR	06-16-71

4TH INFANTRY DIVISION

1.	SSG Dickie Waine Finley	2/4th LRRP	10-21-68
2.	SP/4 Luther Anderson Ghahate	2/4th LRRP	10-21-68
3.	SGT Michael Eugene Lawton	E/58 LRP	12-01-68
4.	SGT Kenneth Charles Hess	K/75 RGR	02-08-69
5.	PFC Nathaniel Irving	K/75 RGR	02-08-69
6.	CPL Frank William Humes	K/75 RGR	07-08-69
7.	SSG Wallace Fred Thibodeau	K/75 RGR	07-19-69
8.	CPL Eddie Dean Carpenter	K/75 RGR	11-13-69
9.	SGT Luis A. N. Hilerio-Padilla	K/75 RGR	11-13-69

10.	PFC Robert John Silva	K/75 RGR	11-27-69
11.	SP/4 Kenneth James Smolarek	K/75 RGR	11-27-69
12.	SGT Michael William Lyne	K/75 RGR	01-07-70
13.	SP/4 La Roy Frederich Roth	K/75 RGR	01-07-70
14.	SP/4 Charles R. Willard Jr.	K/75 RGR	01-07-70
15.	SSG William H. Bartholomew Jr.	K/75 RGR	01-23-70
16.	SP/4 Dean Allen Borneman	K/75 RGR	01-23-70
17.	SSG Luther James Doss Jr.	K/75 RGR	04-30-70
18.	SP/4 Frank Edward McClellan	K/75 RGR	06-04-70
19.	SP/4 Earl David Broach	K/75 RGR	08-03-70
20.	PFC Evelio Alfred Gomez	K/75 RGR	08-19-70
21.	SP/4 Antonio Ambrosio Grau	K/75 RGR	08-30-70
22.	SSG William Eugene Roller	K/75 RGR	09-07-70
23.	CPL Frank Howard Miller Jr.	K/75 RGR	09-19-70
24.	SP/4 Roy Christopher Olgyay	K/75 RGR	09-19-70
25.	SSG Robert Wilber Toler Jr.	K/75 RGR	12-05-70

1ST INFANTRY DIVISION

1.	SGT Rudolph Algar Nunez	1st Div LRRP	06-13-66
2.	SSG George Frank Knowlton	F/52 LRP	11-19-67
3.	SFC Robert Levine	F/52 LRP	12-15-67
4.	SGT James Patrick Boyle	F/52 LRP	04-17-68
5.	SSG Jackie Glen Leisure	F/52 LRP	05-12-68
6.	PFC Edwin Everett Carson	F/52 LRP	10-21-68
7.	SGT William Paul Cohn Jr.	F/52 LRP	10-21-68
8.	PFC Gerard Coyle	F/52 LRP	10-21-68
9.	SP/4 Lester Allan Doan	F/52 LRP	10-21-68
10.	PFC Michael Allen Randall Sr.	F/52 LRP	10-21-68
11.	PFC Steven Paul Sorick	F/52 LRP	10-21-68
12.	PFC James Allen Boots	F/52 LRP	11-13-68
13.	PFC Gerard James Blume Jr.	F/52 LRP	11-21-68
14.	PFC Arnold Lee Roy Mulholland	F/52 LRP	11-21-68
15.	SSG Anthony Felix Washington	F/52 LRP	11-21-68
16.	SP/4 Reynaldo Arenas	F/52 LRP	12-31-68
17.	SP/4 Robert David Law	I/75 RGR	02-22-69
18.	SSG Enrique Salas Cruz	I/75 RGR	02-27-69
19.	SP/4 James Terry Liebnitz	I/75 RGR	02-27-69
20.	PFC Gary L. Johnson	I/75 RGR	02-28-69
21.	SGT Anthony G. Markevitch Jr.	I/75 RGR	04-16-69
22.	SGT Robert Allen Roossien	I/75 RGR	05-12-69
23.	CPT Michael Patrick Reese	I/75 RGR	05-14-69
24.	SP/4 Charles Edward Smith Jr.	I/75 RGR	08-30-69
25.	SGT Bernard Ambrose Propson	I/75 RGR	09-05-69

9TH INFANTRY DIVISION

1.	SSG Kenneth Ray Lancaster	E/50 LRP	01-03-68
2.	PFC Thomas Wayne Hodge	E/50 LRP	01-24-68
3.	PFC George Jonathan House	E/50 LRP	02-11-68
4.	SP/4 William Francis Piaskowski	E/50 LRP	03-14-68
5.	SSG Johnston Dunlop	E/50 LRP	04-16-68
6.	MSG Joseph Melvin Jones	E/50 LRP	04-16-68
7.	SP/4 Herbert Lee Vaughn	E/50 LRP	05-25-68
8.	PFC James L. Dillard III	E/50 LRP	09-13-68
9.	SSG Herbert Pok Dong Cho	E/50 LRP	09-25-68
10.	CPL Robert John Loehlein Jr.	E/50 LRP	09-25-68
11.	PFC Ronald Kelvin Moore	E/50 LRP	11-04-68
12.	SGT Joseph Philip Castagna	E/50 LRP	12-21-68
13.	SP/4 Richard Roy Bellwood	E/50 LRP	01-25-69
14.	SGT Roman Gale Mason	E/50 LRP	01-27-69
15.	SP/4 Leon David Moore	E/50 LRP	01-27-69
16.	1LT Richard Vickers Thompson	E/50 LRP	01-27-69
17.	SP/4 Irwin Leon Edelman	E/75 RGR	02-18-69
18.	SP/4 Warren G. H. Lizotte Jr.	E/75 RGR	02-26-69
19.	SGT Lonnie Dale Evans	E/75 RGR	04-10-69
20.	SSG Curtis Ray Daniels	E/75 RGR	05-29-69
21.	SP/4 Michael Cory Volheim	E/75 RGR	05-29-69
22.	SSG Herbert Cornelius Frost	E/75 RGR	06-21-69
23.	SP/4 Jonathan Lee Lamm	E/75 RGR	02-11-70
24.	SGT Robert Lamaar Bryan	E/75 RGR	07-13-70
25.	1LT Mark Joseph Toschik	E/75 RGR	08-11-70
26.	SGT Ray Michael Gallardo	E/75 RGR	02-08-72

1ST CAVALRY DIVISION

1.	SP/4 David Allen Ives	E/52 LRP	04-23-67
2.	MAJ David Bruce Tucker	E/52 LRP	10-01-67
3.	SGT David Thomas Dickinson	E/52 LRP	12-06-67
4.	MSG Lewis E. McDermott	E/52 LRP	12-06-67
5.	SP/4 William Robert Critchfield	E/52 LRP	02-27-68
6.	PFC Felix Leon Jr.	E/52 LRP	03-17-68
7.	SGT William Glenn Lambert	E/52 LRP	04-20-68
8.	PFC Robert Joseph Noto	E/52 LRP	04-20-68
9.	SP/4 Richard John Turbitt Jr.	E/52 LRP	04-20-68
10.	SGT Robert Eugene Whitten	E/52 LRP	05-08-68
11.	SGT Juan Angel Elias	E/52 LRP	05-29-68
12.	CPL Donald Robert Miller	E/52 LRP	05-31-68
13.	1LT William Brent Bell	H/75 RGR	03-27-69
14.	SGT Dwight Montgomery Durham	H/75 RGR	04-10-69
15.	SGT Loel Floyd Largent	H/75 RGR	04-10-69
16.	SP/4 Daniel Raymond Arnold	H/75 RGR	05-13-69

17.	SP/4 Lon Michael Holupko	H/75 RGR	07-10-69
18.	SP/4 Daniel Moreland Sheehan	H/75 RGR	07-17-69
19.	SGT Stanley John Lento	H/75 RGR	07-24-69
20.	CPL Archie Hugh McDaniel Jr.	H/75 RGR	07-24-69
21.	SGT Paul John Salminen	H/75 RGR	07-24-69
22.	SGT Kenneth Eugene Burch	H/75 RGR	08-11-69
23.	SP/4 John Charles Williams	H/75 RGR	08-11-69
24.	SP/4 David Torres	H/75 RGR	11-17-69
25.	SP/4 Julius Zaporzec	H/75 RGR	11-17-69
26.	SFC Deverton C. Cochrane	H/75 RGR	06-17-70
27.	SP/4 Carl John Laker	H/75 RGR	06-17-70
28.	PFC Michael Dean Banta	H/75 RGR	10-02-70
29.	SGT Omer Price Carson	H/75 RGR	12-07-70
30.	SP/4 Thomas Washington Lipsey III	H/75 RGR	02-06-72
31.	SP/4 Jaime Pacheco	H/75 RGR	05-25-72
32.	SP/4 Jeffrey Alan Maurer	H/75 RGR	06-09-72
33.	SGT Elvis Weldon Osborne Jr.	H/75 RGR	06-09-72

25TH INFANTRY DIVISION

1.	SP/4 Ervin Leonard Laird	F/50 LRP	02-01-67
2.	SP/4 Larry Paul Blackman	F/50 LRP	02-17-67
3.	SSG Joseph Edward Fitzgerald	3/25th LRRP	05-31-67
4.	SP/4 Carl David Flower	3/25th LRRP	05-31-67
5.	SSG John Andrew Jakovac	3/25th LRRP	05-31-67
6.	SSG Brian Kent McGar	3/25th LRRP	05-31-67
7.	CPL Charles Roland Rogerson	3/25th LRRP	05-31-67
8.	SGT Todd R. Jackson	F/50 LRP	01-30-68
9.	SP/4 John Herbert White Jr.	F/50 LRP	03-01-68
10.	SP/4 Gregory Richard Kelly	F/50 LRP	04-06-68
11.	SP/4 Hubert Arthur Meredith	F/50 LRP	08-01-68
12.	SSG Howard Brown Handley	F/50 LRP	09-13-68
13.	SGT Gary Richard McFall	F/50 LRP	09-13-68
14.	SGT Steven Edward Collier	F/50 LRP	10-27-68
15.	PFC Reid Ernest Grayson Jr.	F/50 LRP	12-28-68
16.	SP/4 Raymond Walter Sullivan	F/50 LRP	01-24-69
17.	SGT Duane Alfred DeVega	F/75 RGR	02-11-69
18.	SP/4 Donald Richard Mayberry	F/75 RGR	03-01-69
19.	CPL Frank Wilder	F/75 RGR	03-01-69
20.	PFC Charles Davis Macken	F/75 RGR	03-08-69
21.	SGT Douglas Ray Pollock	F/75 RGR	03-08-69
22.	SGT Fidel Joe Aguirre	F/75 RGR	03-10-69
23.	SGT John Francis Crikelair	F/75 RGR	08-06-69
24.	SP/4 Ernest Heard Jr.	F/75 RGR	08-07-69
25.	SGT Mack Dennard Jr.	F/75 RGR	09-18-69
26.	SSG Lennis Goddard Jones Jr.	F/75 RGR	11-06-69

27.	SP/4 Kenneth DeWayne Harjo	F/75 RGR	11-18-69
28.	SGT Richard Clark Babb Jr.	F/75 RGR	01-01-70
29.	SFC Alvin Winslow Floyd	F/75 RGR	04-02-70
30.	SSG Michael Francis Thomas	F/75 RGR	04-02-70
31.	SGT Donald Warren Tinney Jr.	F/75 RGR	04-14-70
32.	SP/4 Robert Charles Thompson	F/75 RGR	05-12-70
33.	SGT Donald Allen Davis	F/75 RGR	05-24-70
34.	SSG Robert Bruce Pritchard	F/75 RGR	05-24-70
35.	SGT Milan Lavoy Lee	F/75 RGR	09-19-70

101ST AIRBORNE DIVISION

1.	SSG Donovan Jess Pruett	1/101 LRRP	04-03-66
2.	SSG Percy W. McClatchy	1/101 LRRP	08-13-66
3.	SP/4 David Allen Dixon	1/101 LRRP	05-15-67
4.	SP/4 John Lester Hines	1/101 LRRP	09-15-67
5.	PFC George Buster Sullens Jr.	1/101 LRRP	11-01-67
6.	SP/4 John T. McChesney III	1/101 LRRP	01-23-68
7.	SGT Thomas John Sturgal	F/58 LRP	03-22-68
8.	PVT Ashton Hayward Prindle	F/58 LRP	04-23-68
9.	SGT Thomas Eugene Riley	F/58 LRP	06-02-68
10.	SP/4 Terry W. Clifton	F/58 LRP	11-20-68
11.	SGT Albert D. Contreros Jr.	F/58 LRP	11-20-68
12.	SP/4 Arthur J. Heringhausen Jr.	F/58 LRP	11-20-68
13.	SGT Michael Dean Reiff	F/58 LRP	11-20-68
14.	SSG Julian Dean Dedman	L/75 RGR	04-23-69
15.	SGT Keith Tait Hammond	L/75 RGR	05-05-69
16.	SSG Ronald Burns Reynolds	L/75 RGR	05-08-69
17.	SGT William Lincoln Marcy	L/75 RGR	05-20-69
18.	PFC Michael Linn Lytle	L/75 RGR	10-26-69
19.	SGT Ronald Wayne Jones	L/75 RGR	01-11-70
20.	SSG James William Salter	L/75 RGR	01-11-70
21.	SP/4 Rob George McSorley	L/75 RGR	04-08-70
22.	SGT Gary Paul Baker	L/75 RGR	05-11-70
23.	SSG Raymond Dean Ellis	L/75 RGR	05-11-70
24.	CPL George Edward Fogleman	L/75 RGR	05-11-70
25.	PFC Bryan Theotis Knight	L/75 RGR	05-11-70
26.	SGT David Munoz	L/75 RGR	05-11-70
27.	SSG Robert Lee O'Connor	L/75 RGR	05-11-70
28.	SSG Roger Thomas Lagodzinski	L/75 RGR	05-19-70
29.	SSG John Thomas Donahue	L/75 RGR	05-22-70
30.	SP/4 Jack Moss Jr.	L/75 RGR	08-25-70
31.	PFC Harry Thomas Henthorn	L/75 RGR	08-29-70
32.	SP/4 Lawrence Elwood Scheib Jr.	L/75 RGR	08-29-70
33.	SGT Lloyd Harold Grimes II	L/75 RGR	09-25-70
34.	SGT Robert George Drapp	L/75 RGR	11-16-70

35.	SSG Norman R. Stoddard Jr.	L/75 RGR	11-16-70
36.	SGT Steven Glenn England	L/75 RGR	02-15-71
37.	1LT James Leroy Smith	L/75 RGR	02-15-71
38.	SGT Gabriel Trujillo	L/75 RGR	02-15-71
39.	SP/4 Richard Lee Martin	L/75 RGR	02-21-71
40.	SP/4 David Roy Hayward	L/75 RGR	03-22-71
41.	CPL Joel Richard Hankins	L/75 RGR	03-26-71
42.	SSG Leonard James Trumblay	L/75 RGR	04-06-71
43.	SGT James Bruce McLaughlin	L/75 RGR	04-16-71
44.	CPT Paul Coburn Sawtelle	L/75 RGR	04-16-71
45.	SP/4 Johnnie Rae Sly	L/75 RGR	04-24-71
46.	SGT Gary Duane Cochran	L/75 RGR	05-08-71
47.	PFC Steven John Ellis	L/75 RGR	06-13-71
48.	CPL Charles Anthony Sanchez	L/75 RGR	06-13-71
49.	CPL Johnny Howard Chapman	L/75 RGR	08-20-71
50.	SP/4 Hershel Duane Cude Jr.	L/75 RGR	09-18-71
51.	SP/4 Harry Jerome Edwards	L/75 RGR	01-20-72
52.	SSG James Albert Champion	L/75 RGR	04-24-71
			Missing in Action

I FIELD FORCE

1.	1LT Calvin Arthur Greene	E/20 LRP	12-19-67
2.	SGT Patrick Lee Henshaw	E/20 LRP	12-19-67
3.	SGT John Richard Strohmaier	E/20 LRP	03-12-68
4.	SP/4 Donald Ray Kinton	E/20 LRP	03-25-68
5.	SGT Edward Gilbert Lee	E/20 LRP	05-13-68
6.	SGT Frederick William Weidner	E/20 LRP	05-20-68
7.	SSG Emory Morel Smith	E/20 LRP	06-13-68
8.	SGT Eric Stuart Gold	E/20 LRP	01-05-69
9.	SGT Paul Robert Jordan	E/20 LRP	01-24-69
10.	SGT Elton Ray Venable	C/75 RGR	02-19-69
11.	SSG Ronald William Cardona	C/75 RGR	07-06-69
12.	CPL Frank Daniel Walthers	C/75 RGR	08-01-69
13.	SSG Harold David Williams	C/75 RGR	08-01-69
14.	SSG William Russell Squier Jr.	C/75 RGR	09-13-69
15.	SGT Keith Mason Parr	C/75 RGR	10-26-69
16.	CPL Walter Guy Burkhart	C/75 RGR	11-11-69
17.	CPL Rex Marcel Sherman	C/75 RGR	11-19-69
18.	SP/4 Richard Gary Buccille	C/75 RGR	12-20-69
19.	SGT William Joseph Murphy	C/75 RGR	02-16-70
20.	SSG Steen Bruce Foster	C/75 RGR	05-14-70
21.	CPL James Lee Loisel	C/75 RGR	05-14-70
22.	SSG Michael Edward Kiscaden	C/75 RGR	07-01-70
23.	SGT Hilburn M. Burdette Jr.	C/75 RGR	07-12-70
24.	SGT John William Rucker	C/75 RGR	12-14-70

25.	CPL Edward Earl Scott Jr.	C/75 RGR	02-22-71
26.	SP/4 Kevin Garner Thome	C/75 RGR	02-27-71
27.	SSG Gordon Keith Spearman Jr.	C/75 RGR	03-10-71
28.	SP/4 Lloyd Eugene Robinson	C/75 RGR	06-11-71

II FIELD FORCE

1.	SGT Daniel Hinson Lindsey	F/51 LRP	12-05-67
2.	1LT John H. Lattin Jr.	F/51 LRP	12-15-67
3.	SP/4 Kenneth Ray Blair	F/51 LRP	08-12-68
4.	SGT Jan Victor Henrickson	F/51 LRP	08-12-68
5.	PFC Willie Whitfield Jr.	F/51 LRP	08-12-68
6.	SP/4 Raymond Michael Enczi	F/51 LRP	10-31-68
7.	SGT Richard Walter Diers	F/51 LRP	11-20-68
8.	SSG Larry LaMont Cunningham	F/51 LRP	12-03-68
9.	SP/4 Leslie Donald Rosekrans	F/51 LRP	12-03-68
10.	PFC David Lee Urban	F/51 LRP	12-03-68
11.	SGT Freemon Evans	F/51 LRP	12-04-68
12.	CPL Roy Antonio Aubain	F/51 LRP	01-04-69

☆ ☆ ☆ ☆ ☆

Glossary

AA Antiaircraft.

AC Aircraft copilot.

acid pad Helicopter landing pad.

aerial recon Reconning a specific area by helicopter prior to the insertion of a recon patrol.

AFB Air force base.

air burst Explosive device that detonates aboveground.

air strike Surface attack by fixed-wing fighter-bomber aircraft.

AIT In the U.S. Army, advanced individual training that follows basic combat training.

AK A Soviet bloc assault rifle, 7.62 cal., also known as the Kalashnikov AK-47.

AO Area of operations, specified location established for planned military operations.

ao dai Traditional Vietnamese female dress, split up the sides and worn over pants.

ARA Aerial rocket artillery.

Arc Light A B-52 air strike.

ARTO Assistant radio/telephone operator.

Arty Artillery.

Arty fan An area of operations that can be covered by existing artillery support.

ARVN Army of the Republic of (South) Vietnam.

A Team Special Forces operational detachment that normally consists of a single twelve-man team comprised of eleven enlisted men and one officer.

ATL Assistant team leader.

A Troop or **Alpha Troop** Letter designation for one of the aerorifle companies of an air cavalry squadron.

AVN Aviation unit.

bac si Vietnamese for doctor.

baseball Baseball-shaped hand grenade with a five-meter kill range.

BC Base camp.

BCT　In the U.S. Army, basic combat training every trainee must complete upon entering service.

BDA　Bomb damage assessment.

beat feet　Running from danger.

beaucoup or **bookoo**　French for "many."

beehive　Artillery round filled with hundreds of small metal darts designed to be used against massed infantry.

berm　Built-up earthen wall used for defensive purposes.

Big Pond　Pacific Ocean.

Bird Dog　A small, fixed-wing observation plane.

black box　Sensor device that detects body heat or movement. They were buried along routes used by the enemy to record their activity in the area.

black PJs　A type of local garb of Vietnamese farmers also worn extensively by Viet Cong guerrillas.

blasting cap　A small device inserted into an explosive substance that can be triggered to cause the detonation of the main charge.

blood trail　Spoor sign left by the passage or removal of enemy wounded or dead.

Blues　Another name for the aerorifle platoons or troops of an air cavalry squadron.

body bag　A thick black plastic bag used to transport American and allied dead to Graves Registration points.

break contact　Disengaging from battle with an enemy unit.

bring smoke　Placing intensive fire upon the enemy. Killing the enemy with a vengeance.

B Troop or **Bravo Troop**　Letter designation for one of the aerorifle companies of an air cavalry squadron.

bush　The jungle.

buy the farm　To die.

C-4　A very stable, pliable plastique explosive.

C & C　Command and control.

CA　Combat assault.

cammies　Jungle-patterned clothing worn by U.S. troops in the field.

cammo stick　Two-colored camouflage applicator.

Capt.　Abbreviation for the rank of captain.

CAR-15　Carbine version of the M-16 rifle.

Cav　Cavalry.

CCN　Command & Control (North), MACV-SOG.

Charlie, Charles, Chuck　GI slang for VC/NVA.

cherry　New arrival in country.

Chicom　Chinese Communist

chieu hoi　Government program that encouraged enemy soldiers to come over to the South Vietnam side.

Chinook　CH-47 helicopter used for transporting equipment and troops.

choa ong Vietnamese for "How are you?" or "Good morning." (As spoken to a male.)

chopper GI slang for helicopter.

chopper pad Helicopter landing pad.

CIDG Civilian Irregular Defense Group. South Vietnamese or Montagnard civilians trained and armed to defend themselves against enemy attack.

clacker Firing device used to manually detonate a claymore mine.

CO Commanding officer.

Cobra AH-1G attack helicopter.

cockadau G.I. slang for the Vietnamese word meaning "kill."

Col. Abbreviation for the rank of colonel.

cold An area of operations or a recon zone is cold if it is unoccupied by the enemy.

commo Communication by radio or field telephone.

commo check A radio/telephone operator requesting confirmation of his transmission.

compromise Discovered by the enemy.

contact Engaged by the enemy.

CP Command post.

Cs Combat field rations for American troops.

CS Riot gas.

daisy chain Wiring a number of claymore mines together with det cord to achieve a simultaneous detonation.

debrief The gleaning of information and intelligence after a military operation.

DEROS The date of return from an overseas tour of duty.

det cord Timed-burn fuse used to detonate an explosive charge.

diddy boppin' Moving foolishly, without caution.

didi Vietnamese for to run or move quickly.

DMZ Demilitarized Zone.

Doc A medic or doctor.

double canopy Jungle or forest with two layers of overhead vegetation.

Doughnut dollies Red Cross hostesses.

drag The last man on a long-range reconnaissance patrol.

D Troop or **Delta Troop** Letter designation for one of the aerorifle companies of an air cavalry squadron.

dung lai Vietnamese for "don't move."

Dustoff Medical evacuation by helicopter.

DZ Drop zone for airborne parachute operation.

E-1 or **E-2** Military pay grades of private.

E-3 Military pay grade of private first class.

E-4 Military pay grade of specialist four or corporal.

E-5 Military pay grade of specialist five or sergeant.

E-6 Military pay grade of specialist six or staff sergeant.

E-7 Military pay grade of sergeant first class or platoon sergeant.

E-8   Military pay grade of master sergeant or first sergeant.

E-9   Military pay grade of sergeant major.

E & E   Escape and evasion, on the run to evade pursuit and capture.

ER   Enlisted reserve.

ETS   Estimated termination of service.

exfil   Extraction from a mission or operation.

extension leave   A thirty-day furlough given at the end of a full tour of duty after which the recipient must return for an extended tour of duty.

FAC   Forward air controller. Air force spotter plane that coordinated air strikes and artillery for ground units.

fast mover   Jet fighter-bomber.

field   Anywhere outside friendly control.

finger   A secondary ridge running out from a primary ridgeline, a hill, or a mountain.

firebase   Forward artillery position usually located on a prominent terrain feature used to support ground units during operations.

firefight   A battle with an enemy force.

Fire Fly   An LOH observation helicopter fitted with a high-intensity searchlight.

fire mission   A request for artillery support.

fix   The specific coordinates pertaining to a unit's position or to a target.

flare ship   Aircraft used to drop illumination flares in support of ground troops in contact at night.

flash panel   A fluorescent orange or yellow cloth used to mark a unit's position for supporting or inbound aircraft.

FNG   Fucking new guy. Slang term for a recent arrival in Vietnam.

FO   Forward observer. A specially trained soldier, usually an officer, attached to an infantry unit for the purpose of coordinating close artillery support.

foo gas or **fougasse**   A jellied-gasoline explosive that is buried in a fifty-five-gallon drum along defensive perimeters and when command-detonated, sends out a wall of highly flammable fuel similar to napalm.

freak or **freq**   Slang term meaning a radio frequency.

G-2   Division or larger intelligence section.

G-3   Division or larger operations section.

ghost or **ghost time**   Taking time off, free time, goofing off.

gook   Derogatory slang for VC/NVA.

grazing fire   Keeping the trajectory of bullets between normal knee-to-waist height.

grease   Slang term meaning to kill.

Green Beret   A member of the U.S. Army Special Forces.

ground pounder   Infantryman.

grunt   Infantryman.

gunship   An armed attack helicopter.

H & I Harrassment and interdiction. Artillery fire upon certain areas of suspected enemy travel or rally points, designed to prevent uncontested use.

HE High explosive.

heavy team In a long-range patrol unit, two five- or six-man teams operating together.

helipad A hardened helicopter landing pad.

Ho Chi Minh trail An extensive road and trail network running from North Vietnam, down through Laos and Cambodia into South Vietnam, which enabled the North Vietnamese to supply equipment and personnel to their units in South Vietnam.

hootch Slang for barracks or living quarters.

horn Radio or telephone handset.

hot A landing zone or drop zone under enemy fire.

HQ Headquarters.

Huey The Bell UH helicopter series.

hug To close with the enemy in order to prevent his use of supporting fire.

hump Patrolling or moving during a combat operation.

I Corps The northernmost of the four separate military zones in South Vietnam. The other divisions were II, III, and IV Corps.

immersion foot A skin condition of the feet caused by prolonged exposure to moisture that results in cracking, bleeding, and sloughing off of skin.

incoming Receiving enemy indirect fire.

Indian country Territory under enemy control.

indigenous Native peoples.

infil Insertion of a recon team or military unit into a recon zone or area of operation.

intel Information on the enemy gathered by human, electronic, or other means.

jungle penetrator A metal cylinder lowered by cable from a helicopter used to extract personnel from inaccessible terrain.

KCS Kit Carson scout. Repatriated enemy soldiers working with U.S. combat units.

Khmer Cambodian.

Khmer Rouge Cambodian Communist.

Khmer Serei Free Cambodian.

KIA Killed in action.

Killer team A small LRP/Ranger team with the mission of seeking out and destroying the enemy.

LAW Light antitank weapon.

lay dog Slang meaning to go to cover and remain motionless while listening for the enemy. This is SOP for a recon team immediately after being inserted or infilled.

LBJ Long Binh jail. The in country military stockade for U.S. Army personnel convicted of violations of the U.S. Code of Military Justice.

LDR Leader.

lifer   Slang for career soldier.

LMG   Light machine gun.

LOH or **Loach**   OH-6A light observation helicopter.

LP   Listening post. An outpost established beyond the perimeter wire, manned by one or more personnel with the mission of detecting approaching enemy forces before they can launch an assault.

LRP   Long-range patrol.

LRRP   Long-range reconnaissance patrol.

LSA   Government-issue lubricating oil for individual weapons.

Lt.   Lieutenant.

Lt. Col.   Lieutenant colonel.

LZ   Landing zone. A cleared area large enough to accommodate the landing of one or more helicopters.

M-14   The standard-issue 7.62 caliber semiautomatic/automatic rifle used by U.S. military personnel prior to the M-16.

M-16   The standard-issue 5.56 caliber semiautomatic/automatic rifle that became the mainstay of U.S. ground forces in 1967.

M-60   A light 7.62 caliber machine gun that has been the primary infantry automatic weapon of U.S. forces since the Korean War.

M-79   An individually operated, single-shot, 40mm grenade launcher.

MAAG   Military Assistance Advisory Group. The senior U.S. military headquarters during the early American involvement in Vietnam.

MACV   Military Assistance Command Vietnam. The senior U.S. military headquarters after full American involvement in the war.

MACV Recondo School   A three-week school conducted at Nha Trang, South Vietnam, by a cadre from the 5th Special Forces Group to train U.S. and allied reconnaissance personnel in the art of conducting long-range patrols.

MACV-SOG   Studies and Observations Group under command of MACV that ran long-range reconnaissance and other classified missions over the borders of South Vietnam into NVA sanctuaries in Laos and Cambodia.

mag   Short for magazine.

Maguire rig   A single rope with loops at the end that could be dropped from a helicopter to extract friendly personnel from inaccessible terrain.

Main Force   Full-time Viet Cong military units, as opposed to local, part-time guerrilla units.

Maj.   Major.

Marine Force Recon   U.S. Marine Corps divisional long-range reconnaissance units similar in formation and function to U.S. Army LRP/Ranger companies.

MARS   Military/civilian radio/telephone system that enabled U.S. personnel in Vietnam to place calls to friends and family back in the United States.

Medevac   Medical evacuation by helicopter.

MG   Machine gun.

MIA   Missing in action.

Mike Force   Special Forces mobile strike force used to reinforce or support other Special Forces units or camps under attack.

Montagnard   The tribal hill people of Vietnam.

MOS   Military occupation skill.

MP   Military police.

MPC   Military payment certificates. Paper money issued U.S. military personnel serving overseas in lieu of local or U.S. currency.

NCO   Noncommissioned officer.

NDP   Night defensive position.

net   Radio network.

NG   National Guard.

no sweat   With little effort or with no trouble.

number one   The best or highest.

number ten   The worst or lowest.

Nungs   Vietnamese troops of Chinese extraction hired by U.S. Special Forces to serve as personal bodyguards and to man special strike units and recon teams. Arguably the finest indigenous forces in Vietnam.

nuoc mam   Strong, evil-smelling fish sauce used to add flavor to the standard Vietnamese food staple—rice.

NVA   North Vietnamese Army.

ONH   Overnight halt.

OP   Observation post. An outpost established on a prominent terrain feature for the purpose of visually observing enemy activity.

op   Operation.

op order   Operation order. A plan for a mission or operation to be conducted against enemy forces, covering all facets of such a mission or operation.

overflight   An aerial reconnaissance of an intended recon zone of an area of operation prior to the mission or operation, for the purpose of selecting access and egress points, routes of travel, likely enemy concentrations, water, and prominent terrain features.

P-38   Standard manual can opener that comes with government-issued C rations.

pen flare   A small, spring-loaded, cartridge-fed signal flare device that fired a variety of small colored flares used to signal one's position.

peter pilot   Military slang for the assistant or copilot on a helicopter.

PFC   Private first class.

Pink Team   An aviation combat patrol package comprised of an LOH scout helicopter and a Charlie-model Huey gunship or an AH-1G Cobra. The LOH would fly low to draw enemy fire and mark its location for an immediate strike from the gunship circling high overhead.

pith helmet   A light tropical helmet worn by some NVA units.

point   The point man or lead soldier in a patrol.

POW   Prisoner of war.

PRC-10 or **"Prick Ten"** Standard-issue platoon/company radio used early in the Vietnam War.

PRC-25 or **"Prick Twenty-five"** Standard-issue platoon/company radio that replaced the PRC-10.

PRC-77 Heavier, longer-range radio capable of voice or code communication.

Project Delta Special Forces special unit tasked to conduct long-range patrols in Southeast Asia.

Project Gamma Special Forces special unit tasked to conduct long-range patrols in Southeast Asia.

Project Sigma Special Forces special unit tasked to conduct long-range patrols in Southeast Asia.

PRU Provincial reconnaissance units. Mercenary soldiers who performed special military tasks throughout South Vietnam. Known for their effective participation in the Phoenix Program, where they used prisoner snatches and assassinations to destroy the VC infrastructure.

Ps or **piasters** South Vietnamese monetary system. During the height of the Vietnam War, 100P was equal to about $0.85U.S.

PSP Perforated steel panels used to build airstrips, landing pads, and bridge surfaces, and had a number of other functions.

P-training Preparatory training. A one-week course required for each new U.S. Army soldier arriving in South Vietnam, designed to acclimatize new arrivals to weather conditions and give them a basic introduction to the enemy and his tactics.

Puff the Magic Dragon AC-47 or AC-119 aircraft armed with computer-controlled miniguns that rendered massive support to fixed friendly camps and infantry units under enemy attack.

pulled Extracted or exfilled.

punji stakes Sharpened bamboo stakes imbedded in the ground at an angle designed to penetrate into the foot or leg of anyone walking into one. Often poisoned with human excrement to cause infection.

Purple Heart A U.S. medal awarded for receiving a wound in combat.

PX Post exchange.

R & R Rest and recreation. A short furlough given U.S. forces while serving in a combat zone.

radio relay A communications team located in a position to relay radio traffic between two points.

Rangers Designation for U.S. long-range reconnaissance patrollers after January 31, 1969.

rappel Descent from a stationary platform or a hovering helicopter by sliding down a harness-secured rope.

reaction force Special units designated to relieve a small unit in heavy contact.

rear security The last man on a long-range reconnaissance patrol.

redleg Military slang for artillery.

REMF   Rear echelon motherfucker. Military slang for rear-echelon personnel.

rock 'n' roll   Slang for firing one's weapon on full automatic.

Round-eye   Slang for a non-Asian female.

RPD/RPK   Soviet bloc light machine gun.

RPG   Soviet bloc front-loaded antitank rocket launcher used effectively against U.S. bunkers, armor, and infantry during the Vietnam War.

RT   Recon team.

RTO   Radio/telephone operator.

ruck   Rucksack or backpack.

Ruff-Puff or **RF**   South Vietnamese regional and popular forces recruited to provide security in hamlets, villages, and within districts throughout South Vietnam. A militia-type force that was usually ineffective.

saddle up   Preparing to move out on patrol.

same-same   The same as.

sapper   VC/NVA soldiers trained to penetrate enemy defense perimeters and to destroy fighting positions, fuel and ammo dumps, and command and communication centers with demolition charges, usually prior to a ground assault by infantry.

satchel charge   Explosive charge usually carried in a canvas bag across the chest and activated by a pull cord. The weapon of the sapper.

Screaming Chickens or **Puking Buzzards**   Slang for members of the 101st Airborne Division.

SEALs   Small U.S. Navy special operations units trained in reconnaissance, ambush, prisoner snatch, and counterguerrilla techniques.

search and destroy   Offensive military operation designed to seek out and eradicate the enemy.

SERTS   Screaming Eagle Replacement Training School. Rear-area indoctrination course that introduced newly arrived 101st Airborne Division replacements to the rigors of combat in Vietnam.

SF   U.S. Special Forces or Green Berets.

SFC   Sergeant first class (E-7).

Sgt.   Sergeant.

shake 'n' bake   A graduate of a stateside noncommissioned or commissioned officers' course.

short rounds   Artillery rounds that impact short of their target.

short-timer   Anyone with less than thirty days left in his combat tour.

single canopy   Jungle or forest with a single layer of trees.

sitrep   Situation report. A radio or telephone transmission, usually to a unit's tactical operations center, to provide information on that unit's current status.

Six   Designated call sign for a commander, such as "Alpha Six."

SKS   Communist bloc semiautomatic rifle.

sky   To run or flee because of enemy contact.

Sky pilot   Chaplain.

slack Slang for the second man in a patrol formation. The point man's backup.

slick Slang for a lightly armed Huey helicopter primarily used to transport troops.

smoke A canister-shaped grenade that dispenses smoke used to conceal a unit from the enemy or to mark a unit's location for aircraft. The smoke comes in a variety of colors.

Snake Cobra helicopter gunship.

snatch To capture a prisoner.

Sneaky Pete A member of an elite military unit who operates behind enemy lines.

snoop and poop A slang term meaning to gather intelligence in enemy territory and get out again without being detected.

socked in Unable to be resupplied or extracted due to inclement weather.

SOI Signal Operations Instructions. The classified code book that contains radio frequencies and call signs.

Sp4. or **spec four** Specialist fourth class (E-4).

Spectre An AC-130 aircraft gunship armed with miniguns, Vulcans, and sometimes a 105mm howitzer with the mission of providing close ground support for friendly ground troops.

spider hole A camouflaged one-man fighting position frequently used by the VC/NVA.

Spooky AC-47 or AC-119 aircraft armed with Gatling guns and capable of flying support over friendly positions for extended periods. Besides serving as an aerial weapons platform, Spooky was capable of dropping illumination flares.

spotter round An artillery smoke or white-phosphorous round that was fired to mark a position.

S.Sgt. Staff sergeant (E-6).

staging area An area in the rear where final last-minute preparations for an impending operation or mission are conducted.

stand-down A period of rest after completion of a mission or operation in the field.

star cluster An aerial signal device that produces three individual flares. Comes in red, green, or white.

starlight scope A night-vision device that utilizes any outside light source for illumination.

Stars and Stripes U.S. military newspaper.

stay-behind A technique involving a small unit dropping out or remaining behind when its larger parent unit moves out on an operation. A method of inserting a recon team.

strobe light A small device employing a highly visible, bright flashing light used to identify one's position at night. Normally used only in emergency situations.

TA Target area. Another designation for AO or area of operations.

TAC air   Tactical air support.

tail gunner   Rear security or the last man in a patrol.

TAOR   Tactical area of responsibility. Another designation for a unit's area of operations.

TDY   Temporary duty.

tee tee or *ti ti*   Very small.

ten forty-nine or **1049**   Military form 1049 used to request a transfer to another unit.

thumper or **thump gun**   Slang terms for the M-79 grenade launcher.

Tiger Force   The battalion reconnaissance platoon of the 2/327, 101st Airborne Division.

tigers or **tiger fatigues**   Camouflage pattern of black-and-green stripes usually worn by reconnaissance teams or elite units.

time pencil   A delayed-fuse detonating device attached to an explosive charge or a claymore antipersonnel mine.

TL   Team leader.

TM   Team.

TOC   Tactical operations center or command center of a military unit.

toe popper   Small, pressure-detonated antipersonnel mine intended to maim, not kill.

Top   Slang term for a first sergeant meaning "top" NCO.

tracker   Soldier specializing in trailing or tracking the enemy.

Tri-Border   The area in Indochina where Laos, Cambodia, and South Vietnam come together.

triple canopy   Jungle or forest that has three distinct layers of trees.

troop   Slang term for a soldier, or a unit in a cavalry squadron equal to an infantry company in size.

tunnel rat   A small-statured U.S. soldier who is sent into underground enemy tunnel complexes armed with only a flashlight, a knife, and a pistol.

URC-10   A pocket-size, short-range emergency radio.

VC   Viet Cong. South Vietnamese Communist guerrillas.

Viet Minh   Short for Viet Nam Doc Lap Dong Minh, or League for the Independence of Vietnam. Organized by Communist sympathizers who fought against the Japanese and later the French.

VNSF   South Vietnamese Special Forces.

warning order   The notification, prior to an op order, given to a recon team to begin preparation for a mission.

waste   To kill the enemy by any means available.

White Mice   Derogatory slang term for South Vietnamese Army MPs.

WIA   Wounded in action.

World   Slang term for the United States of America or home.

WP or **willy pete**   White-phosphorous grenade.

XF   Exfil. Extraction from the field, usually by helicopter.

xin loi/sin loi   Vietnamese for sorry or too bad.

XO   Executive officer.

Xray team A communication team established at a site between a remote recon patrol and its TOC. Its function is to assist in relaying messages between the two stations.

Yards Short for Montagnards.

zap To kill or wound.

zipperhead Derogatory name for an Asian.